DENNIS HOPPER

PETER L. WINKLER

DENNIS HOPPER

THE WILD RIDE OF A HOLLYWOOD REBEL

The Robson Press

First published in the United States in 2011 by Barricade Books, 185 Bridge Plaza
North, Suite 309, Fort Lee, NJ 07024

This edition published in Great Britain in 2011 by
The Robson Press
Biteback Publishing Ltd
Westminster Tower
3 Albert Embankment
London
SE1 7SP

ISBN 978-1-84954-165-7

10 9 8 7 6 5 4 3 2 1

A CIP catalogue record for this book is available from the British Library.

Printed and bound in Great Britain by TJ International, Padstow, Cornwall

For my sister, Erica V. Marlowe,
who made it possible for me to write this book.

CONTENTS

"I remember that I was driving along one time away from Dodge City to Garden City, where the big farm was and whipping down this dirt road and goin' about 70, and there's a strong wind coming from the right and I was really leaning into it, really leaning hard with my wheel, but I didn't realize it because I'd been going that way for so long, and suddenly there were some granaries off to the right and it stopped the wind and I went into the ditch. I think that I've been fighting the wind or fighting whatever it is for so long that I really have a great fear that if I stop turning the wheel hard into the wind, if something makes an obstacle, I'll go into the ditch."

"When I was a child, I thought as a child. When I became a man, I still thought as a child [laughs]."

Dennis Hopper, in the documentary
The American Dreamer (1971)

· 1 ·

FIRST LIGHT

A lonely farm boy wonders where the trains are headed and follows them to Hollywood.

"I come from Kansas, which is nowhere. And I hate my parents, who are no one."

Dennis Hopper, introducing himself to writer
Gwen Davis at a Hollywood party in 1956

*D*ENNIS LEE HOPPER was born in Dodge City, Kansas, on May 17, 1936, to Jay Millard Hopper and Marjorie Mae Hopper (nee Davis). "My grandparents were from Kentucky—I'm related to Daniel Boone," Dennis Hopper said. "He was my great-great-great-uncle. Sarah Boone, his sister, was my great-great-great-grandmother."

Jay Hopper managed a grocery store in Dodge City until the outbreak of World War II and served as a lay minister in the Methodist church. After the war, he got a job with the postal service's railway division, guarding the mail on the trains running from Kansas City to Denver. This entitled him to wear a sidearm, which impressed Dennis when he saw his father off at the railroad station and may have influenced the gun fetish that manifested itself in his adult life.

"Well, my father was pretty busy," Dennis recalled. "I mean, I learned more about him at his funeral than I did, really, growing up." Jay Hopper was a shadow in his son's life, "a hard, totally secret man with no words," as Dennis later put it. Child-rearing was left to Marjorie Hopper, a temperamental fundamentalist with 19th-century values who was unprepared for motherhood. The backstroke champion of Kansas, Marjorie was on her way to the Olympics until she became pregnant with Dennis when she was only seventeen.

"It was my mother," Dennis said, "basically, who took care of those things, even though we had a terrible relationship, my mother and I. I mean, she screamed, yelled, and threw things at me. It was a terrible, terrible relationship. I wanted to be an actor. I decided when I was very young, when I first saw movies, that I wanted to be an actor." Dennis' desire to become an actor was anathema to his mother and became the source of constant friction between them.

Brooke Hayward, Hopper's first wife, met his family in the '60s. "Dennis' grandfather was a sweetheart," she said. "I think Dennis was fond of his father, but his mother was a nightmare. She talked endlessly, and you couldn't stop her." "Hopper was the son of an unemotional father and an overly emotional mother," CBS News reported in 2004. "She was wild, very emotional, a screamer and a yeller," Hopper said about his mother. "My mother had an incredible body, and I had a sexual fascination for her. I never had sex with my mother, but I had total sexual fantasies about her."

Until he was ten, Dennis spent most of his time on his grandparents' little twelve-acre farm seven miles outside of Dodge City, where they grew Chinese elms and alfalfa, and kept chickens, cows, and pigs. "It was the dust bowl," Hopper said, "so I had to wear a gas mask to school five days a week because the dust was so heavy in the air, and my grandmother would open the door, and five inches of dust would blow inside. The sky was obliterated by dust storms a lot of the time. There were bread lines and soup lines, and it was really bad. The whole middle of the country had blown away."

"My early memories of Kansas are like, sort of classical stuff," he said. "There was a ditch in front of the house, a lot of weeds, a very fertile place, Kansas. There was a dirt road in front, a mailbox. A country road. I got my first sheepdog from the brother of the Clutters, the family that was murdered years later that Capote wrote about in *In Cold Blood.*"

"I never knew my father or my mother very well," Hopper said. "I very seldom saw my father—which I resented tremendously." Dennis' father joined the military when he was six, and his mother trained lifeguards for the Red Cross and managed an outdoor swimming pool in Dodge City. Dennis' grandmother was his only company during the day, when his grandfather worked on a large wheat farm sixty miles away in Garden City.

"As a little tiny child he didn't have anyone to play with," Marjorie Hopper said. "We didn't live where there were a lot of children, so he only knew children when he was at school. Grandmother read him every child's book in the Dodge City library before he was in kindergarten and was reading him novels."

"Most of the time I spent alone, daydreaming," Hopper said. "I didn't do much; occasionally I cleaned out the chicken house. I watched more than anything else. Wheat fields all around, as far as you could see. No neighbors, no other kids."

With little else to do, Dennis would look at the horizon line or lie in the ditch with his dog, watching the daily procession of flatcars loaded with heavy farm equipment rumble by until they disappeared over the horizon. "I used to spend hours wondering where it came from and where it went to," he said.

"My grandfather and my grandmother Davis were my best friends. I shot a BB gun at the black crows," Hopper recalled in an autobiographical sketch. "I fought the cows with a wooden sword. I hung ropes in the trees and played Tarzan. I listened to Joe Louis fight on the radio. I fed the chickens, pigs, cows. I swam in the swimming pool my mother managed in Dodge. I got a telescope and looked at the sun and went blind for five days. I caught lightning bugs, lightning shows, sunsets and followed animal tracks in the snow. I had a kite. I used the telescope to burn holes in newspapers. The sun was brighter than I was. God was everywhere and I was desperate. I walked on the rails on the train tracks. I shot marbles with an agate shooter. I caught catfish and carp in the river. I wondered what mountains looked like and skyscrapers. I imagined them on the Kansas horizon."

Dennis first discovered the intoxicating effects of mood-altering substances on his grandparents' farm. Grandfather Davis owned an old tractor whose gas tank was on the front, where the radiator is usually found. Dennis' curiosity led him to remove the gas cap and take a tentative whiff of whatever was inside. Becoming more adventurous, he breathed deeply of the gas fumes and went reeling from their dizzying effect. He enjoyed the disorientation and started doing it nearly every day. He would stretch out on the hood of the tractor, huff the gas fumes, and turn on his back. The sky turned into an animated fantasy, with clouds transformed into clowns and goblins. Dennis had his first bad trip one afternoon when he

OD'd on gas. The grill and lights on the tractor were transformed into the face of a terrifying monster attacking him. Dennis' grandfather pulled him away from the tractor as he smashed away at its lights and windshield with his baseball bat. Dennis was so high, he wasn't even aware of what he was doing until his grandparents explained it to him afterward.

Saturdays became special occasions for Dennis when his grandmother treated him to a trip to the local movie theater to see the matinee. She would fill her apron with fresh eggs and walk the six miles into town with him, where she'd sell the eggs at the local poultry shop. She'd use the proceeds to buy tickets to one of the dingy little theaters, where Dennis sat in the balcony, enthralled by the adventures of Roy Rogers, Gene Autry, Smiley Burnette, or Wild Bill Elliott, who was his favorite, because he wasn't a singing cowboy.

"Then all the next week," Hopper said, "I'd live that picture. If it was a war picture, I'd dig foxholes; if it was sword-fighting, I'd poke the cow with a stick. Those dark little Kansas theaters, Saturday afternoons, man, that was big news to me. It was just after the dust bowl, and sometimes I used to say that the first light that I saw was in the movie theater, because the sun was just a little glow. And being in Kansas, there's nothing really to look at. And right away, it hit me. The places I was seeing on the screen were the places the train came from and went to! The world on the screen was the real world, and I felt as if my heart would explode, I wanted so much to be a part of it. Being an actor was a way to be part of it. Being a director is a way to own it."

Riding his broom horse, Dennis announced the start of WW II to the crows on his grandparents' farm. When his father left for military service, his mother perpetrated a strange deception on Dennis that undermined his trust in his parents and authority figures. She took him aside one day and told him that his father had been killed in a munitions explosion during basic training. She was the only member of the family who knew that the story was a ruse to conceal Jay Hopper's duty in a unit of the Office of Strategic Services (OSS) that was active in Burma, China, and India.

Dennis adjusted to the news of his father's supposed death and went on with his life. "I ate raw onion sandwiches in the Victory Garden," he later wrote. "I drove a combine and one wayed. I was William Tell and Paul Revere. I dug fox holes in the field and played war. I was Errol Flynn and Abbott and Costello. I racked balls in the pool ball, smoked cigarettes, drank beer, and ate more onions."

After taking the surrender from Japanese forces in Peiping (also known as Peking or Beijing), Jay Hopper returned to civilian life and rejoined his family, confounding his nine-year-old son with his reappearance. "Now wouldn't that make you a paranoiac?" Dennis later said.

Dennis' family moved to Newton, Kansas, and then to Kansas City, Missouri, after Jay Hopper returned from China. On moving to Kansas City, Marjorie Hopper enrolled Dennis in art classes for underprivileged children at the Nelson-Atkins Museum of Art, which he attended every Saturday for three-and a-half years. Dennis had already started painting in Dodge City, the result of his rebellion against his mother after she enrolled in a dancing school. "But my mother put me in a tap-dancing class with a bunch of *girls*, man," he said. "I had to wear this little white outfit. She was trying to live in another place in another time, but I couldn't do it. I said, 'I'm not going anymore.' So she got me these watercolors, and I learned to do this little mountain and the tree with the roots and the water coming by."

Hopper's art instructor was a member of the Rocky Mountain School of painting that flourished in the mid-to-late 19th-century, whose members specialized in creating large scenes depicting the Rocky Mountains and the natural wonders of the West. When he was eleven, Hopper got his first art critique from Thomas Hart Benton, the hard-drinking American muralist. "Thomas Hart Benton would come in occasionally," he recalled. "He came about three times probably, just to visit the kids. But he wasn't teaching, really. He would just walk through the museum. He walked around, looked at one of my little watercolors and said, 'You're little, so you might be too young to understand what I'm about to say to you, but someday you're gonna have to get tight and paint loose.' " Benton's advice may have contributed to Hopper's later belief that artists had a prerogative to use alcohol and drugs to liberate their creativity.

In November 2009, Hopper told *San Diego Magazine*'s Tom Blair why his family moved to San Diego when he was thirteen. "My aunt lived there," Hopper said, "and my younger brother had bronchial asthma, and they said it would be the best place for him. And I think my mother just wanted to go to San Diego." Hopper told a later interviewer that his family moved because Jay Hopper got a job managing the San Diego post office. The Hoppers put down roots in Monterey Heights, a suburb of Lemon Grove, a quiet little blue-collar town. (The Hoppers lived at 3224 Massachusetts Avenue.) Marjorie Hopper got a job managing the largest outdoor swimming pool in El Cajon and presided over the local genealogical society. Dennis attended Lemon Grove Junior High School and then spent two years attending sessions split between Grossmont High School and Helix High School in La Mesa, which was still under construction. He finished his last two years of high school at Helix High.

Moving to San Diego afforded Hopper his first opportunity to see the mountains and the ocean he could only fantasize about in the flatlands of Kansas. "I'm creative man, because of my big disappointment: seeing real mountains and real ocean for the first time," he later explained. "In movies about Dodge City, they always put in big mountains, but there aren't any. Just endless wheat fields, this fantastic flat horizon line, incredible electric storms, sunsets like the northern lights. Wow, what a bringdown! The mountains in my head were much bigger than the Rockies. I didn't know what I thought I would see when I looked out at the ocean, but I thought I'd see something different. But then, looking out at the ocean, it was the same perspective I had looking out at a wheat field. I remember thinking that that ocean looked very similar to our wheat fields. The Pacific was the horizon line in my wheat field."

During his teenage years in San Diego, Hopper became consumed by his desire to become an actor, which first emerged when he was a child. "I decided when I was very young, when I first saw movies, that I wanted to be an actor," he recalled. "When I was at Nelson-Atkins back in Kansas City, we'd be there for five hours on a Saturday, but we would have an hour to go around the museum. They had a theater in the museum, and during my hour, I used to go in and sketch the actors."

Before he even left Dodge City, Hopper was making precocious complaints to his contemporaries about the constraints Kansas placed on his artistic development. Lin Dee, a childhood acquaintance, recalled, "Many times we heard you say you couldn't wait to leave us . . . You went on to follow your dreams, saying you needed to go for your chance to grow."

Hopper's desire to become an actor was tied up with another idea from his childhood, that becoming a famous artist would relieve his emotional pain. "I as a child was very, very unhappy and very lonely," he said in *The American Dreamer*. "The only way I could stop being unhappy and stop being lonely was to become something like an artist that would be, you know, so creative and so beautiful that everybody would, uh, say 'Wow!' Then I remember like, you know, the loneliness of holding your pillow thinking it's Elizabeth Taylor and thinking it's Leslie Caron and not being able to tell anyone and having to leave the room at school because you're so in love with Leslie Caron you just couldn't bear it anymore or go to the bathroom and cry for a while. The time when you couldn't identify with your parents and you couldn't identify with anyone, any of your surroundings, so you wanted new surroundings and new dreams and new ideas and new people, new things."

The most influential art form in Hopper's childhood was the movies. Hopper believed he could make people go "Wow!" by becoming an actor. But acting wasn't his first choice to achieve fame and fortune. "When I went to Hollywood, though, I was going to be either a matador, a race-car driver, or a boxer," he said. "In Spain, if you're broke and lousy in school, you become a matador. In Italy, you race cars. Here, you box or act. I boxed and got beat up, so acting was the only thing left." (Some of Hopper's studio biographies claimed that he was a Golden Gloves welterweight finalist.)

San Diego became Hopper's gateway to Hollywood, when he discovered the Old Globe Theatre in Balboa Park and the nearby La Jolla Playhouse. "When I moved to San Diego, I told my parents I wanted to take acting lessons, and they were horrified at the idea," he said. "But I started taking classes and started playing small parts at the Old Globe Theatre in San Diego." The teenage Dennis Hopper hated his parents for opposing his plan to become an actor. "I didn't love either one of them, very honestly," he said. "They weren't bad—like, this isn't a monster story—but I just felt out of place. They thought I should be a doctor or a lawyer or an engineer, and that being an actor was a life of becoming a bum—and this was not an acceptable occupation. So we start there, and you can get the rest."

Hopper's high-school friend, Bob Turnbull, who shared Hopper's ambitions and later joined him in Hollywood at his invitation, used to drive around with Dennis in a blue 1930 Chevrolet that Jay Hopper fixed up for him. Turnbull met Dennis' parents only fleetingly. "Whenever he went out to do anything, we always . . . out the door and into a car, never really into his house to meet his folks," Turnbull remembered. "They wanted him to have a normal career, as they called it. He was very embittered by that."

While making *Rebel Without a Cause* in 1955, Hopper told James Dean what compelled him to become a actor. "Because I hate my parents," he recalled telling Dean. "I told him how much I hated my home life, the rules, the regimentation. I felt the same kind of anger, that lack of communication that propels you to do something. I told him what a nightmare my home life had been, everybody neurotic because they weren't doing what they wanted to do, and yelling at me when I wanted to be creative, because creative people 'end up in bars.' "

Dennis reserved his greatest animosity for his mother and told an interviewer decades later that he never loved her. "Dennis lived through an intense relationship with his mother, an energetic Kansas farm girl who, according to Dennis, communicated a passion for material success, a 19th Century sense of guilt, and very little love," *Life* magazine's Brad Darrach wrote. "Man, she thought if I didn't turn out to be a lawyer or a doctor I'd turn out to be a bum," he told Darrach. "And my father didn't care how I turned out. They were always screaming . . . I swore to myself I'd show them."

Hopper tried to escape his parents' disapproval by running away from home. "I was a crazy kid," he said, "mixed up with a wild bunch, delinquents I guess, but I got away from that in acting. I was into the general gang stuff. Petty theft and a lot of misdemeanors." Darrach wrote, "Most of Dennis' friends have invoked this family drama to explain his hangups: his mistrust and rebellion, his lifelong refusal to study or even read, his frustrations that explode as violence, his tendency to look for experience in chemicals instead of in relationships, even to some extent his preference for what is imaginary over what is real."

Dennis Hopper began acting in amateur theatrical productions in 1949, when he joined the Old Globe Theatre's children's repertory group, the Community Theatre's Junior Workshop. (It became the Junior Theatre Wing of the Old Globe Theatre until late 1953 when it became a separate entity operating under the auspices of the San Diego Park and Recreation Department.)

"It was wonderful, because I got to start acting at the Old Globe Theatre when I was thirteen, so I acted there until I was eighteen," he said. Hopper first role came in the Globe's 1949 Christmas production of *A Christmas Carol*. "I played the urchin who comes at the beginning asking for alms and gets run out," he recalled just months before his death in 2010. "At the end, he gets a turkey. So I had to sit from the first act to the last act. [Laughs.] But I got through it." Hopper also opened the Globe's plays. He recalled, "Ringing the bell and going up and down the aisle and chanting: 'Hark ye gentles, hark ye all, time has come for curtain call . . .'"

Hopper played in the Old Globe's Christmas production of William Makepeace Thackeray's *The Rose and the Ring* in 1952. A local newspaper gave Dennis Hopper his first review when he appeared in *Cheaper by the Dozen* in 1954. "Dennis is now pleasing audiences in the role of Frank Gilbreth Jr. in the hit show, 'Cheaper by the Dozen,' running nightly except Mondays at the Old Globe Theatre," the paper reported." "Dennis has good looks, good diction, and an easy stage manner. He is especially liked in his memory narratives with Peg Plimmer, before the scenes in 'Cheaper by the Dozen.' "

After winning a scholarship to the 1954 San Diego National Shakespeare Festival, Hopper was given roles in the Old Globe's productions of *Cheaper by the Dozen, The Merchant of Venice, Othello, and Twelfth Night*, all staged in 1954. "I started playing Shakespeare during the summer," he said. "They'd bring over English directors because the Old Globe in San Diego was a duplicate of Shakespeare's Globe in England, which had burned down. But I worked with some really good English directors. I worked with these guys from time to time during the summer, because you really had to be in college to do that, but there were a lot of parts that they let me play." In the August 6, 1954, edition of the Southwestern Jewish Press, Berenice Soule gave kudos to the Globe's *Merchant of Venice*, writing, "among those besides the above-mentioned who gave excellent portrayals are Eugene Price, Abe Polsky, Miller Bushway, Shirlee Johnson, Robert ONeal, Bob Halverson, Dennis Hopper, William Francis, and Ann Barlow."

Hopper had barely begun acting, but had already set his sights on Hollywood. "But what a place to grow up, what a great place to be," he said, extolling the virtues of San Diego to Tom Blair. "And here I was, thinking, 'I gotta get out of here and get to Hollywood.' Every time I go back to San Diego now, I say, 'What an idiot you were. Look at this idyllic place.' There's nothing more beautiful than the Old Globe Theatre in Balboa Park, and all I was thinking about was 'I gotta get into the movies.' "

In November 1955, the *San Diego Union's* Edward Martin reported on Hopper's then-recent success in Hollywood. "Craig Noel, director of the Old Globe, remembers Hopper with much enthusiasm," he wrote. " 'He was one of the most brilliant young actors we ever had. At the age of 15, he was already an accomplished and finished performer,' Noel said." "He recalls with some amusement the time Dennis tried out for 'Caught in the Act,' (which opened in September 1949) the Old Globe's perennial musical favorite, by doing a serious dramatic play called 'Submerged,' in which he portrayed every character of the men supposedly trapped in a submarine, seven roles in all. After he had concluded Noel told him; 'That was fine, Dennis, but this is a tryout for a musical, not a heavy drama.' 'I know,' grinned the ambitious young actor. 'But I just wanted to try that sketch out before an audience.'"

"Hopper never forgot his days at the Old Globe and is intensely loyal to the local theater," Martin's story continued. "Whenever he returns to San Diego, he takes in a play there and visits back stage. Roberta Ridgely, secretary at the Old Globe, recalls a night not long ago, when Dennis paid a visit to San Diego during the filming of 'Rebel Without a Cause.' He startled Miss Ridgely's mother by calling her home at 1 A.M. to find out where the Globe personnel were staging a party to celebrate the end of the successful Shakespearean Festival."

One of San Diego's local papers published a brief story in December 1953 that touted Hopper's burgeoning acting achievements. The item was head-lined "Scores At Globe," with the subheading "He's 17 and Well on His Way to Stage Success." "Last summer, Dennis pulled curtains and did other backstage work at La Jolla Playhouse," the story went. "During another summer he fried hamburgers by day at the Pasadena Playhouse cafe, and assisted backstage at nights. He also played a juvenile lead in 'Doomsday' at the Pasadena Playhouse. [Hopper later said that he ran away from home the summer he turned sixteen, finding refuge at the Pasadena Playhouse.] This year Dennis played the lead in 'Harvey,' put on at Helix High School where Dennis is a senior student. In December Dennis won a speech contest at State College. He seems to be coming right along as an actor. Or he can be a silver-tongued orator if he wants to go into politics."

Hopper said that he won the Dramatic Declaration for the State of California in the National Forensic League in high school. Hopper's studio biographies claimed that he won three California state forensic competi-tions and recited Vachel Lindsay's poem "Abraham Lincoln Walks at Mid-night" on *Art Linkletter's House Party* TV show to a standing ovation. Helix High's 1954 yearbook notes, "Won several speech contests." When James Lipton, host of TV's *At the Actors Studio,* mentioned Hopper's appearance on Linkletter's show, he chuckled and said, "Wow, you've really done your research."

When Hopper returned to San Diego from Pasadena, he became an apprentice at the auspicious La Jolla Playhouse, a summer theater founded by film and stage actress Dorothy McGuire and her husband, *Life* photographer John Swope, which they operated with the assistance of Gregory Peck and Mel Ferrer. The playhouse presented professional productions of notable plays with paid casts featuring actors from Hollywood like Peck and Joseph Cotten. ". . . I was an apprentice at the La Jolla Playhouse when I was 16," Hopper told Tom Blair. "I picked up props and pulled the curtain, did sound cues and cleaned out the dressing rooms." Hopper told James Lipton, "I got a job cleaning toilets and pulling curtain and driving the prop truck. What a glamorous job that was. I'm very serious. There were all these movie stars. I had never seen a movie star before. I was actually cleaning their toilets."

The La Jolla Playhouse also introduced Hopper to Vincent Price, a connoisseur of fine art who became an important influence on his artistic development. Hopper's boss there was Hank Milam. Milam, an interior designer, worked with another interior designer, Mary Price, Vincent Price's wife, and lived in the couple's guesthouse near Beverly Hills. " . . . Vincent Price had actors over all the time, so I'd pick them up and drive them," Hopper said. ". . . actress Susan Kohner, agent Paul Kohner's daughter, was the other apprentice. We were around the same age, and they'd let us do backstage stuff until finally they gave me a couple of walk-ons."

"When at eighteen, I moved to Los Angeles under contract to Warner Bros.," he said, "one of the few people I knew here was Hank, who was then living at Mary and Vincent's house—they had a great Spanish house in Beverly Glen with a working kiln and huge art collection. When I came by, Bill Brice was making these great butterfly tiles for their pool. But even though I'd secretly dabbled in abstraction as a kid and in high school, when I went to Vincent's house and saw Richard Diebenkorn, Emerson Woelffer, a small Jackson Pollock, and a Franz Kline, these were the first real abstract pictures I'd ever seen. At one point, Vincent gave me a painting—of a head I think, I'm not sure by whom—and said he thought I would eventually become a collector."

Hopper couldn't wait to get out of school to pursue an acting career. "Anyway, I was terrible in school, because I didn't like reading," he later said. "I've read maybe eight novels in my life. I'd rather live it, man, get out in the street, get it *on*. I thought, I already know more than most of these kids," Hopper said, explaining why high school bored him. "Why should I study other people's ideas, when I can find everything just by using my ears and eyes? Teachers hated me, because I was so involved with acting that I didn't study or anything."

Hopper later told his friend, Lisa Law, the source of his antipathy to formal education and the received wisdom found in books. When his family moved to Newton and then to Kansas City, Dennis was placed in schools more progressive than the ones he'd attended in Dodge City and fell behind academically. "When I went from Dodge City to Newton, I was put in a corner with lima beans and a dunce cap on my head because I didn't know anything about mathematics," he said. "When we moved to Kansas City, I was really behind in reading. I didn't have the technical ability to add, subtract, multiply, read, and do the kind of things that I had gotten left out of. I think art and acting and those things became the way that I could express myself. So my whole drive became art, and I considered acting and being in movies and theater and painting and poetry—all of those things are what I was all about."

"I was kicked out of Art, Drama, and Social Studies, which were a requirement to graduate, because I'd written this thing about being amoral, not believing in society's mores, and that only people who break society's mores can make change, and that people who read and got their lines out of books and got their ideas out of books would not have any original ideas. The academic world and the act of actually reading a book was for people who didn't have a life. I had built up this whole defense about the fact that I danced through it all without having to really apply myself in any of these areas because of being backward and not wanting to feel like a fool."

"Peg Lemmer, his junior high English teacher, remembered him as an indifferent student who spent most of the time daydreaming or leaving early to attend Old Globe Theatre rehearsals," *The San Diego Union* reported in 1991. Lemmer recalled, "In desperation I said, 'Dennis, if you don't give your classes any attention, what ever are you going to do to make a living when you grow up?' "

Hopper's classmates at Helix High remember him as a likable student with average grades who was only enthusiastic about acting. Phyllis Gollehon says that Hopper "sailed through" his classes because of his talent for memorization. "His heart was really was not in the school," Bob Turnbull recalled. "His heart was to get out of school and get into Hollywood. That was where his focus was all the time. To me, he was an average student. I had a couple of classes with him. I was about as average as they came, so I could recognize another average student."

Rurik Kallis, a student who was a year younger than Hopper, set off a stink bomb in chemistry class one day, infuriating the teacher and driving the class out on the lawn. "Dennis thought that was great," Kallis said. "He was glad to get a day out of class." Hopper's classmate, Cecil Munsey, said that Hopper routinely blew off his schoolwork. "Dennis already knew what he wanted to do and what he was good at." Munsey recalled how they'd often ditch classes together. Someone in the school parking lot would say, "Who's up for Tijuana?" and a small group of truants would gather for an impromptu trip to the nearby border town where they'd drink in the bars and furtively peer into the doorways of brothels. According to Munsey, Hopper, who wrote poetry, would get loaded on beer and tequila and jump on the bar, as if ascending a stage, to recite what Munsey called Hopper's "Beatnik poetry."

Hopper's pal, Ed Sorrels, remembers the trips to Tijuana. "Oh God, did we ever, that and we'd go up to the snow in the morning and the beach in the afternoon. The bunch that I ran with, with Hopper dead now, I'm the last remaining guy. But the girls are all dead. He [Hopper] was fun, and he was wild. There was a group of us that was beyond the pale, if you will." Sorrels, who held a variety of jobs as a teenager, said, "I always had a dollar in my pocket and a set of wheels. We got around and had a lot of fun. That was what grown-up San Diego was like then. Just below Grossmont, there was a cleared off pad. Grossmont sits on a hill relative to the El Cajon Valley. There was this pad out there, where nobody used to bother ya. We used to park out here, three, four, five of us. And I had an old '46 Dodge four door, and we'd sit out there, and just get drunker 'an shithouse rats, at least for kids. We used to drink vodka and chase it with beer, Smirnoff Blue Label. You don't know what drunk is when you're that age. If you drink enough to puke, you've had a really good evening."

"He was like me—a wild child—and we had a lot of fun looking for the bottom of a beer can or bottle of vodka," Sorrels said of Hopper, "but he was also very serious about his craft. He didn't run with us as much as the group did because he was down at the Old Globe, La Jolla, what have you, working on his craft, even at fifteen and sixteen. He always knew what he wanted to do with his life, which he was amazingly successful with as we have witnessed through the years."

Hopper's classmate, Phyllis Gollehon (aka Trinity Mason), performed with him in school classes and for various service organizations in San Diego. After learning Hopper had died, Gollehon wrote a letter to him, addressing Hopper as if he was still alive. "It seems only yesterday that we were on our way to performances either with the Helix High School Choir or we were teaming our talents for the USO, as well as performing in various other venues that included the Navy Hospital in Balboa Park and the Army-Navy YMCA," she wrote.

Gollehon also became Hopper's sole confidant, whom he entrusted with his innermost feelings. "Sometimes," she wrote, "you would come and sit on my front doorstep where we talked about many things . . . some frivolous, though mostly serious. During one of those serious talks, you told me I was easy to talk to and you spoke of things you did not share or relate to others. Although you said I was very talented, you were quite sure I would someday become a psychologist." (Gollehon later became a spiritual psychologist.)

Hopper's doorstep sessions with Phyllis Gollehon soon became a regular occurrence. Sometimes he would call her the night before to ask if he could visit her the next day. She always said yes. "He did the talking," Gollehon said. "It was easy for him to open up to me." Gollehon recalled that Hopper was desperate to talk to someone who would entertain his deepest concerns and take them seriously, something his parents were unwilling to do. "He was looking for someone to help him understand who he was," she said. Hopper often complained that his father was emotionally unavailable and couldn't give him the masculine support he felt he needed. Gollehon listened sympathetically when Hopper expounded on his acting and artistic ambitions. He also revealed to her how he sought spiritual solace from his hikes in the mountains near San Diego, especially when they were covered in winter's fresh snowfall. "I know underneath there was so much more to Dennis than any of us really knew," Gollehon said. "I think I do. I think I touched into that when we were teens."

Hopper's classmates said that he was not a troublemaker, but Gollehon remembered him constantly disrupting classes. "He was given the boot from every class, even at one time or another from choir," she said. She recalls that Hopper sometimes seemed to be acting out something from his private stream of consciousness. "It played out in his mind, but made no sense. He was lonely and sought attention. Other times, he was bored and acted disruptive like a third-grader."

Dianne Kaderli (nee Leirsey) shared the honor of being voted Most Likely to Succeed with Hopper and went on to become a schoolteacher in Lemon Grove. In 1990, the *Los Angeles Times* reported "Kaderli, who lives with her husband and two children in Del Cerro, remembers her rowdy friend (who later starred in 'Rebel Without a Cause') as sweet, sensitive and incurably idealistic." "He was the classic class clown," she said. "He was real funny, always making little remarks, being very dramatic, especially at inappropriate times. As a teacher, he's made me more empathetic with students like that. He was *so* creative, and so I appreciate students like that, having known Dennis." Ed Sorrels laughed with delight when he recalled Hopper disrupting Mr. Schwendiman's English class, saying, "Yeah, he wasn't usually alone. I was probably right alongside of him. Just raisin' hell, we used to raise hell."

"I was incorrigible," Hopper confessed with pride. "I got kicked out of Speech and Social Studies. But as a makeup, I did an art correspondence course with Berkeley. I had so many correspondence courses going because I had been kicked out of so many classes. I was antisocial and amoral. I thought it was the way to go."

Jacquelyn Craig, who was in Drama and Choir with Hopper, said, "I know he was frequently in trouble because he knew what he wanted to do, and it wasn't sitting in class. I never saw it, but I heard about it. He did wholeheartedly put himself into the drama class. We knew that Dennis was very talented and very dedicated. He was the director of a one-act play, *Sham*, and he had a mature professionalism about him. But he could also really cut up, too. I always found Dennis to be very nice. He was a cutup, but not a rude person." Craig, who noted that everyone at school simply addressed Dennis as "Hopper," doesn't remember him acting in school plays much because he was always pursuing opportunities outside of school. Hopper acted in the Associated Student Body's production of *Charley's Aunt* in 1953 and had the lead role in the A.S.B.'s production of *Harvey in 1954*. The school's yearbook, the *Tartan*, noted, "This show enjoyed record breaking attendance, and was enjoyed by students and adults alike."

Sham was actually directed by Donna Zaisser and was one of three one-act plays presented by members of Helix High's drama classes under the direction of dramatic coach John Schwendiman at Helix High's Fletcher Auditorium on Friday, March 20, 1953, at 8 p.m. The plays were staged under the sponsorship of the Fletcher Hills Presbyterian Church's Sunday school as a fund-raiser for a new church building. One of the local newspapers reported, "The third and final plot, 'Finger of God,' answers the dramatic question, 'Can a criminal bury his past deeply enough to resist future temptations?' Dennis Hopper will direct this tense drama as well as act the part of Strickland, a successful broker with a dubious past. Benson, a valet who believes in double dealing, will be enacted by Bill Johnson, and Anne Engfelt will play the part of Strickland's secretary."

"He was extremely talented even as a junior high school student," Dianne Kaderli recalled. "He always used to do plays or readings in class. Even in the eighth grade, he was doing *The Hairy Ape,* a monologue by William Bendix.[1] He could do Hamlet's soliloquy, and it was marvelous. This was as an eighth-grader. You could tell he was going to be great. He wasn't as active in high school. Already, he was immersed in the San Diego Junior Theatre, or he was doing parts for the La Jolla Playhouse or pulling the curtain at the Old Globe. He was so wrapped up in drama that he stopped going to class. He was kicked out of a few classes. You could tell where his heart was; it wasn't in school."

While Hopper had a circle of acquaintances, none of his Helix classmates recall him having a best friend. "He was a loner, in the sense that he didn't really pal out with all the cool people on campus," Bob Turnbull said. Jacquelyn Craig and Phyllis Gollehon said that Hopper was so wrapped up in acting that he never had a girlfriend. "I know Dennis liked the girls, but was so driven to be an actor, he did not want anything that might take his focus off his goal," Craig said. "I was impressed by his determination and desire for what seemed to be a glamorous profession."

Hopper may not have had a steady girlfriend, but Ed Sorrels said that didn't stop Hopper from losing his virginity before he graduated from Helix. "There were young ladies around Lemon Grove who were available," Sorrels said. "There was a young lady over in Lemon Grove, that, how do I put this nicely, put out for the troops. She was a year behind me in school. It wasn't that she was particularly his girlfriend or anything, she

---

[1] *The Hairy Ape* is Eugene O'Neill's 1922 play. A low-budget film version of O'Neill's play, starring William Bendix and Susan Hayward, was released by United Artists in 1944.

wasn't anybody's girlfriend, but he wasn't without female companionship from time to time."

Hopper's senior portrait in the 1954 edition of the *Tartan* reads, "HOPPER, DENNIS LEE 'Hopper'—our very talented actor . . . favorite class is Drama . . . Won several speech contests . . . A.S.B. Play 2,4 . . . Choir 3,4 . . . Drama 2,3,4 Speech 2,3,4, . . . 'You'll Never Walk Alone.' " Though Hopper won several school debating contests and was proud of having one of his poems published in the school newspaper, the *Highlander*, his crowning achievement at Helix High was getting voted Most Likely to Succeed, with an accompanying photo in the school's yearbook. "He was just the obvious choice," Jacquelyn Craig said. "A lot of people in our class just knew that he would make it."

"Everybody could tell there was something special about him, especially as a thespian," Bob Turnbull said. Hopper told Tom Blair, "I was in the men's room—just came out from playing football, and a guy said I heard you're most likely to . . . And I punched him. I thought he was putting me on. I think I was kicked out of school right after that."

Hopper wasn't kicked out of high school. He was one of Helix High's 308 students who participated in graduation ceremonies at San Diego State College's Greek Bowl at 8 P.M. on June 17, 1954. Bob Turnbull remembers walking together with Hopper to collect their diplomas.

Rurik Kallis said that Hopper's classmates voted him Most Likely to Succeed because "Nobody else had a movie contract." Kallis heard talk around school that Hopper and a friend went to Hollywood over their Easter break in 1954, and Hopper returned with a screen test and an agent. Dennis Hopper always maintained that he made his first trip to Hollywood after graduating from high school. Phyllis Gollehon and Bob Turnbull did not recall hearing anything about Hopper's Easter trip to Hollywood, but Cecil Munsey said that Hopper, Turnbull, and possibly a third person, "Went up to Hollywood and got some leads there." (Turnbull says he did not accompany Hopper.) Turnbull says that Hopper may have been accompanied by his friend, Jerry Hauft. (Sadly, Hauft died two months before I spoke with Bob Turnbull in June 2010.)

Gollehon recalls hearing that Hopper was spotted by a Hollywood scout during one of his performances at the Old Globe Theatre. Bob Turnbull says that David Weisbart, who produced *Rebel Without a Cause* (1995), spotted Dennis Hopper during one of his performances at the La Jolla Playhouse.

Hopper always said that John Swope and Dorothy McGuire gave him his entree to Hollywood. They befriended him after being impressed by his performance in a bit part in the La Jolla Playhouse's production of *Double Indemnity*. After he spent the summer of '54 working at the playhouse, McGuire and Swope came to see Hopper play Lorenzo in the Old Globe's production of *The Merchant of Venice*. Hopper made an appointment to see Swope, who wrote him a letter of recommendation to Ruth Burch, the casting director for the Hal Roach Studios in Hollywood.

Hopper would have hightailed it to her office right then, but Swope left for Europe, where he wasn't available to confirm his letter. Hopper spent the next six months trying to see Ruth Burch, but couldn't get an appointment without an agent or membership in the Screen Actors Guild. He said, "It was a Catch-22 beyond any." Hopper scraped together some money with Billy Dwyer, a friend from high school who was a singer, and they rented an apartment in Los Angeles. One day, Hopper decided to accompany Dwyer to his dance class. There was an agency next door run by a powerful agent and producer named Helen Ainsworth. "So Billy was in taking a lesson," Hopper said, "and I walked into the agency and showed them my letter. There was a young agent there named Robert Raison, and he said, 'Let me see that.' He looked at the letter, and then he said, 'Can you do anything?' So I did one of my dramatic declarations that I had done in high school, and it flipped him out. He got me in to see Ruth Burch, who gave me a ten-line part in *Cavalcade of America* [a TV series] as a Civil War amputee who is dying, and I got my Screen Actors Guild card. It cost about $200, and I didn't have the money, so I borrowed it from the agency."

Raison, who had an affinity for representing offbeat, promising new-comers like Jack Nicholson, took Hopper on as a client. Hopper's big break came when he played a teenage epileptic in an episode of the TV series *Medic* (1954–1956). Hopper beat out thirty-two other actors for the part when he pretended to have a seizure in the office of *Medic*'s casting director.

Rurik Kallis told me a story that makes one wonder if Hopper could have auditioned for *Medic* on the Easter trip to Hollywood he was rumored to have taken. Kallis heard about one of Hopper's practical jokes. Hopper and several friends were browsing the aisles at Marston's Department Store when Dennis suddenly fell to the floor. One of Hopper's friends, who was in on the gag, yelled, "He's having an epileptic seizure!" Store employees summoned the police, and an ambulance was dispatched. Hopper quickly got up and ran out of the store. He was already gone by the time the police and ambulance arrived. Was Hopper's department store seizure a rehearsal for the one he faked for *Medic*'s casting director?

Whether Hopper actually scored a part on his Easter break or only after leaving San Diego remains a minor mystery. I suspect that he couldn't contain his enthusiasm about getting a letter from John Swope and told everyone within earshot about his good fortune, which time has transformed into different stories for different listeners. Hopper's mother said, "He was eighteen, they had $200, and he went to Hollywood. We didn't want him to go. We said, 'When you run out of your $200, you come home, or you call us. We'll come and get you.' He had no car, nothing. Before Christmas, he did a *Medic* show, and he came out smelling like a rose."

· 2 ·

YOUNG REBELS IN LOVE

Dennis Hopper hits Hollywood, hits the sheets with Natalie Wood, fights with Nicholas Ray and falls under James Dean's spell.

Success in Hollywood came remarkably easy for Dennis Hopper. It began on the day that he auditioned for *Medic*. Hopper didn't stand out from the other actors anxiously awaiting their turn to audition until he was called in to the casting director's office. After a little small talk, Hopper suddenly fell to the floor, feigning an epileptic seizure. Hopper was so convincing, the casting director was afraid that he was really having a seizure. His hand reached for the phone just as Hopper suddenly jumped up, dusted himself off, and smiled broadly. The casting director stuck his head out the door and told the thirty-two other actors waiting in the corridor they could go home. Hopper had the role. Hopper's episode of *Medic*, "Boy in the Storm," was quickly filmed in December 1954.

In "Boy in the Storm," Hopper plays the role of seventeen-year-old Robert Allan Maxwell, an epileptic whose parents were killed in a plane crash when he was two years old. Robert is placed in the care of his wealthy aunt, Flora, on her estate. Lacking any understanding of Robert's disorder, his aunt keeps him hidden away from the world to protect their family's reputation from the stigma of his epilepsy. Upon her death, Robert is placed in a medical institution under the benevolent care of Dr. Moore (Nelson Leigh), where he becomes infatuated with his young nurse, Nan (Evelynne Eaton). While reciting the sixth of Lord Byron's "Stanzas to

Augusta" to Nan, his way of expressing his hopeless love for her, Robert suffers a grand mal seizure.

When he recovers, Nan hides her affection for him to make a treacly little speech, telling him not to devote his love to any one thing, but to love each of the things and people he will encounter in his life with a special love. Nan chokes back her tears at the episode's conclusion as she and Dr. Moore send Robert off with his new foster parents. The show's epilogue has the fictional Dr. Konrad Styner (Richard Boone) leave the audience with the takeaway that epilepsy is not a sign of insanity or evil, but is a "disability that is as logically explainable as a lame leg."

Playing Robert Maxwell, Dennis Hopper looks amazingly fresh and dewy, and is by turns awkward, anguished, and innocently wide-eyed. When it comes to Maxwell's seizures, the show's money shot, Hopper delivers. His body becomes rigid, he falls down, and he even foams at the mouth. It may not be authentic, but it's spectacular and must have impressed audiences in 1955 who had never seen the real thing.

The $300 Hopper made from doing *Medic* wasn't enough to sustain him in Hollywood until the show aired and new roles came his way. "I stole milk from porches, occasionally I'd hit an orange juice," he said. He reluctantly returned to his parents' home and took a job until Hollywood beckoned. "I didn't know what to do. My folks thought I was crazy. They were always against this 'acting stuff.' Around Christmas time, I got a job for the telephone company going door-to-door, asking people for their old phone books so I could give them new ones. I wore a little suit that I bought at Sears & Roebuck. But out of all San Diego, the area I get is Lemon Grove—where I live! It was pretty funny. There was a lot of, 'Oh, Hopper's here. You want my phone book? Weren't you in *Cavalcade of America*?' And my friends kept saying, 'But I thought you were an actor!' So it was a little embarrassing, but I paid back the agency."

Hopper's entire family gathered around their TV set on January 3, 1955, to watch *Medic*, leaning forward in their chairs to capture every nuance of Dennis' performance. Dennis' beloved grandmother remarked that his mock seizures looked a lot like what happened when he huffed gasoline vapor from the gas tank of his grandfather's tractor. Even Hopper's parents were impressed, expressing reserved appreciation for their son's debut.

Medic was a popular show with film industry insiders. Hopper claimed that all seven movie studios clamored for him the moment that *Medic*'s end credits faded. (Only three of them called.) Columbia Studios, ruled over by the legendarily coarse mogul Harry Cohn, was the first to contact Hopper's agent and invite Hopper for an interview. Cohn's office was designed to intimidate nervous supplicants who eagerly sought favors from "King Cohn."

"I donned my tie and my suit and went with my agent to Columbia Pictures," Hopper recalled. "Now, I'd never been in a studio. It was all really new. Max Arnow, the head of casting, brought me into Cohn's office—a long room filled with Academy Awards. [Cohn] had a psychological ploy of having a very long room with his desk at the end. And behind that desk were these rainbow effects of these Academy Awards. And sitting at the desk with us is Abe Schneider, whose son, Bert Schneider, eventually gave me the money to make *Easy Rider* [1969]. Abe was second in charge and eventually became the head of Columbia."

"So Harry Cohn is sitting there, smoking a cigar," Hopper said. "He's like, 'Come on in, kid!' By the time I got to this desk, this long walk there, I was sweating and found a crack in the ceiling. I was really nervous. I had never seen an Academy Award, much less been in a studio. It was really something." After the usual pleasantries, Cohn addressed Hopper. "I saw you last night in this show kid, and I gotta tell you, you're really natural, really natural. You're the most naturalist actor I've ever seen since Montgomery Clift. We're going to make a big star out of you. So tell me, kid, whatcha been doing? Watcha been doing recently?"

Hopper answered, "Well, I've been playing Shakespeare."

Cohn erupted. "Shakespeare? Oh my God, Max, Max, Max, give the boy some numbers [money], put him in school for six months or a year, and take all that Shakespeare crap out of him. I hate Shakespeare. We can't have any of that. That Shakespeare guy, God, that's not natural at all. That's really broad stuff. We don't do that in movies."

"At that point, I stopped looking at that crack in the ceiling," Hopper said. "I focused on him, I stopped sweating, and I said, 'What the fuck are you talking about? You're telling me I have to go to fucking school to learn how to be a movie actor?' I mean, that was just it—I told him to fuck himself, basically. [In a number of interviews, Hopper said that he just told Cohn, "Go fuck yourself."] So I was banned from the studio. I was kicked out of the studio right then. I was escorted out the door, man. My whole agency was banned." Fortunately for Hopper and his agent, there were still two studios left to try.

Warner Bros.' casting director told Hopper, "If you to go see Nick Ray, and he puts you in *Rebel Without a Cause*, then we'll put you under contract with the possibility of you playing the son in *Giant* [1956]." Nick Ray took a look at Hopper and said, "Yeah, you can be in it."

However, the route from *Medic* to Warner Bros. wasn't quite as direct as Hopper believed. Jim Nelson, an assistant director on *Medic*, who was the neighbor of David Weisbart, *Rebel*'s producer, smoothed the way for Hopper's successful interviews at Warners. "I called David and told him I just saw this kid, and he was unbelievable," Nelson recalled. Less than three weeks after the broadcast of "Boy in the Storm," Dennis Hopper had done what other actors struggle for years without achieving—land a contract to a major studio, which assigned him to their next two films starring Hollywood's hottest new actor, James Dean.

On Thursday, January 20, 1955, one of San Diego's newspapers ran a small story headlined "San Diego Actor Gets Warner Role." After noting Hopper's upcoming roles in *Rebel* and *Giant*, the story concluded, "Nice way to start a film career." On March 17, the *Hollywood Reporter* reported: "Dennis Hopper, Warners contractee, will make his screen debut in 'Jagged Edge,' playing a college student who becomes involved with a dance hall girl portrayed by Shelley Winters." (The film was released under the title *I Died a Thousand Times*.)

Some sources credit Hopper with appearing in director Nicholas Ray's offbeat Western, *Johnny Guitar*, which was released on May 27, 1954. "I was never in *Johnny Guitar*," Hopper told *The Onion A.V. Club*'s Noel Murray. "And it's everywhere in my bio. I know why that happens. Nick Ray directed it, and Nick Ray directed *Rebel Without a Cause*, and I was in *Rebel Without A Cause*. I wasn't even in Hollywood when he made *Johnny Guitar*." Hopper did appear on-screen before *Rebel* in an uncredited cameo in *I Died a Thousand Times* (1955), a color, widescreen remake of the Humphrey Bogart classic *High Sierra* (1941). "I was with Dick Davalos, who played James Dean's brother in *East of Eden*, and we had just a few lines. We're dancing the mambo with Shelley Winters, and Jack Palance comes in. He grabs me, throws me against the wall, and says, 'Hey, that's my girl.' And I say, 'Hey buddy, hands off.'"

Nick Ray cast Hopper as "Goon," one of the lesser members of the teenage gang that harasses James Dean's character in *Rebel Without a Cause*, which Warner Bros. originally planned as a low-budget, black-and-white exploitation film to cash in on the public's growing interest in juvenile delinquency. "When he made *Rebel Without a Cause*," David Dalton wrote, "Dennis Hopper looked like he hadn't even started shaving yet, but there was that hint of madness in his eyes."

Though Hopper's role in *Rebel* is small, he has a few moments of his own. His genuinely surprised, pissed-off reaction when Corey Allen, imitating a crab, pinches his nose during the planetarium lecture, is spontaneous and amusing. Hopper's manic gum chewing before the chickie run, where he eagerly anticipates some kind of violence happening, and his delighted chuckle near the end of *Rebel*, as he looks forward to torturing the recumbent Plato (Sal Mineo), have a kind of naïve malevolence that foreshadows the full-blown psychosis of *Blue Velvet*'s Frank Booth, who Hopper would play thirty years later. But Hopper's most important scenes took place off-screen, when sixteen-year-old Natalie Wood, who was already fucking forty-three-year-old director Nicholas Ray, propositioned Dennis. And then Hopper met James Dean, who transformed his conception of acting and directing, and remained an inspirational figure to Hopper throughout his life.

Ray was still in preproduction for *Rebel* in February 1955 and had not settled on an actress to play Judy, one of the three middle-class teenagers whose tribulations within their dysfunctional families eventually bring them together. The director's unconventional methods and lifestyle set him apart from the usual Hollywood crowd. A bisexual, misogynistic womanizer addicted to alcohol, drugs, and gambling, Ray also possessed a keen eye and an unusual sensitivity to the emotional honesty of his actors' work. During interviews with actors he was considering for *Rebel*, Ray skipped the usual chitchat. Instead, he asked them about their family life, especially how they got along with their father.

Warners submitted numerous actresses to Ray for the role of Judy, including Debbie Reynolds and Margaret O'Brien. Both were too conventional and goody-goody for his taste. O'Brien told him she loved her parents and teachers. It wasn't what he wanted to hear. The studio mentioned Natalie Wood, but Ray initially dismissed her. He only later discovered that Natalie Wood was living a family psychodrama similar to Judy's in *Rebel Without a Cause*.

Natalie Wood's parents, Nick and Maria Gurdin, were Russian émigrés who fled the turbulence and vicissitudes of the Bolshevik Revolution. Nick was an emasculated alcoholic who occasionally worked as a
carpenter. Maria was a superstitious dreamer without the means to realize
her yearning for material comfort and fame. Maria found a way to do
this after she read about a local ten-year-old girl who won a role in Alfred
Hitchcock's *Shadow of a Doubt* (1943), filmed in the Gurdins' hometown
of Santa Rosa, California.

When a Hollywood crew arrived in Santa Rosa to film the ironically
titled *Happy Land* in June 1943, Maria paraded four-year-old Natalie,
pigtailed and cute as a button, around the set before pushing her to sit
on director Irving Pichel's lap. Natalie charmed the director by singing
an old Russian folk song. After Pichel used Natalie in a brief walk-on
role, Maria moved the family to Hollywood, where she maneuvered the
reluctant Pichel to cast Natalie in her first speaking role, in the Claudette
Colbert-Orson Welles melodrama *Tomorrow Is Forever* (1946).

Natalie was in a transitional phase of her life when she tested for *Rebel*.
She was physically ripening, too mature to play children, yet too young to
play leading roles against older male stars. Natalie's life at home was tough to
cope with, making her eventual performance as Judy an emotionally autobiographical exercise. Nick Gurdin periodically erupted in drunken rages
and chased his wife around the house with a butcher knife. Maria controlled
Natalie's every move with an encyclopedia of prohibitions to obey. Anything
that could diminish her daughter's earning power as an actress was verboten.
Maria restrained Natalie's desire for independence and interfered with the
few tentative relationships that she formed with boys her own age.

Wood rebelled against these constraints when her agent, Dick Clayton,
who also represented James Dean, showed her an early draft of the script
for *Rebel Without a Cause*. "I guess I was going through my first rebellion,"
Wood said in 1974. "Natalie thought that being grown up meant being
free of the rules," said Nick Adams, a diminutive blond with a small role
in *Rebel* who attached himself to Wood. "For a few months she spent most
of her time rebelling against everything and everyone." "I was a rather
dutiful child," Wood said, "and when my parents read the script of *Rebel*,
they said, 'Oh no, not this one,' because it showed parents in a rather
unsympathetic light, and yet I read it, and for the first time in my life, I
said, 'Oh, wait a minute. I have to do this! I love this, I love Judy,' and I
felt very much of a connection, identification with the part."

Determined to impress Ray, Wood showed up at his office at Warner Bros. as her idea of how a sexy, mature woman should look. Heavily made up, wearing the slinkiest dress she could find, and perched on high heels, she threw herself at Ray, but it did little to change his impressions of her as a child actress. "But after Nat's interview," he wrote, "she left, and outside waiting for her was this kid with a fresh scar across his face, so I said, 'Let's talk again.' She seemed to be on that kind of trip." Ray took Natalie to a posh restaurant, where he seduced her in the company of a girlfriend she had brought along for moral support. Natalie quickly ended up in Ray's bed in his poolside bungalow at the Chateau Marmont hotel on the Sunset Strip, where he enjoyed afternoon trysts with pliable young actresses, most notably Marilyn Monroe.

Ray agreed to give Wood a screen test. Since he knew better than to bother James Dean with this, and Dean was in New York at the time, he employed Dennis Hopper for screen tests with the actresses who were candidates for the role of Judy (including Jayne Mansfield, one of Ray's lovers, who was briefly under contract to Warner Bros.). Ray conducted the tests on a rainy evening to see if CinemaScope and black-and-white film could capture such extreme conditions.

"By the time we were finished, Natalie and I both felt like wet unhappy animals," Hopper recalled. Natalie Wood became infatuated with Dean before *Rebel* when they did a TV show based on Sherwood Anderson's "I Am a Fool." When Dean didn't return her interest, Dennis Hopper became Natalie's surrogate for James Dean. Hopper looked similar to Dean, was closer to Wood in age and experience, and shared Dean's self-absorbed seriousness and dedication to the Method school of acting.

The day after the screen tests, the phone rang in Bill Dwyer's apartment, where Hopper was staying. Handing the phone to Hopper, Dwyer said, "It's Natalie Wood! I think you tested with her."A young girl's voice said, "This is Natalie Wood. I tested with you the other night on *Rebel*. Remember? It was raining?" Hopper barely remembered the skinny little girl he tested with. He said, "She had to identify herself to me over the telephone for me to know which one she was because I tested with about ten women that day. She was really funny. She told me I was great looking, and she really liked me, and she wanted to have sex with me—which never happened before or since. Natalie said, 'I'd like to fuck you, but I don't do anything. I just lay there.' I said, 'Uh . . . .' " "Helluva line. In the '50s to be aggressive like that as a woman was really amazing. It was an amazing turn-on to me, for one thing. But it was certainly contrary to any kind of movement, or idea, at the time.

"So she said, 'I have to do a little rehearsing with Nick at the Chateau, but if you pick me up afterward . . .' So I went to pick her up. She gets in the car, and I said, 'You know, I've got a roommate . . .' She says, 'Let's just go up the hill. I know a lover's lane.' So she took me up the hill, and we started linking up, and I started to go down on her, and she said, 'Oh, you can't do that.' I said, 'Why?' She said, 'Because Nick just fucked me.' I thought it was *weird*, O.K.?" Hopper recalled. "At the time, I was eighteen years old! I thought it was strange, I thought it was weird of her to be *doing* it . . . he was having an affair with a minor. It was illegal for me, too, but at least I was only a couple years older."

On another day further in their relationship, a hysterical Wood burst into Hopper's apartment, telling him that a famous actor got drunk, called her a whore, and raped her. Wood then spied a bullwhip Hopper acquired in Texas when he was in *Giant*. Brandishing it, she said, "Let me whip you." It sounds too fantastic to be true, you say? Hopper's Helix High classmate, Gerald Palmer, was surprised to see him at the Jack in the Box drive-through restaurant in La Mesa one evening in late November 1956, when *Giant* was released. Palmer remembers Hopper standing on the corner of University and Massachusetts Avenues where Hopper was showing off trick moves with his bullwhip to a crowd that had gathered. Palmer chatted briefly with Hopper before moving on. He later heard that someone from the crowd borrowed the whip and bested Hopper, expertly moving around a scrap of paper with the whip.

Natalie Wood became Dennis Hopper's Hollywood tour guide, tooling around town in her pink Ford Thunderbird with Hopper and Nick Adams. They placed their hands and shoes in the imprints of the screen immortals at the entrance to Grauman's Chinese Theatre. Natalie introduced Dennis to her favorite hangouts: Googie's, a twenty-four-hour diner designed by futuristic Los Angeles architect John Lautner, and the Villa Capri, frequented by Humphrey Bogart and Frank Sinatra. Most important for Wood, James Dean was a habitué of both restaurants.

Natalie, Dennis, and Nick alternated between a search for seriousness and frivolity. Hopper said they attended foreign films, "trying to find another way of, like, working. We were very ambitious to change things." Suzanne

Finstad, Wood's biographer, wrote, "The Dean acolytes adopted angst as an artistic affectation, and Natalie cheerfully suffered with them: 'What we used to talk about was how unhappy we were. Whoever was the unhappiest, whoever came closest to suicide the night before, he was the winner.'"

Adams, Hopper, and Wood thought of themselves as the logical successors to the great names of show business and began emulating what Hopper called "wild, crazed Hollywood icons." Hopper said, "It was almost as if we were naïve to the point, 'If people did drugs and alcohol and were nymphomaniacs, then that must be the way to creativity, and creativity's where we wanna be. We wanna be the *best*.' She [Natalie] always wanted to be the best."

"We were always envious of the generations *before* us," he continued. "In the '50s, when me and Natalie and Dean and Nick Adams and Tony Perkins suddenly arrived, we all sort of felt like an earlier group of people who thumbed their noses at Hollywood tradition, people like John Barrymore and Errol Flynn, both of whom, of course, died as alcoholics. It seemed a romantic, a colorful way to go. God, it was a whole group of us that sort of felt like the earlier group—the Barrymores, Flynns, Sinatras, Clifts—were a little further out than we were. I mean we heard of the orgies that John Garfield used to have, the Hollywood roulette. It seemed wilder. So we tried to emulate that lifestyle. In a strange way, we were trying to emulate some sort of past glory."

Dennis Hopper and Nick Adams rented a house in the Hollywood Hills on Rothdell Trail, a winding side road off of Laurel Canyon Boulevard, where Adams discovered Hopper's penchant for guns. Adams told Andrew J. Fenady that he was reading a magazine one afternoon when he heard a tremendous explosion and a bullet whizzed by his ear. Adams ran into the next room to see Hopper, giggling, holding the smoking .44 Magnum pistol that he had just fired. The house on Rothdell Trail became the setting for outré episodes where Hopper, Adams, and Wood tried to be wilder than their legendary predecessors.

"For instance," Hopper said, "once Natalie and I decided we'd have an orgy, you understand?" Dennis, Natalie, Nick, and his girlfriend were joined by other members of Natalie's inner circle. "Several showed up and girls, too," recalled Bob Turnbull, who was there. "It was kind of a big event. She wanted to have an orgy, she just wanted all kinds of guys doin' her. She just wanted to have the old champagne bath."

"And Natalie says, 'O.K., but we have to have a champagne bath,' " Hopper said. "I think she had heard that Jean Harlow or somebody had had a champagne bath. So Nick and I went and got all this champagne, and we filled the bathtub full of champagne, and we said, 'O.K., Natalie, we're ready for the orgy.' Natalie takes off her clothes, sits down in the champagne, starts screaming." Why did Wood scream? "Well," Hopper said, "because it burned her pussy. Set her on fucking *fire*, you know." Hopper and the others raced the agonized Wood to the nearest emergency room. "It was a very expensive burn. That was our orgy, you understand? I mean it seemed like none of these things really worked out. Still, that kind of experience didn't stop us from trying to be as far out as we could. We partied a lot."

"Of course, she [Natalie] had other times, too, when Dennis, Nick, and I would be enjoying her company, as well," Turnbull said. "She was just a wild and crazy gal. It was just her style. She was just very friendly, but oversexed. But in a likable way, not a slutty way, if that makes sense. She was a very classy girl. She just had a whole different outlook on the morality of one's life. She was a nice person, very polite, just a very free-flowing spirit."

Nicholas Ray was still testing actresses for the role of Judy in late February 1955. Natalie was anxiously awaiting a phone call from Ray on February 22 confirming that the part was hers. Dennis Hopper suggested that she and her friend Jackie Eastes meet him at Googie's. Wood proposed that they go to the Villa Capri for a glass of wine to calm her nerves. The trio piled into Hopper's car and spent the evening drinking wine until the restaurant closed at 11 P.M. Hopper insisted on buying a bottle of whiskey at a liquor store before driving up Mulholland Drive and parking. Eastes said that they sat there, "drunkenly looking at the stars," and saw Hopper guzzle half the whiskey before she passed out. When Eastes woke up, Wood was standing outside the car vomiting while Hopper muttered, "It's all my fault, I shouldn't have bought that bottle."

Deciding to return Natalie to Googie's to pick up her car, Hopper turned cautiously onto rain-slicked Laurel Canyon Boulevard, a serpentine, two-lane mountain road. Hopper emerged from a curve only to collide head-on with a driver who had crossed the center line. Hopper's car flipped over, throwing the trio on the road like a stack of pancakes—Hopper landed on

Eastes, who was on top of Wood. As people emerged from their homes to assist the accident victims, Hopper got up and walked around, repeatedly mumbling, "Oh man, this is all my fault," while Eastes screamed at Natalie to wake up.

At the hospital, Wood, who had suffered a concussion and kept passing out, insisted that the police call Nick Ray, not her parents. Eastes said that she told Hopper to call Ray, "because he communicated on our level. We needed a spokesperson because we obviously had been drinking, and it didn't look good." Ray called his own doctor and Natalie's parents to the hospital. When Ray encountered Hopper in the corridor, he lashed out at him. "Ray grabs me and throws me against the wall. I was trying to explain to him, and I guess he was hysterical, and he slapped me very, very hard, pushed me against the wall, and said, 'Shut up, and straighten up.' "

Wood insisted on seeing Ray before her parents. When he approached Natalie's bed, she pulled him close and said, "Nick! They called me a goddamn juvenile delinquent. *Now* do I get the part?" Eastes and Hopper overheard Ray tell Wood's doctor, "Take good care of this young lady, she's the star of my next movie." In a gallant touch, Nick Ray had a dozen roses delivered to Natalie on March 30, 1955, the first day of production on *Rebel Without a Cause*. When Hopper discovered this, "He completely freaked out, calling her all kinds of nasty names," said actor Frank Mazzola. Maybe Natalie didn't tell Hopper about her affair with Ray on their first night together, as he later claimed.

Hollywood columnist Sidney Skolsky's daughter, Steffi Sidney, who played a gang member in *Rebel,* was impressed by Hopper's performance on *Medic* and became his confidant during the filming of *Rebel Without a Cause.* In 2007, she said, "When I got to interviewing with Nick Ray, because Dennis was in the office, I found out that Dennis had been put under contract by Warner Bros., and I had my best girlfriend with me at the time, who was Susie Strasberg, who knew Nick Ray. We were spending the afternoon together, so I said why don't you come up with me to Nick Ray's office, and I'll have this talk with him, and we'll be on our way, and Dennis was there, and the three of us talked a little bit, and when I walked out, I was very impressed. I said this young man is not only talented, but, gee, his knowledge of film and theater and books and art and music . . . I said it's so nice to have somebody so young be as knowledgeable as that. I mean, I was brought up in Hollywood and always with older people. Susie came from a theatrical family. I came from a movie-theatrical family."

Hopper confided in Sidney in much the same way he had with Phyllis Gollehon back in Lemon Grove. "Dennis and I could really communicate on things," Sidney said. "When we had to test and had wardrobe things and stuff like that, we talked some more. It was very nice, and he was a very good-looking guy. I got a crush on him, not only from his talent, but from his intellect. I think in some ways, he thought the same thing because we had lovely, wonderful conversations, and that's when he told me all about being in love with Natalie and her mother and Nick Ray and all of that. Nick was just terrible to him over the loudspeaker. There was always a P.A. system on the set because you're always called to do your scene if you're in your trailer, or if Nick was up on a boom, he had a bullhorn, and it would always be 'Mr. Hopper,' you know."

Dennis Hopper told Sidney that he went looking for Natalie at Ray's bungalow one evening and caught Natalie and Nick having sex. "He told me about being love with Natalie and what he was going to do because Nick hated him," Sidney said. Hopper told her that he visited the Chateau Marmont equipped with his gun to confront Ray, who, fortunately, wasn't at home that night.

Ten days into production, studio executives decided to shut down *Rebel Without a Cause* and start over. Impressed by the critical reaction to *East of Eden* (1955), they decided that their new hot ticket, James Dean, was too good for a cheap little black-and-white B-movie. They told Ray that he should start filming from scratch in CinemaScope and color. Dennis Hopper got into trouble with Ray almost instantly on Monday, April 11, 1955, when Ray started shooting the scenes involving Jim Stark's (James Dean) altercation with Buzz (Corey Allen) and his gang at the Griffith Planetarium.

Beverly Long, who played the blonde, pony-tailed member of Buzz's gang in *Rebel*, said that after filming scenes inside the planetarium, assistant director Don Page told the kids to go outside and take a short cigarette break. Hopper told Long he was going to get a hot dog because he was hungry. Long tried to stop him. She said, "They're going to start shooting any minute." Sure enough, Hopper was nowhere to be found when Page yelled, "Places, everybody." The studio's call sheets for the day note, "Corey Allen and Dennis Hopper left set. Could not find in time to complete shot." None of the other actors recalls Allen's absence.

According to Long, "School buses started arriving from the city school system, and they threw us out. And they had to leave their huge cranes behind, and they never got their shots. Dennis cost them, I don't know, $50,000. He cost them a lot of money."

Hopper returned, oblivious to what had happened. Ray, standing on the observatory's front steps, told Hopper he was fired. "Steve Trilling, a Warner Bros. henchman, came up with his big cigar and informed Nick, 'We can't fire him. He's under contract here,' " Long recalled. "So Nick said, 'Well, I'm not going to direct him anymore' and gave all of his lines to Jack Grinnage. So from the planetarium on, you'll notice Dennis has nothing to say." Long's memory fails her here. Hopper has several lines of dialogue near the film's conclusion when he, Grinnage, and Frank Mazzola are in a car, discussing whether they should pursue James Dean to the abandoned mansion where he's taken refuge with Natalie Wood and Sal Mineo.

Tensions between Hopper and Ray flared again when *Rebel*'s chickie run scenes were filmed on May 13 and 14, 1955. (Steffi Sidney insisted that the scenes were completed in one evening.) Shooting took place on Friday and Saturday night at the Warner Ranch, a high plateau located twenty miles from the studio. "The day of the chickie run scene," Hopper said, "Natalie's parents had arrived on the set, and Nick suddenly started yelling at me and sent me to my trailer, in front of her parents. She [Wood's mother] knew about Natalie and Nick, didn't like it, but kept quiet about it because he was the director. But she made a fuss about Natalie and me to an executive at the studio, and I was told to lay off."

Hopper resented being singled out while Ray "came out pure as the driven snow." "Which is when I realized that the reason I was getting into this kind of problem with Nick was because of Nick Ray's relationship with Natalie and my relationship with Natalie. I realized that I could be expendable in Nick Ray's world. That he could blame me and get off. I wasn't gonna let it happen."

Hopper confronted the director. "I said, 'Nick, I know you've been fucking Natalie. You're now using that against me. I know that you've told the studio that I'm having an affair with her. This has gotta *stop,* or I'm gonna beat the shit out of you right now.' And I took some sort of boxing pose. Ray said, 'See, that's your problem. You have to use your fists. You can't use your brain. Someday you're gonna have to start using your brains.' And he turned and walked away. At that point, I lost my aggressiveness."

With his run-in with Ray behind him, Dennis Hopper fixed his attention on James Dean. Hopper's glimpses of Dean before *Rebel* left him unimpressed. As soon as Hopper won his contract with Warner Bros., he went to see *East of Eden*, the only one of Dean's movies that was released before his death. Hopper was walking down a hallway with Robert Raison on his way to Nick Ray's office when he encountered Dean coming in the opposite direction. "You've got to understand, Hollywood, at this time, was all suits and ties," Hopper said. "These guys were old-school gentlemen. They smoked cigars, but they were gentlemen." Clad in dirty Levis and a turtleneck, the bespectacled, unshaven Dean crept down the hallway, a cigarette dangling from his lips. In a hushed voice, Raison said, "That's James Dean." Though Hopper had just seen him on-screen, he didn't even recognize Dean. Hopper did a double take, exclaiming, "That's James Dean?"

After Hopper met with Ray, he and Raison walked over to the drugstore across the street from Warners, where Dean was sitting at the counter. Dean would pour a heap of sugar on a spoon, then watch it dissolve when he stirred it into a cup of coffee. He did this several times before Raison told Hopper, "Let me introduce you." Raison approached Dean and said, "Jimmy, this is Dennis Hopper. He's going to be in the movie with you." Ignoring Raison and Hopper, Dean continued pouring sugar into his coffee.

Hopper's confidence in his acting prowess was shaken after he started watching Dean work. "I thought," Hopper said, "I was the best actor in the world, pound for pound—I mean the best *young* actor. I was really good, I had incredible technique, I was incredibly sensitive. I didn't think there was anyone to top me. Until I saw James Dean. And then I'm on set, and the first thing we're doing is the scene in *Rebel* at the police station where he gets arrested. And suddenly, Dean starts making siren sounds. When they search him, he starts to laugh because it's tickling him, and I'm thinking, 'Where the hell is this on the page? Where is this coming from, man?' I'd never seen anyone improvise before."

"Watching Dean act was like watching someone pull miracles out of the air. He fascinated me. Because he was working internally, and I was working externally. I was an actor who'd come out of Shakespeare. My experience of acting was line readings, precise gestures, knowing what you were going to do next. Everything I was doing was preconceived, although it looked very natural. Dean completely disregarded any direction in the script. He would do a scene differently every time. It came straight out of his imagination, his improvisation. I didn't understand how he was arriving at those conclusions because he was having real emotional feelings, real emotional reactions. He also had a way of physically expressing himself that I'd never seen another actor do. I didn't know what he was doing, but I knew it was great."

Hopper attempted to get close to Dean and talk to him about his technique. But Dean preferred to sequester himself in his dressing room, smoking marijuana and playing classical music. "I tried to get to know him. I started by saying 'Hello.' No answer. He wouldn't talk to people on the set. He would be into himself, into his thing. He'd lock himself up into his dressing room."

Hopper made his move during a break in filming. "Finally, about halfway through the picture, in the chickie run, it was at night," he recalled, "and I grabbed him and literally threw him into a car, and I said, 'Look, I really wanna be an actor, too. And I wanna know what you're doing, what your secret is.'" Dean calmly looked through his glasses at Hopper and asked, "Why?"

" 'Because,' " Hopper said, I want to be a great actor.' So he asked me very quietly why I acted, and I told him what a nightmare my home life had been. Anyway, Jimmy and I found we were both neurotic and had to justify our neuroses by creating, getting the pain out and sharing it."

"I thought I was the best young actor in the world," Hopper said, "but I didn't even understand what he was doing, that I was flabbergasted by his spontaneity, his ability to do scene after scene different each time without changing the words." Hopper asked Dean, "Do I have to go to New York? Do I have to see Strasberg?" [Lee Strasberg was the director of the Actors Studio in New York.] Still smarting from the brutal critique Strasberg gave Dean when he was at the Actors Studio, he said, "No, you're too sensitive. Strasberg will destroy you."

"No, no, take it easy," Dean told Hopper. "Just listen to me and I'll help you along." "It was, in a strange way, a closer friendship than most people have," Hopper said, "but it wasn't the kind of thing where he said, 'Let's go out and tear up the town.' Sometimes we'd have dinner. Also, we were into peyote and grass before anybody else. What we really had was a student-teacher relationship, the only one he ever had, as far as I know. He helped me with my acting, and I watched him get old in *Giant*. That was our relationship. We didn't hang out together or go out together. It wasn't a buddy-buddy hang-out thing. He started watching my takes after that. I wouldn't even know he was there. He'd come up and mumble, 'Why don't you try it *this* way?' And he was always right."

"Do things, don't show them," Dean advised Hopper. "Stop the gestures. Well, if you're smoking a cigarette, don't act smoking a cigarette, just smoke it. You know, you feel like smoking, smoke it. It will be very difficult doing the simplest things at first, like drinking a cup of coffee. Doing anything will be very difficult in the very beginning, but you must start at that simple reality."

Hopper recalled these revelatory exchanges with Dean twenty years after they took place. But Hopper was still uncertain about why he wanted to act while filming *Rebel*. In her memoir, actress Susan Strasberg, Lee Strasberg's daughter, wrote, "Dennis Hopper, also appearing in *Rebel*, gave me a copy of Rilke's *Letters to a Young Poet* and talked to me about his inspirations as an actor, bemoaning that he had consulted a psychiatrist who had told him he was not neurotic enough to need therapy. Dennis asked, 'If I'm not sick, how can I be a good actor?' And I, reassuringly, said, 'You *are* sick Dennis. Believe me, you are!' "

James Dean's relationship with Nick Ray, like his style of acting, was unlike anything Hopper had seen in his brief career. It affected him as powerfully as Dean's acting advice and ruined his ability to accept direction. It appeared to Hopper that Dean completely dominated Ray and called the creative shots on the set. Hopper watched as Ray indulged Dean's whims, like the time he allowed Dean to prepare for his scene in the police station with his parents by staying in his dressing room for what seemed like hours, drinking red wine and blasting Wagner's "The Ride of the Valkyries" on his phonograph over and over.

When Dean received a cut behind his ear while filming the knife fight with Corey Allen, Nick Ray yelled, "Cut, Cut," and summoned the first-aid man to stanch the trickle of blood flowing from behind Dean's ear. "Jimmy got furious when Nick stopped that scene," Hopper recalled. "He started yelling at Nick, 'What the hell are you doing? Can't you see I'm having a *real* moment? Don't you *ever* cut a scene while I'm having a real moment. What the fuck do you think I'm here for?' "

Commenting on the scene in *Rebel* where a drunken Jim Stark (Dean) is booked by the police, Hopper said, "Then he's searched, and this angry, drunk guy is suddenly ticklish? Where'd that come from? I'll tell you where it came from. It came from genius, that's where it came from. And that was all him. Nobody directed him to do that. James Dean directed James Dean."

Jim Backus, initially skeptical about Dean's excessive preparation, also fell under his spell. "May I say that this is the first time in the history of motion pictures that a twenty-four-year-old boy, with only one motion picture to his credit, was practically the co-director," Backus told *Variety*. Over the years, Backus and Hopper's opinions that Dean directed *Rebel* have hardened into an urban legend.

Leonard Rosenman, who composed the music for *East of Eden* and *Rebel Without a Cause*, said, "No, Jimmy was just one character in the story. Nick had a much broader concept. He had the sets, the photography all working at the same time." Beverly Long felt that Dean and Ray enjoyed a nice collaborative relationship.

"Ray, of course, directed, cajoled, humored, diapered, and powdered James Dean to great effect in *Rebel Without a Cause*," William Russo wrote. "No one ever gave Ray credit for Jimmy Dean's performance." In 1967, Ray wrote, "While I was working on *Rebel*, I came across a note of [Elia] Kazan's when we'd worked on *A Tree Grows in Brooklyn* [1945], and the note said: 'Have to be careful. Fuck acting. Don't direct a natural.' I've always believed that. A director shows the way. He does not manipulate his actors." Nicholas Ray's directorial style and willingness to indulge Dean convinced Backus and Hopper that Dean directed *Rebel Without a Cause*.

"I always thought he did direct *Rebel*," Hopper said in 2010. "I mean, Dean would set the camera. He'd rehearse the scene. Isn't that what a director does? Well, Nick Ray had worked for Elia Kazan, so he came out of Kazan's way of working. He was a great admirer. Nick Ray was intelligent enough to let Dean do what he did. You know, it's one thing to think you're the director and you have to get involved with everything, but when the fuckin' thing is working, you have to have that ability to step back and let it work. If what Dean wanted to do was intelligent, then Nick Ray would let him do it."

Filming on *Rebel Without a Cause* finished at 2:45 A.M. on May 27, 1955. The family feeling Ray engendered among the cast even extended to

Dennis Hopper that morning. Ray, Hopper, Natalie Wood, Perry Lopez, and Roger Donoghue got into Ray's Cadillac and followed James Dean on his motorcycle to Googie's.

Dennis Hopper had no time to reflect on what transpired while making *Rebel* or recharge his creative batteries. He and Dean were both eleven days overdue in Marfa, Texas, where *Giant* was being filmed. And Marfa would prove to be a far cry from the comfort of Hollywood.

· 3 ·

FROM GIANT TO HELL

Dennis Hopper tries to live out James Dean's legacy and ruins his career.

GIANT'S OUTDOOR SCENES were filmed in June and July 1955 in Marfa, Texas, a drought-stricken cattle town of 3,000 residents located in southwest Texas, about an hour's drive from the Mexican border. The town had one hotel and two movie theaters that showed Mexican films. The cast and crew rose at dawn and worked until darkness fell. "It was hotter than Hades out there," recalled *Giant's* production manager, Tom Andre.

Dennis Hopper had become James Dean's shadow after breaking through his protective armor on the set of *Rebel Without a Cause*. "He's just this guy who keeps following me around," Dean told his friend, John Gilmore. "Dennis quickly became docile around Jimmy on the set, apologetic and sometimes silent," Gilmore recalled.

Actors Studio alumnus Carroll Baker arrived at Warner Bros. for *Giant*, her first film role, while *Rebel* was still in production. Dean greeted Baker and showed her around the studio before taking her on a wild motorcycle ride to his private hideaway on the backlot. Dean brought his bike to a stop at a set that was a replica of a small American town, complete with a house with a white picket fence. Dean and Baker were laughing at the way the wind whipped up by their motorcycle ride split her dress open when he suddenly hugged her—until he saw something that abruptly changed his mood to cold fury.

Dennis Hopper was sitting on the front porch of the house. "It's my fault," Dean said. "I told him. Now he's here all the time!" "It's his place now, so go and meet him," Dean angrily commanded Baker. "Maybe it was because Jimmy told me to, but I walked over to Dennis and introduced myself," Baker wrote in her autobiography. "He looked up only briefly from contemplating his boots and then reassumed his 'James Dean' attitude. But he was only a mimic. There were no thoughts in his head worthy of boot contemplation. The troubled pose was just that: a pose."

Dennis Hopper's scenes in *Giant*, where he plays Jordan Benedict III, the teenage son of Bick Benedict (Rock Hudson) and Leslie Benedict (Elizabeth Taylor), were all shot on Warner Bros.' sound stages in Burbank after the film company returned from Texas. Hopper had very little to do in Marfa except to watch James Dean, who no longer objected to Hopper hanging around him. "During the filming of *Giant*, however, Dennis got a little closer to Jimmy, who was encouraging anyone to take his side against the 'others' who were making problems for him on the Texas locations," John Gilmore recalled. If observing Dean in *Rebel Without a Cause* was Hopper's freshman course in Method acting and upstaging directors, then *Giant* became his master class in bad behavior and directorial disrespect.

James Dean scandalized bystanders in Marfa with his loutish behavior and got away with it. And Hopper had a ringside seat. Dean's first scene in *Giant* with Elizabeth Taylor takes place when dirt-poor Jett Rink (Dean) invites Leslie Benedict (Taylor) to tea at his clapboard shack. Plenty of Marfa's locals watched the filming from the periphery of the outdoor location. To create Rink's unease with Leslie Benedict, Dean kept his bladder full before shooting commenced. But his technique didn't work. Intimidated by Taylor's star status, Dean flubbed several takes. He suddenly turned away from Taylor, walked a couple of hundred feet away, unzipped himself, and urinated on the ground in front of about a thousand strangers. Then he went back and got the scene on the first take.

Even Hopper was aghast. On the drive back to town, he asked Dean why he did it. "If you're nervous, your senses can't reach your subconscious, and that's that—you just can't work," Dean said. "It was Elizabeth Taylor. I can't get over my farm-boy upbringing. I was so nervous that I couldn't speak. I had to pee, and I was trying to use that, but it wasn't working. So I thought that if I could go pee in front of all those people, I would be able to work with her." Public urination was one of Dean's favorite shock tactics. Most likely, Dean just wanted to throw Taylor off balance and upstage her.

On another day, Rock Hudson emerged from his trailer just as Dean and Hopper strolled by. Dean suddenly leapt onto Hudson and French-kissed him. "Jimmy. I've seen you do some pretty crazy things, but what was that about?" Hopper asked. "Ah, he's a fairy," Dean replied.

James Dean had campaigned for the role of Jett Rink in *Giant* because George Stevens directed Dean's idol, Montgomery Clift, in *A Place in the Sun* (1951) and was considered one of Hollywood's great directors. Dean's enthusiasm for *Giant* and Stevens eroded rapidly in Marfa. Dean had been at the center of *Rebel Without a Cause*, and Nick Ray involved him in its production. Dean was in nearly every scene in *Rebel*. For Stevens, Dean was just one of the cast of *Giant*, deserving no special consideration. As Jett Rink, he only had about a total of thirty minutes of screen time in the three-hour-and-eighteen-minute-long film. Dean was often forced to sit idle in Marfa's heat, in costume, all day long, in case Stevens decided to use him. Dean and Stevens clashed over their respective working methods. Stevens didn't understand or like Dean's improvisatory methods or the plasticity of his performance, his way of doing different things in each take, which is exactly what Dennis Hopper sought to emulate.

Hopper witnessed Dean's growing contempt for Stevens, who became Dean's symbol for all directors. Dean told Hopper that he hated how acting forced him to be a director's puppet. "He couldn't stand being interrupted every five seconds by some idiot behind the camera," Hopper said. "He was too caught up in the role to be stopped abruptly and made to start again. *Jimmy wanted to be in charge.*"

Back in Hollywood, Dean caused a major blowup after he failed to show up at the studio one Saturday for shooting. After showing up for a previous Saturday morning call ready to work, only to be left cooling his heels in his dressing room, Dean decided to keep Stevens waiting. Studio functionaries spent half the day trying to locate him. Even Elizabeth Taylor was enlisted to check out some of Dean's haunts to see if he was there. Stevens bawled Dean out in front of the cast after he returned to the set. Stevens called him on the carpet in Jack Warner's office and threatened to kick Dean out of Hollywood after the picture was finished, but Dean remained unbowed. Dean related the meeting to Hopper, where he told Stevens and Warner, "I may be working in a factory, but I am not a machine. I stayed up all night Friday to do that scene. I prepared *all night* for that scene. I came in ready to work, and you kept me sitting around all day. Do you realize I'm doing emotional memories?"

Dean promised them that for every day he didn't work, he would skip a day, then two, then three. "And you're *not* going to stop me from working. Now let's get back to the set." "And you know something?" Hopper recalled. "From then on, when they called Jimmy in to work, he worked. He never sat around after that." This was another object lesson for Hopper.

Shortly after returning to Hollywood from Texas, Dennis Hopper participated in a delightfully ironic event. While Hopper, Nick Ray, and others privately took turns getting it on with Natalie Wood, Hopper and Wood were chosen as Hollywood's fresh young faces to adorn Disneyland's opening-day parade on July 17, 1955. The nationally televised event was hosted in part by Ronald Reagan.

"Strangely enough, I was at the opening of Disneyland," Hopper told *Variety's* reporter Strawberry Saroyan in 2005. "Natalie and I rode in the parade. Nixon was governor of California. He led the procession." (Goodwin Knight was then-governor of California. Richard Nixon was vice president of the United States.)

Eighteen-year-old Jack Nicholson, a mail clerk at MGM's animation department, watched the parade from the sidelines. "Hopper, who was under contract to Warner Bros. at the time—as was Wood—recalls being eager for official duties to end so he could check out the rides," Saroyan wrote. Hopper remembered particularly enjoying a celestial-themed ride. "We took off in a rocket, and we were in the stars, and it was really wonderful. Full of technology and full of things I'd never seen before," he told Saroyan. Hopper loved Disneyland and returned for another live televised special on June 15, 1959, appearing with Richard Nixon and Clint Eastwood.

Hopper got back to work after that brief respite. Unlike James Dean, Dennis Hopper worked well under George Stevens' direction. Perhaps Hopper's insecurity about living up to the demands of his first major role in a star-laden, prestige production blunted his rebellious tendencies. "Then he was going off to do *Giant*, which was a big thing for him, and he was really scared," Steffi Sidney told author Randall Riese. "I don't think he was intimidated," Sidney later told me. "I thought he was more excited to be in Texas and working with Stevens and Jimmy Dean and Elizabeth

Taylor and those people. I think he was extremely excited about it. He did write me from the set and just dropped a postcard or two. He was always very upbeat about it."

Before Hopper shot his first scene, Stevens gave him the star treatment to loosen him up and practically put Hopper on a pedestal. "I was really nervous the first day on the set, and he sat me down and started talking to me about where I was from, introduced me to people, made me relax, and finally said, 'Look at the way you're sitting. I like the way you're sitting,' and suddenly I was in the scene, and it was like talking to him. Once, he said to me, 'I don't care how much you think. I *like* thinking actors. But don't ever let me *know* you're thinking.' "

Stevens wasn't as pleased by James Dean's effect on Hopper, who became less compliant after one of his impromptu acting lessons with Dean. "You've been watching that Dean guy again. You two guys are screwing me up," Stevens groused. "He and Dean fought like dogs," Hopper said. "Then he got on me, too, because everything that Dean did was somehow my fault." Unlike Dean, Hopper's respect for Stevens survived the filming of *Giant*. Hopper later cited Stevens as one of the two directors he learned the most from (Henry Hathaway was the other). "The most underestimated is George Stevens," he said. "I learned a lot from him on *Giant*, watching him. His way with actors. I had the most respect for him. Always did. His arguments were not wrong."

Dennis Hopper had only one brief scene with James Dean in *Giant*. Accompanying his parents to the opening of Jett Rink's Emperador Hotel, Jordan Benedict III (Hopper) is outraged when the hotel's beauty parlor denies his Mexican wife (Elsa Cardenas) service. Jordan hurls a perfume decanter at a mirror bearing the initials JR. In Stevens impressive use of crosscutting, Jordan pursues Jett Rink to the banquet being held in his honor. Before the assembled guests, Jordan confronts Rink, who punches him out while his flunkies hold Benedict's arms.

Hopper was intimidated by the scene's demands on his abilities. He turned to Steffi Sidney, not Dean, for advice on how to play the scene. "I remember toward the end of the film, Dennis came up to me and said, 'You know, I have this scene that I have to play in *Giant*, and I just don't know what to do,' " Sidney recalled. " 'I'm just not a violent person. I don't know how to do it.' And I said, 'What's that?' And he told me about the scene in which he comes in and smashes the mirror because they won't seat his wife. Anyway, he said, 'I just don't know how to do that.' And I said, 'Well, just think of Nick Ray.' And he said, 'You're right.' "

James Dean finished his last scene in *Giant*, where he delivers Jett Rink's drunken monologue to a deserted banquet hall, on September 23, 1955. Hopper claims that Dean then retreated to a Trappist monastery in Malibu for three days. When Dean came back, he paid a visit to the studio. It was one of the few times Hopper ever saw him dressed in a suit and tie. Dean asked Hopper if he had read Mark Twain's novella *The Mysterious Stranger*. "It was as if he was saying goodbye to people," Hopper said.

"That night," Hopper recalled, "we went downtown to the old restaurant Sinatra used to go to, Villa Capri. And Dean said, 'I saw what you did today. I wish Edmund Kean could have seen you. And John Barrymore.' Because he said, 'Today you were great.' And I started to tear up. And tears started coming down my face. He said, 'It's very sweet. You're showing appreciation for what I'm saying, but when you really become a fucking actor, you'll have to leave the room to cry. Then you'll be there.' "

In the late afternoon of Friday, September 30, 1955, James Dean was killed in an auto accident as he drove his exotic Porsche Spyder to Salinas to compete in a race to be held there the next day. Natalie Wood, in New York to act in a television show, was enjoying dinner with Dick Davalos, Nick Adams, and Sal Mineo. The conversation inevitably fell to discussing James Dean. Adams opined that with Jimmy's penchant for dangerous sports like bullfighting, riding horses, and racing cars, Dean wouldn't live past thirty.

At the same time, Dennis Hopper and Robert Raison were attending a play in Santa Monica. The play hadn't started when Raison excused himself to take a call. When he returned, his face was ashen. Raison told Hopper, "I have to tell you something, but promise me that you'll stay here in the theater." Hopper said, "Is it someone in my family?" Raison said, "No, but are you going to stay here?" Hopper said, "Yeah." Raison said, "James Dean was just killed in a car accident." At that moment, the lights on stage went out and a spotlight illuminated an empty chair. An incredulous Hopper punched Raison and cried "Liar!" just as the spotlight came on.

Singer Toni Lee Scott, an amputee who received James Dean's sympathetic attention after they met at Googie's, knew Hopper and tells a different story in her memoir. Scott claims that Steffi Sidney telephoned her, to tell her that Dean had just been killed in a car accident. Scott then went straight to Hopper's home. Scott says that Hopper, who worshipped Dean, slapped her in disbelief when she told him Dean was dead.

Scott claims that James Dean's benevolent ghost haunted her and Dennis Hopper, and even saved his life. "Late one night, Dennis came into my bedroom and touched my foot so I would wake up without being frightened," she wrote. "Because so many people lived in the apartment and were always coming and going at odd hours, we left the door unlocked to avoid hassles over keys. 'What's the matter, Dennis?' I asked. 'I can't sleep in my bedroom, Toni. Can I use the twin bed?' 'Why can't you sleep in your bedroom?' He hesitated, then blurted it out. 'Because he's there, in my closet.' 'Dennis,' I said, 'he's here too, don't you know that?' He sensed what I had. 'Yes, I know that now, but can't I stay? That way, we'll be able to face him together.' 'Of course, you can stay, Dennis,' I replied, 'but remember, he loves us. He'd never do anything to hurt us. He just wants us to know he's around if we need him.'

"One day shortly afterward, Dennis was driving down a steep hill on the way to the studio when his brakes gave out," Scott wrote. "He didn't know what to do. Panicked, he turned around to see if there were other cars behind him, in case he had to swerve into another lane. And saw Jimmy sitting in the back seat, very relaxed, with his arms along the top of the seat. 'It's all right, Dennis,' he said. 'Just pull the emergency.' Dennis did and stopped the car. When he looked back, Jimmy was gone. When he came home, he told me what had happened. He didn't expect me to believe him. But I did. And still do."

It is difficult to overstate the importance of James Dean's influence and the impact of his death on Dennis Hopper's life. Hopper once spoke about Dean as if he was recalling the love of his life: "I was with him almost every day for the last eight months of his life and then he died." Nearly every interview with Dennis Hopper includes one of his elegiac laments for James Dean.

"The most personal tragedy in my life was James Dean, you know. I was nineteen years old, and I had such admiration for him," a tearful Hopper said in 1987. "I was haunted by the death of Dean, which had been the greatest emotional shock of my young life. He taught me so much. When he died, I felt cheated. I had dreams tied up in him, and suddenly, that was shattered. The alcohol and drugs brought me temporary escape. That was the first major thing that really affected me. It affected me for years after. I mean it really did. Even now I still . . . you know, I question. I mean, I can go to Europe, I'm going to Sweden, I go into a nightclub, and there's James Dean, Humphrey Bogart, Marilyn Monroe on the wall. Going to Paris, there he is . . . and yet I just feel rather cheated personally. I feel cheated personally and I just . . . it just leaves me sort of empty and not . . ."

"His death blew my mind," he said. "Because I really believe in predestination—that something protected gifted people until they could realize their potential. My life was confused and disoriented for years by his passing. My sense of destiny destroyed—the great films he would have directed, the great performances he would have given, the great humanitarian he would have become, and yet he's the greatest star and actor I have ever known."

Phyllis Gollehon saw the effect Dean's death had on Hopper when he returned to Helix High in June 1956 to speak to their graduating class. "When he got up to talk, it was embarrassing," she recalled. "He really hadn't prepared. He was not the Dennis I knew at all, and all he could talk about was how great James Dean was and how much he missed him. There was really nothing of substance to get people prepared for graduation. He was incoherent. It's hard to know when I saw him where the drugs started and James Dean . . ."

James Dean once sent a photo of himself taken while making *East of Eden* to Barbara Glenn, his girlfriend in New York. The photo shows Dean leaping off a train, seemingly able to fly. Dean's inscription on the photo reads, "Try and catch me. You might think I have to come down from up here, don't you? I hate all earthlings." It is the superhuman Dean of that photo that Hopper recalled to interviewers, not a real person. In the short time Hopper knew him, James Dean appeared to transcend earthly constraints. Dean defied actors, directors, and studio publicists with impunity. Then his death sealed him away from the inevitable ravages of age and the poor creative choices that diminish every actor and director.

Hopper might not have made Dean his role model if he had lived to disappoint him. Instead, Dennis Hopper became convinced that he was the natural heir to Dean's unfulfilled plans. Hopper made the mistake of confusing Dean's personal attributes with his artistic ability. To Hopper, Dean's professional success validated his personal excesses. Hopper was convinced that Dean succeeded because of, not in spite of, what Dean's friend, Bill Bast, called Dean's habit of playing brinksmanship in every area of his life. That included Dean's aggressive disrespect for directors and studio executives, casual drug use, and reckless driving.

"Dean was the symbol," Hopper said. "I was just a follower. When I came to Los Angeles, Montgomery Clift and Marlon Brando were getting their way and changing things. I adapted their ways because they worked. I wasn't (any of those three), but I was very conscious of a way of life that was evoked through their behavior. I didn't feel that 'the life' separated from 'the work,' and I thought that by emulating that lifestyle, I'd probably be able to work in the same way. I still maintained my own personality, but I was suddenly driving a sports car, wearing Levis and T-shirts, riding motorcycles, playing bongo drums, hanging out in coffeehouses, and listening to jazz. And drinking. Because Montgomery Clift did. I justified all my drinking and drug-taking by what my favorite actors, directors, musicians, and writers did."

James Dean was like an exotic potion that delivered short-term euphoria, but slowly poisoned anyone who imbibed it. Hopper's idolatry of Dean unleashed his worst incipient tendencies. For Dennis Hopper, a solipsistic dreamer with a remarkable lack of self-awareness, the effects of embracing Dean's dark side soon began to show. "It was after Jimmy's death several weeks later that Dennis began to change," John Gilmore wrote. "His agent and mine at the time, Bob Raison, said, 'Dennis has undergone a metamorphosis. He's lost who he was, and he's being replaced by this troublesome, unbalanced person.' "

"Dennis was peeing in the long trough in a men's room on the Warners lot one afternoon, telling me how he saw in some way that the duty to carry on Jimmy's enigmatic rebellion had fallen upon his shoulders. Very much alone in this presumption, he said, 'Only they don't know it yet,' and wagged his penis in the direction of the front office. 'But they're going to find out, man.' "

Gilmore saw what Hopper did with a letter Warner Bros. sent him detailing what his lateness to the set cost the studio. "Satisfied that they were at odds, just like it had been with Jimmy at the end, Dennis framed the letter and hung it next to a small painting Vincent Price had given him of a round, sickly green, grotesque face, like a freak or a wind-god, with distorted, blown-out cheeks and crazy, sleepless eyes. The trouble he caused the studio was all part of Dennis' 'break for freedom,' as he put it, bragging that Warners understood they had another volatile talent on their hands who needed 'special handling—the same as Jimmy Dean.' "

Jack Nicholson, who was then a nobody scrounging around for work, sometimes dropped by Hopper's house to cadge some cheap wine and a joint. He listened to Hopper's diatribes against the Hollywood establishment. "But even soused or stoned," Gilmore wrote, "Jack couldn't applaud Dennis' 'mumblings about rebellion,' which he saw as rationalizations for an 'ill-chosen course of action.' When Dennis went outside to where he'd hidden the dope to roll another joint, Jack said to me, 'Man, this is suicide! What the fuck's he doing?' He stared apprehensively at the studio letter on the wall."

Perhaps the blandishments of success at an early age caused Hopper to lose his bearings. Maybe his success came too easily. After performing in only two TV shows, Hopper was under contract to Warner Bros., got acting lessons from James Dean, and enjoyed a torrid affair with an underage starlet that was enriched with the drama of Hopper's enmity toward her older lover, who was directing him in his second film. By his own admission, Hopper arrived in Hollywood "with no worldly experience. I was a good actor, but that's about it."

"When I met Dennis, he was young and innocent and very un-Hollywood," Steffi Sidney said. "I think he was just a very earnest actor who hit Hollywood and worked hard to find what he could. Then he got under contract to Warner Bros., and all the frills came, and sometimes at nineteen that may not be as easy as you think, and when you have a star like Natalie approaching you, he thinks he's in seventh heaven. I think from there on in, it was downhill for him. Until he found himself again."

Gilmore witnessed Hopper's recklessness when he accompanied him to see a burlesque show in downtown Los Angeles. "Driving with Dennis in his little red Austin-Healey sports car could be scary," Gilmore wrote. "Always giving it gas when the light was turning yellow, he never looked both ways before racing ahead. At a bus zone, he'd block traffic to tell the waiting commuters he'd seen the bus several blocks back, and it was on the way. They would thank him, and he'd pull away laughing. I never understood the prank—one of many he'd claim he was pulling to 'put people on.'

"Hopping signals, he had to blow a couple of joints on the way, then sat stiffly anxious when the short, big-nosed comic in baggy balloon pants teetered around the girls, stepping on a fart bag for laughs." Hopper reacted apathetically until a pockmarked girl with a scarred stomach came on stage. "Something about her so enraptured Dennis that he began at once grabbing and pulling at his crotch," Gilmore recalled. "A couple of bums edged off, thinking he was some sort of queer, and soon the assistant manager came down the aisle and asked us to leave the theater. In the lobby, Dennis yelled, 'I'm Dennis Hopper, man. I'm with Warner Bros., and I'll have your fucking job!' The guy said that if he was such a hotshot, he wouldn't want the job in the first place, but if Dennis didn't leave the lobby immediately he'd call the cops. 'We don't allow no jacking off in here!' "

Gwen Davis, a young writer, got to know Dennis Hopper around this time. She remembered her first encounter with him, which took place shortly after James Dean had died. Davis was at a party where Marlon Brando was supposed to make an appearance. Brando never showed, but Ben Gazzara and Anthony Perkins, who was being touted as the next James Dean, were there. Davis was in the garden when a stocky young man suddenly pushed his way through the bushes and said, "I crashed this party. Fuck everyone!" Davis was taken aback by Hopper's f-bomb. Such language was not used in casual conversation back then.

"Hi," Davis managed to reply. "I come from Kansas, which is nowhere," Hopper said. "And I hate my parents, who are no one." Davis and Hopper went from the party to Googie's, where, Davis recalled, Dennis told her he "had spent numberless hours with Jimmy Dean, who had been his 'best friend.' " To Davis, Hopper was "one of the most original, deliberately offensive, and unintentionally funny people I'd ever known. He liked to think of himself as the hero in *The Sun Also Rises*, his balls having been cut off by an insensitive society, failing to recognize his genius."

One of Hopper's stunts involved coming over to Davis' house, which stood across a narrow lane from Adams and Hopper's. Hopper would attach a long length of rope to the guardrail of Davis' porch, and swing over to his porch, yelling "Fuck Errol Flynn!" Annoyed by Davis' crush on Perkins, Hopper stole the cardboard likeness of Perkins that stood in front of Grauman's Chinese Theatre to promote his film, *Friendly Persuasion* (1956). The next morning, Davis awoke to see Hopper in her backyard, sitting on a rock next to Perkins' cutout. "You'd still rather have him?" a grinning Hopper asked Davis. When she said yes, Hopper drove away angrily to meet up with Natalie Wood.

There seemed to be no limit to Hopper's eagerness to violate social conventions. "After bringing him into the home of a literary critic who was a close confidant of mine, I found out, to my very young and inexperienced horror, that Dennis had bedded the critic's wife," Davis wrote. "It was one thing my writing lurid sex scenes; quite another finding out they took place in real life. My God, I was young, but bear in mind that Dennis was even younger."

After a year of postproduction, *Giant* opened at New York's Roxy on October 10, 1956, to almost unalloyed praise. Most critics paid obligatory attention to George Stevens, Rock Hudson, and Elizabeth Taylor, but focused their attention on James Dean's final performance. Hollis Alpert set the tone in the October 13, 1956, issue of the *Saturday Review*. In a review headlined, "It's Dean, Dean, Dean," Alpert wrote, "But it is the late James Dean, as Jett Rink, that the audiences will be watching—and there are many who will be watching him with fascination and love."

Dennis Hopper's performance would have been mentioned favorably in other circumstances, but reviewers ignored him. Though George Stevens acclaimed Hopper as "one of the brightest young actors in the business—one destined to go far," his performance was lost in the backwash of hysteria over Dean. Twenty years later, *Giant* and George Stevens' critical stock had declined, while appreciation for Hopper's performance had risen. Discussing the second half of *Giant*, James Dean biographer John Howlett wrote, "After the epic style and vision of the first half of the film, this contrived melodrama is a sad anti-climax, only kept alive by the vitality of Elizabeth Taylor's performance, and the occasional glimpses of Dean and Dennis Hopper."

Hopper balked at the studio's plans for him to take Natalie Wood to *Giant*'s New York premiere. "I went to the premiere of *Giant*," he said, "and the studio wanted me to take Natalie, and I wanted to take Joanne Woodward, and nobody ever heard of Joanne Woodward, and I insisted. So when I arrived at the premiere of *Giant*, they wouldn't interview me because I was with Joanne Woodward, and they said, 'Who are you, his secretary?' " (Jayne Meadows and Chill Wills briefly interviewed Hopper and Woodward outside the theater for the live television coverage of the premiere, though Meadows and Wills didn't know who Woodward was.)

After the screening, Hopper and Woodward attended a party held at the swank Copacabana nightclub. Sitting at Jack Warner's table, they were ignored, while all eyes were on Elizabeth Taylor—when she wasn't in the women's bathroom. Taylor's husband, Mike Todd, kept sending Hopper to fetch her from the bathroom. When Hopper objected, Todd, who was very angry, said, "You're younger, you can go yelling back there, if I do that . . .

Go see what she's doing in there." Woodward finally asked Hopper to take her back to her apartment. When he tried to follow her in, she wouldn't let him and pushed him down a flight of stairs. "I never figured that out, until later she told me that Paul [Newman] was waiting for her in her apartment," Hopper said. "This was before they were married."

Though Dennis Hopper had adopted James Dean's contempt for Warner Bros.' publicity apparatus, he happily cooperated with the gimmick they thought up for *Giant*'s Los Angeles premiere on October 17. Hopper and Natalie Wood went to the event on a double date with Dennis' younger brother, David, escorting Natalie's younger sister, Lana. Like Dennis, David wore a tuxedo and Lana wore a dress that matched Natalie's. Photos taken at the premiere show an unusually happy, open-faced Dennis Hopper beaming at the camera. While newsreel cameras covering the opening whirred, Natalie surprised Dennis with an enthusiastic kiss. Putting aside their understandable interest in Dennis' performance, Hopper and Wood watched the film with rapt attention, lost in admiration for their friend, James Dean, stung by the poignant realization that they were seeing him for the very last time.

Dennis and Natalie's affair cooled after *Giant*'s premiere. Her infatuation with James Dean, and, by extension, Dennis Hopper, had spent itself. Natalie was constantly seen and photographed with a new beau on her arm, whether he was a studio-arranged date like Tab Hunter or someone she had a genuine affinity for. Wood's stand-in on *Rebel*, Faye Nuell Mayo, said, "Natalie had a lot of boyfriends, this was part of her exploring to find out who she was." For his own part, Hopper played the field, dating starlets Ursula Andress (Dean's last girlfriend) and Joan Collins. "None of these affairs were too serious," he said. "I don't think there was a starlet around who could have been had in those days that I didn't have," he boasted.

Elvis Presley arrived in Hollywood nearly a year after James Dean's death to make his first movie, *Love Me Tender* (1956). Presley was obsessed with James Dean and sought out anyone with a connection to him, including Nick Adams, Dennis Hopper, and Natalie Wood, who Elvis dated. Unlike Nick Adams, who invited himself to Memphis and into Elvis' entourage, Dennis Hopper never joined Elvis' Memphis Mafia, as his inner circle came to be known. "It was his first film," Hopper said, "and he wanted to know about James Dean. He came to see me before he saw anyone else. So I spent a couple of weeks with him." Hopper learned some interesting things about Elvis when he kept company with the singer.

"I remember when Elvis Presley came to Hollywood for his first picture, we met, and he told me he was worried because the script called for him to hit Debra Paget," Hopper recalled. "And he said to me, 'Man, I never hit a woman before.' I said, 'Just pretend you're slapping at a bothersome fly.' He said, 'No, I can't hit a woman!' And I suddenly realized it wasn't a question of motivation. Elvis actually believed that he had to hit the girl in this scene!" When Elvis told Hopper he had to fight another actor, but felt he could take him, Hopper patiently explained to him, "That you never actually hit anyone in a movie, that it was all faked, but the film was cut in such a way as to give the impression that it actually happened. Now, he believed that movie fights were real, and that movie bullets were real, and when I explained that they weren't, he got *very* pissed off at me! He thought I was kidding him. He couldn't accept the fact that he had been deceived all these years by movies."

Hopper also remembered how Elvis enjoyed the sexual opportunities available to him in Hollywood. "It was in the '50s," he said, "pre-Pill and pre-pantyhose. It was a little more difficult to score, is what I'm tryin' to say. But Elvis didn't have that problem. So I went to see him in the Beverly Wilshire, and he had six women waiting for him, all who I knew and all who I knew didn't fool around, and all who were going in for a quickie. So he would take one in, another twenty minutes, another one would go out and in there. And I said, 'Elvis, are you fucking all those women?' He said, 'Yeah.' And I said, 'How the hell do you get it up, man?' And he said, 'Well, they all different, ain't they?' "

Hopper's escapades with Presley couldn't distract him from his growing frustration with his stalled career. Hopper's role in *Giant* should have been the jumping-off point for a series of good roles in other pictures. Instead, Warner Bros. seemed to lose track of Hopper, using him as fodder in a variety of thankless film and TV roles. The twenty-one-year-old Hopper was typically miscast as Napoleon in producer Irwin Allen's film, *The Story of Mankind* (1957). "Playing Napoleon, glum and Method-y in a sub-Brando way," Stephen Rebello wrote, "Hopper strokes a bust in his likeness and lusts to be emperor, muttering, 'A man is only as great as his fellow men will allow.' " Based loosely on the nonfiction book of the same title, *The Story of Mankind* made heavy use of stock footage to illustrate a pageant of famous historical episodes, relying mostly on aging stars posed stiffly against obviously fake sets. The measure of the film can be taken by noting that Harpo Marx played Sir Isaac Newton.

Even after the success of *Rebel Without a Cause* should have pointed the way, Warner Bros.' executives failed to exploit Hopper's obvious resemblance and devotion to James Dean. Warner Bros. paired Hopper and Natalie Wood in an episode of their TV series, *Kings Row*, and loaned them out to do an episode of *The Kaiser Aluminum Hour*, but never put them in a film. Instead, the studio's new "romantic" couple became Wood and Tab Hunter, the handsome but vapid actor to whom Warner Bros. was giving a star buildup.

Even Hunter complained about the lack of direction he received from Warner Bros., which he says, was at a "crossroads." "Other than its huge success with Natalie and me, Warner Bros. was hurting," Hunter wrote in his memoir. "It was confused about what kind of movies to make, during a period when new trends were shaking things up: competition from television, the influence of foreign films (both on filmmakers and viewers), the shift toward realism and naturalism, the cultural changes brought on by rock and roll—Warners wasn't too swift picking up on any of these. Studio executives could see the writing on the wall, but had a lot of trouble translating it. It was a cautious and conservative company."

Perhaps because *Giant* was commonly thought of as a Western, and Western films and TV series were then a booming genre, Hopper found himself playing young gunfighters who sometimes expressed angsty self-doubt about their deeds. In 2007, he told talk-show host Tavis Smiley, "It was the time of John Wayne and Kirk Douglas and Burt [Lancaster]—they were all doing Westerns. Westerns were the big films of that time."

Warners cast Hopper in the guest-starring role of Billy the Kid in an episode of their TV series, *Sugarfoot* (1957–1961), hoping to spin off a twice-monthly television series about Billy the Kid starring Hopper. "When I was under contract to Warner Bros.," he told Smiley, "everybody was doing a television series, and I just didn't want to do a series of my own. I just felt that I'd get stuck there, and I'd never get into feature films, and that's where I wanted to be. I was wrong about that. Jim Garner and Steve McQueen, all of them came out of series. So they kept putting me into guest-starring parts, and in guest-starring parts in television, you usually play the bad guy 'cause the good guys are already on the series. So I came in as the villain most of the time, and that was fine."

Hopper appeared as Billy Clanton in John Sturges' colorful, robust *Gunfight at the O.K. Corral* (1957), among a large cast headed by Burt

Lancaster and Kirk Douglas. He played two scenes with Lancaster and had a lot of fun with the film's stunt crew, who played a running practical joke on Hopper. They'd approach him and convince him that the police were about to arrest him for getting a girl he was having a fling with pregnant. One time, they hustled him away from the film's climactic gunfight scene and back to his hotel room to protect him from the police. This carried on for several days until Hopper finally wised up and said, "Come on! There's no police."

Hopper played Hatfield Carnes, a flippant, arrogant killer pitted against the town sheriff in *The Young Land*, a decently made B-Western that gave eighteen-year-old Patrick Wayne, John Wayne's son, his first starring role. Carnes is arrested and put on trial for drawing on a Mexican in the cantina of a one-horse town in the newly formed state of California. A mild amount of tension builds as Carnes awaits trial, hoping his cronies will break him out of jail while the town's Mexican population waits for the arrival of a judge (Dan O'Herlihy) to see if he will dispense justice to the gringo who killed one of their own. Whether he was telling the prosecutor he's already killed five men by casually holding up one hand or leaning back in his chair and smirking while listening to the judge, Hopper had some effective moments in the film. Directed by Ted Tetzlaff, Hitchcock's cinematographer on *Notorious* (1946), *The Young Land* was made by Disney's Buena Vista division in 1957, but sat on the shelf until Columbia Pictures rescued it for a 1959 release.

Hopper looked cool playing a young gun who helps Lucas McCain (Chuck Connors) defeat corrupt forces out to take control of the town of North Fork in the "The Sharpshooter, (broadcast on September 30, 1958), the pilot episode of the classic TV series, *The Rifleman* (1958–1963). Hopper also guest starred in another *Rifleman* episode, "Three Legged Terror," (broadcast on April 21, 1959) as the artistically gifted nephew of an abusive farmer (John Hoyt). What Hopper remembers best about *The Rifleman* was the opportunity to meet Sam Peckinpah, another wild talent who wrote the series' pilot and directed four of the show's episodes. "This was before he'd directed anything, but he was still on set whispering, 'Do this, do that,'" Hopper said. "Sam and Steve McQueen—we all smoked grass. So Sam was the only one that we could go into his office and smoke grass at the studio."

Hopper complained publicly about Warner Bros.' mishandling of his career. An article in the March 1, 1957, edition of the Hollywood *Citizen*

News reported that Hopper was unhappy because Warner Bros. wouldn't let him study acting in New York. "I finished *Giant* two years ago," he told a reporter while lunching with seventeen-year-old Venetia Stevenson in Warner Bros.' Green Room. "And since then I've done two bits and some television. I watch other guys with no more talent, getting pictures and buildups in other studios."

Hopper's frustration culminated in 1958 when he was cast in the film *From Hell to Texas,* directed by Henry Hathaway. It was a role he didn't cherish. "The part was the weak son of the bad man, and I didn't want to do it, but the studio said go on and do it," he said. Hopper tried to exercise the creative prerogative he believed Brando, Clift, and Dean enjoyed. That was unheard of for an actor of Hopper's stature.

"They were the only ones," he said. "At that time, everything was so staid and locked in. In most major studio productions, actors were just directors' puppets, and you had to do every line reading, every gesture their way. Then Brando demanded the right to block his scenes. Dean demanded to block his own scenes. Montgomery Clift. The three of them demanded that kind of thing. And so you had these people coming in and blocking their own scenes and making their own moves and doing their own emotional things and not repeating the same thing over and over, but doing it differently from a closeup to a long shot and yet knowing enough to still have something to match and cut to. I tried that, and they kicked me out."

"He was a big time director, Hathaway," Hopper said. "He'd come up as a carpenter, then as a prop man and director. He was one of those tough, old-school directors. So it was a major fight. We fought and fought throughout the whole picture. He wanted me. He thought that I was the best young actor he'd seen. But he wanted me to imitate Marlon Brando in timing and gestures, and he gave me his line readings and his approach to acting. I walked off the picture three times."

"I must say, Hathaway had a reputation," said Don Murray, who played the lead role in *From Hell to Texas.* "I had heard about Hathaway, going into this film, of being a very, very volatile director and getting very angry and having all sorts of emotional outbreaks himself on the set, sort of like Otto Preminger, very dictatorial in his ways. So I think right away they were going to come into conflict because Dennis Hopper was a Method actor, the kind of a performer who would feel his way through the part and not come to a strong characterization right away. I think that was bound to upset Henry Hathaway, and when you add his volatile nature, it's not a good combination."

Murray recalled that Hopper would "sort of mumble and experiment" in rehearsals. "And Hathaway couldn't really get an impression of what he was going to do," he said. "On quite a few of the takes, he would not give a performance that Hathaway thought was acceptable because I think Hathaway realized, as we all did, that he really was a good actor. He had been in *Giant* and was really forceful in that, and I think Hathaway had that image in mind. But Hathaway was not getting what he wanted. Hathaway was not prone to giving you readings unless he thought that you didn't understand what he was saying, and then he might give you readings."

Murray recalls watching Hathaway film twenty-two takes of a scene involving Hopper, when Hopper called Hathaway "a fucking idiot" to his face and stormed off the set. "But Hathaway printed a lot of those takes," recalled R. G. Armstrong, a stage actor who made his movie debut playing Hopper's father in *From Hell to Texas*. Armstrong said that Hathaway did tell Hopper how to move and read lines. Hathaway yelled at Hopper when he rejected his direction. "Get yourself another fucking actor," Hopper told Hathaway before stalking off the set. Armstrong, who was awestruck by Hopper's defiance, said that Hathaway would then throw his arms out in front of him, as if to say, "What can I do with him?"

By day, Hopper complained to Murray that he felt Hathaway was dictatorial. "Hathaway would come to me at night and say, 'I just don't understand this young man. I don't know how to reach him. What am I going to do?' " Murray said. "What I would say to Hathaway is to exercise patience and just keep on going for what he wants. The very rebellious nature that Dennis Hopper has as a person is exactly what the role has. He's the spoiled brat of a wealthy rancher who's unjustifiably started a vendetta against my character and is very, very undisciplined and a brat, but that's the quality you want to get from him, you want to use that quality. I think that Hopper ended up very good in the film because that's exactly what comes across in the film."

Murray suggested that Hathaway should try to resolve his differences with Hopper over dinner. It didn't work. Each time Hopper walked off the picture, Hathaway begged him to come back, inviting him to wonderful dinners where he charmed him. "He was the most charming man you'd ever meet at dinner," Hopper said. When Hopper discussed his ideas for the following day's scenes, Hathaway said, "Sure, sure kid. Whatever you say." On the set the next day, Hathaway was a monster again, yelling and screaming at Hopper. "Mr. Hathaway, last night at dinner, you said I could try this," Hopper reminded him. Hathaway told him, "Forget that, it's fuckin' dinner talk, kid. We're makin' a movie here, now get the fuck over there, and hit your mark, and say your lines like I tell ya!" On at least one occasion, Hopper punked Hathaway. "If you really wanted to drive him crazy," Hopper said, "you'd put a paper cup in the scene. 'Paper cup in a fuckin' Western! They didn't have fuckin' paper cups in the Old West, goddammit!'"

Yelling at actors was evidently Hathaway's style. In 2011, Kim Darby and Glen Campbell, who costarred with John Wayne in Hathaway's film, *True Grit* (1969), recalled the director's bellicose manner. Though Hathaway had been pleasant to Darby at their first meeting at the studio, he yelled at her on the first day of shooting. "He was an old prop man, and he usually focused on the prop man, and he would just yell at him no matter what he did," Darby said. "It got me so off guard. I just got up and went back to my dressing room." After a talk with Hathaway in her dressing room, Darby said, "Henry, I'll do anything you want, just don't yell at me again." "After that day," she said, "we went along swimmingly."

When Hathaway yelled at Glen Campbell one day, he told the director, "You know, I can get on a horse and get out of here and get in my car and go back to L.A." "He kind of looked at me," Campbell recalled, "and said, 'Well, I have been tough on you.' That was Henry Hathaway."

If his battle with Hathaway wasn't enough trouble, Hopper was also conducting an affair with married actress Diane Varsi during filming. "In fact," Don Murray said, "I remember one time, her husband burst in on them and picked up a chair and attacked Dennis Hopper with it. And Hopper was defending himself with his feet. Dennis Hopper ended up with all sorts of bruises." R. G. Armstrong recalled how Hopper also enlisted Varsi in his rebellion against Hathaway. She was less demonstrative with Hathaway than Hopper. Varsi merely turned her back on Hathaway when she balked at his direction.

Hathaway confronted Hopper on the last day of shooting. "I had a ten-line scene with my father [in the film]," Hopper recalled. "And Hathaway came on the set and said, 'You know what these things are over there?'

And I said, 'Yeah, those are film cans.' He said, 'Yeah those are film cans. There's enough film in there to shoot for four months. And you're going to do the scene my way. You're going to pick up the coffee cup and put it down. You're gonna read the lines this way. And you can do it that way, or you can make a career out of this one scene in this one movie because I own 40 percent of this studio.' He said, 'We're here now to stay. We'll send out for lunch, send out for dinner, we're here. Sleeping bags will be brought in. This is it.' "

"We started at seven in the morning," Hopper said. "About eleven o'clock, Steve Trilling, who was then head of production for Warner Bros., called and said, 'What's going on over there? Just do what Hathaway says, and get back over here.' At two o'clock in the afternoon, Jack Warner called and said, 'What the fuck is going on?' He said, 'Do what fucking Hathaway says, and get back over here.' Dinner came."

By ten o'clock, Hopper buckled. "I couldn't figure out another way to do the scene," he said. "By this time all the executives from Fox—Warner, everybody—were all there. It was big news. 'You want to see Hathaway and Hopper freaking out? Come on over.' I said, 'Just tell me what you want.' And I broke down and started crying. I said, 'Just tell me one more time what you want.' I did the scene." Hathaway came over to Hopper, and without removing his cigar from his mouth, said, "Kid, there's one thing I can promise you: you'll never work in this town again." "I said thank you very much and walked out of the studio," Hopper said. "And I was dropped by Warner Bros. And that was the end of my career in Hollywood."

"After the film Warners canceled my contract. They had labeled me as a troublemaker, a rebel. Most actors in Hollywood were just directors' puppets. The old-line directors hated us for trying to introduce something new. When it was successful, when the critics raved about it as something fresh, they hated us even more. Of course, I didn't have anything like the muscle of a Brando, so I lost my argument with Hathaway."

Dennis Hopper became convinced that he was blacklisted by the studios because of his showdown with Hathaway. Brooke Hayward said, "Baloney! Dennis just wouldn't take direction." John Gilmore believes that Hopper was the victim of an industry-wide trend. The Hollywood studios had embarked on a campaign of retrenchment, seeking to cut their losses when the competition from television caused movie attendance to plummet. "There was no need for unnecessary trouble," Gilmore wrote. "The so-called 'rebels' were weeded out, those 'misfits' who could create unbalance in the flow toward picture prosperity. The troublemakers were sifted out through a kind of blackballing that had quickly gone into effect after Jimmy Dean's death."

Hopper asserted that the paucity of his work after *From Hell to Texas* came from an undeserved reputation as a difficult actor. "Young Dennis Hopper says a misguided Hollywood notion that he's a 'rebel' is costing him important screen roles," Joe Finnigan reported in the January 23, 1960, edition of the *Los Angeles Examiner.* "I was influenced by Jimmy, and I believe my friendship with him hurt my career," Hopper told Finnigan. "Jimmy, a fine talent, wasn't the easiest guy in the world to work with. That's no secret."

"Dennis, who has turned in some first-rate performances, said some filmland folk believed he 'was cut from the same pattern' as Dean and automatically put him down as hard to get along with," Finnigan wrote. "After Jimmy was killed, a lot of people in this business who didn't like him, took their anger out on me," he told Finnigan. Hopper still believed this in 1990 when he told Stephen Rebello, "They really couldn't do anything to Dean. When he died, whether it was conscious or unconscious, they could do to me what they couldn't do to a major star."

"The industry was lenient," John Gilmore wrote, "and forgave unspeakable things in the name of genuine, salable talent, but the consensus was that Dennis Hopper didn't have any such talent. His pranks had cost the studio money that couldn't be backed up with any sort of commercial delivery, and so he was simply dumped. It was all very easy—no one cared. But Dennis hit the unemployment line hard, joining the rest of us out-of-work actors in a crowded, desperate town."

After warring with Henry Hathaway, Dennis Hopper was happy to return to the warm embrace of the La Jolla Playhouse for their production of Thornton Wilder's play *The Skin of Our Teeth.* Hopper played his mother's (Cloris Leachman) miscreant son among a cast that included James Whitmore and Eartha Kitt. *The Skin of Our Teeth,* which opened on June 23, 1958, was one of eight plays presented by the playhouse that summer, each running for one week. Director Sherman Marks told his friend, Lamont Johnson, the play's producer, that Hopper was "one cocky son of a bitch."

Roughly three years after Dennis Hopper hit Hollywood with little experience and a chip on both shoulders, Hollywood hit back hard. Hopper treated his termination by Warner Bros. as a liberation. "I wanted to get away from Hollywood and also study acting," he said. It was as good a time as any for him to head to New York, where, despite James Dean's warning, Hopper was determined to join the Actors Studio.

· 4 ·

HARDLY WORKING

An underemployed Dennis Hopper turns to photography and collecting pop art to satisfy his creative drive. Hopper marries a Hollywood princess and loses her to alcohol, drugs, and violence, but gains Easy Rider.

"*I*T WAS ALWAYS my obsession to try and make the characters real, from the time I was very young," Dennis Hopper said. "I mean, the first two great performances I saw were all in one week. I saw Montgomery Clift in *A Place in the Sun* [1951], and I saw Marlon Brando in *Viva Zapata!* [1952]. I had never seen them act before, and it really twisted my head around. Before that I had been doing Shakespeare. I had been doing classical theater, so I had been impressed with Orson Welles and John Barrymore and a very broad kind of acting. And to see Montgomery Clift and Brando, who were so subtle and so real, it just blew me away."

The effect of Brando and Clift's performances, and Hopper's personal relationship with James Dean, compelled him to seek out the source of their genius for acting. Dennis Hopper and his peers were convinced that the secret to Brando, Clift, and Dean's performances could be found in their training in the Method acting techniques originated by Konstantin Stanislavski that Lee Strasberg practiced at the Actors Studio in New York. (None of the three actors really spent much time there, especially Dean, who rarely participated in classes at the studio after Strasberg's withering critique of his first scene.) Hopper took up residence at New York's bohemian Chelsea Hotel and waited six months before finally gaining admission to Strasberg's acting class. Hopper competed with dozens of applicants for the select honor, for only a handful of students were rewarded with membership in the studio each year.

"Dean told me not to go study with Strasberg," Hopper said. "He felt that if I just learned how to do things and not how to show them, then I had enough natural talent to get by. The second that he died, my teacher was gone. When he died, I felt a little lost, and I went immediately to New York and studied with Strasberg. He had a tremendous effect on me.

"First of all, he never told you anything really. He'd sit in his class and watch you. And you learned by just being there. But he was a very quiet guy, and we'd do scenes, and he would criticize the scenes. Lee Strasberg taught me about sense memories, emotional memories. The senses control the brain. So how do you trick your subconscious? You get rid of all the tension areas, go back, try to recall every sense, and one sense will bring it all back.

"He was a very strange man. I'd get in the elevator with him every morning for almost five years and say, 'Good morning, Mr. Strasberg.' I never got a good morning back from him during those five years. He'd have this newspaper, and he'd clear his throat. He'd never speak to anyone until class began, then he spoke, talked, and did his thing, but when class was over, he was back into himself. He was a very tough guy. He was strict. I saw three-quarters of the people studying with him taken off the stage in a straitjacket to the booby house or the funny farm when they suddenly hit their emotional memory."

Hopper immersed himself in the cultural riches New York offered, haunting its art museums and galleries. "When I was studying at Lee Strasberg's, I used to go to MoMA [the Museum of Modern Art] every day to look at Cezanne and Matisse, go through the whole collection," he said. "I was born visual and started seeing really early on. It had to do with Kansas, that horizon line. With nothing to look at, I had to become visually creative."

When he wasn't memorizing the MoMA's collection, Hopper hung out with Beat poets Allen Ginsberg and Peter Orlovsky, and spent his evenings in the city's jazz clubs, becoming friends on a first-name basis with jazz musicians like Miles Davis. "When we were kids, Miles Davis and I used to spar together. I was in my early twenties. He was a little older. We'd box, and he'd say profound things, and I'd say, 'Oh, so what? So what?' 'So what' was just something I would say all the time because I had no fucking answers. One night, I came into the club he was playing in Los Angeles—we'd all gotten kicked out of New York for the drug problems—and he said (raspy voice), 'I've written a song for you, Dennis. I want you to hear it now. It's called 'So What.' Really a good song.' The album was called *Kind of Blue* and 'So What' was on it. So that one sticks."

In interviews, Hopper gave the impression that he relocated to New York to study at the Actors Studio, but he kept one foot firmly planted in Hollywood, where he kept a duplex. Hopper performed in fifteen episodes of various TV series and two movies between his dismissal from Warner Bros. and his return to Los Angeles in 1961 after his marriage to Brooke Hayward. He commuted to New York, the costly coast-to-coast air travel financed by his fees from TV guest shots and roles in low-budget films. (Peter Fonda was being paid a surprisingly generous $7,000 to $11,000 for five to seven days of work for guest-starring roles in one-hour TV dramas around the same time.)

Though Hopper always maintained that he studied with Strasberg for five years, his studies at the Actors Studio ended when he married Hayward and they settled in Bel Air, a posh suburb of Los Angeles where the couple resided until she left Hopper in 1968. Although Hayward flatly declared, "Dennis had nothing to do with the Actors Studio," she could have been unaware of his work there before she met him. It's a curious statement because, in her memoir, Hayward recounts joining Strasberg's classes in the fall of 1959.

Despite the bad reputation that Hopper earned after his blowup with Henry Hathaway, MGM signed him to a five-picture contract in 1959. MGM's contract with Hopper minimized their risk, paying him only when he made a film, instead of putting him on a weekly salary. Hopper's only MGM film was *Key Witness* (1960), which starred Jeffrey Hunter and Pat Crowley as a suburban couple whose lives are turned upside down when Hunter witnesses a street gang kill a man and decides to testify against their leader, William "Cowboy" Tomkins (Hopper). Cowboy and his gang (which includes Hopper's fellow *Rebel Without a Cause* cast member Corey Allen), terrorize Hunter and Crowley in an ultimately unsuccessful attempt to prevent Hunter from testifying. Filmed in CinemaScope and black-and-white, *Key Witness* was a cheaply made, small-scale film that offered little more than contemporary TV dramas and earned little at the box office. Charles Wolcott's jazzy title music remains the film's strongest element.

Key Witness was a creative dead end for Hopper, who was stuck playing a hopped-up punk four years after his similar role in *Rebel Without a Cause*. A little independent film came along that promised something more, something Hopper could get excited about. Thirty-five-year-old Curtis Harrington had worked with avant-garde filmmaker Maya Deren, directed several avant-garde short films of his own in the '40s and '50s, and appeared with Anais Nin in Kenneth Anger's film, *Inauguration of the Pleasure Dome* (1954). After working as producer Jerry Wald's assistant on films like *Peyton Place* (1957), Harrington hoped to strike out on his own as a feature-film director. Harrington planned to make an atmospheric, moody horror film along the lines of producer Val Lewton's *Cat People* (1942). Hopper responded enthusiastically to Harrington's ideas and agreed to star in his new film after viewing his short films.

In Harrington's *Night Tide* (1961), Hopper plays Johnny Drake, a lonely young sailor on leave who becomes fascinated with a dark-haired, exotic young woman named Mora (Linda Lawson) he glimpses in a jazz club one night. By day, Mora wears a fake mermaid's tail and swishes around a giant fish tank as "Mora the Mermaid" in a sideshow act on the pier. Johnny encounters a series of local characters who gradually fill him in on Mora, including retired sea captain Murdock (Gavin Muir), who adopted the orphaned girl from the Greek island of Mykonos. Sheltered by Murdock, Mora is socially inept—she serves Johnny cold mackerel for breakfast. Murdock has convinced Mora that she is a member of a race of sea-dwelling sirens and is responsible for the disappearance of her two previous boyfriends. When Johnny and Mora go scuba diving, she swims away from him, cuts her own air hose, and drowns. During a raging thunderstorm, Johnny discovers Mora's lifeless body floating in her tank at the sideshow where Murdock tries to kill him. The police suspect Johnny of her death until Murdock makes a convenient eleventh-hour confession of killing Mora's boyfriends.

Night Tide betrays its very meager $50,000 budget (Hopper said it was $28,000). Filmed around Venice, California, and nearby beach locations, *Night Tide* strives for atmosphere, but just looks visually drab with an underpopulated cast. There is little action as the story unfolds in a series of expository scenes directed at an unvarying pace. The "Is Mora a siren or isn't she?" mystery is bogus and generates little suspense. *Night Tide* could have used more of its penultimate scene's *Sturm und Drang*, however cliched the thunderstorm is. *Night Tide's* most interesting scene takes place when Johnny visits Mora and takes a nap on her sofa while she showers. She emerges from the shower and embraces Johnny, who suddenly finds himself in the strangling grip of an octopus until he awakens from his erotic nightmare.

Curtis Harrington, who had never directed a feature before, was pleased to rely on Hopper, who contributed his filmmaking experience to help Harrington guide his actors' performances. Linda Lawson didn't find Hopper's assistance helpful. He creeped her out. Hopper said that Lawson's future husband, John Foreman (the business partner of Paul Newman who produced *Butch Cassidy and The Sundance Kid* [1969]), hovered behind him during filming, just out of camera range, to make sure he didn't grope her too much in their kissing scenes.

"Dennis was very talented and so excited about playing a lead in Curtis' film, which was done for no money at all, so we all pitched in to make it work," Lawson told writer David Del Valle. "I invited Dennis over to run lines one afternoon, and when he arrived at my apartment, he walked in and went straight back to my kitchen and climbed under the table and would not come out. He was really scary when he chose to act like this. Afterwards, we worked together only on location or with Curtis present. I warned Dennis that if he acted that way again, I would walk off the film. The end result was Curtis really did not like me that much in any case, and we never saw each other again once the film was wrapped. It is bittersweet now since I get so much fan mail about that film, and now it is a cult film with articles being done about it all the time, but it was not a pleasant experience for me because of Dennis being in such a weird place emotionally."

Harrington said that Hopper was on his best behavior until the final day of filming *Night Tide* arrived. Hopper fell apart emotionally when he confronted the realization that the film was over. "Boy, I remember this day—sort of," Hopper said. "I was so drunk, I could barely stand. It was our last day on the picture. And then I had a terrible motorcycle accident that night and ended up in the hospital. Well, it had been an incredible experience for all of us. It was like a death. I always feel that the end of a film is a death of some kind. It's a birth, and it's a death, all at the same time. Since Jimmy Dean died on *Giant* two weeks before we finished the film, it was always really difficult, the endings of films. But especially on a film like this because we had all really created something. I mean, it was really a creative endeavor, and none of us had ever had that kind of freedom, really. There was no such thing as freedom in movies at that time. This was really our endeavor, and it was a wonderful thing. I got so drunk, then got a woman on the back of my motorcycle, then went off and had an accident and ended up in the hospital for ten days." (Hopper's bike skidded out on an oil patch on Sunset Boulevard while his girlfriend was riding with him.)

Night Tide remained unreleased until 1963 because of union complaints (the film was a nonunion production) and a financier who wanted his investment returned. On his DVD commentary with Harrington, Hopper boasts that *Night Tide* was the first American film made outside the studio system "in the streets" and stayed on *Time's* list of ten best films for an entire year. Hopper introduced the film at the opening of Henri Langlois' Cinémathèque Française in Nice on July 4, 1976. Hopper and Langlois went to the beach that afternoon. With characteristic grandiosity, Hopper compared his plight in Hollywood to that of Rembrandt. He told Langlois how Rembrandt, the most famous painter in Holland, had his paintings put in people's basements and was banished to obscurity because he had an affair with a maid, until his paintings were rediscovered three hundred years later by British scholars. That night, Langlois related the Rembrandt story and introduced Hopper as "the guy who screwed Hollywood."

In May 1961, Franchot Tone called Hopper to New York to replace James Caan, who was playing Tone's son in the play, *Mandingo*. "Franchot Tone had wanted me to play his son," Hopper said, "but they hired Jimmy Caan over his wishes, and he said, 'All right, I'll tell you what I'll do: I'll let him rehearse for two weeks, and then I'm going to replace him with Dennis Hopper.' And they said, 'Fine.' " A lurid play about slavery set on an Alabama plantation in 1832, *Mandingo* was later adapted into the infamous 1975 blaxsploitation film featuring James Mason and boxer Ken Norton. *Mandingo* was performed only eight times, from May 22 to May 27, but that was long enough for Hopper and actress Brooke Hayward to become smitten with each other. "We had to rehearse the first two or three days," she recalled. "On the third day, Dennis said, 'I think I'm going to marry you.' I thought it was quite a flattering thing to be told."

Brooke Hayward was, in the trite phrase, genuine Hollywood royalty. Brooke was the daughter of actress Margaret Sullavan, who had been briefly married to Henry Fonda before becoming the wife of agent and producer Leland Hayward. Brooke spent her first ten years growing up in Brentwood, California, an upper-class enclave of the Hollywood community. In his review of Brooke Hayward's memoir, *Haywire*, Gerald Clarke wrote, "Worshiped by his children and idolized by his five wives, he [Leland] exuded vitality; he was incomplete without a telephone in his hand, making a million-dollar deal or selling a Garbo, a Fonda, or a Hemingway. Mother was Margaret Sullavan, the husky-voiced star of the '30s and '40s. Though she was not a classic beauty, men found her bewitching: 'The fairest of sights in twinkling lights is Sullavan with an a,' rhapsodized Ogden Nash." Leland Hayward loved making deals more than fatherhood, which compelled Margaret to divorce him after ten years of marriage and take her three children with her.

Being a Hayward was hard. Brooke's life was shadowed by tragedy. Margaret Sullavan died on January 1, 1960, of a drug overdose that was officially determined to be accidental, though many suspected suicide. Brooke's sister, Bridget, committed suicide nine months later. (Her brother, William Hayward, fatally shot himself on March 9, 2008.)

Brooke attended the posh Greenwich Academy and then Vassar with her Hollywood neighbor and friend, Jane Fonda. "Brooke always was the one who wanted to be the actress," Fonda told journalist Al Aronowitz. "I didn't want to be an actress. She was always the one everybody said was going to be a big star. She's the one, you know, and I was much too shy." "Jane remembers once riding in a car with David O. Selznick and listening to him tell Brooke that she had star quality, that she was beautiful, that she was glamorous, and that she would become a great actress," Aronowitz wrote. "Jane remembers that Selznick didn't say anything to Jane. Later Brooke and Jane found themselves both in Lee Strasberg's acting classes."

Dennis and Brooke began cohabiting at her spacious apartment on Central Park West after *Mandingo* closed. "At the time, your dad was very much into painting, and he was in his black-paint period. My apartment was covered in black oil paint," Hayward later told her daughter. "The floor was covered with black paint a foot thick with embedded cigarette butts and beer cans." "It was like one big oil painting, and not a very good one, either!," Hopper said. Leland Hayward and Brooke's stepmother, Pamela

Harriman, weren't able to interfere with Brooke's courtship. Brooke said, "They were in Europe, thank God."

"He was an incredibly colorful character in those days, a reel sweetheart," Brooke Hayward said of Hopper. She also found his intense devotion to the arts highly attractive. Peter Fonda, who met Hopper at the wedding reception his sister, Jane, threw for Brooke, said, "And I thought, 'This guy is looney tunes, but he sure is interesting.'"

"I think he [Hopper] operated under the illusion that he could do anything that he wanted and that he was a free, independent spirit," Hayward said. "He was on the cutting edge. Dennis had an eye and an ear for what was happening at that time. He was on the scene. If you wanted to know something about what the scene was, Dennis could tell you."

"Dennis made me read Huxley's *Doors of Perception*," she said, "and it did sound a bit thrilling, all these colors and all that. So I agreed to take some mescaline, which, as I remember it, was one of the most horrific experiences. He intrigued me further with the concept that what he was really interested in was film directing, not acting at all, film directing. And that he was a superb photographer, although he didn't have a camera. I had to take it on faith that he was a superb photographer. All he wanted was a camera. Dennis used to walk down the streets of New York, and I could tell that he might be a very good photographer because he was framing everything with his hands. He'd say, 'Look at this!' and I'd look through the frame of his hands."

Hayward called her father in Europe to ask his expert opinion on the best camera to purchase. She then spent the last $351 in her bank account on a Nikon for Dennis, who wore it constantly until he abandoned photography when he began directing *Easy Rider* in 1968. "But I figured it was worth it," she said, "because he might be good. Well, he was good. He has the best eye of anyone I ever saw."

Dennis and Brooke returned to Hollywood for supporting roles in a TV show. "My agent got me some minor role in a television show," she said, "so Dennis and I went to California. I think Dennis and I had to do something on TV with Groucho Marx."[2] Back in Los Angeles, Brooke decided to introduce Dennis to her parents over lunch at the swank Beverly Hills

---

[2] Hayward, Hopper, and Marx appeared in *The Hold-Out*, an episode of *General Electric Theater* that the CBS network broadcast on January 14, 1962, after Hopper and Hayward were already married.

Hotel. Dennis and Brooke arrived at the hotel on his motor scooter. "I'd had my driver's license taken away for five years because I had so many tickets," he said, "and I wasn't able to drive, so I had a motor scooter."

It was not a successful meeting. Pamela Harriman was always trying to fix Brooke up with prominent men she thought were suitable candidates for marriage. Harriman wanted Brooke to marry someone like David Brinkley or John Frankenheimer, who were then at the top of her list. Leland Hayward was appalled by Hopper. (He disapproved of Hopper's raincoat, for one thing.) Dennis said, "I would like to ask for your daughter's hand," and Leland Hayward had what Brooke Hayward called a minor nervous breakdown. She said, "He stumbled around and said, 'I think you've got to come back to New York!' I think he thought that if he got me back to New York, he could collar me."

Hopper then told Leland Hayward how he got out of the army. Hopper had told Brooke that the night before his induction, he had a dream that he was the reincarnation of Jesus Christ. "I wrote a thing that they interpreted as being that," he recalled. "I wrote, 'Would Christ do this?' Would Christ go and wear a uniform and behave like all these other people? Would he go out and kill people because you wanted him to? No, he wouldn't do that. So, why should I? They read this, and they gave me a Section Eight—'Get him out of here! He thinks he's Jesus!' "

Leland Hayward continued trying to dissuade Brooke from marrying Hopper. He told her, "I am a producer. I don't like actors. You are going to end up hating each other." He called Brooke at 6 A.M. the day of the wedding and said, "Brooke, it's not too late to call it off." Dennis and Brooke were married on August 9, 1961, in the church at 60th Street and Park Avenue in New York. Leland Hayward made a last ditch effort to convince his daughter to reconsider her decision. Tom Mankiewicz witnessed him walk up the aisle and whisper in Brooke's ear before she recited her vows of marriage. Leland told her that she could still get out of the marriage.

"Father came with Pamela," she recalled. "They came, and then they walked out." "Pamela and Leland left us outside the church, just standing there!" Hopper said. "Jane [Fonda], sort of embarrassed, looked at Johanna Mankiewicz and her husband, Peter Davis, and Peter Fonda, and said, 'Oh, why don't you come over to my place, and we'll have a little something.' So we went over to her apartment. It was small, and there were about eight of us. We had a few sandwiches and sat around and talked and drank. It was very pleasant. That's when Peter and I actually met."

Dennis, Brooke, her two children from her previous marriage, and their Scottish nurse lived in Hopper's L.A. duplex while the couple searched for a home of their own. Hopper had haunted New York's art museums and galleries when he lived there, feeding his appetite for avant-garde art. Back in Los Angeles, Dennis channeled the creative drive that once went into acting by throwing himself into painting, photography, and poetry. These art forms offered him freedom from outside interference with his creative vision and a purity of artistic expression that commercial filmmaking lacked.

Hopper realized that, as an actor, he was merely an interpretive artist. "I was doing somebody else's screenplay, and there was a director there telling me how to do it," he explained. "So at best, I could call myself an artist, but at best, I was still interpreting. But a fine artist was not an interpretive artist because he was creating something. He was creating a one-of-a-kind thing in his special view. So that's how I got involved in art."

Hopper's friend, artist Ed Ruscha, recalled that Hopper was a fixture of California's "minuscule but vital" modern art scene when he met him in 1961 or 1962. "He had an exhibit at the David Stuart Gallery, which was a few doors north of Ferus (the Ferus Gallery)," Ruscha said. "He was just always around, always taking pictures and making things. I remember visiting him, and he said, 'Let me show you my garage.' It was jammed with these sculptures he did. The thing I appreciated was he was so kind of restless, and then you say, 'God, he's had more than one life.' I mean, here he checks in with all these great performances in movies, but he always comes back to art."

Disaster struck just two weeks after Brooke and Dennis rented a little house on Stone Canyon Road in the Hollywood Hills and prepared to personalize it. At approximately 8:15 A.M. on November 6, 1961, the hot, dry Santa Ana winds whipped a burning trash pile in Sherman Oaks into a conflagration that raced through the dry brush surrounding the hillside homes in Brentwood and Bel Air. Sheets of flame up to fifty feet high raced up the canyon, and cinders carried by the winds landed on the flammable wooden shingle roofs of homes nearby. The Hoppers' house was the first on Stone Canyon Road to burn. Dennis manned his water hose in a vain attempt to save his home while Brooke took their one car to retrieve her two sons from school. The Bel Air fire eventually consumed more than 6,000 acres and 484 luxury homes.

Hopper became a minor hero that day by running up and down the neighborhood, getting others out of their homes. He even rescued the occupant of a burning home. "Everybody had abandoned this house with the roof on fire, and I kept thinking, 'Somebody's in there,' " he recalled. "I ran in, and this woman was sitting on the toilet. I said, 'You've got to leave.' 'No, no, I'm staying, I'm staying. I don't care.' Anyway, I got her out of there, and that's when, I guess, they took the picture." Hopper was photographed emerging from the woman's house holding paintings by Picasso and Juan Gris under each arm. The photo was published in a two-page spread in *Paris Match* with the caption, "Unidentified man, hero of Bel Air fire."

The Hoppers lost everything in the fire, including Margaret Sullavan's modern furniture and the ancient Asian tapestries that Jay Hopper collected while fighting in China alongside Mao during World War II. Three hundred of Dennis Hopper's paintings were destroyed, as well as six hundred manuscript pages of his poetry. Only a Milton Avery painting that Sullavan owned survived. "But thank God I don't have to look at those terrible paintings I'd made!," Hopper said. "They'd still be around haunting me." Hopper's photographic negatives, which were in the gallery where an exhibition of his photos opened the night of the fire, were spared. Hopper and Hayward regarded their losses as a cleansing experience. Brooke Hayward discovered she was pregnant the day after she lost her home.

The couple briefly became Beverly Hills nomads after the Bel Air fire. They stayed with Vincent and Mary Price until the Prices kicked them out for lack of room. Then David O. Selznick and Jennifer Jones welcomed the Hoppers into their home, allowing them to live in their guesthouse. Brooke Hayward said that David O. Selznick loved Dennis. "He was going through a very similar thing that I was—he couldn't get a job, either," Hopper said. "I mean, he was David O. Selznick! He later died of a heart attack in a bank asking for a loan."

Dennis Hopper couldn't bring himself to paint after the Bel Air fire destroyed his canvases. His interest in painting shifted from creating to collecting. Hopper had already met some of L.A.'s emerging artists in the mid-'50s through his friendship with James Dean. Dean liked to watch Mr. Chang, an eccentric street performer who wore an old Confederate general's uniform and gave badly accented readings of Shakespeare in front of Grauman's Chinese Theatre for the loose change listeners tossed in his cap. Dean brought Hopper along to Mr. Chang's poetry reading one night at Stone Brothers Printers, a printing workshop that was then the nexus for L.A.'s avant-garde artists. Hopper met art critic Walter Hopps, poet Robert Alexander, and artists Ed Kienholz, Wallace Berman, and George Herms there. After Dean died, he just started hanging out with them.

Hopps, Kienholz, and Alexander founded the Ferus Gallery in West Hollywood in 1957, which became a vital force in L.A.'s contemporary art scene when Irving Blum replaced Kienholz's stake in the gallery and took over its direction in 1958. Hopper's involvement with the Ferus group led him to become a pioneering collector and enthusiast of pop art before the term was even invented.

Andy Warhol showed Blum several *Campbell's Soup Can* paintings when Blum visited him in New York in 1962. Blum, who gave Warhol his first West Coast exhibition in July of that year, recalled telling him, " 'You should show these in California.' I knew he was thinking his friends were in New York, and he didn't know that many people on the West Coast. I took his arm and said, 'Andy, movie stars come into the gallery.' He said, 'Let's do it.' The truth was that no movie stars ever came into the gallery. Dennis Hopper did." "He (Hopper) bought one of my first paintings, *Standard Station*," Ed Ruscha said. "He was an early collector, one of the very few people in Hollywood who bought modern art."

"In 1962 everybody was talking about 'the return to reality,' " Hopper said. "I was a third-generation abstract expressionist, which we all were, really. We were looking at a lot of the Bay Area figurative painters, but really felt that they were just rehashing a lot of the old stuff. It wasn't a return to reality. It was nothing new."

"I walked into the Ferus Gallery one day," he recalled, "and Irving Blum, who was running the gallery said, 'Dennis, I want to show you something.' He showed me two slides, one of which was of a soup can, and the other was a cartoon. It was Andy and Roy Lichtenstein. I went crazy, started jumping up and down, and said, 'That's it! That's it!' Irving said, 'That's what?' I said, 'That's the return to reality!' Irving said, 'What are you doing tomorrow?' So we went to New York the next day, went to Andy Warhol's studio, and met Roy Lichtenstein, Jasper Johns, [Robert] Rauschenberg, [James] Rosenquist, I saw the whole thing. That was it. I bought a Roy Lichtenstein called *Sinking Sun* for $1,100, which I later lost in a divorce. A year and a half ago [2007], it sold for $17,870,000. I bought one of Andy's soup cans out here, and I've been collecting since."

Brooke Hayward gave birth to her daughter, Marin, on June 26, 1962. Dennis Hopper purchased one of Andy Warhol's iconic *Campbell's Soup Can* paintings that day for $75. "People have always assumed that I bought one of Andy's soup can paintings from the Ferus show," he said, "but I didn't. I bought it from John Weber who was then running Dwan Gallery. It was hanging over his desk, and so when I inquired, he said he'd sell it to me for $75—$25 less than Irving's asking price."

Hopper also bought two works by Ed Kienholz. He paid $125 for *The Society Girl, Quickie*, which was made up of a female mannequin's head and one hand attached to an old roller skate, with the hand fixed so that its outstretched finger appeared to be picking the mannequin's nose. (Hopper later told National Public Radio's Terry Gross that he paid $30 for *The Society Girl, Quickie*.) The other Kienholz was a big wooden construction called *White on the Side*.

Hayward said that Dennis jubilantly announced, "I've just bought a major painting from Irving [Blum], a soup can, a tomato soup can! It cost $75," as the couple's daughter was presented to them at the hospital. "What the hell are you going to do with it? I guess you're going to have to put it in the kitchen," Hayward said. Hopper said, "No, it's going in the living room—it's fabulous!" Hayward later claimed that their motivation to collect art was born of the losses they suffered in the Bel Air fire. An insurance agent told her, "Here is what is going to hold its value if you ever have another fire: silver, paintings, and antiques. Everything else you can throw away." "So that's why we bought paintings," she said, "including the famous Andy Warhol tomato soup can that Dennis bought for $100."

"My agent came in and looked at these things," Hopper recalled, "the soup can painting, this mannequin on a roller skate picking her nose, and this big wood black-and-white construction abstract thing, and he said, 'You should be embarrassed. You're married to Margaret Sullavan and Leland Hayward's daughter. Obviously she has money, and you don't, and you're squandering it by buying this junk. Now, either you respect that and get rid of this junk immediately, or I'm leaving, and I'm not going to be your agent anymore. And I said, 'Goodbye then.' So that was the beginning of my collecting. And I only collected works by artists who I thought were going to be important. I never collected one where I thought, 'Oh, I really like this.' First of all, I'd wished I made them. It was a sort of criterion, the way I approached it."

In April 1963, Dennis and Brooke purchased their new home, located at 1712 North Crescent Heights in Beverly Hills. Igor Stravinsky, Marlon Brando, and Bob and Toby Rafelson were just some of their neighbors. Their home became an eclectic showcase of pop art that Dennis collected and antiques that Brooke Hayward picked up at bargain prices in L.A. shops. A Hammond organ, a circus poster, a horse from a merry-go-round, and a glitter ball hanging from the ceiling turned their entrance hall into a tiny ballroom. Hopper used the foyer for the setting where he photographed Ike and Tina Turner posing with a giant inflatable Coke bottle for the back cover of their record album, *River Deep, Mountain High,* which Phil Spector produced. The Hoppers' residence became talked about enough to be featured in an article in *TV Guide,* which wrote that the couple "live amid an outlandish collection of eye-catching objects of every description." One critic called the house "the Prada of Pop."

Hopper's first act after moving into his new home was to throw a party for Andy Warhol and Hopper's other artist friends. Hopper set the tone for the party by suspending a fourteen-foot-long Mexican papier-mâché clown with firecrackers hanging off of it from the ceiling. He papered the downstairs bathrooms with billboards, and set up a hot-dog stand to serve his guests hot dogs and chili. "We drove to a billboard place called Foster & Kleiser," Irving Blum recalled. "And we looked at several of the sheets they would plaster on billboards. They were enormous, but they would fold them flat. Dennis bought three or four. We went up to Crescent Heights, where he and Brooke lived. He began putting them up as wallpaper—a giant hamburger in his bedroom. Drove Brooke mad. But he caught the pop sensibility before it was a sensibility."

"Well, first of all," Hopper said, recalling the party, "I don't think anybody had ever been in our house before. It was entirely 'pop.' We had Lichtenstein . . . we had Frank Stella . . . we had Kienholz . . . we had Andy Warhol . . . we had Ed Ruscha. So, one year after his soup-can show at Ferus in Los Angeles—the first pop-art show of an individual artist anywhere in the world—Andy comes to Hollywood and sees an environment that actually accepts this kind of new art. It was a very thrilling thing for everybody at that point. Because it was the first time anybody saw a collection like this together with antiques and with the kind of outrageous stuff that we had found."

" 'OOH! AAH! OOH! AAH!' That's all Andy ever said," Hopper said, remembering Warhol's reaction to the scene. "I never heard Andy make a sentence. He was wonderful to be around, but he was always 'OOH! AAH! OOH! AAH!' " (Hopper made a brief appearance in Warhol's *Tarzan and Jane Regained . . . Sort of* (1964), which Warhol filmed at John Houseman's swimming pool and various other locations around L.A. in October 1963, when he had his second show at the Ferus Gallery. Hopper also appeared in *The Thirteen Most Beautiful Boys* (1964), a compilation of some of Warhol's silent screen tests.)

Brooke Hayward said that the highlight of the party came when Claes Oldenburg's wife, Patty, knocked *The Society Girl, Quickie* off a cabinet, decapitating the mannequin's head from the roller skate. (Terry Southern, the coauthor of the scandalous bestseller *Candy* and Stanley Kubrick's film *Dr. Strangelove* (1964), recalled Hayward's three children upsetting the (supposed) $1,700 Kienholz when he visited the Hoppers for *Vogue* magazine in 1965. " 'Brooke,' said Hopper tersely, 'we may be on to something here!' And, seizing his camera, he began to photograph it rapidly from several angles.")

Photography replaced painting as Hopper's artistic salvation after the Bel Air fire, satisfying his compulsive need to create when acting jobs became scarce. In *The American Dreamer*, the documentary about Hopper that was made when he was editing *The Last Movie*, he described how the dearth of work following his fight with Henry Hathaway affected him. "Man, I felt like a fly killing itself on a window."

"He briefly did some experimentation with color, but rejected it in still photography because he found himself being seduced by color for color's sake—which reduced his concentration on composition, form, and content," art curator Henry Hopkins wrote. "His first studies in 1954 were abstract arrangements of existing objects—walls, torn posters, street signs—rather than people and events (Images of this type still remain among his favorite subjects.)"

Hopper used Kodak's Tri-X, a high speed black-and-white film that gave him the ability to shoot quickly under a range of lighting conditions. "I'd already been a painter, and I started taking photographs not of people, but of walls and of things where I had no depth of field," he said. "I would shoot flat on so I had a painting surface, so I'd shoot flat on a wall or flat on something, and it would become like the surface of a painting." Hopper was using his camera the way an abstract expressionist used his paintbrush, producing images that commented on the two-dimensional nature of the medium.

"Los Angeles is visually one of the uglier places in the world," he said, "built to last until the next earthquake. So I started looking at walls, and the walls started really becoming my life, talking to me about dying, decay, forms of indifference. They became Duchamp, became the accident. They became that dangerous word beauty. I paid attention to the human scratches, and they became like life to me. Like John Cage, I was very much into the aesthetic of chance."

"Like me, Dennis' art grows out of alienation and the theme of frustration in modern life," said Ed Ruscha. "Dennis always responded to city anxiety, graffiti, etchings on walls expressing the frustration of urban life. That still turns him on and really rings his bell."

Hopper told Ruscha that he thought of his photos as "readymades," Marcel Duchamp's neologism for mass produced or found objects that become art when an artist says they're art. (Duchamp's most famous readymade is *Fountain*, a ceramic urinal he signed "R. Mutt 1917" in black paint and displayed upside down on a pedestal in his studio.) "The whole idea of the readymade and that the artist of the future could be somebody who points their finger and says 'It's art,' and it'll be art," Hopper said. "I think of that with my photographs. I think of them as 'found' paintings because I don't crop them, I don't manipulate them or anything."

Hopper, who was using photography as a way of learning to direct movies, recalled the advice James Dean had given him. When Dean discovered that Hopper was a fellow photographer, he told him, "If you're going to take pictures, don't crop them." Hopper said, "Why not?" Dean said, "Because you're probably going to want to direct films someday, and you can't crop film, so learn how to frame full frame, full negative." "So from that day on, I didn't crop my photographs," Hopper said. "I was learning to work within the frame of movies."

Hopper's next choice of photographic subjects was a natural extension of his interest in modern art. "It started with me just hanging out with artists," he said. "When I was a young guy, some people went to the beach, some people went to play tennis, and I went to art galleries.

I was a gallery bum, associating with Walter Hopps, Ed Kienholz, Wallace Berman, who was busted for pornography, the whole Ferus Gallery crowd. They used to call me 'the tourist' because I always had the camera hanging round my neck.

"I didn't photograph actors much because actors hate to be photographed. They are being photographed all the time. But artists didn't mind it at all, so I started photographing the artists. They wanted me to take photographs. They wanted posters and things. I worked so little during those eight years. It was really embarrassing. I thought, 'Well, if I'm not going to be able to work as an actor, I might as well be able make something that's going to be credible.' So I took photographs of Martin Luther King and Selma, Montgomery, as history and selecting artists that I thought would make it. So in my mind, by taking photographs of the artists, I felt, in some strange way, I would be doing history a favor."

"He photographed all of the artists we showed—Bob Irwin, Billy Al Bengston, Ed Ruscha—and I used his photographs as announcements," Irving Blum said. Word of Hopper's photographic talent filtered back to New York, where editors at *Harper's Bazaar* and *Vogue* hired him to shoot celebrity layouts with established stars like Paul Newman and Dennis' other friends, like Jane and Peter Fonda.

By the mid-'60s, Brooke and Dennis seemed to be living a perfect life, ensconced in a kind of phantasmagorical world of their own design, which Terry Southern described for *Vogue*. "The Den Hoppers are tops in their field," he wrote. "Precisely what their field is, is by no means certain—except that she is a Great Beauty, and he a kind of Mad Person."

Southern's captions for the photos accompanying his article aptly describe the Hoppers' fantastic abode. "Up in the Hollywood Hills, above the Sunset Strip, Mr. and Mrs. Dennis Hopper (portraits, above left) have a house of such gaiety and wit that it seems the result of some marvelous scavenger hunt, full of improvised treasures, the bizarre and the beautiful and the banal in wild juxtaposition, everything the most of its kind.

"On the wall, a Lichtenstein 'mad scientist' canvas. Above right, a French pitcher, Mexican paper flowers spilling from metal bowls, an art nouveau panel. Below, the view from the kitchen window of a 750-pound fibre glass sedan, part of a billboard retrieved from a junkyard, the effect reminiscent of a line from Terry Southern's *The Magic Christian*—'There's power to spare under this baby's forty-foot hood.' The throne chair in the corner was a studio prop. Opposite page, below, on the dining room walls, a 1907 Budweiser girl and a Chéret poster. In the hall, one of several street-lights in the house. On the living room wall: a Marcel Duchamp found object; above it, the Mona Lisa in duplicate by Andy Warhol.

"Everywhere in the Hopper house the point is to amuse, to delight. Dominating one room, an Edward Ruscha painting of a Standard station, all line and energy. To the left, a streetlight; to the right, a Tiffany poppy light and a Bruce Conner drawing. Not showing: a shiny white-enamel and black-leather barber chair. Opposite page, below, Brooke Hopper with her children outside the house, which is itself a kind of jungle gym of the imagination, a house which seems always subtly to compliment its guests. 'Look,' it seems always to say, 'what we have found now to divert you.' "

Gail Gerber was a Canadian ballet dancer who moved to Los Angeles in the mid-'60s to widen her career horizons as an actress. A cute blonde who looked good in a bikini, Gerber played beach bunnies in several films like the Elvis Presley vehicle, *Girl Happy* (1965). Gerber met Terry South-ern when she had a small role in *The Loved One* (1965), which South-ern had adapted from Evelyn Waugh's novel. She responded to Southern's approach and quickly became the married writer's companion until his death in 1995.

"We stayed friendly with Brooke and Dennis (Terry, always with the nicknames, called him 'Den'), and we'd go to the house for dinner," Ger-ber recalled in her memoir. "Brooke would serve something wonderful and wisely go to bed. Dennis and Terry would retire, drinks in hand, to the living room, which had a disconcerting dentist's chair. I would find a cozy sofa and watch Dennis and Terry talk. Dennis would expound on his idea of how Shakespeare should be spoken and rant on about a film he wanted to direct called *The Last Movie*, which he eventually managed to make. Terry loved madness and people behaving badly (and you couldn't get any madder or badder than Hopper). Terry would draw this behavior out and then go home and write 'fiction.' "

Thanks to her parents, Brooke Hayward moved easily among Holly-wood's venerable elite, who invited her and Dennis to their parties. Many of them were undoubtedly curious to meet her new husband, who might introduce them to the latest cultural trends. But Dennis did nothing to endear himself to his hosts. Still hurting from his experience with Henry Hathaway, who embodied the Hollywood establishment to Hopper,

Dennis confronted them, convinced that they were denying him the opportunities he needed to realize his creative genius.

"We'd go to these parties where you'd have the crème de la crème of Hollywood," Hayward recalled, "and he'd tell them that when he ran things, heads were going to roll, they'd be in chains. Some day he'd make a movie, and the old dinosaurs would be slain." Hopper was still emulating James Dean. "He was also a guerilla artist who attacked all restrictions on his sensibility," Hopper said. "Once he pulled a switchblade and threatened to murder his director. I imitated his style in art and in life. It got me into a lot of trouble."

Desperate for work, Hopper would get high at parties and corner a producer, imploring him, "Why am I not directing? Why am I not acting?" "Who wants to deal with a maniac like that?" he later said. "To tell the truth, it's just plain difficult for me to be in society—to be a social being," he explained. "New York and Hollywood are hard for me, where you have to go and sit in a producer's lap at those parties. Oh, I can do it for a while, but then I find I'm acting. I think it's my worst performance. I try to be polite and courteous, and then, sure enough, I get pissed and blow it. Let's face it, I can't stay on my best behavior for long. I don't have the social amenities to make it or enjoy it."

"I'm an introvert by nature. Social things are not my best. I would prefer sitting quietly rather than thinking that I have to make some sort of conversation to prove myself, advance some philosophies. I was always unbearably shy. That was probably one of the reasons that I drank and took drugs." (Unbearably shy? This from the man who displayed himself completely naked in four films.)

Meanwhile, Hopper toiled in episodes of TV series like *Bonanza*, *Gunsmoke*, *Surfside 6*, *Wagon Train*, and *Petticoat Junction*, whose casting director demonstrated his sense of humor by hiring Hopper for the episode "Bobbie Jo and the Beatnik" (broadcast January 7, 1964). According to the *Onion A.V. Club*, this episode of *Petticoat Junction* "spoofs Hopper's reputation in the industry, casting him as a hard-edged Greenwich Village poet ready to blast the show's small-town rubes for their hypocrisy—until he gets offered $2,000 to write a dog-food jingle."

Most of the series Hopper guest-starred in were hackneyed potboilers, but a few aspired to social relevance. He starred in the *Twilight Zone* episode "He's Alive" (broadcast January 24, 1963), playing the neo-Nazi

Peter Vollmer, who finds no success in attracting followers until a shadowy figure, who is soon revealed to be none other than Adolf Hitler (Curt Conway), begins advising Vollmer on tactics. Although Rod Serling wrote this episode of the classic series, the already weak story suffers additionally from having to fill the one-hour format that *Twilight Zone* used in its fourth season.

In his authoritative book, *The Twilight Zone Companion*, Marc Scott Zicree notes the unreality of Vollmer's character, a committed neo-Nazi who is also devoted to an elderly concentration camp survivor played by Ludwig Donath. Zicree calls the story "just one long editorial," writing, "Dennis Hopper lacks the personal magnetism to be believable as a charismatic leader. Speeches which are intended to be hypnotic seem merely shrill, although the audience is clearly supposed to be mesmerized."

Hopper played a racist Marine in "To Set It Right," a topical episode of *The Lieutenant* (1963-1964), an hour-long series depicting life during peacetime at Camp Pendleton, the U.S. Marine training base in California. "To Set It Right" featured Nichelle Nichols (the mistress of series creator Gene Roddenberry, who cast Nichols as Lieutenant Uhura in his next series, *Star Trek*) in her first role as the wife of a black Marine (Don Marshall) who attacks the corporal (Hopper) who used to gang up with other bigots to harass him when they attended high school together. The two antagonists ultimately learn to work together to further their platoon's interests. The Pentagon withdrew their cooperation from the series after they read the script for this episode (written by future *Star Trek* writer-producer Gene L. Coon under his pseudonym, Lee Cronin), and NBC refused to air the episode because of its controversial racial theme.

Hopper got involved with black Americans' struggle for full civil rights when he joined the Rev. Martin Luther King Jr.'s march from Selma to Montgomery in March 1965. "How's a white guy like you end up not just taking pictures at the march, but participating in this?" black talk-show host Tavis Smiley asked Hopper in 2007. "How did you get pulled into the movement in that way?" "Well, I was born in Dodge City, Kansas," he said, "and I was just raised that the only people you should be prejudiced against are people who are prejudiced, so I didn't have any of that kind of upbringing."

Hopper first met King at the Chateau Marmont, where Hopper was living, soon after Rosa Parks famously refused to surrender her seat on a

bus to a white passenger on December 1, 1955. Sidney Poitier led Hopper
to a room at the hotel one evening where he met Parks, Harry Belafonte,
and King, who was soliciting support from the show-business community.
Hopper recalled being the only white person in the room.

Several days before the start of King's march in 1965, Hopper was out
walking with some friends in Hollywood when Marlon Brando pulled
up alongside him in his limousine and rolled down his window. Brando
said, "What are you doing?" Hopper said, "Nothing." Brando said, "How
would you like to go to Selma and Montgomery? We're having a little
march." Hopper said, "Great."

Hopper grabbed his Nikon and joined Reverend King's civil-rights
march, witnessing and photographing history in the making. It was quite
the opposite of throwing hot-dog and chili parties for inarticulate Pop
artists in your home in Beverly Hills. State and local police attacked six
hundred marchers with billy clubs and tear gas on March 7, 1965, a day
which came to be known as "Bloody Sunday." Under the protection of
the Alabama National Guard, federal marshals, and the FBI, the marchers reached a campsite at the City of St. Jude, a Catholic complex on the
outskirts of Montgomery, on the evening of March 24.

The following day, 25,000 people marched to the steps of the state capi-
tol building to hear Dr. King address them. "Joan Baez and I, we'd walk
through a bomber's row, which was really—we were passive resistance,"
Hopper recalled, "but there was a lot of violence going on all around us,
and it was pretty scary, actually, going in there. There were helicopters flying everywhere, and people screaming and yelling at us waving Confederate flags. It was something to be remembered. But King got up and spoke,
and it was just—he was great."

The omnipresent threat of violence during the march worsened Hopper's innate paranoia. "He had revolutionary delusions," Brad Darrach
wrote. "He accumulated weapons. He was convinced the FBI was having
him shadowed. Sometimes at night, he took a gun and stalked through the
suburb where he lived in search of government agents who weren't there.
He found a portrait of Jesus that looks almost exactly like Dennis Hopper.
It still goes everywhere with him, and he was convinced that, like Christ,
he was going to die in his thirty-third year."

Hopper also began taking karate lessons, ostensibly for self-defense. In
the '60s, dabbling in karate and other martial arts became a popular pas-

time of actors that advertised their hipness in the photos illustrating their magazine profiles. One day, karate practice became a comedy of errors for Hopper and his friend, actor Robert Walker Jr. Their instructor, Hungarian-born Emil Farkas, who was Phil Spector's bodyguard, broke Hopper's toe and Walker's nose in the same session. "We were practicing karate, and we learned just enough to cause him enough trouble that he had to do that," Hopper said.

Hopper couldn't have been more surprised when his next offer of work came from his nemesis, Henry Hathaway. Hathaway, who was directing *The Sons of Katie Elder* (1965), a Western starring John Wayne and Dean Martin, had Hopper come in for an interview. Wayne and Hathaway took pity on Hopper. "Well, his reason for hiring me was because he and John Wayne, the Duke, heard that I'd married a nice Irish woman, Brooke Hayward," he said. "They knew her mother, Margaret Sullavan, who was a nice Irish woman. I'd married her daughter, and we had a daughter of our own, so it was about time for me to go back to work. That was Hathaway's way of putting it to me in the office. 'But you know,' Hathaway said, 'Wayne doesn't dig any of that Method shit, so if you're gonna use any of that Method shit, get out of here, kid.' I said, 'Mr. Hathaway, I'm a much better actor now than I was then, and I just want you to work with me.' Hathaway said, 'It's not me, you understand. I like that Method shit, it's Wayne.'

"So I arrive on the set in Durango, Mexico, and it's my first day on the picture, and Hathaway gives me every line reading and every gesture. And he says, 'Now, roll the camera,' and I do every line reading and every gesture the way he told me. At the end of it, he says, 'Cut.' He's crying, and he has a cigar in his mouth, says, 'That's great kid, that's great, your just so wonderful, so wonderful.' I said, 'You see Henry, I told you, I'm a much better actor now than I was eight years ago.' And Hathaway says, pointing to his head, 'You're not a better actor, kid, you're just smarter, you're just smarter.' "

Hopper had spent some time analyzing Hathaway's directorial technique since they clashed while making *From Hell to Texas* and thought he had figured out the source of his problems with the director. "Hathaway would give you directions for very strange, uncomfortable movements," he said. "But he had everybody moving like that, so if you weren't doing that, you were in another movie. Now I realize he seldom dollies his camera.

He goes from one still shot to another. It's the style of [Howard] Hawks and others. You begin to realize that what he's doing is getting *you* to move because his camera doesn't move. It's the simplest way to make movies and often a good way. You shouldn't overcomplicate the medium."

After appearing in Hathaway's *True Grit*, Hopper said, "Henry Hathaway taught me a great lesson, a lesson I don't think I was able to accept until that point in my life, but one I've never forgotten. Don't fool with the director! He's the man in charge, and he gets what he wants. Just imagine what a mixture of styles and effects you would get if everyone was doing his own thing as an actor in a movie—what confusion! I love Henry now. I made *True Grit* for him, and there's nothing I wouldn't do for him." When Hopper attended Hathaway's funeral in 1985 ("There were about seventeen people there," he said), his widow told him, "God, I'm amazed you're here, but Henry loved you so much and talked about you all the time." "I learned more from him than from any other director," Hopper said.

Between minor roles in major films like *The Sons of Katie Elder*, *Cool Hand Luke* (1967), and *Hang 'Em High* (1968), Hopper continued acting catch-as-catch-can in low-budget genre films. He reunited with Curtis Harrington for American International Pictures' (AIP) science-fiction film, *Queen of Blood* (1966), which writer and director Harrington called a "seven-day wonder." Hopper played an astronaut who becomes one of the victim's of the title character, an alien ambassador who subsists on blood and lays pulsating eggs. *Queen of Blood* incorporated special-effects footage from superior Soviet SF films that Roger Corman licensed into an original story that Harrington filmed for $50,000 at a poverty-row rental studio using nonstars like Hopper and John Saxon and the elderly Basil Rathbone, who died little more than a year after the film's March 1966 release.

While on location in Durango for *The Sons of Katie Elder*, Hopper wondered about the impact of an American movie crew's intrusion on the indigenous population. "I thought, my God, what's going to happen when the movie leaves and the natives are left living in these Western sets?" Hopper's observation became the inspiration for his passion project, *The Last Movie*, the film that he eventually made in 1970.

Hopper approached Stewart Stern to write a screenplay based on his idea. "According to Stern," *Esquire*'s Robert Alan Arthur wrote, "one day Dennis Hopper, 'a really wonderful guy,' dropped by the house with an original idea for a picture and needed to see what a proper screenplay page looked like. The first result was a collaboration where Stern shaped a screenplay from Hopper's idea; the final result, the picture, was a disaster."

Stern had known Hopper since *Rebel Without a Cause*, which Stern had written. "In the aftermath of *Rebel*, there was a group of us that became close," he said. "That included Jimmy Dean, and Dennis was at the edge of that." Hopper and Stern kept running into each other at the home of James Dean's friend, Arthur Loew Jr., or at the Chateau Marmont, where Paul Newman and Joanne Woodward were staying. "We were friendly with Joan Collins because she was going with Arthur Loew," Stern recalled. "We were always kind of together, either around the Chateau pool or up at Arthur's. Anyway, Dennis was one of the kids.

"And he and I got to be friendly after Jimmy Dean died. He was very funny, very attractive, and very irreverent. He was a great audience. He would laugh at anything. And also very mystical, in a funny way. He used to love to go down to Tijuana and see the famous bullfighters down there. One night, just on a whim, he said, 'What'll we do tonight?' I said, 'I don't know.' And he said, 'Why don't we do something extreme?' So we drove down to Tijuana with the top down." ("Dennis was supposed to be the lead in the first play I ever did," Jack Nicholson said. "But he went to Mexico to learn bullfighting instead, so I was pretty happy when our paths crossed again.")

Stern, who admitted that he had a love-hate relationship with Hopper and fell out with him over *The Last Movie*, has varied his opinion of Hopper over the years. (The portion of Stern's papers dealing with *The Last Movie*, which are deposited at the University of Iowa's Special Collections Department, have been sealed until both Hopper and Stern's deaths at Stern's request.) In 1988, when interviewer Margy Rochlin asked Stern if he'd collaborate with Hopper again, he said, "Anytime."

"He [Hopper] fascinated me because he had ideas before anybody else did," he told Rochlin. "I always thought they were silly ideas. He would point out paintings that he thought were art, and I would get infuriated because the art seemed to have no history, tradition, background. I felt many of the artists he admired seem to come from nowhere. I felt they were sort of starting from each other. History was suddenly being looked upon with great contempt."

Stern revised that opinion shortly after Hopper's death in 2010. "The serious photography and all the things he really was, and that amazing instinct he had . . . he was really at the cutting edge," he said. "He would say he was a genius, and I would say, 'Well, it's much more polite if somebody else decides that and says that about you than if you go around telling everyone that you are.' But he was."

"It was never quiet around Dennis," he said. Stern recalled what happened at a party one night at his home when his guests included William Inge and Beatrice Lillie. "Dennis was on this roll that night, he thought he was the greatest poet in the room," he said. "He was shouting this gibberish that he was making up on the spur of the moment, and none us could hear anybody who had any sense there. There was a lot of interesting conversation going on, and Dennis just ignored it." Joanne Woodward suddenly grabbed the wooden handle of an antique copper bedwarmer Stern had and hit Hopper on the side of his head with it. That got his attention. "He began railing and screaming," Stern said, "talking to Paul Newman, Woodward's husband, saying 'I'm a better actor than you are, Newman, and I'm a better actor than she is.' And Paul just said, 'Dennis, get well soon.' "

Stern was uncomfortable with the friends that Hopper surrounded himself with when he wrote the screenplay for *The Last Movie*. "I never really fit in with his group, I was older," he recalled. "I thought it was just nonsense when he and Peter Fonda and Bobby Walker would get together and everybody would be smoking joints. I just thought they got stupider and stupider as the evening wore on. But they all seemed to think they were brilliant."

While Stern manned the typewriter in his Hollywood home, Hopper ranted, smoked joints, and paced behind him as they exchanged ideas for his film. "I bet you could really write if you had a little joint," he told Stern. Stern said that marijuana made him hallucinate. "There's something called a bong," Hopper said. "You inhale it over water." So Hopper occasionally blew some smoke down the snorkel of a scuba mask that Stern wore while he typed. Though Stern got nearly as stoned as Hopper, he turned out a ninety-eight-page treatment titled *The Last Movie or Boo Hoo in Tinsletown*. No one in Hollywood was the least bit interested in *The Last Movie* or anything else Hopper had to offer. "I was looked on as a maniac and an idiot and a fool and a drunkard," he later said. Peter Fonda tried using his connections to get the screenplay produced, but got nowhere with it.

After meeting at Brooke Hayward's wedding reception, Fonda and Hopper became friends whose creative ambitions intertwined. Fonda was trying to escape his famous father's shadow and change the image created by his roles in movies like *Tammy and the Doctor* (1963), which he derided as *Tammy and the Schmuckface*. Hopper wanted, more than anything else, to direct films. Hopper, actor Ted Markland, and screenwriter Joe Steck visited Fonda at his home one afternoon in late 1965. The discussion fell, as it often did, to the subject independent filmmaking. Hopper jumped off the sofa, excitedly saying, "Everyone talks about making an independent film, but nobody's willing to go through with it."

Fonda accepted his challenge. He put Hopper and a stand-up comedian and writer named Don Sherman on the payroll of his company, Pando Productions. Fonda, Hopper, and Sherman met each day, swapping ideas and dialogue that a secretary took down in shorthand. By mid-December, they had completed a comic screenplay, *The Yin and the Yan(g)*, a pop-art musical fantasy, which Fonda claims was so funny it brought him to tears.

At the beginning of 1966, Fonda and Hopper embarked on an expedition to Manhattan to pitch *The Yin and the Yan(g)* to moneyed interests outside Hollywood's studio system. (Hopper said that they were trying to find someone to put up the money for *The Last Movie*.) To their eventual detriment, they took a confrontational attitude toward the very people they were hoping would fund their film. "A few years ago, I let two guys [Hopper and Fonda] off at the airport, on their way to New York, and they weren't going to play diplomacy," Fonda's friend Owen Orr recalled. "They were going to lay the fucking facts on the goddamn line to a lot of heavy people, breadwise. And say, 'Look, man, we're going to save the movie industry, and we're not going to play any fucking games, and we're not going to play *your* games.' And they left, and then Dennis turned back to me and said, 'Man, we've got to get it, or it's the death of the movie industry.' "

By day, Fonda and Hopper met with potential investors. They partied at night with Mick Jagger, Salvador Dali, Andy Warhol, Nico, Timothy Leary, Larry Rivers, Robert Rauschenberg, and Huntington Hartford, the heir to the A&P supermarket fortune. Hopper later planned to make *Second Chance*, a film about his and Fonda's trip to New York and their efforts there to raise money to make *The Last Movie*. *Second Chance* was going to rebuke the people who turned down Fonda and Hopper's requests for money. "These big producers who didn't like the sound of the picture," Hopper said. "And that's one thing the picture will do, man—give me a chance to *show* these frivolous men, man, who laughed at us then. We were asking Carter Burden, man, we were asking Huntington Hartford, we asked George Plimpton, man, these cats who could have written the bread off their undershirts: everybody Peter knew, and everybody I knew, and I was very well-married at the time."

Hopper made it seem as if the things that he and Fonda experienced during their trip all happened in one day when he recounted them to *The New Yorker*'s James Stevenson in 1971. Their adventures began when they met Huntington Hartford. "I guess he'd been doing a lot of acid because he had somebody painting psychedelic stuff all over his apartment," Hopper recalled. (The meeting with Hartford may have taken place at the apartment of Van Wolf, an entrepreneur who set up some of Fonda and Hopper's meetings with investors. In his memoir, Fonda describes Wolf's "wild" apartment: "Van's (Wolf) apartment was being painted by some blissed-out hippie to look like the miasma of an acid trip.") "It was totally crazy. So we get in there, and I'm explaining the film to him and asking him for money to make the movie, and he says, 'You're so passionate about this. I'll tell you what: I'm going to give you the money.' And I'm like, 'Wow.' But then he says, 'All you have to do is levitate, right now, in front of me.' I said, 'Fuck you. I'm out of here. I wouldn't fuckin' levitate in front of you if I could.' "

Fonda and Hopper left Hartford and walked outside into the snow where they watched a pigeon with a broken wing making tracks in the snow. Their sad contemplation of the broken pigeon ended when a German marching band went brassily oom-pahing down the street. They sat with a civil-rights activist at the Russian Tea Room, who told them that black power was in and that it was all over for "whitey, man." They watched helicopters landing on the roof of the Pan Am Building. They entered a gallery where there was an exhibition of nothing but broken mirrors. The gallery owner was crying. All his famous artists had left him that day and gone to other galleries. "I'm ruined," he said. "They all left me. What will I do?" Hopper recalled "Peter's father's limousine dropping Bobby Walker and me at this church, and us trying to get into the church on acid, and everything is covered with black crepe because the Pope has just left."

Fonda and Hopper then stumbled on what seemed like a historic discovery at the apartment of Fonda's friend, Darlene de Sedle, as they prepared to go out for dinner one evening with Hopper's friend, art curator Walter Hopps, who happened to be in town. When Fonda arrived at de Sedle's place, he found a teary-eyed Hopps on the sofa, while an excited Hopper tried to explain things to Fonda. Hopper and Hopps were talking art over cups of coffee when Hopps noticed a painting on the wall that he said looked like a copy of a panel from the Mérode Altarpiece, a triptych painted by the 15th-century Flemish artist Robert Campin. De Sedle told them, "It's not a copy. The other two pieces of the triptych are somewhere in my closet." Hopper and Hopps scrutinized the three panels, which Hopps estimated were worth $8 million if they were authentic. De Sedle said that she'd sell them to bankroll Fonda and Hopper's film.

"See, it was painted in 1425 by this man by the name of Robert Campin, who was known as the Master of Flémalle," Hopper told Tom Burke in 1970, explaining Campin's significance. "Campin was the man who gave art a second chance by using oil paint, which had been used previously for sketches, and gave religion a second chance by depicting Christ born in a Flemish kitchen. He thought that artists should control all the communications in the country; and, uh, there was this unpopular war going on at the time involving the artists' guilds, and it stopped all communications. Then, uh, Robert Campin took over, in a sort of bloodless coup. And what he did was, he saved art, man. He gave art a second chance." (Peter Fonda claims that the Mérode Altarpiece was once referred to as *The Annunciation* or *The Second Chance*.)

Hopper's film, *Second Chance*, was to begin by reenacting Fonda and Hopper's drive to the airport where an impassioned Hopper tells Fonda, "We've gotta save the movie industry, man. *We* gotta save it, or it's all over for the movies!" "And that's what the picture is about," Hopper told Burke. "Do you dig, man? For fifteen years, I had been telling the movie studios it was all over for them. 'You are dying, man,' I shouted, and they laughed at me!" Do you get it, man? Hopper saw himself as the Robert Campin of the movies.

Fonda and Hopper took the triptych to be examined by scholars at the Columbia School of Art. When an elderly expert who was supposedly the head curator at the Louvre became tearful and began excitedly muttering in French while examining the painting, the scholars requested Fonda and Hopper to leave it to be X-rayed and have the paint tested. "Man, don't you get it man," Hopper told Fonda, taking him aside. "They're going to keep the painting, man, and when they find out it's the original, they'll keep the real one and give us back the counterfeit one, man." (The triptych that is displayed in the Cloisters, a section of the Metropolitan Museum of Art, is thought to be a contemporary copy of Campin's original.) They returned the panels to de Sedle.

In the lobby of the hotel where Hopper was staying, a black junkie prostitute handed him a copy of *The Gospel of Thomas*,[3] which became his spiritual touchstone. "I was an atheist at that point," he recalled, "and it was pretty far out, but we read it aloud, and I couldn't find anything in it I couldn't believe. Doubting Thomas—he was the one who stuck his hand in the Wound. It starts out, 'These are the secret words which the living Jesus spoke. Whoever finds the explanation of these words will not find death.' There's only one law you have to abide by; 'Don't lie and don't do what you hate.' "

Fonda and Hopper returned to Los Angeles empty-handed and shelved *The Yin and the Yan(g)*.

A year after Stern wrote the treatment for *The Last Movie*, Hopper spoke to Phil Spector about producing the film. After negotiating with Hopper, Stern, and their agents for an entire day, Spector agreed to put up some money to fund research and pay Stern to expand his treatment into a screenplay. "Spector was a terrifying man, extremely wrapped up in himself," Stern recalled. Hopper and Stern completed a 119-page screenplay three days after getting the go-ahead from Spector.

Hopper's first choice for the leading role in his film was Montgomery Clift. After Clift died on July 23, 1966, Hopper lined up a cast that included Jason Robards Jr., Jennifer Jones, and Jane Fonda. Then Hopper decided that he was going to star in his own film. Brooke Hayward and Stewart Stern both remember that Spector withdrew his support for the film at the last minute when his accountant advised him that the project was too risky.

"No, he didn't pull out," Hopper told *Vanity Fair* magazine in 2001. "Phil said, 'I'm going to do this myself, because we've gone to everybody and we've been turned down. And I said, 'How much money do you have in the bank?' and he said 'I've got a million five.' And I said, 'Well, there's

---

[3] *The Gospel of Thomas* is a collection of 114 sayings attributed to Jesus. The Coptic text, dated at around 340, was discovered in Nag Hammadi, Egypt in 1945.

a great possibility that this movie may cost a million two hundred thousand.' He said, 'That's all right. I'm going to risk it,' I said, 'Phil, I can't let you do that because if the movie isn't successful I've wiped you out, and I'm not going to feel comfortable doing that.' It was one of the hardest things I ever did."

Pulling the plug on *The Last Movie* devastated Hopper. "It was tragic, quite tragic," Hayward recalled. "It destroyed some huge central part of his ego. If it had been made, then he wouldn't have fallen into the abyss." Withdrawing *The Last Movie* from Spector sent Hopper into a downward spiral of increased drinking and, Hayward claimed, heavy LSD use. "I was into peyote and drinking, and I'd fly into uncontrollable rages," he recalled. "Not exactly a good basis for a marriage." Hopper's violent rages left Hayward fearing for herself and her children. During this nightmarish period, Hopper often resembled Frank Booth, his psychotic character in *Blue Velvet* (1986). "That's the way you would have seen Dennis behaving any number of nights in the sixties," Hayward said.

Hopper made another effort to realize *The Last Movie*. Designer Tony Duquette organized a black-tie dinner at his Beverly Hills home for fifty or sixty guests to introduce Dennis to tobacco heiress Doris Duke, whom Hopper hoped would finance his film. Brooke Hayward drove her Checker cab to Duquette's party alone because Dennis was in San Francisco's Haight-Ashbury district participating in the first Human Be-In, which was held on January 14, 1967. The Human Be-In was something of a trial run for the Woodstock Festival two years later. Under banners and flags decorated with images of marijuana leaves, fifty thousand people gathered before a stage to be addressed by Jerry Rubin, Timothy Leary, Richard Alpert, poet Gary Snyder, Allen Ginsberg, Michael McClure, and Zen master Shunryu Suzuki Roshi.

In his memoir, Peter Coyote wrote, "Fifty thousand people took drugs, danced, painted their faces, dressed in outrageous costumes, crawled into the bushes and made love, fired up barbecues, pitched tents, and sold wares—crystals, tie-dyes, hash pipes, earrings, hair ties, and political tracts. Fifty thousand people played flutes, guitars, tambourines, tablas, bongos, congas, sitars, and saxophones, and sang, harmonized, and reveled in their number and variety, aware that they were an emergent social force."

Hopper was already immersed in the Haight-Ashbury scene before the Human Be-In. "When I was a photographer for *Vogue* magazine, they gave me an assignment to photograph groups," he recalled. "So I photographed the Grateful Dead, the Jefferson Airplane, and Lovin' Spoonful, The Byrds, some others. I went up to San Francisco and got involved in the whole Haight-Ashbury scene with people I knew from Kansas—Michael McClure, Bruce Conner. I was in San Francisco almost every weekend with the free-speech movement, and a lot of my activities meant going through Berkeley.

"Berkeley was on fire. Stopping the war. Everything I was involved with at that time came out of Berkeley and San Francisco more than anywhere else." Hopper adopted a hippie appearance and persona, which found its way into his character in *Easy Rider* against Peter Fonda's wishes. "In 1967, when we started writing *Easy Rider*, I was the only hippie in the group," Hopper said. "Peter was not a hippie. Peter wanted me to have short hair in *Easy Rider*. The whole hippie scene and all that—Peter didn't want it in the movie. That was because of my involvement in San Francisco."

Hopper arrived late for Duquette's dinner, straight from the Be-In. His appearance alarmed his wife. "He had a three-day growth of beard," she said, "he was filthy, his hair was crazy—he'd started growing a ponytail— he had one of those horrible mandalas around his neck, and his eyes were blood-red. Dennis was altered forever."

Duquette suggested that Dennis, Brooke, and Irving Blum should take Duke back to her home. Doris Duke sat beside Dennis as he drove the cab while Hayward and Blum huddled in the back. Duke became terrified of them after listening to Hopper explain why socialism should replace the failing democratic system. Duke fled the cab and pushed the button that activated her electric gates the moment that she reached her home. She scooted under the gates as they rose vertically and disappeared, to the delight of the cab's occupants.

Unlike that evening's conclusion, Hopper and Hayward's deteriorating marriage was no laughing matter. While he pursued his goal of becoming a director, the couple was being driven apart by his alarming behavior, which was exacerbated by his use of alcohol and drugs. "Dennis was an alcoholic and a druggieholic," Hayward said. Hopper set fire to his house several times after falling asleep drunk with a lit cigarette between his fingers. One night, Hayward was awakened by the smell of smoke and discovered Hopper's room engulfed in flames. She pushed him out of his flaming bed, saving his life.

The marriage reached a turning point on the afternoon that Hopper broke his wife's nose. "He was furious because I criticized one of his photographs," she recalled. "He had shown me some proof sheets, and I said, 'Well . . . ' and I was kind of in a rush—I had to pick the children up from school—and it was sort of a swipe. I don't think he intended to do anything."

"During our marriage, I was an alcoholic, and the alcohol did make me violent," he admitted. "And we were having problems. Problems that I wasn't old enough to understand. We had a lot of problems, emotionally, the two of us, and I was unable to deal with any of it, much less my own emotional catastrophe, but ours together was way over my head. I was way out of my league. I didn't have it, you know? I just wanted to make a movie, get on with things."

"There was a moment when I became violent with her," Hopper said. "And she was probably afraid of me after that. That was a very young and stupid mistake because I didn't understand her illness. She was manic-depressive, and I couldn't cope with it. It was hard. She would be up and talking at a party, performing, and the second the last person left the room, she would fall into this deep funk." Hopper said that Hayward would shut herself up in her room for days at a time, refusing to even talk to him through her locked door. Hayward wasn't drinking or taking drugs, but Hopper claimed that she had to be hospitalized after gulping down a handful of pills and attempted to commit suicide twice. (Hayward denies this.)

Hayward says that "the floodgates opened" after Hopper broke her nose. She drove her Checker cab to a theater near their home one evening to watch Dennis rehearse the role of Billy the Kid in his friend Michael McClure's controversial play, *The Beard* (1965), where, Peter Fonda says, "Billy rips off Jean Harlow's panties and eats her out—in heaven." After the performance, Hayward told Hopper, who was "completely crazy" with stage jitters, that she needed to return home to her children. Hopper, who badly wanted her to stay, jumped on the hood of her cab and kicked in the windshield in front of onlookers. A terrified Hayward had to wend her way back home without a windshield.

A fortuitous confluence of events eventually led from the rut of exploitation films Hopper was trapped in to his breakout project, *Easy Rider*. Prolific B-moviemaker Roger Corman was producing his Hell's Angels story, *The Wild Angels* (1966) and required his lead actors to actually ride motorcycles in the film. Corman's first choice for his film's leading man,

George Chakiris (who won an Academy Award for Best Supporting Actor for *West Side Story* (1961), couldn't ride a chopper. Peter Fonda eagerly accepted the role under Corman's conditions, claiming that he made the entire film stoned.

Written by Charles B. Griffith, who also wrote two of Corman's best films, *A Bucket of Blood* (1959) and *The Little Shop of Horrors* (1960), *The Wild Angels* portrays the outlaw antics of a group of Hell's Angels led by Heavenly Blues (Fonda). "The film's beer-swilling, pot-smoking, and unfocused brawling may have become screen clichés in record time," critic Mark Deming wrote, "but they were newer and more shocking in 1966, and the film's rough, unpolished visual style gives it a ring of truth missing from most of the films that followed in its wake."

Though *The Wild Angels* is really pretty crummy, it confirmed Corman's Midas touch for exploiting hot trends when it cleaned up at the box office. *The Wild Angels'* success spurred a series of biker films and was the precursor to *Easy Rider*. Dennis Hopper starred in *The Glory Stompers* (1968), while Jack Nicholson costarred in *Hell's Angels on Wheels* (1967). (Hopper later said that his behavior drove *The Glory Stompers'* director, Anthony M. Lanza, to a nervous breakdown, leaving Hopper to finish directing the film. Some picturesque long shots of bikers riding over sand dunes and on a highway against a reddish setting sun are uncharacteristic of the rest of the film's prosaic direction and suggest Hopper's handiwork.)

Flush with the success of *The Wild Angels*, Corman moved on to another topical subject, LSD. *The Trip* (1967) starred Peter Fonda as a disaffected director of commercials who hopes LSD will transform his life. Jack Nicholson, whose career as an actor hadn't taken off, wrote *The Trip's* screenplay. A bearded Bruce Dern, resembling the young Francis Ford Coppola, played Fonda's acid trip guide. Corman gave Dennis Hopper the role of Max, the drug dealer who provides the film's other characters with their LSD and becomes the hippie high priest in Fonda's LSD hallucinations.

"I wasn't doing acid until I got the part of an acid dealer in *The Trip*, the one that Bruce Dern and Peter Fonda buy from," Hopper said. "I thought 'Well, if I'm dealing it, I better understand what it is.' I took acid very late because I had already done peyote, and I said what do I want to do this chemical for? One is like eating a flower, and one is like eating an IBM machine. I had a really great trip. Amazing."

"Dennis needed a job," Fonda said, "and he was very pleased to get this one. People didn't want to hire Dennis because he was a tough cookie to work with." "Dennis, who was recommended by Peter, since they had been trying to do films together, gave an exceptional performance as Max," Corman recalled. "The scenes in his hippie drug den worked wonderfully. He got Max's stoned apocalyptic ramblings down right. I let them improvise a little and have some fun and make the dialogue their own. As a joint passes around a circle of hippies seated on the floor, Dennis has lines like 'Anyway, I'm flashing, and I'm strung out in the stream and then the fuzz drive by. I say, 'Hey, baby, get a hold of yourself and pull yourself in, man, 'cause this is it.'

"This shot was a complicated circular dolly movement in the middle of the group as each friend took a hit. Peter Fonda insists to this day it was not real grass. I wasn't listening too closely to Dennis because of the intricacy of the shot. When it was over, I said, 'Print.' The soundman came to me and said, 'Dennis just broke the all-time record. He used the word 'man' thirty-six times in one speech.' 'Great,' I said. 'Print it, man.' "

Hopper's role in *The Trip* eventually put him in the director's chair on *Easy Rider*. Hopper and Fonda formed a second unit and filmed the sequences in Nicholson's script that Corman decided not to shoot. "I thought we needed the script's desert sequences," Fonda recalled, "so I told Corman that I'd gotten some cameras and a friend who could operate them and that we needed the footage. I knew that if I just asked him for some money, he'd say no, so I said I had part of it covered, and Roger bought us the film. Then I rented a camera and found a cameraman and drove out to the desert, and Dennis directed it. So we shot for a couple of days in Yuma to Big Dune and back toward L.A. I ran up and down dunes and stood there and did freaky numbers—whatever he wanted me to do. Dennis got some beautiful, beautiful stuff of me in the dunes, with water behind me, water going into my profile and bursting behind me, water lit by the sun. We pulled off some of what I felt were the best shots of the film. Roger used it all."

Peter Fonda was trying to wind down in his hotel room one evening in late September 1967 after spending the day promoting *The Trip* at a movie exhibitor's conference in Toronto. High on beer and grass, he was staring at one of the publicity stills from *The Wild Angels* that he was obligated to autograph for an exhibitor when the idea for *Easy Rider* suddenly hit him. He phoned Hopper, who was surprised to hear from him after a recent argument they'd had. Fonda outlined his story to Hopper and invited him to come aboard his project as its director. Hopper's work on *The Trip* convinced Fonda that he possessed the crazy vision that the film needed.

By January 1968, they had secured the participation of screenwriter Terry Southern and financing from Raybert, Bob Rafelson and Bert Schneider's company, which produced the hit TV series *The Monkees* (September 1966–March 1968), and were about to start filming the Mardi Gras festival in New Orleans. Though Brooke Hayward never interfered with Hopper's career choices, her open contempt for *Easy Rider* was another source of marital discord.

Hayward and Hopper had one of their typical exchanges over his pet project when she drove him to the airport in late February to leave for New Orleans. Brooke considered *Easy Rider* just another one of Hopper's "biker-druggie" films, which she hated. "I've known Peter all my life," she said. "He can't act. You're going after fool's gold." "That didn't read too well with me," Hopper said. "Brooke is groovy, we even have a beautiful little girl, but you don't say that to me about something I've waited fifteen years—no, all my life—to do." Only days after the release of *Easy Rider* in July 1969, Hopper told journalist Tom Burke that he decided to divorce his wife when she derided *Easy Rider* on the way to the airport. Hayward called Hopper's claim, which he repeated to *Vanity Fair*'s Bob Colacello shortly before his death, "idiotic."

Brooke Hayward left Hopper shortly after he returned to Los Angeles from New Orleans, the sudden culmination of a series of events. Peter Fonda and Terry Southern phoned her from New Orleans as location shooting there on *Easy Rider* wrapped, warning her that Hopper had become dangerously unstable. They advised her to take her children and vacate her home before he returned. Fonda told her that the Mardi Gras footage was dreadful, that he couldn't work with Hopper anymore, and that he would have to fire him from the film. Loathe to cut and run, Hayward stayed in the home with her children.

Hopper retreated to his bedroom for several days after returning from New Orleans, fearing he had blown his only opportunity to direct a film. "The dying swan," Hayward quipped, "holding court in his bedroom." Hopper finally roused himself to attend a screening of the New Orleans footage with Brooke and the parties involved in the film. "It was just an endless parade of shit," associate producer William Hayward said. (Hayward's low opinion of the New Orleans footage didn't stop him from keeping his share of *Easy Rider*'s profits.) "It was just dreadful stuff, murky, the camera work wasn't any good," Brooke recalled. "The talent I knew Dennis had, and Peter knew Dennis had, that we'd seen in the second-unit stuff for *The Trip* that he'd shot, none of that was there. There was a terrible silence in the editing room."

Hopper became increasingly edgy in the days following the screening, when Brooke assumed that Peter Fonda was searching for Hopper's replacement. (Actually, Fonda and William Hayward held a meeting with Bert Schneider and tried to quit the film.) "He was now drinking a great deal," she recalled about Hopper, "and doing a lot of different drugs, which did not help his state of mind, and he was under the gun. He was violent and dangerous. Exceedingly dangerous."

Hopper came home one evening with his buddy, artist and experimental filmmaker Bruce Conner, whose editing techniques Hopper used while cutting *Easy Rider*. While Conner played the Hammond organ in the foyer, Hopper yelled at his wife because she fed the last portion of hot dogs and beans to their children, leaving nothing for him. Hopper threatened Brooke, Marin started screaming, and Brooke's little son Jeffrey bravely interposed himself between Dennis and his mother. Fearing more for her children's safety than her own, Hayward persuaded Conner to contrive a ruse to get Hopper to leave the house long enough for her to gather the children and flee. Hayward and her children hid at a variety of friends' homes, always making sure Hopper couldn't find her.

Hayward hired a divorce lawyer and impressed on him the importance of getting a restraining order to keep Hopper out of their home. Then her brother, William, called her to tell her that Hopper had just been arrested by the police for possession of marijuana. "You're not going to believe this," he said, "but Dennis has just been arrested for smoking dope on the Strip, and he's in jail."

"They stopped me only because my hair was somewhat long," Hopper recalled, "and I was driving an old car. They said that I'd thrown a roach out of the car, which I had *not*. Well, I did have this roach in my *pocket*. Then, in court, they produced as evidence not *my* roach, which was wrapped in *white* paper, but somebody else's roach, which was wrapped in *black* paper. How ludicrous, man! It was dark. They couldn't have even *seen* a *black* roach."

When Brooke told her lawyer that Hopper was in jail, he told her, "Great. Go back to the house," which she did. Hopper's pot bust would facilitate the issuance of a restraining order. Bert Schneider bailed Hopper out of jail, and sent him out of town to scout locations for *Easy Rider* with Paul Lewis, the film's production manager.

"So that's how I survived," Hayward said. "It was just luck. If Dennis had been replaced, I'm sure he would have killed me." Sometime later, Hopper and Lewis broke into the house to retrieve the art that Hopper believed was rightfully his, but Hayward had already removed it. She filed for divorce from Hopper and got a restraining order against him. Leland Hayward called his daughter the day that she filed for divorce. He told her, "Congratulations on the first smart move you've made in six years."

Brooke Hayward charged Hopper with extreme cruelty, claiming that he had a violent temper and struck her on several occasions. She also charged him with using marijuana and LSD. The court granted Hayward's divorce in February 1969, on the lesser grounds that Hopper used "rude and abusive language" in front of their daughter. Hopper withdrew his cross-complaint after the couple agreed to a court-approved property settlement. The settlement awarded Hayward possession of the couple's home, all of Hopper's beloved pop art, and custody of her children.

The only possession of Hopper's she refused to pursue was her community-property share of the then-speculative profit from *Easy Rider*, which she considered worthless. Hayward changed her tune in 1997, telling author Peter Biskind, "When we got divorced, I probably could have gone for half of his cut from *Easy Rider*, but I refused to take a nickel from him, because I didn't want him coming after me with a shotgun and shooting me." (In 2010, Brooke Hayward told me that Hopper never kept guns in their house when they were married.)

Dennis Hopper walked out of court with little more than the rights to *Easy Rider*. He told Tom Burke that he relinquished his house and art collection in exchange for his share of *Easy Rider*'s profits. It turned out to be a stroke of incredible good luck that proved to be his ticket to ride. *Easy Rider* would end up paying Hopper dividends for years to come and would become the foundation of his cinematic legacy.

· 5 ·

EASY RIDER

The long, strange story of how Dennis Hopper went from being a Hollywood pariah to the hottest director in town in only two short years.

"One of the stars was a drunken hippie, one of the writers was an acid-fried biker, and the director was a paranoid control freak. The bad news was all three of them were Dennis Hopper."

Anonymous

"It was an incredible moment," Hopper said, referring to the success of Easy Rider. *"But that is all it was. A moment."*

*S*UCCESS HAS A thousand fathers. Failure has none. Long after its success was proven, more than one person has come forth to take credit for creating *Easy Rider*. Decades after its 1969 release, the exact circumstances of *Easy Rider*'s origin, the authorship of its script, and the details of its production still remain subject to competing claims. *Easy Rider*'s associate producer, William Hayward, commented, "The whole thing has been like a Rashomon experience, the whole movie, the entire production. Everybody's got an entirely different story on the thing."

Dennis Hopper's old acquaintance, John Gilmore, maintains that actor George Macready's son, Michael, paid him to write a screen story titled *Out Takes* that was the basis for *Easy Rider*. (Interestingly, Hopper's unpublished memoir was also to be titled *Out Takes*.) Gilmore described his story in his memoir. "About two buddies who score big on a cocaine deal and head out for New Orleans on motorcycles—riding abreast on the highways as I'd once ridden with Jimmy Dean. The two guys in the story get hooked into a lot of freaky action-ideas I'd noted down on my New Orleans expedition. In *Out Takes*, it's Errol Flynn's 'grim reaper' that's tracking them, littering the road-ways with reminders of death. At the end, the guys lose the bikes outside a whorehouse in the French Quarter, wind up stealing a '59 Cadillac convertible, and chance to cross paths with death on an otherwise deserted highway. Both heroes get blown away by the shotgun blasts of a total stranger."

The rights to *Out Takes* reverted to Gilmore when Macready lost his funding. Gilmore says that he took *Out Takes* to Hopper, who responded enthusiastically and showed it to Peter Fonda. Fonda and Hopper agreed that if AIP green-lighted the project, Gilmore would write the film, and Hopper would direct it. They assured Gilmore that AIP would pay him for his story and give him a screen credit, even if they refused to hire him to write the screenplay. When Gilmore visited Brooke Hayward to retrieve a surfing script he had left with Hopper, Hopper told him that the deal with AIP was dead. Then Hopper said that he and Peter Fonda were developing Fonda's idea, called *Riding Easy*, whose storyline sounded almost identical to Gilmore's, and they had hired Terry Southern to develop a treatment. Deprived of any credit or compensation for his story, Gilmore still feels that Hopper cheated him of his rightful due.

Michael Macready told me that he never met anyone named John or Jonathan Gilmore. Likewise, he had no interaction with Peter Fonda or Dennis Hopper. Macready recalled that he could rarely get into the editing suite he rented at Ryder Sound Services at the same time that *Easy Rider* was in postproduction because Fonda and Hopper were tripping on LSD in there and left the settings on the editing console messed up whenever they departed.

Peter Coyote, who was a member of the San Francisco Mime Troupe and a small group of activists called the Diggers in the late '60s, claims that he was present when *Easy Rider* was born. In late 1968 or early 1969, the Diggers' leader, Emmett Grogan, Coyote, Peter Berg, and a Hell's Angel named Sweet William (Bill Fritsch) drove to Los Angeles to attend a meeting of music-industry executives. The executives wanted to organize a benefit for the Diggers featuring The Beatles, whose ticket proceeds would be donated to charity. (Grogan excused himself during the meeting to rifle the coatroom.) "I guess if they were the light," Coyote wrote, "we were the dark—leathers slick with oil and road dirt, edgy, armed, and not about to have our name co-opted by a bunch of Nehru-shirted aesthetes whose monthly tab for weed and cocaine equaled any of our annual incomes."

The Diggers remained in L.A. after the meeting, staying with Ravi Shankar's manager, Benny Shapiro. After rejecting the executives' offer, the Diggers' mystique spread around Hollywood. "The Diggers reputation as cutting-edge social thinkers had spread fairly widely; now our refusal to accept money and our ability to quash or create events had amplified our status as underground 'heavies,' " Coyote wrote. "From our point of view, freedom involved first liberating the imagination from economic assumptions of profit and private property that demanded existence at the expense of personal truthfulness and honor, then living according to personal authenticity and fidelity to inner directives and impulses."

"One night Peter Fonda, Brandon De Wilde, and Dennis Hopper visited Benny's to check us out," Coyote recalled. "These guys were our age, sons of the film community, caught somewhere between their home base and their imaginings of free life, seeking to connect with a pure strain of the underground. We discussed 'what was happening' for some time and how it might be translated into film (still never accomplished, as far as I'm concerned) and we passed scenarios and ideas back and forth as they picked our brains for stories. Chat was easy and things felt good. Then Sweet William took the floor, magnificent in his Angel colors, his hard-chiseled face and poetic eyes mesmerizing those of us who knew him well.

" 'You know what I'd do?" Sweet William said. "I'd make a movie about me and a buddy just riding around. Just going around the country doing what we do, seeing what we see, you know. Showing the people what things are like."

"This," Coyote wrote, "was the germinating idea for the hit movie *Easy Rider*, a film about which I have complicated feelings." The idea of two free-spirited buddies sharing their adventures while traveling around the country was hardly original anymore by the late '60s when *Easy Rider* was made. It is the premise for Kerouac's *On the Road* (published in 1957), which had been housebroken and formulized for the white-bread TV series *Route 66* (1960–1964). (There's another problem with Coyote's account of the genesis of *Easy Rider*. Coyote recalls coming to L.A. with the Diggers in late 1968 or early 1969. *Easy Rider* began production on February 23, 1968, and was released on July 14, 1969.)

Coyote also gives the Diggers' presence in Hopper's life credit for ruining his marriage. "Some time later," Coyote wrote, "Emmett, Peter, Billy, and I were cooking smack in his living room forest of pop and op art when his wife at the time, Brooke Hayward, walked in, appraised the scene, and left for good, precipitating a long downhill spiral for Dennis." Hayward denies the story, but says she was not delighted when Hopper let a group of Hell's Angels sleep over at her home.

"Of the three actors who visited us at Benny's that night," Coyote recalled, "only Dennis Hopper would leave the safe havens of his known haunts and run around with us during the rest of our stay. Offscreen, in those days Dennis was a passionate and half-crazy seeker of truth, something like the photographer he played to perfection in *Apocalypse Now* (1979). I came to think of the others as beautiful hothouse flowers that could not withstand the rigors of unprotected environments."

Peter Fonda created the kernel of *Easy Rider* on the evening of September 26, 1967, while he was attending a movie exhibitors' convention in Toronto to promote *The Trip*. Earlier that day, he was in the audience when MPAA (the Motion Picture Association of America, which instituted the movie-rating system) President Jack Valenti addressed a group of exhibitors. "My friends, and you are my friends," Valenti began. Then Valenti looked right at Fonda as he said, "It's time we stop making movies about motorcycles, sex, and drugs." Instead, Valenti encouraged his audience to make more movies like *Doctor Dolittle* (1967).

That aroused Fonda's rebellious instincts. That night, Fonda was out of marijuana, depressed, and tired of promoting a film he disliked. He was disenchanted by what he felt was AIP's emasculation of *The Trip*. They inserted an antidrug message in the film during postproduction. AIP had superimposed an image of glass shattering over the film's final closeup of Fonda gazing outward at the beach on the morning after his LSD trip. Fonda drank several Heinekens and took a sleeping pill to try to get some rest in a hotel full of noisy conventioneers. (He later said that he also smoked some "doobs.")

"I was a little bit loaded and looked at a picture on the table that was left for somebody's cousin," he told *Playboy*'s interviewer, Lawrence Linderman. "It was a photograph from *The Wild Angels* of actor Bruce Dern on a chop. I looked at the photo for a while and then thought what it would look like if, instead of two guys on one cycle, I had each of the guys on a bike. And suddenly I thought, that's it, that's the modern Western. Two cats just riding across the country, two loners, not a motorcycle gang, no Hell's Angels, nothing like that, just those two guys. And maybe they make a big score see, so they have a lot of money. And they're going to cross the country and retire in Florida.

"Anyway, they get to Florida, and they've got the money, and it's together, and they're about to get to the farm or get to the boat when a couple of duck poachers in a truck rip them off cause they don't like the way they look." The hunters taunt the first biker and shoot him. (The bikers had no character names or identities when Fonda first conceived the story.) His buddy straps him on his bike and starts to ride for help. The hunters decide, "We'd better go back," leaving audiences to expect they're returning to help the bikers. Instead, in what Fonda thought would be a shocker, they blow away biker #2.

"We changed a lot of details later, of course," Fonda said, "and there was no Captain America or anything else yet." (Except for the premise of two bikers who make a killing on a dope score and decide to retire, just about everything else Fonda told Linderman was in his original story, including some dialogue and the shock ending, were only written later by Terry Southern—creative hindsight is an amazing thing.) Fonda said, "But I thought fuck it's *right* because we've got all the things backers want. We go for dope, we go for motorcycles, we go riding across the country, we'll even get some sex here and there—but we can do all these things really honestly."

Fonda called Hopper, even though he vowed never to speak to Fonda again after a recent fight that took place when he showed up at Fonda's home, demanding to be made the director of a record album Fonda was to perform on and produce. "He went ballistic and screamed at me that everyone was stealing his ideas and other unintelligible things," Fonda recalled. When Hopper wouldn't stop his tantrum, Fonda hurled a tape recorder on the floor at his feet, smashing it to bits. Hopper paused, then told him, "You're a fucking child, man! I can't believe this! You're out of your fucking mind, and I'm not going to talk to you anymore, man!"

Fonda said that he called Hopper from Toronto anyway because "Dennis Hopper was the only guy crazy enough to know what I was talking about, even crazier than I am." Hopper's handling of the desert sequences in *The Trip* inspired Fonda's confidence in his directorial potential. "The footage was beautiful," he said. "Dennis could have done the whole movie like that, which is why I knew he'd be perfect for *Easy Rider*. He had the passion, and he had the ability to see form and substance much better than I. He understood framing. I was still learning, watching him, shooting every kind of still shot you can imagine. Directing is a verb, not a noun. It's just like acting."

Brooke Hayward recalled that Dennis was in one of his funks, retreating to his bedroom for three or four days, when Fonda phoned him. "Around three o'clock in the morning, Peter called me," Hopper said. "He was up in Toronto promoting *The Trip* at the film festival up there. So Peter says that he's just talked with James Nicholson, no relation to Jack, and Sam Arkoff, who ran AIP, and I told them this idea for a movie." Hopper said, "Man, wow, Jesus! I'm sure glad you called me, man, 'cause I was never going to speak to you again, you know, man." Fonda said, "Fuck that man." He told Hopper the film's story. Hopper said, "That's great, man! Fucking great! What do you have in mind?" Fonda said, "You direct it, I'll produce it, we'll both write and star in it." Hopper said, "You . . . ah . . . want me to direct?" Fonda said, "Fucking A, man! They said we could both act in it, and you could direct. What do you think?" Hopper said, "They actually said they'd give you money for that?" "Yeah," Fonda said. Hopper said, "Terrific, man. If they really said they'd give you the money, it sounds great to me." Fonda recalled, "Hopper thought for a second and said, 'Listen man, the score, we gotta make it a *cocaine* score.' Hopper was already thinking about details. 'Sure, man, right, a cocaine score. I'll talk to you tomorrow, when I get back to L.A.' And that's how *Easy Rider* got started. I looked at that photograph and went for it."

Fonda and Hopper were convinced that they had come up with a sure-fire moneymaker. Fonda's *The Wild Angels* made $16,000,000 in the U.S. alone. Hopper's *The Glory Stompers* earned $3.5 million. Fonda believed *Easy Rider* could be made for $300,000 and combined the biker films' appeal with an additional X-factor. Fonda said, "I kept thinking about this seventeen-year-old kid coming up to his friends, saying, 'Hey man, you have to see this flick. These guys, they smuggle coke across the border, and then they get on these chops, these wild, far-out bikes, and then they ride and they get high—I mean *really* high—and at the end of the movie, well, they just get shot. Like *that*, man, just because they're there at the wrong time.' And then the other kids are gonna go see the film."

Fonda said that he and Hopper developed a twelve-page outline titled *The Loners* by walking around Fonda's tennis court, brainstorming, and high-fiving each other when they came up with a good idea while Fonda's daughter, Bridget, rode her tricycle around them. Fonda said that's when Hopper created the character of George Hanson, the Southern alcoholic lawyer memorably played by Jack Nicholson in *Easy Rider*, and worked out the logistics of the drug sale at the beginning of the film.

"When Peter talked about the marijuana being smuggled in the beginning," Hopper said, "it was too big a load. I couldn't figure out how two guys on dirt bikes were gonna haul any kind of marijuana worth selling, get a lot of money, and retire in Florida. And heroin to me, at that time, was out of the question. I felt it was not a drug I wanted to promote. And I thought, 'Let's do cocaine, nobody has cocaine, it's called the drug of kings, it's gotta be really expensive.' We bring the cocaine in. And then we can do it in small like battery packs. So, we all thought that was a great idea."

Fonda and Hopper took their outline to Sam Arkoff and James Nicholson at American International Pictures, to whom Fonda owed a final film on a three-picture contract. "Under the guise of doing a biker movie, they could maybe pull off a movie that might be more interesting," Terry Southern said. "Dennis would be able to make his debut as a director in one fell swoop. It seemed possible under these auspices, whereas he couldn't get arrested ordinarily. Under the setup where Peter Fonda owed AIP this picture, it would be possible to get this different approach in under the wire. He persuaded Peter to go along with this. 'We'll get Terry to write the script!' I had this good reputation off of *Dr. Strangelove* and *Candy*."

AIP were skittish about the story's unsensational depiction of hard drugs and were worried about how much responsibility Hopper could handle. AIP decided that Hopper could choose to direct the film or costar in it, but not do both. As Jack Nicholson said, "You know Dennis, you don't exactly just turn over money to him and say, 'No problem, you know what I mean?'"

Fonda went off to the French coastal village of Roscoff in October '67 to appear with Jane Fonda in the Roger Vadim-directed segment of the film, *Spirits of the Dead* (1968), a trilogy loosely based on the writings of Edgar Allan Poe. (The film is a must-see for its concluding story, "Toby

Dammit," directed by Federico Fellini, with a mesmerizing Terence Stamp playing a demon-haunted movie star.)

Right after his visit to the set of *Barbarella* (1968) in Rome, where he was one of that film's seven credited screenwriters, Terry Southern dropped by Roscoff to discuss the editing of *Barbarella* with its star, Jane Fonda, and her husband and director, Roger Vadim. When Southern asked Peter Fonda what he was up to, he told him about Dennis Hopper and their embryonic film. When he told Southern they were seeking a writer, Southern eagerly offered his services. Fonda said, "Terry, your fee is the same as the budget, man." Southern replied, "No, no, no. You don't get it! It's the most commercial story I have ever heard. And a real pip of an ending! I'm your man!"

Gail Gerber recalls Peter Fonda visiting her and Southern in their New York home on a rainy evening in November 1967 to discuss his project. (In the early '90s, Southern told his biographer, Lee Hill, that Fonda and Hopper were both present at this meeting.) According to Gerber, Fonda's idea for the film concerned "two daredevil race-car drivers being exploited by greedy promoters, but when Fonda realized that he owed American International Pictures one more biker film, it then morphed into a tale about two bikers who score some dope, go on a road trip, and have a series of 'interesting incidences.' "

"Well, right at the beginning Dennis and Peter had just this one idea, right?" Southern said. "Listen, this is their contribution to the whole thing. These two guys, Peter and Dennis, at first they were going to be in cars, so they could do stunts in cars. It was going to be called "Barnstormers" or something. This is what they came to me with. So we changed it to motorbikes, but the idea then was that they would score some drugs and—this is when people are just beginning to realize you can make big money in drugs—so they buy some coke in Mexico, sell it, ride their bikes to Florida, buy a boat, and leave the American rat race. Sail off into the sunset. The entertainment aspect of the film, presumably, was to be their pilgrimage from Mexico to Key West. *That was it.*"

After Fonda and Hopper discussed their story, Southern swept the air with his hand and told them how good the title *Easy Rider* would look on a marquee. Fonda later said that Southern's title was a boon to the film and explained its meaning. "An 'easy rider' is the guy who is the prostitute's boyfriend, her lover," he said. "He sits at home drinking beer and watching television. When she comes back home, he has sex with her. He's got the easy ride. She takes care of him."

"They said we want you to write this, and we're going to defer any money in exchange for splitting 10 percent three ways," Southern recalled. "For a variety of complicated business reasons, I wasn't in a position where I could defer so they said you can get $350 a week for ten weeks in lieu of that. So I had to do it that way. So I never had a piece of it which turned out to be very lucrative." Gail Gerber insists that there was a verbal understanding that Southern would receive some share of the film's profits. Though Southern expressed trepidation over Fonda's choice of Hopper to direct, he agreed to go ahead with his involvement.

Why did Southern agree to write *Easy Rider* for such a paltry salary when he was at the peak of his career? He needed the money. Southern lived large, spent generously on others, and carelessly managed his financial affairs. Southern's enthusiasm for *Easy Rider* may also have been prompted by a sudden drought of offers of film work, despite his cowriting credits on *Dr. Strangelove*, *The Cincinnati Kid* (1965), and *Barbarella*. (Gerber claims that she and Southern later discovered that FBI harassment chilled Hollywood's interest in him.)

Gerber says that Peter Fonda returned after the New Year and stayed with her and Southern for about a month while he and Terry worked in earnest on fleshing out Fonda's story into a treatment. Southern would recline on his couch, pencil and legal pad in hand, while Fonda paced the room, exchanging ideas with him. They brought in an experienced typist to transcribe Southern's pages, which he then worked on into the morning hours.

Hopper joined Southern and Fonda for two weeks, staying with Southern and Gerber. "So we began smoking dope in earnest and having a nonstop story conference," Southern told Mike Golden. "The first notion was that they not be bikers, but a duo of daredevil car drivers barnstorming around the U.S. being exploited by a series of unscrupulous promoters until they were finally disgusted enough to quit. Then one day, the dope smoke cleared long enough to remember that Peter's commitment was for a motorcycle flick, and we switched over pronto."

"Dennis would rant and rave, using a lot of four-letter words, and the typist would break into tears and run sobbing out into the night," Gerber recalled. "Terry would have to call the typing pool the next day and get another typist." Gerber claims that it was Southern who suggested changing the drug that bikers Wyatt (Fonda) and Billy (Hopper) sell from marijuana, which would be too bulky to profit from in the small quantity the bikers could carry, to cocaine. Southern later insisted that he created the character of George Hanson and serendipity provided the campfire scene where he tells Billy and Wyatt about UFOs and space aliens.

Southern said that he, Fonda, and Hopper agreed "that a Southern establishment-figure was needed for the film." Southern told Lee Hill, "The idea of meeting a kind of a straight guy, which turned out to be the Jack Nicholson role, was totally up to me. I thought of this Faulkner character, Gavin Stevens, who was the lawyer in this small town. He had been a Rhodes scholar at Oxford, Heidelberg and had come back to this little town to do whatever he could there. So I sort of automatically gave the George Hanson character a similar sympathetic aura. I wrote the part for Rip Torn, who I thought would be ideal for it. When shooting began, we went to New Orleans and Rip was going to come, but he couldn't get out of this stage commitment in this Jimmy Baldwin play, *Blues For Mr. Charlie*." (Torn was rehearsing for Jack Gelber's play, *The Cuban Thing*, which closed on its opening night of September 24, 1968, when a Cuban resistance group bombed the theater. *Blues For Mr. Charlie* was first performed (with Torn) on April 23, 1964.)

Southern's typist was a devotee of the late George Adamski, who claimed to have communicated telepathically with Venusians and traveled on their spaceship. When Fonda, Hopper, and Southern took a break from work, she regaled them with monologues about how Venusians in various guises lived among humans to surveil them and avert a nuclear holocaust. Southern wrote, "Her attitude toward their presence was one of such total conviction, and her enthusiasm so fervent, that it had a very appealing effect. I recorded several of these soliloquies, had a transcript made of the tape and gave it to Hopper, along with the script, before he went on location—where the sequence in question was filmed. I doubt that he misplaced either."

During story sessions, Fonda objected to the scene where his character visits a New Orleans whorehouse. "Hopper and Southern wanted the characters to go to a whorehouse," he wrote. "I felt that Captain America didn't need to buy sex—in this decade, it would come to him whenever he wanted it. I was being stubborn, but Hoppy [Fonda's nickname for

Hopper] finally convinced me that we'd do it for the lawyer, to fulfill his greatest wish. Hoppy told me that my job, as an actor, was to get us out on the street, as soon as possible, back to where the action was. I relented."

Southern also devised the ending where Wyatt and Billy are killed. Southern recalled, "It wasn't until the end that it took on a genuinely artistic dimension—when it suddenly evolved into an indictment of the American redneck, and his hatred and intolerance for anything that is remotely different from himself—somewhat to the surprise of Den Hopper. And when Dennis Hopper read it he said, 'Are you kidding? Are you going to kill off both of them?'

"So I said, 'Well, that's the only way it can be, because otherwise we're not saying anything, it's just a little odyssey by a couple of irresponsible hippies. So they've got to serve some purpose, make some point.' I think for a minute he was still hoping they would somehow beat the system. Sail into the sunset with a lot of loot and freedom. But of course, he was hip enough to realize, a minute later, that it [their death] was more or less mandatory." As a parting gesture, Southern presented bound copies of his treatment to Fonda and Hopper, who returned to Hollywood to seek financing for the film.

Fonda tells a somewhat different story in his memoir. He recalls flying Hopper up to New York in late 1967 where he and Hopper spent only five days in story conferences with Terry Southern. Hopper claimed that was scouting locations for the film in the South when he discovered that Fonda and Southern had written only three pages of the screenplay. So he dropped everything and flew to New York. What happened next has become part of *Easy Rider* lore.

Peter Fonda, Gail Gerber, Terry Southern, Don Carpenter, and Rip Torn were enjoying drinks and appetizers at a New York steakhouse when an agitated Hopper suddenly appeared at their table. Gerber's recollection of Hopper's appearance supports his claim to have come to New York straight from scouting locations. "Dennis soon showed up in full *Easy Rider* regalia—long hair, bushy mustache, and fringed buckskin jacket." Hopper confronted Fonda and Southern. "What the fuck is happening, Peter? Why aren't you guys writing? Man, you don't know how rough it's been out there." Then he complained about his encounters with intolerant Texans. "Man, I've been lookin' for shootin' locations in Texas, and man, I'm lucky I'm still alive. Those motherfuckin', redneck bastards." He asked Torn, "Hey Rip, you're from fuckin' Texas, aren't you?" Torn, a Texas native, said, "Yes, but don't judge all bastards by me."

Torn tried to mollify Hopper by extending his hand in friendship. Hopper swatted it away, pushed Torn, and said, "Sit down, you motherfucker." Then he grabbed a steak knife and pointed it right between Torn's eyes, a few inches from his forehead. Torn grabbed Hopper's wrist and twisted it, making him drop the knife. Torn picked it up and pointed it at Hopper's chest, causing him to jump back and knock over Fonda. (Over the years, Hopper claimed that Torn pulled the knife on him, occasionally telling the story on talk shows. Fonda said that Hopper and Torn grabbed each other's shirts and brandished butter knives.)[4]

Hopper said, "I've got a buck knife. You wanna have a knife fight?" Torn said, "I'll wait for you in the street. Bring your knives. Bring your guns. Bring your pals, and we'll find out in about three seconds who the punk is" and walked out. Concerned that Hopper might really have a gun, Torn stood between two cars with the lid of a trash can that he picked up. He planned to throw it at Hopper like a Frisbee and then run like hell. But Hopper never left the restaurant. (Torn had good reason to worry. Hopper's hippie regalia included a leather satchel he wore where he secreted a .45 semiautomatic pistol.)

Hopper claimed that he fired Torn from the film, but Fonda recalled that Torn hadn't even been formally hired when the incident took place. "I already had a theater contract signed, and if they'd got the movie together in the right time frame, I'd have been happy to do it. I didn't turn it down," Torn told the Guardian's John Patterson in 1999. He also told Patterson that the rumor that he quit the film plagued his career long after the scene at the restaurant.

In 2008, Torn told reporter Spencer Morgan that he quit Easy Rider after a bizarre encounter with Norman Mailer that took place one evening on New York's 23rd Street. Mailer and Torn found themselves walking toward each other when they heard gunfire and ducked behind a lamppost. Four armed gangsters had cornered someone they'd already wounded.

---

[4] The truth finally emerged in court years nearly thirty years later. In 1994, Hopper told *The Tonight Show*'s Jay Leno that Torn pulled a knife on him at the restaurant. Torn then sued Hopper for slander. The judge in Torn's case awarded him $475,000 in damages and lawyer's fees in 1996. When Hopper appealed the judgment, he was fined an additional $475,000 in punitive damages.

They shot their prey dead after he came out from under a car, threw his gun out, and put up his hands. The gangsters recognized Mailer and asked who Torn was. Mailer said, "He works for me. We're talking about a job we're getting ready to do. Can we leave now?"

Mailer asked Torn about the new film he heard that Terry Southern was writing. Torn said, "They're not going to pay me anything. They only offered me scale." Mailer said, "How much money you want?" Torn said, "$3,500." Mailer said, "I'll give you $3,500." Torn ended up acting in Mailer's film *Maidstone* (1970), which became infamous for the scene where Torn actually hit Mailer on the head with a hammer and Mailer bit Torn's ear.

According to Peter Fonda, story meetings between himself, Hopper, and Southern continued without incident after the dispute in the restaurant. Southern wanted Fonda to record their story on audio tape, which would then be transcribed and typed up. Fonda suggested that since Hopper was the film's director, he should do it. "I wanted to hear what he wanted to see," he wrote. Fonda went out and purchased a tape recorder for the night of the "Big Speak," as he called it. Southern brought along a young British photographer, Michael Cooper, so that someone new to the story would be listening.

Everyone assembled had cognac shots and waited for Hopper to begin. He picked up the mike, broke out in a sweat, and was unable to perform. Fonda took the mike from him and told the story to Cooper. "Forty minutes later, as I was wrapping it up, a strange noise slipped from Terry's mouth," Fonda wrote. "With cigarette ash all over his jacket lapels, Terry, who had been in a trance, croaked, 'Wait till you hear this ending, my friend.' The tape was transcribed by Terry's secretary and edited down to twenty-one pages. Dennis and I headed back to Los Angeles, and after Christmas, we showed the pages to Sam Arkoff and Jim Nicholson . . ."

Fonda and Hopper fared badly with AIP. Arkoff and Nicholson told them that it was unacceptable for a film's heroes to deal hard drugs like cocaine. Couldn't it be grass or maybe hashish? Fonda explained that two motorcycles couldn't haul enough grass to generate Wyatt and Billy's big score. AIP was imposing unacceptable limitations on Fonda, even after he accepted Roger Corman as the film's executive producer. (In his autobiography, Corman claims that Fonda and Hopper originally brought their story to him, and he agreed to produce the film for AIP. He also claims that Fonda had a back-channel deal with Jack Nicholson. If Nicholson could sell Bob Rafelson and Bert Schneider on the film, he'd get to play the part of George Hanson.) Still skittish about Hopper's reliability, AIP now decided that they could seize the film if he ran three days over schedule. Fonda couldn't accept AIP's restrictions and knew that he and Hopper would have to look elsewhere to find financing for their film.

Fonda, Hopper, and their friend, controversial playwright Michael McClure, received a friendlier reception when they dropped by the offices of Raybert in mid-January 1968 to pitch Bob Rafelson a twenty-minute film based on McClure's story, *The Queen*. Fonda, Hopper, and McClure would each direct for one day and play Dean Rusk, McGeorge Bundy, Robert McNamara, and LBJ sitting around a table in evening gowns as they feast on live lobsters while planning the assassination of JFK.

Bob Rafelson and his wife were Dennis Hopper's neighbors, and Rafelson had also met him at the New York apartment of Buck Henry's girlfriend. Jack Nicholson was also on Raybert's premises. After writing the screenplay and producing the soundtrack album for the Monkee's first, and mercifully, last film, *Head* (1968), Nicholson had been rewarded with an office at Raybert.

Bert Schneider popped into Rafelson's office while Fonda was pitching *The Queen*. Schneider pulled up a chair beside Fonda and said, "How much do you need for that movie?" Fonda said, "Sixty. Real cheap. Can't lose." Then Rafelson asked, "Peter, how's that motorcycle movie coming?" Fonda started telling him about the problems he was having with AIP. Schneider looked quizzically at Rafelson, who filled him in on *Easy Rider*. Rafelson looked at Hopper and told Schneider, "This guy is fucking crazy, but I totally believe in him, and I think he'd make a brilliant film for us." Fonda recalls Hopper and McClure going to Jack Nicholson's office to smoke a joint, leaving him to discuss the film's budget with Schneider. Echoing Terry Southern, Rafelson told Schneider, "I'm telling you, Bert, it's the most commercial story I've ever heard!" Schneider said, "How much do you want for this motorcycle thing?" Fonda knew he wanted to do it for $500,000 or less, but was unprepared for Schneider's question. Since Roger Corman made *The Wild Angels* for $360,000, Fonda quoted Schneider the same figure.

Hopper remembered the decisive meeting this way. "Peter couldn't help but talk about what was then called *The Loners*, and by then, we had a full outline. Schneider left the room, then Rafelson left, who came back and said, 'Can I see you in my office?' So we went in, and he said, 'Call Schneider at home tonight. I think he's going to give you the money and let you act in it and direct it.' And Schneider said, 'Yeah, it's a go.'"

According to Fonda, Schneider proceeded more cautiously. He asked Fonda to come to his home that evening and tell the film's story to a group of his friends that Fonda called Schneider's "brain trust." Fonda left Schneider his tape recording of the story at the end of the evening, which he sent to another advisor in New York. Fonda was in Schneider's office a few days later listening while he reamed out a contractor over the phone for his shoddy workmanship and threatened litigation. Schneider then placed a call to his advisor in New York, asking him what he thought of Fonda's tape. Schneider put the call on the speakerphone, from which Fonda heard Schneider's friend praise his story effusively. Schneider told Fonda to bring Hopper to his office the next day. After they arrived, Schneider said, "What do you both want for this project?" Fonda looked at Hopper and said they wanted one third of the picture. Fonda told Schneider, "We oughta go to Mardi Gras 'cause we'll have 100,000 people in costume we won't have to pay for."

"And Bert wrote the check for $40,000 to go shoot Mardi Gras," he recalled. As Schneider cut the check, he told Hopper, "This is your test. I'm giving you this money to shoot this 16mm thing. If this works, fine. If it doesn't, you're not going on with this picture." Fonda and Hopper celebrated the start of their first production with a drink at a local bar, where they couldn't stop hugging each other in jubilation.

Production on *Easy Rider* got off to a shaky start when Peter Fonda miscalculated the starting date for Mardi Gras, leaving only a week before the festival to recruit technicians and a production crew, instead of the month-long breathing spell he had counted on. William Hayward, who Hopper hired at $150 a week as associate producer, saw trouble coming. A meeting for the crew was held in Hayward's office the evening before they departed for New Orleans. The atmosphere was casual, the planning was slipshod. "All right man, we don't have a gaffer," Hopper said near the end of the meeting. "Who wants to be the gaffer, man?" A girl hired to shoot still photos volunteered. That was cool with Hopper. "Fine. You want to do that? I can dig it. You'll light the picture," he said. "I knew then there would be trouble, because being a lighting gaffer is a real honest-to-God fucking job that requires some expertise," Hayward said.

At 6:30 A.M. on the cold, wet Friday of February 23, 1968, Dennis Hopper convened a production meeting in the parking lot of the crummy airport motel in New Orleans where the film's cast and crew were staying. Hopper hectored them for two hours until his voice gave out. "I was really keyed up," he recalled. "As far as I was concerned, I was the greatest fuckin' director that had been in America." Hopper looked at everyone and told them that he was the only creative person on the film. They were only there to do his bidding. "This is MY fucking movie, and nobody is going to take MY fucking movie away from me," he said. "Having a meeting for Dennis was like having an audience," Hayward said. "There was no way he was going to listen to anybody else. It was all about his speeches." Peter Fonda quietly told several of the sound men to start recording Hopper's ego trip. Fonda was aghast. The film company's permission to participate in the Mardi Gras parade required them to be present when it began. They had already missed the start of the parade.

"We were supposed to be in the parade," Karen Black recalled. "If you look at the film carefully, you'll see that we're never in the parade. There's one shot where I'm in the parade." Black explained why. "Get into the Winnie," she said, "in search of the Mardi Gras parade . . . The Winnebago never found the Mardi Gras parade, and there are reasons for that." (The cast and crew rode around in a Clark-Cortez motor home, not a Winnebago.) "Everyone was stoned out of their minds. Dennis was just shooting, like getting, he's gonna get New Orleans, man, which he did."

It was déjà vu all over again the second day except that Hopper's tirade only lasted an hour. It's a miracle that anything got accomplished. "I was hellbent to make a movie—I mean, talk about obsession," Hopper said. "I didn't give a fuck if I ran over people in the street. If they got in the way, then they'd better get out of the way—that was my objective, and that's what I did. I was crazy, there's no question about it. We shot for four days. [Fonda recalls six.] I literally walked people through the streets. It was like the Bataan Death March."

Hopper had invited five of his friends who owned 16mm cameras and had directorial ambitions to accompany him to New Orleans and shoot the Mardi Gras festival. "The one thing you must not do is shoot any film unless I tell you to," he instructed them. "Well, every time I turned around, they were shooting another thing, you know." Hopper was obsessed with making a perfect film, driven by the fear that Bert Schneider would cancel the project and his one chance to direct would slip through his fingers. "It was a nightmare," he admitted. "I was a maniac."

Hopper brandished loaded pistols at meetings and rambled on about imaginary enemies. "We're all out of our minds—half of us were on acid," recalled Seymour Cassel, one of Hopper's camera assistants. "We'd go to a meeting in the conference room, Dennis and Peter are sittin' up there. Dennis said, 'We gotta be careful because they know what we're doin'.' I say, 'Dennis, who knows what we're doing?' He said, 'The government.' I said, 'The government? Well, why, what are we doing?' 'They know that we're here to make this movie.' Well, how do they know what the movie's about? We don't have a fuckin' script. How the fuck can they know that?' 'They know, man. Man, they know because of who we are.' I said, 'Who are we, man?' "

Crew members wilted under the pressure of coping with Hopper's combative behavior. "A lot of people quit," William Hayward said, "so they started to come back about the second or third day, and they'd all come by the office and just tell me these horror stories about what happened." Hopper later admitted that filming in New Orleans was a complete disaster. At the end of the first day of shooting, Peter Fonda, like the rest of the company, was exhausted and saddened. He had just remembered it was his birthday. He took a shower, smoked a joint, and joined Karen Black and Toni Basil in their room. He picked up Black's guitar and began to play when they heard a commotion outside.

Dennis Hopper became enamored with the shimmering reflections of neon in a pool of rainwater and wanted to film it with Barry Feinstein's $30,000 three-lens ARRIFLEX movie camera. When Feinstein, who was serving as cinematographer, refused to relinquish it, Hopper began kicking Feinstein, a former Golden Gloves champion. As Hopper grappled with him, they crashed through the door into Basil and Black's room. Hopper smashed Black's guitar over Feinstein and threw a TV set at him. At one point, Black said, Hopper was sitting on Feinstein, telling him, "I love you, man! Man, I love you!"

Fonda pulled Hopper off Feinstein and into his room. He gave Hopper, who had been doing uppers and wine all day, a joint and 1,000 milligrams of the sedative Placidyl. When Hopper fell face forward on the coffee table, Fonda lifted him onto his bed and began removing his boots. Hopper sat bolt upright and said, "Don't ever take off my boots again!" Fonda gently put Hopper's socks and boots back on after he fell asleep.

On the next-to-last day of shooting, Hopper and Fonda filmed the scenes where their characters take two prostitutes (played by Basil and Black) to a cemetery and drop acid. Terry Southern was present during shooting in New Orleans, supplying dialogue as needed, since a full screenplay was yet to be written. At that morning's meeting, Southern told an out-of-control Hopper, "The cacophony of your verbiage is driving me insane." Until his involvement in *Easy Rider*, Southern had made a habit of being on the set throughout the shooting of any film that he wrote. When filming in New Orleans wrapped, he returned to New York to complete the screenplay for *Easy Rider*, but terminated his involvement with the production of the film.

Fonda recalled, "Later he told me he could not afford to stay on as a coproducer for $350 a week plus expenses *and* put up with Herr Director's rules of the game." (When Fonda returned to Hollywood, he divided the share of *Easy Rider*'s future earnings that he claimed Southern had been promised between his Pando Productions and William Hayward. When Hopper discovered this, he became furious, and later sued Fonda over what he believed was an unequal division of the film's profit.)

During their on-again, off-again friendship, Fonda became comfortable enough with Hopper to confide a family secret to him. Fonda's mother slashed her throat with a razor while confined to an asylum when Peter was ten, something that he only discovered years afterward from a stranger. Hopper said that he found an Italian statue of liberty on a tomb in the cemetery in New Orleans and wanted Fonda's character to climb into its arms and talk to it like it was his mother, asking her why she abandoned him by killing herself. "That to me was talking to the statue of liberty and saying, 'Are you just a piece of paper? Is liberty just a piece of paper,' " Hopper recalled. "I thought of those things as being symbolic of what was happening in the country." (The use of the Italian statue, as well as most of the actions of the film's characters in the cemetery, were described in a page of screen directions that Terry Southern wrote in his trailer on location before the scenes were filmed.)

Fonda told Hopper he had no right to ask him to expose something so personal and sensitive on camera. When that didn't convince Hopper to let it go, Fonda told him that his character in the film, Captain America, had no parents, sprang fully formed from the earth, and was just an idea. After arguing strenuously with Hopper, Fonda said, "Give me one good reason to do it." A tearful Hopper said, "Because I'm the *director*, man!" Finding Hopper's logic unassailable, Fonda clambered up the statue and began talking to it, really getting into his character's emotions. His concentration was broken when Hopper started arguing with Barry Feinstein about some camera directions. Fonda looked down at Hopper and yelled "Shut up." (Fonda's digression stayed in the finished film.)

Fonda felt that Hopper abused his confidence by demanding that he use his mother's suicide in the film, an act that broke their friendship. "Their big schism seemed to have come down in New Orleans," William Hayward said. "They never were the same after that. And they argued considerably throughout the remainder of the picture. They started out as great pals, and they didn't end up great pals, at all. But they could pretend they were great pals to the outside world, and they did for years."

When Fonda returned to Los Angeles, he and Hayward met with Bert Schneider and Jack Nicholson on March 1, hoping to get out of the film. Fonda and Hayward apologized to Schneider and offered to refund his money. "Hopper's obviously lost it," they said. "Listen to this." Then they played the recording of Hopper's outburst in the cemetery. "And I was screaming, yelling, fighting," Hopper recalled. " 'I asked for a yellow light and a red light and a green light. That's all I asked for in this cemetery, where the fuck are they?' This maniac screaming, 'I'm gonna win the Cannes Film Festival and blah, blah,' crazy out of my mind, and 'Who's over there?' and starting fights in the middle of the street, and they're recording me, nobody's doing anything, just recording me."

"You know," Schneider said, "he really sounds excited, but did he ask for those lights, and why weren't the lights there? You know, I hired him to direct this movie, and I'm not replacing him." Schneider believed that Hopper had been let down by poor planning and said, "I think Dennis deserves a second chance." Even after the fiasco in New Orleans, Schneider remained committed to gambling $360,000 of his own money on *Easy Rider*. (Hopper said *Easy Rider*'s budget was $340,000, while William Hayward said it was $501,000.) Schneider's decision was made easier by the fact that his father, Abe Schneider, had succeeded Harry Cohn as the president of Columbia Pictures upon Cohn's death in early 1958. Bert already had a guaranteed distribution deal in place for *Easy Rider* with Columbia when he gave Fonda and Hopper the go ahead.

Easy Rider's production was temporarily shut down while a professional crew was hired, and a cinematographer was recruited to replace Barry Feinstein. Hungarian-born László Kovács was initially reluctant to become the film's cinematographer. He had already photographed *Hell's Angels on Wheels* and another biker film, *The Savage Seven* (1968). Kovács told Dennis Hopper he'd had his fill of them until Hopper convinced him that *Easy Rider* wasn't just another biker film. Paul Lewis became *Easy Rider's* production manager. "I had done a series of pictures with Jack Nicholson," he said. "Jack and I were talking one time, he says, 'Have I got a thing for you. A great, great picture for you to do. It's a bike picture, and it's with two crazies, but at least you have one guy there who will drink with you.'"

According to Peter Fonda, he and Dennis Hopper returned to New York in early March to meet with Terry Southern to write *Easy Rider's* screenplay. "The three of us sat on a couch in Terry's small office," Fonda wrote in his memoir. "We would all discuss a scene, then Hopper would dictate it to Terry's secretary, starting at the beginning and working our way through the story. And this is probably the genesis of his notion that he alone had written the screenplay."

Contrary to Southern, Fonda claims that Hopper introduced George Hanson's dialogue about UFOs and aliens on April 4, 1968, the day that Martin Luther King was assassinated. Fonda says that Hopper was inspired to create Hanson's speech by a book on UFOs that he was engrossed in at the time. "After this collaboration," Fonda recalled, "the script still had to be put into a real screenplay structure with exterior (EXT), interior (INT), and other shooting directions inserted."

There was one matter left before filming could resume: casting another actor to replace Rip Torn in the role of George Hanson. Introduced to the strains of "Born to be Wild" at Jack Nicholson's AFI Life Achievement Award ceremony in 1994, the tuxedo-clad Peter Fonda and Dennis Hopper explained how Nicholson won the role. "I'm the guy who didn't want Jack in *Easy Rider*, all right?" Hopper said. "You're lookin' at the schmuck right here, O.K.? I went in to Schneider, Schneider said 'Ya gotta use Jack,' I went into the office, and I said, 'I can't use him, he's not right for the part,' and Bert said, 'Listen, I've asked you for absolutely nothing, you're running wild out there, use Nicholson!' I said, 'O.K., but you're screwin' up my movie, O.K.?'" (Hopper only learned subsequently that Schneider sent Nicholson to keep an eye on him.)

A ponytailed Peter Fonda alluded to Rip Torn when he said, "Actually,

I'm going to tell you how Jack really got the part. Dennis and I had an actor in mind who we had been in collaboration very early in the process, and when it came time to principal photography, the man wanted forty-five-hundred dollars, and I didn't have forty-five-hundred dollars. I said to this fellow, 'You know, everybody's getting scale but me,' and he said, 'Well, what are you getting?,' and I said, 'Nothing.' And Jack, who was willing to do a part for scale, agreed to work for us, and scale at that time was $392 a week." Doing a John Wayne impression, Fonda said, "I'll tell you one thing, mister. It was the best $392 I ever spent."

With a completed screenplay in hand, Fonda and Hopper filmed *Easy Rider* in seven weeks (Hopper claimed it was four and a half), shooting the film's scenes in continuity—in the same order that they take place in the script. *Easy Rider* begins in Mexico, where Wyatt, a.k.a. Captain America and Billy pull into a desert junkyard on their choppers and buy a load of cocaine from a dealer. (The scene was filmed in Taos, New Mexico.) Fonda said that Hopper was delighted by the idea of "buying junk in a junkyard." Hopper pointed out that the cocaine was never identified as such (they used baking soda).

Billy and Wyatt sell their stash to a wealthy customer (Phil Spector) and his bodyguard at the Los Angeles International Airport. The scene was filmed at an unused side road that Fonda spotted once when he flew over the airport in John Lear's Learjet. Spector contributed himself, his black Rolls Royce, and his own bodyguard, saving the production the cost of renting a vehicle and two actors. The incessant roar of commercial jets landing every few minutes deafened the actors and spooked Spector, who ducked whenever a plane flew over. Wyatt places their bankroll into a plastic tube hidden in his motorcycle's American flag-emblazoned teardrop-shaped gas tank. Fonda later commented that this was "money fucking the flag."

Billy and Wyatt hit the road, only to stop at a ranch to fix Wyatt's flat tire. A farmer (Warren Finnerty), his Hispanic wife, and their kids share their meal with the bikers. Admiring the bucolic scene, Wyatt tells the farmer, "You've got a nice place. It's not every man that can live off the land, you know. You do your own thing in your own time. You should be proud." ("And Bert Schneider, everyone, wanted the farm sequence out of the picture," Hopper recalled. He refused to cut it. "The farm is my history, my life. It's where I'm from.")

In an intentional parallel to the Westerns of John Ford, *Easy Rider* includes a moment where Billy and Wyatt climb a hill and stand silhouetted in the sunset against the iconic buttes of Monument Valley. They pick up an enigmatic hitchhiker (Luke Askew) and take him to a ragtag commune. (When the New Buffalo commune in Taos refused to allow filming there, Fonda and Hopper filmed the scenes in Malibu, using friends to populate what someone called the "Styrofoam" commune.)

Witnessing the communards planting seeds in the parched soil, Billy says, "They ain't gonna make it. They ain't gonna grow anything here." In the film's most fatuous moment, Wyatt says, "They're gonna make it. Dig, man. They're gonna make it." (Fonda admitted that that line and the commune scenes were the weakest ones in the film. He scoffed at the notion that a return to primitivism was a solution to society's ills.)

Billy and Wyatt frolic in the hot springs with two girls from the commune. "I knew that Peter and I and the girls we meet would never be seen totally nude in the nude swimming scene," Hopper said, "because I wanted to show the over-forty crowd that it is possible to play like innocent children in the nude without getting into sex. Even simple nudity would have killed the point." Wyatt considers staying at the commune, but an impatient Billy nags him that they'll miss Mardi Gras. Before he leaves, the hitchhiker gives Wyatt some tabs of LSD, instructing him to use them when he feels the time is right.

Billy and Wyatt are jailed when they ride their bikes in a small town's parade. Their cellmate is George Hanson (Jack Nicholson), an ACLU lawyer sleeping off one of his frequent drunks. The son of a prominent local figure, Hanson is on friendly terms with his jailers and springs himself, Billy, and Wyatt. Hanson impulsively joins them on their trip, having intended several times to visit Madame Tinkertoy's House of Blue Lights, a legendary New Orleans brothel.

When a motel owner turns off his vacancy sign as they ride up, the trio camp out in the woods. Billy and Wyatt introduce Hanson to marijuana. Hanson is afraid it will lead to harder drugs and must be shown how to inhale the smoke to benefit from the drug's effect. (The actors smoked marijuana in this and other scenes in *Easy Rider*, which helped endear the film to potheads and earn the condemnation of straight society.) When Billy says that he just saw a UFO, Hanson accepts his sighting and tells his companions that the government knows that Venusians have lived among us for decades, but conceals the truth to prevent the inevitable social chaos that would result from its disclosure.

Billy, Wyatt, and George get an unwelcome reception at a diner when a bunch of rednecks in a booth make cracks about them that Hanson calls "country witticisms." "Look like a bunch of refugees from a gorilla love-in," one says. "It looks like they're standin' in fertilizer," says another. When the deputy sheriff asks, "What'cha think we ought to do with them?" the man wearing the CAT hat (Hayward Robillard Jr.) ominously predicts, "I don't damn know, but I don't think they'll make the parish line."

A gaggle of giggling teenage girls in another booth is fascinated by the exotic visitors and follow them outside when they leave. The scenes in the diner are among *Easy Rider*'s strongest, thanks to the use of actual patrons of a racially segregated diner in Morganza, Louisiana, to play the customers in the film. Hopper, who discovered the cafe while scouting locations for the film, told the production's advance man not to recruit actors from local theater groups. "I want real people," he said. When Hopper returned there for filming, he was dismayed to see a group of local actors, all dressed up and ready to perform.

"When the three of us arrived at the restaurant, we were without the company," Fonda recalled. "The background players were expecting a movie crew, not three grungy bikers. They had no idea we were the producer and director, as well as the three main leads. A small group of men, gathered around a pop machine (one of the ones that opens like a trunk) were full of comments. 'I kin smell 'em. Kin yew smell 'em? I kin smell 'em.' " Hopper whispered to Fonda, "Those guys! We want them." "You've got to be kidding," Fonda said. "I can't ask those guys. They'll kill me." "Those are the guys I want for the movie," Hopper insisted.

Fonda and Hopper approached them just as the film company pulled up outside. "Listen," Hopper said, "we're playing three really bad men. We've just raped a thirteen-year-old white girl outside of town. There is nothing you can say about us that would be too bad. If you would just say things like you were saying when we came in, it would be perfect." When Hopper reassured the men that he was really from Hollywood and told one that the film was something his mother could go see, they agreed to cooperate. The local deputy sheriff was particularly eager to sign up. It seems that everybody wants to be in the movies.

The men's hostility and the girls' curiosity toward the bikers in the film wasn't acting. It was genuine. The men resented the girls' interest in Fonda, Hopper, and Nicholson. Their antagonism only deepened when some of the film crew danced with the black customers in the back of the diner, preferring the selections on their jukebox and their freer attitude. The sheriff told Paul Lewis, "Either you get them out of there, or I'm putting them in jail.

Taking their cue from the bigots, Wyatt, Billy, and Hanson leave the diner. That night, by the campfire, Hanson ruefully laments, "You know, this used to be a helluva good country. I can't understand what's gone wrong with it." When Billy says the rubes are scared of their appearance, Hanson says, "Oh, they're not scared of you. They're scared of what you represent to them. What you represent to them is freedom." After bedding down, Billy, Hanson, and Wyatt are attacked by unseen assailants, presumably the men from the diner. Billy runs them off, but he and Wyatt discover that George Hanson has been clubbed to death.

Wyatt and Billy proceed to Mardi Gras. They indulge in a rich meal (it looks like beef stroganoff) at a posh restaurant. While Billy consumes his food with unself-conscious gusto, Wyatt appears preoccupied. They pay a visit to Madame Tinkertoy's brothel. (The scene was filmed in a private home in Hollywood.) Wyatt and Billy take their whores (Toni Basil and Karen Black) outside where they mingle with Mardi Gras celebrants, ending up in a cemetery at daybreak. All four consume the LSD the stranger gave Wyatt at the commune. Wyatt and Billy then return to the road. That night, they have a fireside exchange about the meaning of their cross-country trip. The final line became the subject of much debate when *Easy Rider* was released.

Billy: (smoking pot, laughing) "We've done it. We've done it. We're rich, Wyatt. Yeah, man. Yeah. Yeah, we did it, man we did it. We did it. Huh. We're rich, man. We're retired in Florida now, mister. Whew."
Wyatt: (adjusting his bedroll) "You know, Billy. We blew it."
Billy: (befuddled) "What? Huh? Wha-wha-wha—That's what it's all about, man. I mean, like you know—I mean, you go for the big money, man—and then you're free. You dig?"
Wyatt: "We blew it. Good night, man."

The next day, two rednecks in a pickup truck harass Billy as he rides on a country road. The passenger in the truck, Roy, (another nonactor who Hopper recruited from a gas station), says, "Pull alongside, we'll scare the hell out of him." He points his shotgun out the window at Billy and says, "Want me to blow your brains out?" Billy gives him the finger. Roy says, "Hey, hippie, why don't you get a haircut?" and fires, blowing Billy off his motorcycle. Wyatt circles back to him. He takes his jacket off to cover his mortally wounded friend, who says, "I got 'em. I'm gonna get 'em." (Hopper's dialogue is nearly unintelligible—Fonda says Hopper's line is "We're going to get there.")

Roy says, "We'd better go back." Wyatt rides off for help and sees the truck heading back toward him in the opposite lane. Roy fires a second blast (which is seen from the camera's point of view), and Wyatt's riderless bike flies off the road, a fiery plume coming from its engine. The film's last image is an aerial shot of Wyatt's bike burning by the side of the road, which becomes an insignificant speck on the landscape as the camera ascends, revealing a bending river paralleling the curving road.

Two and a half weeks after location photography wrapped, a biker gang stole the film's remaining motorcycles from the garage of stunt driver Tex Hall. The theft reminded Fonda and Hopper that they'd forgotten to film the final campfire scene where Wyatt says, "We blew it." Fonda set up a quick shoot in the mountains of Santa Monica to get the scene. Hopper and Fonda argued vehemently over how the scene should be played. Fonda told Hopper, "I just want to say 'We blew it man.' " Hopper said, "No, no, man. We've got to be more specific. We've got to say something specific about how we blew it, man." Fonda: "I don't think so. I feel that we should say very little." Hopper: "Listen, man, we've got to say we've blown our heritage, you know, man, like when we went for the big bucks and the drugs, ya dig man?"

After fighting for fifteen minutes, Fonda reluctantly agreed to shoot the scene both ways. He and Hopper hugged each other outside their trailer to reassure the crew that their dispute was just the exercise of two nutty Method actors preparing for their scene. Hopper was so taken by Fonda's first reading of "We blew it" that he wanted to shoot fifteen or sixteen more takes of Fonda reading the line and forgot his own version entirely.

Hopper eventually took credit for Fonda's version of the scene. "It's funny," he said in 1987, "Peter said he never understood why I had him say that line. He asked me on the set, and I said, 'Just do it.' " "In 1987 he said in an interview that I had never understood why he wanted me to read that line, *that* way," Fonda fumed in his memoir. "Give me a fucking break, Dennis. Twenty-seven years later, Dennis still believed that he and he alone wrote the screenplay for *Easy Rider*. One can imagine the love-hate relationship I've had with him all this time. Of course I wanted him to direct the film. I hired him! Who else had the passion? Of course I didn't think twice about his vow never to speak to me again. Of course I go to see all his work, and I call him to tell him how much I liked it. Of course I go into his editing rooms, at his invitation, and watch his latest work being put together. Of course he wasn't the sole writer of the screenplay to *Easy Rider*. Of course he still thinks he was. Of course he thinks I cheated him. Of course I didn't. Not my way of life."

With principal photography completed, the tasks of editing and scoring the film remained. Working with editor Donn Cambern, Hopper was given the opportunity to supervise the first cut of the film. Hopper later told Nicholas Ray that he spent a year sleeping on the floor of a pool house on a $140-a-month salary while cutting the film. The sheer amount of film facing Hopper was daunting. He shot hours of footage on location because he lacked the facilities for printing and screening his dailies.

Hopper loved every foot of film he directed and couldn't bring himself to leave any on the cutting-room floor. His version of the diner sequence alone ran for twenty minutes. He was loathe to cut any of its footage because the sheriff and his pals' invective was such a rich source of material. During editing, Hopper received an offer of a small role in *True Grit* from its director, Henry Hathaway. "No, I don't want to do it, I'm editing," he said. Bert Schneider said, "C'mon, man, go and work for the old man. I won't touch the movie while you're gone. He wants you for five days, just go and do it."

Impressed by the tractability that Hopper demonstrated on *The Sons of Katie Elder*, Hathaway brought him back for *True Grit*, the star vehicle that finally brought John Wayne his Oscar. It was Robert Duvall, the film's lead villain, who now reportedly clashed with Hathaway. (It seems that Hathaway was destined to be plagued by disagreeable Method actors. Robert Duvall had studied acting with Sanford Meisner, who had taught at the Actors Studio before breaking with Lee Strasberg. After that, Meisner taught his own method derived from Stanislavski's teachings.)

Though Wayne invited Hopper on his yacht for drinks and showbiz schmoozing, he represented the leftist politics that so irritated Wayne. "I was certainly in John Wayne's world," he recalled. "He used to arrive on the lot via helicopter from his minesweeper that he had moored in New-port Beach. He'd have a .45 strapped on his side, wearing army fatigues, and that's the way he'd arrive to work every day. This one day he arrived, and he wanted to know where 'that Pinko Hopper was hiding.' I was actu-ally in Glen Campbell's trailer, hiding from him. He was screaming, 'My daughter was out at UCLA last night and heard [Black Panther] Eldridge Cleaver cussing, and I know he must be a friend of that Pinko Hopper! Where is he? I want to talk to him!' So he wasn't literally running around with a gun looking for me. He was walking around with a gun at his hip, but I think he wanted to have a political discussion, as opposed to com-mitting actual manslaughter. Anyway, nothing ever came of it. That was just Duke."

Hopper finally arrived at a four-and-a-half-hour cut of *Easy Rider,* which he was convinced should be released as a roadshow presentation with an intermission and reserved ticket sales at first-run theaters, a treatment given only to films like *Lawrence of Arabia* (1962) or *2001: A Space Odys-sey* (1968). Bert Schneider finally told him, "The film's too long. We're not going to destroy your movie, but I want you to take a holiday." Schneider paid the airfare for Hopper and his girlfriend to spend Christmas in Taos, where he was encouraged to work on the film's Mardi Gras footage. "Den-nis could go dick with this stuff," William Hayward said, "fuck around with it forever, think he was doing something, and we could go on and finish the movie."

In Hopper's absence, Donn Cambern, Henry Jaglom, and Jack Nich-olson managed to whittle his epic-length cut of *Easy Rider* down to an economical ninety-five-minute running time. William Hayward dreaded screening this version of *Easy Rider* for Hopper after he returned to L.A. Hayward knew that cutting Hopper's film was tantamount to cutting into his creative soul. After watching the diner scene, Hopper complained, "You ruined my film. You made a TV movie out of it." Knowing his brother-in-law's temper, Hayward was worried what he would do when the film was over. When the lights came up in the screening room, Hopper, with tears in his eyes, told Hayward, "That's beautiful. That's amazing. Don't ever, ever let me cut another foot of film."

"After they had seen a couple of screenings of it on the coast," Terry Southern recalled, "I got a call from Peter saying, 'Well, we've got this print. I think we've got a nice little picture here. Dennis and I want to get our names on the writing credits, but in order to do that, you'll have to notify the Writers Guild to say that it's all right.' Well, one of them was the producer and other was the director, so there was no way the Writers Guild was going to allow them to take a screenplay credit unless I insisted.

"You see, it is practically *impossible* for a director, or a producer, to get a screenplay credit because if a script goes to arbitration, the Writers Guild requires proof that they contributed *over fifty percent* of the total of the script. Too often producers and directors will muscle themselves into a screenplay credit through some under-the-table deal with the writer. Now, whenever a director or producer wants a share of the screenplay credit, it *automatically* goes to arbitration, *unless* the writer—that is, the *real* writer—specifies otherwise, which is what I would always do. In other words, I would *give* them the credit, which they could not have gotten by any other means.

"Neither of them are writers. They can't even write a fucking letter. They [the Writers Guild] said I would be crazy to allow it and wanted to be assured I wasn't being coerced or bribed in any way. Because they hate the idea of these 'hyphenates'—you know, writer-producer, director-producer . . . because of that history of muscle I mentioned. It wasn't fair, but it didn't matter to me at the time because I was ultra secure. I had *Candy* and *Dr. Strangelove*. I said sure that's fine. I didn't mind. So I spoke to the Writers Guild. Anyway, we were great friends at the time, so I went along with it without much thought. So I actually did it out of a sense of camaraderie, said that they could use it, and would help them out. [Southern told Gail Gerber, "The lads need a break."] Hopper's always been extremely insecure, and I gave him credit because I wanted to pull him out."

Hopper immediately disputed Fonda's cowriting credit. Bert Schneider told Fonda that Hopper wanted Fonda's name removed from the writing credits. Fonda was willing to take a story credit to placate Hopper, but he wouldn't accept a compromise. Schneider explained to Fonda that Hopper was hoping for an Academy Award nomination for Best Original Screenplay, not one for the Best Adapted Screenplay. Fonda kept his shared screenplay credit. "Dennis has always resented the fact that I hired him," he said, "that it wasn't his own original idea."

The final element to be added to *Easy Rider* was the film's soundtrack. During editing, a temporary track using preexisting rock songs was used. "I knew that I wanted to use songs that were already popular, rather than a new score," Hopper said. Peter Fonda brought in Crosby, Stills & Nash to compose an original score. Hopper later claimed that he told Stephen Stills, "Anybody who rides in a limo can't comprehend my movie, so I'm gonna have to say no to this, and if you guys try to get in the studio again, I may have to cause you some bodily harm." Fonda said that Hopper undermined the deal because it had been Fonda's idea. In a 2003 documentary on the making of *Easy Rider*, Fonda said that Crosby, Stills & Nash bowed out when they decided that they couldn't improve on the film's existing soundtrack.

Fonda said that all the groups approved the use of their songs in the movie, although The Band called him at 3 A.M. after the screening to say their song, "The Weight," was the only good one and wanted to write the movie's entire score. Bob Dylan was the only holdout. Dylan initially refused the use of his song, "It's Alright Ma (I'm Only Bleeding)," because he thought it would leave viewers feeling hopeless. Dylan suggested changing the film's ending. He told Fonda and Hopper, "Well, reshoot the ending and have Fonda run his bike into the truck and blow up the truck." Then he complained that he didn't like his harmonica-playing in the song.

By way of analogy, Fonda told Dylan about the scene in *Easy Rider* where he talks to the statue in the graveyard. "It embarrasses me every time I see it," he said. "It makes me very, very upset, but because it's there, and because I was convinced to do it at the moment, and then convinced to leave it in the film, I have to hear 'Suicide remarks are torn/From the fool's gold mouthpiece the hollow horn.' My mother cut her throat in an insane asylum, Bobby. I want to hear those lines. It blew his mind. He had no way to argue that."

Due to contractual commitments with his record company, Dylan couldn't give Fonda the right to use his recording of the song, so he told him to get Roger McGuinn to perform a cover version for the film. Dylan asked Fonda, "What's the end of the movie mean to you?" "I wasn't ready for that question," Fonda said. He told Dylan, "Well, ah, you know, you see the road, the road that man built, you see what happened on that road, and there's the river, you see God's road and what happens on that road. Which is the road to travel?" Dylan grabbed a pad and jotted down the lyrics to "The Ballad of Easy Rider." Dylan said, "Give this to McGuinn. He'll know what to do with it." McGuinn added some lyrics, and arranged and performed the song, which is heard at the end of *Easy Rider*.

Following *Easy Rider*'s release, rock critic Robert Christgau wrote, "Hopper, who took most of the responsibility for the music, doesn't even collect records—and that is interesting, because *Easy Rider* is the only film I know that not only uses rock well—though that is rare enough—but also does justice to its spirit. Rock composers don't work well on order and aren't good at background music. He resisted pressure to commission a soundtrack because he understood the profound emotional value of known songs. In many respects, *Easy Rider* is similar to *Nothing But a Man*, which contracted its music from Motown. Both films are low-budget treatments of oppressed subcultures that rely on music for cohesion and spiritual succor." (*Nothing But a Man* (1964) was a pioneering film, the first with an almost entirely black cast intended for an integrated audience, depicting a black man's struggles to assert his integrity in the racist South of the mid-'60s.)

"I think *Easy Rider* might have been the first time that someone made a film using found music instead of an orchestral score," Hopper recalled. "No one had really used found music in a movie before except to play on radios or when someone was singing in a scene." Hopper's use of what he called found music wasn't precedent setting. Kenneth Anger scored his experimental film, *Scorpio Rising* (1964), with songs by The Angels, Ray Charles, The Crystals, Ricky Nelson, Elvis Presley, Martha Reeves & the Vandellas, and Bobby Vinton. Though *Scorpio Rising* wasn't a commercial feature, *The Graduate*, which was released on December 21, 1967, was scored with previously released songs by Simon and Garfunkel. (Halfway through filming, director Mike Nichols' brother gave him a copy of Simon and Garfunkel's 1966 album, *Parsley, Sage, Rosemary, and Thyme*. Nichols commissioned the duo to record several new songs for the film, but only used "Mrs. Robinson.")

"But I wanted *Easy Rider* to be kind of a time capsule for that period," Hopper said, "so while I was editing the film I would listen to the radio. That's where I got 'Born to Be Wild' and 'The Pusher,' and all those songs. Orson Welles told me, 'Don't get confused. Use your best shots, and if the music works, it works, if not, then it doesn't. But always cut to the image.' So I didn't cut the film to the music—I cut it to the picture. But later, when I put 'Born to be Wild' on there, it just worked, man."

Bert Schneider managed to enter *Easy Rider* into competition at the 1969 Cannes Film Festival, where Dennis Hopper was given the newly created award for Best Movie by a New Director. Peter Fonda showed up at *Easy Rider's* Cannes premiere wearing a rented Union Cavalry general's uniform, symbolizing his view that the United States was on the verge of a new civil war.

Hopper was surprised to see Nick Ray wandering around the festival trying to unload the rights to Dylan Thomas' *The Doctor and the Devils,* an original screenplay that Ray once hoped to direct. Ray had changed a lot since directing *Rebel Without a Cause,* enduring a series of personal and professional problems that culminated in a heart attack he suffered while directing the historical epic, *55 Days at Peking* (1963) in Spain. By the time Hopper encountered him, Ray was a shambling wreck. He had lost most of the sight in one eye, which he covered with a patch. Unemployable as a director, Ray was penniless and consumed by his addictions.

Ray asked Hopper for $500. After he explained to Ray that he'd been sleeping in a friend's pool house and living on $140 a month, Ray said, "Well, go to Schneider and ask for the money." Hopper borrowed the money from Bert Schneider and gave it Ray, who came back an hour later, asking for an another $500. Hopper said, "What you talking about?" Ray said, "I lost it in the casino across the street." Hopper let Ray stay at his home in Taos for about six months while he was editing *The Last Movie, where* Ray ran up something like $30,000 in phone calls to Europe and in searching for Howard Hughes, who he hoped would finance his film project. Hopper finally got rid of Ray by getting him a job teaching film at Harpur College in Binghamton, New York.

Easy Rider became a phenomenal hit just days after its July 14, 1969, release. "We made all of our money back the first week. In one theater," Hopper said. Australian film scholar Dean Brandum recently wrote, "The combination of a fine marketing campaign (including the enigmatic tag-line; 'A man went looking for America. And couldn't find it anywhere . . .'), a soundtrack of popular rock music, and the Cannes prize of best film from a new director, which gave it a legitimacy that separated it from the biker movie pack, saw ̄*Easy Rider* achieve $19.1 million in rentals against its paltry $501,000 budget. It was to be Columbia's highest grossing film of the year and would rank as Hollywood's twenty-eighth most successful film of the decade. Without the film's canny exploitation campaign and the might of the studio's distribution arm, it is highly doubtful that *Easy Rider* would have achieved such wide spectatorship and resonance." (Peter

Fonda says that the film didn't receive a TV or major print-ad campaign.) Nevertheless, there was an element of spontaneity underlying *Easy Rider*'s success that defies pat explanations such as Brandum's. *Easy Rider*'s striking and unforeseen success prompted *The New York Times* to scramble to respond, publishing Tom Burke's profile of Hopper on July 20.

To everyone in Hollywood except Hopper, *Easy Rider* was a fluke hit that perplexed those seeking the reasons for the film's success, especially the antediluvian studio heads to whom *Easy Rider*'s values were anathema. "Nobody thought that *Easy Rider* was going to become a seminal film, though," Henry Jaglom said. "I thought it was just another bike movie."

"And there had been a lot of dialogue about *Easy Rider*," Charles Mulvehill recalled, "because they were having all kinds of problems putting it together, and this bunch of hippies had gone out, and they were stoned, and they made this movie, and it was never gonna go together, and they'd spent, you know, six, seven hundred thousand, whatever it was, and that was kind of the rap on the movie, that at least we heard. And then it went out, and it was boffo. I mean, it was genuine shock."

Peter Fonda recalled, "Bert's father, Abe Schneider, resigned as chairman of the board of Columbia, stating that if *Easy Rider* was the way the industry was going to go, he did not understand it and did not want to be a part of it. He told me he thought I was talking about him when we identified the antagonist."

Peter Fonda, Dennis Hopper, and Terry Southern have each offered their interpretations of *Easy Rider*'s meaning. Only Southern seemed certain of the message he wanted to leave in writing the film. "It wasn't until the end that it took on a genuinely artistic dimension—when it suddenly evolved into an indictment of the American redneck, and his hatred and intolerance for anything that is remotely different from himself," he said.

"The thrust of the film, from my point of view, the philosophical position is that it's supposed to be an indictment of the blue-collar thing, the truck-driver people of America, for their intolerance and their support of the Vietnam War. It's supposed to be an indictment of the worst part of mainstream Middle America, as personified by those two assholes in the pickup truck. Bigotry incarnate. And the final sequence is, I guess, the ultimate statement about that mentality, where these two assholes don't like their looks."

For Fonda and Hopper, the ethical implications of *Easy Rider* have proven more elusive. For Fonda, Wyatt's line "We blew it" was *Easy Rider's* moral statement, though he's offered different explanations of it over the years. "Not just that the actors were really smoking grass and driving their own bikes," he said at a press conference after *Easy Rider* was released. "There was something more real. Our own mistakes, which were real. *Easy Rider* started to be, we were going to say, 'My God, see what society was doing to the outcast, to the outlaw.' We were assuming the great stance of the outlaw. Halfway through, we took a look at the outlaw and figured, he blew it too." "My movie is about the lack of freedom," Fonda said. "My heroes are not right, they're wrong."

Reviewing *Alice's Restaurant* (1969) and *Easy Rider* for *The New York Review of Books* in 1970, Ellen Willis wrote: "I saw why the movie affected me the way it did: beyond the melodrama of groovy kids vs. rednecks is an emotion that more and more of us, young and old alike, are experiencing, the overpowering sense of loss, the anguish of *What went wrong? We blew it—how? Easy Rider* is about the failure of America on all levels, hip and straight. Billy and Wyatt on their bikes, riding free down the open road, are living another version of the rugged individualist frontier fantasy, and the big dope deal that made them financially independent is just Hip Capitalism. It won't work, and by the end of the movie, Billy knows it. [Wyatt knows it, not Billy. Willis confuses Billy and Wyatt throughout her review.] The key line of the film is his admission, 'We blew it!' "

In 1987, Dennis Hopper offered what has become the standard interpretation of "We blew it." "Because we three colorful characters were *criminals*. We smuggled drugs, we used amoral ways to buy our way out of the system. That's why we blew it, we blew our inheritance." Of course, by the time he said that, Hopper had overcome the destructive effects of drug addiction and had become a supporter of the Republican Party. Drugs were just part of a counterculture that he seemed to reject in toto.

Luke Askew, who played the enigmatic hitchhiker in *Easy Rider*, suggested that Billy and Wyatt really had no values. "When we first started doing mescaline, came before acid, actually, we were just looking for a different take on things," he said. "When hard drugs started to come in, dealt by people who had absolutely no values whatsoever, that was the beginning of the end of it."

Fonda and Hopper weren't as convinced of the criminality of using or dealing drugs when they made *Easy Rider*, at least compared to what they saw as the greater crimes of society. "We were living in a society that was amoral," Hopper recalled in 2003, "because we could no longer believe in the mores of the society and that we were all breaking the laws of society. Because of smoking marijuana, and the kinds of things we were doing in the '60s, it seemed like everyone was outside of the law at that time."

In 1969, Hopper, who was then into every drug imaginable, said, "Together, we're symbols of this country today—Captain America, man, is *today*'s leader—and when the small-town lawyer joins up with us, you have a real American cross-section. As we watch them, we think of them as nice kids, but they're actually in their early thirties, an age when the Establishment says they should be working, contributing. Instead, they're peddling dope. Because that seems no worse to them than the Wall Street tycoon spending 80 percent of his time cheating the government."

When he conceived *Easy Rider*, Peter Fonda viewed Billy and Wyatt's actions in positive terms. "We go for dope, we go for motorcycles, we go riding across the country, we'll even get some sex here and there—but we can do all these things really honestly," he told *Playboy* in 1970. "I saw it all in my mind, and to me, it reflected the anarchy of the individual, which I think is beautiful, as opposed to the anarchy of society, which is so incredibly awful. The powers that make society's rules break them better than we can imagine—much better than I could by copping a joint, whether its somebody's cock or somebody's reefer. Compare breaking rules like that with our Government denying civil rights, killing innocent people, doing nothing about the hunger and disease of the poor, destroying our environment.

"And then I wondered about the beauty of this individual anarchy and what meaning it really had. I wondered, in fact, if what these guys were up to had *any* reflection of freedom. And then I found that it didn't. What I felt I shot down—which most people didn't pick up—was the idea that I represented anything that should be glorified or emulated. Well, I didn't, which is why Wyatt finally says to Billy 'We blew it.' Literally, within the story, we blew it when we went for the easy money and then thought we could retire." [Fonda despises the idea of retirement.]

"In a broader sense," Fonda said, "not just America, but the rest of the world had blown it by basing life solely on economics. " 'Easy Rider' is a Southern term for a whore's old man, not a pimp, but the dude who lives with a chick," he told *Rolling Stone* magazine's Elizabeth Campbell in 1969. "Because he's got the easy ride. Well, that's what happened to America, man. Liberty's become a whore, and we're all taking the easy ride." (Fonda told Campbell that he voted for Eldridge Cleaver for president in 1968.)

"I wanted to be enigmatic about it," Fonda finally said in 2003, "and I still today want to be enigmatic about it. I mean, this is what had happened when I said we blew it without explanation. Everybody in the theater says 'What does he mean when he says we blew it?' Well, the whole point is, we don't let anybody out of this picture that way. You can't put it under the seat in the theater. You have to truck it home with you and figure it out. 'What did we do, why did we say that, what happened? We were with these guys. They were so cool, and (snaps fingers) they're gone.' "

Dennis Hopper was convinced that *Easy Rider* owed its success to its verisimilitude. In making *Easy Rider*, Hopper felt he was on a personal mission to dispel the prejudice directed against hippies that he experienced when he traveled the country. Hopper became their misunderstood representative. Wherever he went, Hopper was singled out for opprobrium by members of Nixon's silent majority. "Every restaurant, man, every roadhouse we went in, there was a Marine sergeant, a football coach who started with 'Look at the Commies, the queers, is it a boy or a girl?' " he told Tom Burke. "We expected that. But the stories we heard along the way, man, true stories of kids getting their heads broken with clubs or slashed with rusty razor blades—rusty blades, man—just because they passed through towns with long hair.

"And not just in the South. In Montrose, Colorado, where we made *True Grit*, I went into a bar and immediately a guy swung at me, screaming, 'Get outta here. My son's in Vietnam,' and the local sheriff was right behind him, screaming that *his* son was in Vietnam, and I said, 'Now wait a minute,' that I was an actor and there with the movie, whereupon the boys' high-school counselor started screaming to get out, that *his* son was in Vietnam. And I thought, 'What if I wasn't an actor, what if I was just traveling through and was thirsty?' So I said, 'O.K., I'm hitchhiking to the peace march,' whereupon eight guys jumped me. Incredible, but true, I swear."

Hopper seemed proudest of *Easy Rider*'s matter-of-fact depiction of drug use and its popularization of cocaine. "*Easy Rider* wasn't a movie that pushed drugs," he said. "It was a movie that showed aspects of the drug culture that was catching on with the masses, rather than being the exclusive domain of so-called 'degenerates,' artists, and musicians. For years, the 'in group' had smoked and done the stuff without anybody knowing.

"I mean, *Easy Rider* was the first time people smoked marijuana and didn't go out and kill a bunch of nurses or something. They sat around and had a good time. It was the introduction to something. It was also the first time cocaine was ever smuggled in a motion picture. Cocaine was used, and people had never heard of it. I was already using cocaine myself by this time, though in the movie we used baking soda. Suddenly at the end of 1969, at the beginning of 1970, cocaine was as common, if not more common, than heroin on the street. It was called the drug of kings before that. So suddenly, cocaine was introduced. Suddenly, there were parties in Hollywood where everybody's going around with silver trays with marijuana on them and little things with cocaine on them. And it was sort of like everybody was out of the closet."

"Certainly much of it was enjoyable, even memorable," Ellen Willis wrote. "Dennis Hopper, playing Peter Fonda's egotistical, slightly paranoid friend, gave a thoroughly convincing performance, the only realistic portrayal of a head I've seen on film. The dope-smoking scenes were beautifully real. Most movies that acknowledge the existence of grass (*Alice's Restaurant* included) tend to treat it with oppressive reverence; in *Easy Rider*, as in life, stoned people were, for one thing, very funny and, for another, very happy."

Willis seemed to be the only writer who criticized *Easy Rider*'s treatment of women, part of a what she saw as a larger failure of the counterculture. "One of the major flaws of the counter-culture is that for all of its concern with the dispossessed, it is as oppressive as the surrounding society toward the female half of the race," she wrote. "It treats women as 'chicks'—nubile decorations—or mothers or goddesses or bitches, rarely as human beings. *Easy Rider* is an almost embarrassing commentary on the hip male's contempt for women. As in most Westerns, the world of our two existential cowboys is almost exclusively male: thus the issue of sex does not have to be confronted. The women who enter their domain are strictly two-dimensional figures. Women who show any sexual interest in them—one of the communards, a group of giggling teen-age girls—are portrayed as ridiculous. When they stop at a New Orleans whorehouse as a tribute to their dead friend, the lawyer, who had recommended it, only Wyatt, the more frivolous of the two characters, is at all eager to sleep with a woman; Captain America is far above such concerns." (Dennis Hopper's Billy is the one eager to have sex with his whore (Karen Black), not Peter Fonda's Wyatt.)

"I always thought it was filmmaking, not myth," Hopper said of *Easy Rider*. "It's about a time and place. A time capsule. The counterculture was becoming the culture at that time. So I thought I was making a film for everyone. It was meant to entertain, but also deal with our lives. We'd gone through the whole '60s, and the '60s had been such a fascinating time," he said. "And there had been no movies made that had anything to do with our reality. The movie that was made the year that we made *Easy Rider* was Doris Day and Rock Hudson made *Pillow Talk*. [*Pillow Talk* was released in 1959.] The young kind of movies being made for kids were *Beach Blanket Bingo* [1965], you know, with Frankie Avalon. They had very little to do with the reality of Haight-Ashbury or the reality of the hippie love-ins. So much was happening at that moment. The visual arts were exploding. The music was exploding. All these creative things that happened, basically, this was tapping into the end of it. Pop art had already happened. Rock 'n' roll had already happened. The Summer of Love was over."

"*Easy Rider* was never a motorcycle movie to me," Hopper said. "A lot of it was about politically what was going on in the country." That's a strange pronouncement. America was being torn by assassinations, race riots, campus revolts, and its involvement in Vietnam in the late '60s, yet none of that is reflected in the film. "Fonda and Hopper never think politically at all," Ellen Willis wrote. "In private life Guthrie [Arlo Guthrie, star of *Alice's Restaurant*], Fonda, and Hopper are all more or less apolitical, and the movies reflect their personalities. Furthermore, I'm not at all sure that their attitude is not shared by the majority of adherents to the hip life style."

"The film's politics are one problematic element," Lois Rudnick wrote in 2001. "The film's intentions often seem confused and contradictory. Captain America a.k.a. Wyatt (Earp), played by Fonda, and Billy (the Kid) played by Hopper, are named after American heroes who are part of the popular pantheon of Anglo-American culture. But they assumed their identities and costumes as part of a carnival act, and they are drug dealers who feel they owe absolutely nothing to anyone. If they are subversive of established norms of dress and behavior—wearing long hair, refusing to work, taking drugs, having sex when and where they feel like it—their actions and dialogue hardly suggest a revolution of any meaningful sort in terms of the social and political movements of the 1960s mentioned in reviews of the film."

With its countercultural elements now passé, *Easy Rider* comes off today as little more than a picaresque movie scored with an album of golden oldies, whose schematic narrative is driven by the tension between the laid-back seeker Wyatt and hedonistic, materialistic, and suspicious Billy. Fonda's blandly handsome, inexpressive Wyatt is a sphinx. Dennis Hopper's Billy is a dopehead doofus, though Fonda thought that Hopper gave the film's best performance. The film momentarily comes alive with Jack Nicholson's charming, affecting performance as George Hanson, which made him the film's long-term beneficiary. *Easy Rider's* leisurely atmosphere still renders Billy and Wyatt's violent deaths unexpectedly shocking, though they are foreshadowed by Hanson's murder.

More than forty years after its release, *Easy Rider* has become little more than a cultural relic. A clip from *Easy Rider* is an obligatory element of every documentary about the 1960s because *Easy Rider* represents the baby boomers' nostalgic gateway to their own past. Widely available on home video, *Easy Rider* has been reduced to just another cheap commodity. Even the establishment finally recognized *the film*. In 1998, the American Film Institute chose *Easy Rider* as #88 on their list of the top 100 American films. That year, the Library of Congress added a print of *Easy Rider* to the United States National Film Registry for being "culturally, historically, or aesthetically significant."

Ellen Willis presciently wrote, "Nevertheless, it is clear to me that if we want to survive the Seventies, we should learn to draw strength from something more solid than a culture that in a few years may be just a memory: 'Remember hair down to your shoulders? Remember Janis Joplin? Remember *Grass*, man? Wow, those years were really, uh, *far out!*' " She could have added, "Remember *Easy Rider*? Man, was that movie bitchin!"

· 6 ·

WINGS OF WAX

Universal Studios gives Dennis Hopper creative control over his dream project, The Last Movie. *High in the Peruvian Andes, Hopper shoots forty-eight hours of film, spends sixteen drug-fueled months editing it, and creates a career-ending bomb.*

"I remember we were drunk at this press conference in Lima, and a reporter asked Dennis if he had stopped doing drugs. He said, 'Why would I stop doing drugs just because I'm in Peru?' "

Paul Lewis, the producer of The Last Movie

*D*ENNIS HOPPER ALWAYS believed he was a genius, but few believed him. In the lean years between his clash with Henry Hathaway and his triumph with *Easy Rider*, his proclamations were met by most listeners with skepticism or outright derision. Hopper had the occasional supporter among his Hollywood connections, though, including Stewart Stern and Joanne Woodward. When Hopper was in his twenties, Joanne Woodward said, "Dennis is a genius. I'm not sure of what, and I'm not sure Dennis knows of what. Certainly not acting. But he is a genius."

Jack Nicholson thought so, too. "We'd finished our shooting in Taos, and we had a Sunday afternoon off," Hopper recalled. "So Jack and I went up with some of the guys, and we ended up taking acid at D. H. Lawrence's tomb. We'd laid down there, we were watching the insects. I was watching the insects, anyway, and Jack was laying next to me, and we were laying in front of D. H. Lawrence's tomb, looking up at the sun, and I said,

'Jack. Wow, we're just like those insects.' He says, 'Nah, you think so?,' and I said 'Yeah, man, just that insignificant.'

"So later that night, Jack and I ended up with this beautiful young Spanish-Indian woman, and she took us up to a hot springs. And we were up there, naked, enjoying the water and so on under a big full moon and I had my knife out there, some drunk came out of the thing to try to grab the young girl. I pulled the knife and scared Jack and the young girl and the drunk and myself, so like at that point, the girl got in the truck, and Jack said 'Let's run.' And so we had her drive the truck, and we ran in front of the truck in the lights. We were in front of the lights, running naked on this mountain, and Jack said, 'Insects, man? We're geniuses, is what we are, we're geniuses like Lawrence, man.' I said, 'Yeah, Jack, really?' Jack said, 'Yeah.' I said, 'Wow.' The next morning, when we woke up, we found ourselves halfway up a tree."

"We're a new kind of human being," Hopper told Brad Darrach. "In a spiritual way, we may be the most creative generation in the last nineteen centuries." Now a certified counterculture guru, Hopper was even invited to a seven-day conference on predicting the future with director Louis Malle, futurist Herman Kahn, child psychologist Bruno Bettelheim, anthropologist Robert Ardrey, and Peter Desmond. For Hopper, the capper came when he attended the Academy Awards ceremony in early 1970, where he, Peter Fonda, and Terry Southern were nominated for Best Original Screenplay for *Easy Rider*. Attired in a Western jacket, cowboy boots, and a Stetson, Hopper attended the event with Michelle Phillips. (Phillips had recently divorced John Phillips, the leader of the musical group The Mamas & the Papas, of which she was a member.)

Jack Nicholson, who was nominated for Best Supporting Actor for his performance in *Easy Rider*, accompanied them. Neither Hopper nor Nicholson won, but Hopper savored his newfound status among big shots like Cary Grant, John Wayne, and Elizabeth Taylor, who Hopper hadn't seen since *Giant*'s premiere. Hopper told *The New York Times*' Guy Flatley, "I went up to congratulate him [Wayne] when he won his Oscar, and he took one look at me, and he called me a communist. Then he asked me to come out on his yacht—it's actually a minesweeper—and he'd explain to me why he's worth a million per picture."

After making *Night Tide*, Hopper became convinced that the studio model of filmmaking was obsolete, and *Easy Rider*'s success only drove his point home. Speaking in a voice that Brad Darrach described as "the high hostile whine of a teen-ager who figures his ideas will be ignored or rejected by indifferent adults," Hopper said, "Man, the movies are coming out of a dark age. I mean, for forty years the uncreative people told the creative people what to do. But now we're telling them, like forget those big budgets. The only thing you can make with a big budget is a big, impersonal, dishonest movie. The studio is a thing of the past, and they are very smart if they just concentrate on becoming distribution companies for independent producers. We want to make little, personal, honest movies. So we're all taking small salaries and gambling on a cut of the gross. And we're going to make groovy movies, man. We're taking on more freedom and more risk. I think we're heroes. I want to make movies about us."

All around Hollywood, Abe Schneider's counterparts were trying to comprehend what the success of *Easy Rider* portended. After World War II, the once-thriving movie studios were like balloons suffering slow leaks. The U.S. Supreme Court's decision in *United States* v. *Paramount Pictures, Inc.*, 334 US 131 (1948) forced the studios to divest themselves of their theater chains, which formerly guaranteed the distribution of studio product on their financial terms. Then the ubiquity of television deprived the studios of the captive audience that once filled their theaters. Studio facilities were increasingly given over to television production.

The predominantly younger viewers of the 1960s rejected the studios' creatively exhausted Westerns, musicals, and wheezing comedies that failed to reflect the reality of their lives. "Nobody had ever seen themselves portrayed in a movie," Dennis Hopper said. "At every love-in across the country, people were smoking grass and dropping LSD, while audiences were still watching Doris Day and Rock Hudson." When a series of big-budget musicals—*Camelot* (1967), *Doctor Dolittle* (1967), *Finian's Rainbow* (1968), *Hello, Dolly!* (1969), *Paint Your Wagon* (1969), and *Sweet Charity* (1969)—failed commercially, even the hidebound movie moguls were forced to look to *Easy Rider* as the exemplar of a new business model.

Unable to divine the source of *Easy Rider's* success, they simply concluded, as Peter Bogdanovich said, "Wait a second, wait a second, maybe these guys know something we don't know." Studio executives fell over themselves in their stampede to turn filmmaking over to relatively unknown, untested talent, who they assumed were in tune with the needs of the youth audience.

Dennis Hopper said, "Well, I mean, suddenly they thought everybody that could ride a bicycle and deliver a script was certainly a candidate for being a director at that point. Since I had directed, it must mean anybody could direct. The dinosaurs that held on to the industry so tightly for so long that, very honestly, it was time for new blood to get in there and be able to go on and make some films."

Primed to follow up *Easy Rider* with his next masterstroke, Hopper resurrected Stewart Stern's screenplay for *The Last Movie*. *The Last Movie* tells the story of Kansas (Dennis Hopper), a stuntman employed by a Hollywood company filming a B-Western about Billy the Kid in a village in the Peruvian Andes. They return to Hollywood after another stuntman is accidentally killed while shooting the final scene of the movie. Believing that other film crews will soon flock to the village to make movies there, Kansas stays behind with his girlfriend Maria (Stella Garcia), a local whore, and dreams up various moneymaking schemes.

When the Indians watched the filming of the Hollywood Western in their village, they witnessed what they took to be a miracle. An actor who was shot and apparently killed while the cameras rolled suddenly got up unharmed and removed his bloodied shirt after the director yelled "Cut." Convinced by this that the act of making movies confers magical powers on its participants, the Indians create a cargo cult, hoping to invoke the return of the Hollywood company and the prosperity it brought them.

They construct wicker replicas of movie cameras, lights, and boom mics, and mimic the actions of the departed film company by reenacting scenes from the Western. Like Elvis Presley, they don't understand the distinction between real violence and the pretend violence in movies. They throw real punches and shoot real bullets when they make their movie. The village priest (Thomas Milian) enlists Kansas to explain the difference between make-believe and real violence to the Indians, but they don't understand him. Worse yet, they have been seduced by the thrill of the real thing.

At the cantina in the town near the village, Kansas meets Neville Robey (Don Gordon), a friend who is convinced he's located a gold mine that he and Kansas can develop if they can only raise $500 in seed money. Kansas becomes a tour guide for a wealthy American broom manufacturer (Roy Engel) and his jaded wife (Julie Adams) he meets at the cantina. He takes them to the local nightclub/whorehouse where he rescued Maria from her pimp. When Maria begins nagging Kansas for middle-class American luxuries like a refrigerator, a swimming pool, and a fur, he prostitutes himself to the manufacturer's wife for $500 and her fur stole, which he gives to Maria.

When the ore from the mine is determined to contain insufficient gold to make refining it profitable, Kansas returns to the village. The Indians shanghai him into playing a character combining Billy the Kid and Christ, who they plan to sacrifice at the conclusion of their new movie, a cross between a Western and a passion play. Even the priest has decided to acquiesce to the villagers' deadly pageant, hoping it will help them restore the indigenous values that the Hollywood company corrupted.

"It's called the *Last Movie*, and it's a story about America and how it's destroying itself," Hopper said. "The hero is a stuntman in a lousy Western. My character, Kansas, stays behind when the company leaves because he wants to settle down in a little adobe hut, but he's taken over by phony dreams of building a big tourist hotel, an airport, even of building a ski run where it never snows, of finding gold and making a million dollars, all corrupt dreams which turn his life into a lie.

"He's Mr. Middle America. He dreams of big cars, swimming pools, gorgeous girls. He's so innocent. He doesn't realize he's living out a myth, nailing himself to a cross of gold. But the Indians realize it. They stand for the world as it really is, and they see the lousy Western for what it really was, a tragic legend of greed and violence in which everybody died in the end. So they build a camera out of junk and reenact the movie as a religious rite. To play the victim in the ceremony, they pick the stuntman. The end is far-out."

"*The Last Movie* is about reality and unreality and responsibility in making movies," he told reporter Winfred Blevins when he was on location in Peru. "It's about violence. All those Westerns Hollywood made for years promoted violence as a way of life." "Hopper originally wanted Henry Hathaway and John Wayne for the director and star of his Western-within-a-movie," Blevins wrote. "Hopper sees them as the two most-famous purveyors of violence." Hopper told Guy Flatley that John Wayne reminded him of Kansas. He said, "What do you think—is it possible not to like the man? You know, he's like the character I play in *The Last Movie*. Naïve, innocent, blindly American, a guy with preconceived ideas about everything. Paranoid and afraid of anything that's different."

Blevins also revealed Hopper's "far-out" ending, which confused and alienated the film's audience. "Hopper now seems inclined to change the ending for yet another switch on 'reality.' After the Indians kill him, the stuntman gets up and asks someone off-camera if he got the death scene O.K. on film."

Hopper elaborated on his idea to Tom Burke. "Well, first, man, I want to make the audience believe; I want to build a reality for them. Then, toward the end, I start breaking down that reality. So that it, uh, deals with the *nature* of reality. I don't know whether I'm going to die or not at the end, but at the very end, you'll see lots of cuts of old movies, like W. C. Fields and Mae West and so on. Universal, which put up the money, they've got a fantastic old film library, man. I can do anything I want with it. Then the film jerks and cuts and tears, and you see the leader numbers again, so that, uh, it doesn't matter if Kansas dies or not, it's the *film* that dies."

Hopper took *The Last Movie* to Raybert, which had become BBS after Steve Blauner joined the company when *Easy Rider* was in postproduction. (BBS stood for Bert, Bob, and Steve.) Confident that they would have other successful films besides *Easy Rider*, and weary of Hopper's craziness, Rafelson and Schneider were disinclined to produce *The Last Movie*. Blauner got to know Hopper, loved his enthusiasm, and became friends with him. He thought BBS should gamble on Hopper, but eventually broke with him over his decision to play Kansas.

"I wanted Henry Hathaway [to play the Hollywood director in the film]," Hopper said, "because I'd made three films with him, and he'd blacklisted me! He was going to, but then he felt his health wasn't good enough." Hopper replaced Hathaway with the inimitable Sam Fuller, whose amusing performance as the director makes one wish Hopper's entire film had been about the making of the Hollywood Western. John Wayne turned down Hopper's offer to play Kansas, leaving him to continue his search for a lead actor. Bob Hinkle, Hopper's dialogue coach on *Giant*, recalled what happened when Chill Wills' agent found out that Wills had agreed to be in the film. "No!" Wills' agent told him. "You go down there in South America with Dennis and all those drugs, and you'll have a mess on your hands. You don't want to have anything to do with that."

There was talk of casting Ben Johnson as Kansas or even Hopper's fleeting idea of having Willie Nelson play the character. Hopper sauntered into BBS' offices one day and announced that he was going to play Kansas. Steve Blauner, an outspoken, bearlike man, exclaimed, "Kiss my François

Truffaut, motherfucker!" "The only way the movie works," Blauner said, "is the way it's written. [Stern's script described Kansas as a grizzled veteran stuntman.] This is a guy where it's over for him, he's a broken-up stunt-man, it's Joel McCrea or somebody, but it's not Dennis, some guy that you can't feel sorry for him, so go getta job. Dennis wants to play it? It'll ruin the picture." Hopper explained that his decision to play Kansas was dictated by practicality, not vanity. "I'm playing the lead part myself," he said. "Originally, I didn't want to, but after I tested a number of actors, I finally decided it was easier to do it myself than explain to another actor what I wanted."

Hopper may not have realized it, but he was a spaced-out version of Kansas. On location, he told *Los Angeles Times* reporter John C. Mahoney about his dream of living the simple life six months of the year in an adobe hut in Peru without electricity or running water and butchering his own steaks. At the same time that he was telling this to Mahoney, the actor was importing premium Argentinean beef for himself and his stoned groupies at the European-style hotel where he was staying in Cusco and paying black-market prices for vicuna ponchos. Liberally sprinkling his conversation with the words "schizophrenic" and "paranoid," Hopper told Mahoney that he was related to Daniel Boone and predicted apocalyptic scenarios befalling America within five years—American film distribution ending, all-out vio-lence in the streets, Americans choking on unbreathable air.

In Peru, Hopper would pull on a joint and ramble philosophically to journalists. "Bergman is the greatest," he told Brad Darrach. "He's got it all together, man . . . We think the Indians are primitive because they believe that hairy men come out of the mountains at night and carry off stragglers, but real people came out of hills around L.A. and murdered Sharon Tate . . . I see areas of light and shade first of all and color as an afterthought. Light is my obsession. I feel it as an elemental source of power, like a kind of cosmic coal. It makes things grow, it makes things die. It can turn into anything—a plant, an idea. Movies are made of light. Just think of the power of light to transform itself into everything we are and can imagine!"

Hopper's resemblance to Kansas became even more pronounced after he finished shooting the Billy the Kid Western in *The Last Movie*. When Michelle Phillips returned to the United States with the other actors who played the cast and crew of the Western, Hopper got himself a Peruvian odalisque. Pilar, who didn't speak a word of English, moved in to Hopper's hotel room, where she would sit quietly while he entertained friends and journalists, looking on with quiet concern when he snorted cocaine from a tiny spoon.

When the other Hollywood studios declined to finance *The Last Movie*, Hopper wound up at Universal Studios, arguably the studio least receptive to art films. "It was a miserable place to be," said Tony Bill, who produced *The Sting* (1973) at Universal. "It was the coldest and most impersonal experience I've ever had in the business. They gave a giant victory party for *The Sting* and told me I couldn't bring my children. I refused to go."

Universal was ruled over by Lew Wasserman, who *Slate* magazine called "The Man Who Ruined Movies." "But even during the drug-induced brilliance of 1970s Hollywood," *Slate*'s Walter Shapiro wrote, "Wasserman's taste at Universal was always conservative, middle-aged, and middlebrow. Wasserman's entire career was built around an unspoken credo: The deal, no matter how cynical, is an end in itself." Wasserman's commercial mentality led him to suggest employing a studio hack to direct *Jaws* (1975) instead of Steven Spielberg, but also led him to invent the blockbuster mode of marketing when Universal opened *Jaws* in hundreds of theaters simultaneously while saturating TV with ads.

Like his peers, Wasserman didn't understand why movies like *The Graduate* and *Easy Rider* appealed to younger audiences, but said, "We've got to find out." At Universal, Hopper dealt directly with Ned Tanen, who Wasserman charged with overseeing the new division the studio created to emulate BBS by producing a small number of inexpensive, unconventional films aimed at the youth audience. Conservative as it was, Universal was doing poorly at the time and wasn't about to miss the chance to exploit the pent-up demand for Hopper's follow-up to *Easy Rider*. They gave him a budget of from $850,000 to $1 million and full creative control, including the right of final cut.

"More people are getting the chance to make pictures," Hopper said. He shrewdly observed, "But the same people are putting up the money. They figure they can do it cheaply, and there's no great risk. They like the new publicity image it gives them. Universal gave me autonomy on my picture as long as we didn't go over budget. They didn't have script approval or cast approval or anything like that. I even control the choice of the theaters in the first two major cities when it opens, and I have to approve the advertising before it can run."

Hopper's salary while making *The Last Movie* was to be $500 a week, but was entitled to 50 percent of the film's gross profits, with restrictions. Universal could replace him if he exceeded the film's four-month shooting schedule. If he went over budget, the overruns would come out of his share of the film's profits. Hopper would forfeit any profit if he spent more than a million dollars on his film.

"At first I wanted to make *The Last Movie* in Mexico," he said, "but the government put too many obstacles in my way. Censors on the set for the way the Indians were represented. The Mexicans wanted me to have a censor on the set. Ridiculous. To make a movie in Mexico, you have to make sure that all the children are wearing shoes. I couldn't show poverty. I thought, 'Man, I've gone all this way to be free, and I'm going to be stuck with someone telling me what I can shoot?'

"I ran into Alejandro Jodorowsky. I'd helped him get *El Topo* (1970) distributed. He said, 'Why don't you go to Peru?' I said, 'I thought Peru was a jungle.' He said, 'Nah, there's great mountains there, the Andes.' So I went to Peru. I looked for locations all over and wasn't able to find the right one, although I found the country the most beautiful of any I have ever seen. I finally decided to visit Machu Picchu and go home.[5] Then in the office of the travel agency, I suddenly saw a picture with just the elements I wanted. A village of Indian farmers, a church on a big square, adobe huts, the peaks of the Andes in the distance. Chinchero was perfect! Every Sunday about twenty-five hundred people come to a big market. Otherwise, it's nothing but a hamlet with Indian farmers, shepherds, llamas, a rural area with striking scenery. Most of the Indians have never seen a movie. They didn't even know how to fire a pistol. Rifles yes, but they had never seen handguns before."

Following his arrival in Lima in late 1969 to begin preproduction on *The Last Movie*, Hopper granted an interview to *La Prensa*, whose reporter solicited his opinions of "homosexualism" and marijuana, which was illegal in Peru. Smoking a joint, Hopper said that people should do their thing and admitted that he had lived with a lesbian, which was groovy.

---

[5] The remains of an Inca city located on a mountain ridge nearly 8,000 ft. above sea level, Machu Picchu lies about fifty miles from Cusco, a city in southeastern Peru that was once the capital of the Inca empire. ("Cusco" is the currently accepted spelling.) Chinchero, once the summer resort of the tenth ruler of the Inca Empire, is situated at the hypoxia-inducing altitude of 12,500 ft.

Hopper's interview outraged leaders of the clergy and ruling junta, who revoked freedom of the press a day later.

Hopper's actors and crew soon followed him to Peru to disturb its equilibrium. John Buck Wilkin, who wrote and performed songs for *The Last Movie* and Hopper's documentary *The American Dreamer*, joined them after an impromptu meeting with Hopper. "I was lucky enough to be day-running with [Kris] Kristofferson, who asked me if I wanted to meet him. Uh, yeah! We went to a modest two-bedroom rental apartment in North Hollywood, forget the street name. I played Dennis a few songs, and he said, 'Do you wanna go to Peru with us next week?' Well, yeah!

"It was a mixed bunch of cast and crew that rallied together about midnight to catch an APSA Air Lines jet to Cuzco, Peru, where Hopper was all set to film the movie he thought would be his masterpiece. There were about forty of us, including Peter Fonda in a big shearling coat, since it was winter in South America. Also Michelle Phillips, who would later marry Dennis for a week. Probably some of the people I had previously met at the party the year before and assorted actors, hippies, and technicians from Hollywood."

Ten minutes after the APSA Boeing 707 carrying Hopper's company took off, they started smoking pot until the plane's atmosphere seemed more smoke than air. They even tried to get the stewardess to turn on. In 1970, Henry Jaglom wrote in his diary, "Grass air everywhere; guitars and giggles. An incredible assortment of freaks are heading south with me to be in Dennis' film." "The plane trip down to Peru was one of the scariest things I've ever been in," Jaglom said in 2003. "Here was a plane full of strange people, including myself, but they were all so loaded, and walking up and down the aisles and singing and dancing, and the plane was rocking. It was really a ship of fools, you know. It's amazing that anybody got out of that thing alive."

The cast and crew's in-flight bacchanal later generated repercussions that required Hopper's personal attention. "A funny thing happened on the plane on the way down to Peru," Wilkin recalled. "The booze came out, the guitars, then the weed. Seemed natural enough. I had been in Carnegie Hall when it was filled with smoke to hear The Byrds, Burritos, and the Holy Modal Rounders. Anyway, word came down to Peru from Robert Mitchum in Los Angeles through his son Jim, who was in the cast, that the FBI and Interpol were looking for the people who were passing the grass on the plane. So Dennis called all the men in one at a time to get their stories straight. Seemed a stewardess ('flight attendant' title not yet born) had ratted out the party, and they were looking for certain individuals."

"One night," Peter Fonda wrote, "Hopper rushed into our hotel full of paranoia and demanded that we give him all the drugs we had, right then, because the federales were going to bust the cast and crew. He was like a frenzied preacher working a crowd." Everyone in the hotel handed over their drugs to Hopper, except Fonda, who put a used sock inside a rumpled paper bag. Hopper took the collected booty and took off in his pickup truck.

Those who gave up their drugs assumed that he wanted it all to himself, but Fonda says that Hopper genuinely believed the rumor about the federales. Hopper later said that he forgot where he hid the stash. "When our part of the film was finished," Fonda recalled, "most of us were ready to fly back to the States. A day before we departed, Jim Mitchum received word from his father, Big Bob, that we were all going to be searched thoroughly when we returned to the United States."

As soon as the freaks deplaned in Cusco, they invaded its elegant Victorian hotel and went in search of more drugs, especially Hopper's recent discovery, cocaine. Grass was illegal in Peru and difficult to obtain because the local Indians didn't use it much. The best was imported from Bolivia. Fortunately, cocaine was an abundant, inexpensive local resource.

Rolling Stone's Michael Goodwin, who became Hopper's favorite among the many journalists assigned to write about *The Last Movie*, gave his readers the straight dope on cocaine. "Coca leaves (from which cocaine is made) are legal in Peru—you can order them with dinner, and the waiter brings you a big plate from the kitchen. Ostensibly this is done so you can make tea with them (coca tea has long been a mainstay of the Indian pharmacopoeia), but the best way to get off on coca is to chew up the leaves with some lime ash. The lime ash (which is tricky stuff, since it is caustic and can burn your mouth if you use too much) extracts the cocaine from the leaves." Goodwin tried chewing coca leaves for twenty minutes and became numb from the chest up. "Pure cocaine, while definitely *not* legal, is readily available, and a lot less hassle—coke is one of Peru's main exports," he concluded.

By midafternoon on their first day in Cusco, someone in the film unit made a cocaine connection. ". . . and a number of actors laid in a large supply at bargain prices—$7 for a packet that cost $70 in the States," Brad Darrach wrote. "By 10 P.M. almost thirty members of the company were sniffing coke or had turned on with grass, acid, or speed." Most of them were asleep by midnight. At 2 A.M., Darrach was awakened by the screams of an actress in the throes of a bad acid trip.

At 3 A.M., a young woman rapped on his bedside window. Standing on the ledge outside in a rain-soaked nightgown, she asked if she could come in. She turned out to be one of what one reporter called Hopper's "ding-a-lings," a bunch of female groupies who made their own way to Cusco uninvited. Darrach claimed that an actor chained an actress who he thought resembled Joan of Arc to a porch post and lit a fire at her feet. Another actor swallowed five buds of peyote in rapid succession and nearly died. There were rumored to be whipping parties. Writer L. M. Kit Carson recalls someone knocking on his hotel room one evening. When Carson opened the door, some guy he didn't even knew held a bottle out to him and said, "Want some ether? It's really good."

"Of course there was plenty of good cocaine," said Dean Stockwell, who played Billy the Kid in the Western in *The Last Movie*. "The natives there would happily give you leaves to chew on, and there was this little type of rock that's got certain minerals in it, that precipitates the effects out of the leaves, and they all chew it. There was what you'd call processed coke, as well. Was I aware of the amount of drugs being consumed out there? Yeah, oh yeah. But we kept it to ourselves, apart from the leaves, which everyone was doing. We weren't stupid, we were just stoned." "There was a lot of cocaine down there, a lot of cocaine," Russ Tamblyn said. "Every time you turned around, somebody had a spoon."

"Suddenly, your thirty-three, in Peru, with a gang of guys who are living up to their reputations," recalled Kris Kristofferson, who appears near the beginning of *The Last Movie* with a baby face and lanky, greasy hair, singing "Me and Bobby McGee." "In fact, what he [Hopper] did was what he was filming. He was filming the corruption of a little town by movie people, and I mean they *ruined* the town." In 2008, Kristofferson recalled Hopper's behavior for the *Guardian* with awe. "We were down in Peru in this old Inca village, and Dennis was as crazy as he ever was. I mean, I see the guy he's mellowed into now, doing his retirement-fund commercials on TV, and I love Dennis, but back then, he was the most self-destructive guy I had ever seen! He got a priest defrocked because he got him involved in some kind of weird mass for James Dean. He antagonized the military and all the politicians. It was crazy."

"Everyone was aware that Dennis had achieved this enormous success with *Easy Rider* out of nowhere," Dean Stockwell said. "He was absolutely on top of the world. So when people get into a film like that, they feel like they're all of a sudden on top of the world. It was very celebratory."

"It's a circus, of course," Michael Goodwin wrote. "A crew of thirty (more or less), a bunch of friends and hangers-on, lots of groupies (domestic and imported), and hot and cold reporters. There are representatives from *Look*, *Esquire*, *New York Times Sunday Magazine*, *Show*, *New York*, *London Times*, *Ten* and *Rolling Stone*. *Life* and *Playboy* have been here and gone. A media explosion in Peru."

Hopper and his company got away with their debauchery, but the Peruvian government didn't let other visiting Americans share their privilege. On December 24, 1970, *The Village Voice* printed an anonymous letter from an American living in Peru, who wrote, "The absolute cultural insensitivity not only made me sick once again about my country and its fucked-up rich citizens, but have caused the government of Peru to crackdown on longhair tourists. The military [have] started mass shakedowns, round-ups, detentions, drug busts . . ."

In 1970, Hopper complained to Guy Flatley about Brad Darrach's story on the filming of *The Last Movie* that was published in *Life*. "Hopper and his 'Last Movie' crew created something of a scandal on location in Peru," Flatley wrote. "There were many vivid reports of ultra-liberated sexual shenanigans, wild booze bouts, and, particularly, drug-induced pandemonium. According to Hopper, most of the printed accounts of the Peruvian carousing fall into the category of strictly creative writing."

An unrepentant Hopper admitted the veracity of Darrach's article in a 2005 interview. Recalling the filming of *The Last Movie*, he said, "It was shot in seven weeks. The first two weeks were just hard work, getting everything prepared. Then the rest of the cast and a mob of journalists came to join us, and that's when things got out of hand. Things got fairly excessive those next few weeks. Everything imaginable went on. It was one long sex-and-drugs orgy. Wherever you looked, there were naked people out of their fucking minds on one thing or another.

"There was a mountain of coke down there, and we went through it all. But I wouldn't say it got in the way of the movie. I'd say it helped us get the movie done. We might have been drug addicts, but we were drug addicts with a point of view and a work ethic. It was all about the movie. If we were going to take coke and fuck beautiful women, we'd do it on camera. The drugs and the drink and the insane sex, they all fueled our creativity. At least, that's my excuse. If you're gonna be that debauched, it's better to have a good reason."

"That film was never supported and never understood," said Paul Lewis. "But it was literally the height of craziness. We were shooting in Peru at an altitude of 17,000 feet in the cocaine capital of the world. I remember we were drunk at this press conference in Lima, and a reporter asked Dennis if he had stopped doing drugs. He said, 'Why would I stop doing drugs just because I'm in Peru?' " Lewis remarked that the drugs and off-camera shenanigans Hopper was involved in never diverted him from his artistic purpose. "Of course, Dennis did everything else as well," he said. "He was a total maniac, but he never stopped the creative process, no matter what craziness went on." "Dennis is a demonic artist, like Rimbaud," Brooke Hayward told Brad Darrach. "Nothing matters but his work."

"But we used a lot of cocaine on that movie," Hopper said, "and people said how could you make a movie and drink and use cocaine and smoke grass and so on? And Paul said, 'Are you serious?' We were making movies. You know, it wasn't anything—if somebody had said you can't have any drugs, you know, you have to make the movie, we'd have made the movie. Nobody said you can't have any drugs, and we weren't doing anything that interfered with what we thought was our work. So, like, you know, it was always the work. The work was the most important thing, and the drugs and the alcohol and all those things are secondary to it."

Maybe the cast and crew's drug-besotted state helped them ignore the conditions they encountered every day on the film's location. In his diary, Henry Jaglom complained of the illness-producing, unsanitary facilities. He scribbled, "No toilets on location!! Toilet's below filthy, overflowing, disease-ridden, and unusable. No washing facilities. Water is brown and polluted, brown. No soap. Sinks unusable. Feces, urine and vomit mixed with mud everywhere." (Jaglom quit the film after two weeks.) The small hotel rooms were cold, hot water was rare, and there were no bathtubs. There were no stoves or heaters on the set. The actors' dressing room was a frigid stable full of chicken, goat, horse, llama, and pig excrement. The doctor assigned to the film was too busy acting to assist the sick. The company spent two hours each day in a caravan of vehicles that frequently had to be dug out of the muck while they wound their way up the rain-slicked, dangerously narrow, unpaved donkey trail to reach the set in Chinchero.

When they finally got there, they were stricken with altitude sickness. "The quality of the air at 14,000 feet can only be described as psychedelic, but you have to get into it," Michael Goodwin wrote. "Walking more than a few steps, even on level ground, is enough to make you breathe hard; the shortest uphill climb is a major effort." When Goodwin took a breath of pure oxygen from a portable tank, which the cast and crew rarely used, he suddenly felt he had gone from being stoned to being straight. Chuck Bail, the stunt coordinator, said, "I watched László Kovács walk up a little grade in the village, and when he got there, he fell flat on his face, didn't even put his hands out in front of him." Most of the film company was also stricken with diarrhea at one time or another.

Even in Peru, James Dean was never far from Hopper's mind. He had his crew paint the window of a palmistry-and-occult-merchandise store-front built for the Western set with the words "Jimmy's Place. Jimmy's Place reminds you of your destiny. There are other things." Tomas Milian told reporter Alix Jeffry, "When I see Dennis, I see James Dean and I see Dean and I see Dennis. That is very strong." "One does get an eerie feeling watching Hopper," Jeffry observed. "He wears Dean's ring at all times, and when he rubs that ring, he seems to become Dean. Seeing this happen, you feel a shiver creep up your spine. Everyone pretends not to notice, and in truth, it is never mentioned."

"Throughout the shooting of *The Last Movie*," Edwin Miller reported, "Dennis wore a Mexican bronze-and-silver ring bearing the face of an Aztec idol. The ring had once belonged to James Dean. 'It was given to me,' he explains, 'just before the picture by a girl who got it from the lawyer who cleaned up Dean's apartment after he died.' "

Far from Universal's reach and any possible creative interference, Hopper was finally free to do what he first wanted to while directing *Easy Rider*. He discarded Stewart Stern's carefully crafted script, and improvised action and dialogue on the spur of the moment. Hopper said, "In a sense, the movie is a structured improvisation. The script is there, but the dialogue has been changed and improvised by the actors to express their own approach. Each actor you cast subtly affects the whole by the way he reacts to situations or the way he gives his lines."

The day before Hopper started filming, Brad Darrach asked him how closely he would follow the script. "Oh, I'm not afraid to work with an empty head," he replied.[6] "If you can't create out of the moment, you're not creating." Darrach reported, "On the second day of shooting, there was no doubt about it: every scene, every line of the horse-opera sequence that introduces *The Last Movie* was improvised. 'How about we have the young guys against the old guys?' somebody suggested. 'That's cool,' Dennis said right away. In a matter of minutes, he hoked up a story, a ballistic burlesque of a John Wayne Western that somehow managed to involve Billy the Kid, D. H. Lawrence, James Dean and Captain Bligh and the Seven Samurai. By noon, he had put about fifteen minutes of film in the can, and most of it, as somebody said, was 'out of sight.' "

"I call him an instinctive director," Chuck Bail said. "If he saw the sun going down, he'd yell at László Kovács. They'd immediately set something up to get that sunset through a stained-glass window. As things go, that's how he directs. He has a big plan in his mind." Henry Jaglom takes a slightly different perspective on Hopper's method. "The movie was in Dennis' mind, so nobody else seemed to know what was going on or what was happening."

"We were high in the Andes, literally and figuratively, and most of the film was just made up as we went along," said Michelle Phillips. "There was a script, but it wasn't something that we adhered to very closely." Dean Stockwell said that Hopper had no script. "He didn't even make up his mind what I was going to do until we got down there," Stockwell recalled. "He'd outline it, and then we'd go do it. But he was absolutely in control. In his own inimitable way. At that time, he was a piece of work like nobody I've ever known. Dennis was all over the place, all constant energy, you just couldn't shut him up for a second—he had more energy than ten people. He was awesome to be around."

Despite oxygen deprivation, unhygienic conditions, sudden hailstorms, and mud up to a foot deep, Hopper and his company managed to shoot twenty to thirty camera setups every day, a feat even Roger Corman would be hard pressed to match. They maintained this hectic pace twelve hours a day, six days a week, for seven weeks during the rainy season in Peru.

As a director, Hopper was more like Henry Hathaway than Nicholas Ray. Brad Darrach saw how Hopper manipulated his actors when he

---

[6] If that isn't a classic straight line, I don't know what is.

watched him provoke a too-calm Garcia to act hysterical in a scene. Hopper yelled, "Goddammit, Stella, get it on!" Garcia burst into tears and ran off the set. "Get back on camera!" he shouted. "Get back in that scene!" "Stella rushed back and stumbled from one actor to another, sobbing out of control," Darrach wrote. "The camera caught it all, and Dennis came out to comfort her, looking flushed and smug."

"He gets performances out of people by pulling their strings," David Hopper remarked, "and he knows his own pretty well. He's a pretty good behavioral scientist. Dennis will screw an actor up, trip him in delivery or whatever until, if anything, they just break down in not being able to do the structure they know."

Hopper said that he cast nearly all his actors from among his friends because he already understood their psychology. Their friendship with Hopper didn't spare them from feeling his lash. Tom Burke said that Hopper always treated his actresses with "boyish, almost bashful respect." Hopper treated males like a hip Otto Preminger, full of curses and angry threats. In one scene, Hopper calmly endured the first two blown takes. He gently addressed the actor who missed his lines, saying, "Listen, man, now what did I tell you about this shot? Huh, man? Now, please, man. You know we're a little behind. O.K.?" Hopper turned to the crowd watching the scene. "May I have quiet, please? O.K., action—roll it please."

When the actor ruined the next take, Hopper was in his face. He said, "Now, you listen to me, man . . ."

"What a minute, Dennis," the actor protested.

"Wait a minute for *me*, man!" Hopper said. "For *me*! I'll tell you one more time, if you elaborate on *anything* in this shot, we are dead! Just do what we rehearsed, Mr. Actors Studio, or I'll cut off your cocaine supply. Now, GET IT TOGETHER!" The actor blanched, but his next take was perfect.

Hopper commanded a loyalty bordering on devotion from his crew, even after he dragged them to a freezing cold plateau even higher than Chinchero. He spent something like two hours quietly contemplating the area where he planned to shoot Kansas and Neville's gold-prospecting scenes. "I was drawn aside on several occasions and told how exciting it was to be working with a genius," Michael Goodwin wrote. "Clearly, Dennis is considered Hollywood's Great White Hope, at least by the people working with him." "He's a genius," a lighting technician kept telling Tom Burke. "He *feels*, deeper than other men. I love this guy. I'm not queer, but I swear, I love this guy, I almost love him *physically*."

After Brad Darrach left Peru, he heard that Hopper had smashed an irksome person's head through a glass coffee table in the hotel. Hopper reacted so violently to the hotel's eviction order that the manager was forced to hire bodyguards. Near the end of filming, he chose to address a group of revolutionary students who had bombed Cusco's plaza with Molotov cocktails. Peru's government sent an emissary to tell him to muzzle himself or leave.

On the penultimate day of shooting, rumors were flying that the ruling junta was about to be deposed. Hopper began tying up loose ends and completed filming the following day. Posing for a celebratory group photo, he hoisted a bottle and joked, "This picture was not made on mahree-juana. This picture was made on Scotch and soda."

An eerie occurrence capped the final day of shooting, which fell during Lent. The company slept that night in an empty church near the town of Puno. Don Gordon awoke to see weeping Indians holding candles entering the church, one at a time, stepping over the actors in their sleeping bags on their way to pray silently at the altar. Gordon went outside where he saw Dennis Hopper staring at a comet in the night sky. Suddenly, James Dean's ring that Hopper wore broke apart, its pieces falling to earth. Cue the theremin!

Hopper returned to L.A., announced his engagement to Michelle Phillips, and casually informed Universal that he would be spending a year editing *The Last Movie* instead of the three months originally agreed to. He took the forty-eight hours of raw footage he shot in Peru to the new home in Taos, New Mexico, that he purchased in early 1970, which would double as his postproduction facility. Flush with the money pouring in from *Easy Rider*, Hopper purchased the former home of Mabel Dodge Luhan.

A wealthy patron of the arts, Mabel Dodge Sterne moved to Taos with her husband in 1918, where she built a series of adobe houses on a twelve-acre parcel of land. (She later married Pueblo Indian Tony Luhan.) Luhan hosted a veritable who's who of noted artists and intellectuals at her home that included Marsden Hartley, Willa Cather, Aldous Huxley, Robinson Jeffers, Carl Jung, Georgia O'Keeffe, and D. H. Lawrence. Lawrence, who called Luhan's home Mabeltown, wrote, "In the magnificent fierce morning of New Mexico, one sprang awake, a new part of the soul woke up suddenly and the old world gave way to the new. New Mexico was the greatest experience from the outside world that I have ever had."

"Ghost-filled places always fascinated me," Hopper said. "I went to see the house when I was looking for places to shoot *Easy Rider*. It was a mystical experience. When it was time to leave, I couldn't get the door open to get out. I'd been planning to buy a ranch in Elko, Nevada—a working ranch—but when I found out that Mrs. Luhan's granddaughter was willing to sell the house, I decided to go with the aesthetic-and-mud palace in contrast to the working ranch. I decided I was an aesthetic person, and the other was a dream."

Hopper discovered Taos by accident in 1968 while scouting southwestern locations for *Easy Rider*. Leaving Los Alamos on the way to see a commune in Santa Fe, Hopper and Paul Lewis argued about which direction to take on a divided highway, headed north, and ended up in Taos. "I heard that Taos was an artist community, and I didn't want to go to any artist community," Hopper said. "I was looking for a commune to use."

"I just suddenly fell in love with it," he said of Taos. "I mean it was like very mystical to me, and I kept trying to get out of town, and an Indian would come and say the mountain is smiling in you, you must come and see this, you must come and see that, and so on." After shooting part of *Easy Rider* in and around Taos for two weeks, Hopper promised himself that if he ever made any money, he would make it his new home.

Around Christmas 1969, Hopper was staying at the Hotel La Fonda in Taos with his eighteen-year-old girlfriend, Felicia Fergusson, and his friend, Leo Garen. (Felicia was the granddaughter of Terecita Fergusson, the defendant in Taos's most famous criminal trial, where she was accused of cutting off the head of her English lover, Arthur Manby.) Garen, a theater producer and director from New York who knew Dennis from his Actors Studio days, moved to L.A. in 1968 to work on Antonioni's *Zabriskie Point* (1970). It was Garen who found Hopper the pool house where he lived while editing *Easy Rider*, which was on the large estate where Garen was staying in L.A.

After emceeing an LSD party in a house near the hotel, Hopper drove out to see Luhan's home with Garen and Fergusson. Hopper was immediately taken with it, which he connected with the Sacred Mountain that is visible behind it. "Well, they say the mountain is sacred, I really bought that," he recalled. "You know when I went into the house, like light fell right on certain places, and I came outside, and snow was just snowing right where I was standing, you now, and lightning knocked bushes down, you know, I mean it was very bizarre."

Luhan's former residence was a three-story adobe structure with twenty-two rooms that opened to a central solarium. Luhan's compound was made up of the main house (the Big House, as it was often called), five guest houses, a 1,200-foot gatehouse, and a log cabin that Hopper converted into a film-editing facility. (He later joked that the main house, which he nicknamed the Mud Palace, would make a great whorehouse.) Luhan's granddaughter, Bonnie Evans, inherited Luhan's estate, but was unable to maintain it on the weekly salary of $50 she was paid working at *The Fountain of Light*, Taos' hippie newspaper. Evans reluctantly put Luhan's property on the market in late 1968.

Hopper returned to Taos in March 1970 to buy Luhan's house, accompanied by Michelle Phillips and her daughter. Evans was unsettled by Hopper's tense, wigged-out manner and didn't want to sell out to him, but parted with Luhan's house for a sum of between $140,000 and $180,000. (Dennis Hopper claimed the lower figure, his brother the higher figure. Dennis Hopper claimed that Evans doubled her original price for the house when he showed interest in it.)

Hopper intended to create an independent filmmaking commune at the Mud Palace, whose core would consist of his brother David, David's wife Charlotte and their children, Michelle Phillips and her daughter, and personnel involved in postproduction on *The Last Movie*. He spent $80,000 renovating the main house, fixing collapsed roofs, repairing walls, and installing two new septic tanks. He remodeled the house, adding three bedrooms and two bathrooms, and installed a kitchenette apartment in the gatehouse. David Hopper managed Dennis' household and postproduction facilities, and later opened an elaborately designed gallery in Taos where local artisans made pricey Southwestern-style jewelry.

Dennis Hopper moved out of the Mud Palace a year after settling in. He once claimed that he was driven out by the ghost of D. H. Lawrence, who he came to believe was buried in his backyard instead of in a shrine on a nearby mountain slope known as the Kiowa Ranch. "It was more like Tony saying, 'Why don't you come over here where I live, out of this insanity?' " he said. "It was too crazy there. There were so many bedrooms, so many ways in and out of that place, I was just too paranoid for it. It was just like open house for anyone who was hungry. I moved outta there, and into Tony's house (the comfortable guesthouse where Tony Luhan had lived).

Hopper told Guy Flatley, "If you want to talk about the community of Hollywood, though . . . is it dying? Well, I moved to Taos because I don't like the people in Los Angeles, even though they do have nice banks. Hollywood is a very cliquish place. You go to private clubs to see the private people. If you walk on the street at night, the police stop you and want to know what you're up to. Hollywood is so smogged, so swamped, that it's ready to fall into the sea. I tell you, man, you ought to come down here to Taos. It's beautiful. Like Taos is the beautiful place to be."

"I think of Taos as my home. There are less than one million people living above 7,000 feet, and the Pueblo is the oldest inhabited structure in North America," he said. "It's a rather mysterious place. Taos Mountain is one of the seven sacred mountains. And there's the sacred Blue Lake. These things are important to us. If you drilled straight through the world at Taos, you'd come out in Tibet. I get a very strong feeling in Taos."

Bohemians and hippies inspired by Hopper's pilgrimage to Taos flocked there in emulation. "In 1969," author Lois Rudnick wrote, "the hippie population of Taos was estimated to be 2,000, at a time when the native population of the town was 3,500." Jason Silverman wrote, "Already a countercultural destination—the Berkeley of the Southwest—Taos, after 1969, became, as *Parade* magazine wrote, 'a leading candidate for the hippie capital of America.' The film's [*Easy Rider*] success brought in not only new creative energy and splendid art, but also racially charged conflicts and outrageous sex-drugs-and-rock 'n' roll behavior.

"Poet Robert Creeley, who moved to Taos in 1958, called it 'the goyim's Israel,' counting twenty-seven communes there in the late 1960s. Taos—a quiet, religious, centuries-old community—wasn't ready for the hippies. Their town overrun, some locals responded with vigilante violence. Volkswagen buses were torched. Reports of assaults on hippies were routine. The chamber of commerce . . . instructed its members to resist selling to hippies. Doctors complained of strung-out mothers neglecting their kids. The *Taos News* published vicious editorials: 'Hippies are hollow creatures, and their outward manifestations smell.' Worried about attendance by 'undesirables,' the town canceled its annual fiesta—the biggest party of the year. 'Summer of Love?' sniffs Rena Rosenquist, owner of Mission Gallery and a player in Taos's cultural scene since the mid-'60s. 'More like the summer of harassment, police brutality, and racial tension.' Transformed by *Easy Rider* into an international counterculture poster child, Hopper, despite his own efforts, became an emblem of Taos's Hispanics-versus-hippies conflict."

Taos native Larry Torres told Lois Rudnick, "Nineteen sixty-six. I'm fourteen, I suppose, or something like that. And we were told that the hippies were coming, fifty thousand of them. We had visions of fifty thousand longhaired English speakers moving in on us. So suddenly, we are told that fifty thousand hippies are coming out of Haight-Ashbury. We didn't know what Haight-Ashbury was, anyway. But what happened was, they trickled in here . . . without us realizing they had come. Our religion, our traditions, our customs, our way of looking at people are very medieval, still reflected in the language of today, which is very archaic. So we go from a superconservative Hispanic society to an avant-garde society overnight. What happens when you have a society that goes from this to that with no transition or stages?"

Taos' longtime residents reacted to the hippie influx remarkably like the patrons of the Louisiana diner in *Easy Rider*. Hopper later told journalists the story of his conflicts with Taos' anti-hippie locals. "The Indian land runs one foot outside the front door," he said. "The area is predominantly Spanish and Indian. I had a lot of trouble at first from the local Spanish, who didn't want to see an influx of Anglos, especially hippies. Most of the residents live on about $800 a year, 85 percent of the land is owned by the government, and there's a lot of violence. It was bad here when I came here, man, really bad."

Australian director Philippe Mora told interviewer Alex Simon about his experience when he visited Hopper in Taos to interest him in acting in his film, *Mad Dog Morgan* (1976). "[Producer] Jeremy Thomas and I came to L.A. and met Martin Sheen," he recalled, "who wanted to do the lead—everyone actually wanted to do it—and Marty would've been great. Jason Miller, who'd just done *The Exorcist*, wanted to do it. So we ring up Dennis Hopper's agent to see if he was available, and his agent's head nearly popped through the telephone, like in a Tim Burton movie. 'Yeah, he's available!'

"So we took this little plane down to New Mexico, in Taos, and we get out of the plane, and there's Dennis at the end of the runaway, dressed in tattered Levis, holding a rifle, just standing there, and I remember thinking 'That's our Mad Dog!' (laughs) So he takes us to his house in this bat-tered old truck, which was riddled with bullet holes. And I said 'Dennis, what's with the bullet holes?' He said, 'Oh, the Indians have been shooting at me. And that reminds me, you better be in your hotel when the sun goes down because that's when the shootings starts. Ha, ha, ha!' "

As he dropped Mora and Thomas off at Hotel La Fonda, Hopper said, "Check out the nudes by D. H. Lawrence in the front office. Give the guy five bucks to see the dirty pictures, but don't go out after 1 A.M.—that's when the Indians start shooting. G'night, man!" "Later, when we looked at a room full of startling erotic nudes painted by Lawrence (who knew?), gunfire erupted outside the hotel," Mora said. "We sprinted up to our rooms. I slept under the bed. I mean it was just out of control in Taos back then: the booze, the guns, just crazy."

"Suddenly there was me, this movie freak, with my brother and all these hippies around, and the locals didn't dig it," Hopper said. "I symbolized the fact that I could be bringing other people with me. They didn't want that to happen. They didn't care what it took to keep me saying 'This is a dangerous place.' And it is a dangerous place." David Hopper's wife, Char-lotte, and her family were harassed on their trips to town so often that she started carrying a gun in her purse.

Dennis Hopper said, "Every time my brother and I would walk into town, these cars would come swinging around us with guys leaning out yelling, 'Hey, man, we're gonna rape your wife and your sister!' Hippies would be hitchhiking, and when the cops spotted them, they'd call the football team, and those guys would come beat the shit out of them while the cops were watching. After a while, they'd blow their sirens, and when the high school kids disappeared, they'd arrest the hippies. And it's true, man, the guys were getting mutilated and the girls raped."

Hopper finally snapped on June 16, 1970, becoming the hippies' aveng-ing angel. "Finally one night, I said, 'Fuck it,' and got a gun and put it in the backseat of the car." Dennis, his brother, and Dennis' buddies, Owen Orr and Ted Markland, were headed to El Salto Creek above Arroyo Seco, about seven miles north of Taos, which is famous for its waterfalls. (El Salto is Spanish for "The Falls.") They intended to explore a mountain cave beneath one of the waterfalls that D. H. Lawrence used in his story "The Woman Who Rode Away."

When they stopped some teenagers to ask directions, the kids accosted them. Dennis angered them when he mentioned that his brother's wife was Mexican. Hopper said they tried to pull him and his brother out of their car. "Anyway, I got out with the gun in my hand and said 'O.K., everybody up against the wall.' I'd seen too many John Wayne movies, so I made a citizen's arrest and held them at gunpoint until the police arrived." He knocked one of the kids cold and kicked out their car's steering wheel.

"When the police came, they arrested *us* and held us on $8,000 bail. By the time my brother had called the police, there was a lynch mob out there of a good 150 people wantin' to hang our asses. It looked like a scene out of *Viva Zapata*—pitchforks, machetes, the works. The police said, 'We're going to let you out a side door. We can't protect you because of the lynch situation. Then five guys back from Vietnam came in and told me, 'We're going to kill you.' I pointed out to the police that I'd just been threatened. 'Shut up,' they said. That cut it.

"The next day, my brother and I went into the local sporting-goods store and bought every gun in the place. Then I called some stunt men buddies of mine in Hollywood and said, 'Look, I need your help,' cause the staties here sure aren't going to help me.' I also asked for federal help, but that was a joke. Turns out the guys running the general store were undercover feds checking out the communes." (Hopper was later tried for assault with a deadly weapon. Charlotte Hopper recalled how the judge in the trial held up the issue of *Life* magazine that featured Brad Darrach's unflattering cover story on Hopper.)

"So we set up machine-gun nests and rifles on the rooftops—good fields of fire." (A visitor to Hopper's house said that it resembled an armed encampment, with armed patrols on the roof who communicated through walkie-talkies.) After tracing the teens who harassed him to the local high school, Dennis and David Hopper barged into a school assembly. Jumping on the stage, Dennis announced, "Look, I'm here, and I'm going to stay. What's more, there are more freaks coming in over the next few months, and though they may have long hair, they are not the love generation. They're back from Vietnam, and they're hard dudes. Macho is macho, and if this keeps up, somebody is going to get hurt around here. Just because these hippies are dropping acid, that doesn't give you the right to rape their women and cut their balls off. And they're going to have these."

He threw back his poncho to reveal a machine gun. His brother, barring the doorway, repeated Dennis' gesture, saying, "Everybody stay where you are—we're leaving now" as they made their retreat. (The high school principal at the time said that Dennis Hopper's story is a fiction.)

"Well, they listened, and they finally got the message," Hopper said. "After that, I got involved in community activities, and things finally cooled down. I talked to a lot of people, helped with some of the problems, paid for the Teatro Campesino to come in, did some work on behalf of the Indians, helped in the effort to get them back Blue Lake. It made me closer to the community. Anyway, once they decide you are macho, they leave you alone." (Two years later, Hopper was still the occasional target of the locals' hostility. Hopper and his third wife, Daria Halprin, who was seven months pregnant, were on their way to the town of Tierra Amarilla with Chicano activist Reies Tijerina when she and Hopper were thrown to the ground by assailants who began beating him.)

Larry Torres gave Lois Rudnick an insider's perspective on the incident. "Dennis Hopper thought he had made a great many friends in the valley because he made Taos famous, although this is not true. Now the reason they were going up the road, I suspect, was probably to visit El Salto, the seventh of the seven waterfalls that come down the holy mountain. It was [rumored to have been] used in prehistory for human sacrifice. Now Dennis and his friends were going up there, probably to drink and smoke and just commune with the spirit of the old generation. Suddenly the Seco boys decided they didn't want the goddamn hippie on the road, and they got off the truck and were going to beat the hell out of Hopper. Suddenly, our local boys decided these honkies had no right going up there and getting minted and getting under our falls. So they cornered them against the Indian fence [that borders Taos Pueblo].

"These longhairs pulled a gun on our children!" Torres said, describing the locals' outrage at Hopper's actions. "See, the boys never told their fathers that they had plotted to beat the hell out of Hopper. So suddenly I remember there was a meeting at the schoolhouse in Arroyo Seco to see what we were going to do about the hippie problem, and it was decided we'd do something covert. The sheriff, the police department was called in, and they said, 'Do what you want, we won't be around when you do it.' The ringleaders at that time were businessmen in town, and they didn't like the longhairs. It was a communal effort to drive them out."

Undaunted, Hopper purchased the 132-seat El Cortez Theatre in Ranchos De Taos to screen footage from *The Last Movie* while he edited it. Bill

Whaley, who leased and managed the theater, recalled the way that Hopper purchased it, displaying an arrogance that may have provoked Taoseños' dislike of him. "I had a lease and right of first refusal," Whaley wrote in his posthumous remembrance of Hopper. "Hopper bought the building out from under me in the spring of 1970 with the connivance of my attorney, John Ramming, who danced to the tune of a better-paying client. I learned about the sale from a friend, who called me from La Cocina. 'Hey, your landlord is down here drinking and says he just sold the place to Hopper.' When I met later with Ramming and Hopper, the actor said, 'You could sue me, but I need it to edit *The Last Movie*.' And Ramming said, 'We know you're broke.' After all, who was I to stand in the way of great art? Everybody in town was in on the action, taking Dennis Dollars—plumbers, realtors, and layabouts were kissing Dennis' ring.

"Hopper, as if to make amends, offered me free rent for the summer. Later he and his brother, David, hired me to manage the theatre. David was always a gentleman. They sort of played the 'good cop, bad cop' roles. Dennis and I had a few shouting matches about the films I booked for the El Cortez, which, as always, were a mix of foreign, domestic, pop, and exploitation. Who did I think I was to argue with the cultural icon?"

Whaley finally quit when Hopper blamed him for showing *Paint Your Wagon*, which starred Lee Marvin and Clint Eastwood. It seems that students at the nearby University of New Mexico ridiculed Hopper for exhibiting such an unhip movie. (Eastwood sings the song "I Talk To the Trees" in a faint, whispery voice in the film.) "Given the ups and down of his career and confusion underscored about art and life in *The Last Movie*," Whaley wrote, "it's safe to say Dennis never understood the art of film exhibition and the lack of effect of movies on a local or national audience. He told me, 'You shouldn't show Buñuel's *Viridiana* [1961] on a Sunday, either, or *Soldier Blue* [which always attracted a large crowd from Taos Pueblo].'

"The locals liked the silly musical with Clint Eastwood and Lee Marvin well enough, but preferred Mexican movies starring the likes of Antonio Aguilar or Cantinflas in *Por mis pistolas* [1968]. Hardly anyone, much less native Taoseños, attended Buñuel's anti-Catholic art film, which was aimed at the Anglo bourgeoisie, as I told him. Still, Dennis knew better and wanted to censor the masses—paternalist that he was. 'This is a good church-going community,' he said.

"The Taos Pueblo Indians used to fill up the theater for *Soldier Blue*

[1970], the movie about the Sand Creek massacre. As they told me about *Soldier Blue* or even *Flap* [1970], (aka *Nobody Loves a Drunken Indian* with Anthony Quinn), 'we liked to see images of ourselves on the screen, regardless.' Dennis, like most outsiders who attended movies or church or county commission meetings infrequently if at all, wanted to save Taoseños from themselves—as if the natives know little about sin and error in this violence-plagued community."

Whaley, who ended up developing a fondness for Hopper, recalled, "Back then, from under the cowboy hat, which squashed down his scraggly brown locks, Dennis's piercing hazel eyes blazed and his voice frequently cackled above the din at La Cocina as he downed a pisco sour or engaged in raucous conversation at the bar above the Plaza Theatre . . . Dennis frequently turned up at the theater or clubs with movie stars or rockers and musicians in tow. He casually introduced them to me as he passed by the box office: 'Bill, this is Warren Oates.' He and his friends generously supported the efforts of the locals, applauding the efforts of actors in community theater—*West Side Story*, say—or by providing the occasional opportunity for a spontaneous performance by the likes Kris Kristofferson at a local club."

Hopper hadn't even started editing *The Last Movie* when he announced his future projects. In Peru, he outlined his ambitious plans to Tom Burke. "Hey, man, listen to my schedule for the rest of my life: three months to write a movie, two months to get it ready, two months to shoot it, a year to edit it. Then: three months to write, two to get ready . . . dig? *That's* me, *that's* my life! And no vacations, until I'm firmly established!" Hopper said that his next film would be *Me and Bobby McGee*, to star himself and Michelle Phillips as a couple who hitchhike around the country. *Me and Bobby McGee* was set to roll in New Mexico in 1970. Hopper planned to follow it with *Second Chance*, a self-referential film with Hopper and Peter Fonda playing themselves, re-creating their adventures in New York when they tried to get *The Last Movie* made.

In *The American Dreamer*, Hopper wistfully acknowledges that Peter Fonda was the only person willing to give him a chance when he hired him to direct *Easy Rider*. That didn't prevent him from suing Fonda over his share of *Easy Rider*'s profits. On June 24, 1970, *Variety* reported that Hopper filed a lawsuit asking for 3 percent of the net profits on *Easy Rider* in remuneration for the "chore" of writing its screenplay.

Hopper told Guy Flatley, "You know, I'm suing Peter Fonda now, because we started out equal partners on *Easy Rider*, and he ended up 7 points ahead of me. Seven points at $150,000 a point. The movie cost $340,000, and it may end up being the fourth biggest grosser of all time. This year alone, I'll make a million and a half on it—70 percent of which will go to the government. The thing is, I wrote the screenplay in two weeks, and I never got paid a penny for it. At the time, I didn't care. Peter said we could straighten out the financial details later."

When Flatley said, "It seems a shame to end a fruitful relationship on such a bitter note," Hopper explained, "Oh, no, not at all, it's nothing like that. Peter and I have a wonderful relationship. Now that I'm suing him, he calls me more than he ever did before. That's the way it is, you see, when people get guilt feelings. He even offered to buy me a car. And neither of us has even mentioned the lawsuit. Peter and I will always be very close friends, no matter what. Like John Ford and Henry Fonda, like John Ford and Duke Wayne."

Hopper's euphoria suddenly evaporated when the June 19, 1970 issue of *Life* hit the newsstands. Brad Darrach's cover story, which reported Hopper's use of drugs and claimed that he mainlined heroin, caught him flatfooted. "That was the most depressing article I have ever read," he told the *Los Angeles Times*. "I wanted to hide under the bed for three days and not come out."

In full damage-control mode, Hopper emphatically denied Darrach's charges, saying, "The article is not true and most unfair. Man, the only thing I shoot up with is vitamin B-12. My only habit-forming vice is cigarettes. When they [young people] read that Dennis Hopper can take heroin and still write, direct, and act in movies, they will get the mistaken impression that heroin is not bad." He told the *Times* that he wanted to appear on Johnny Carson, Dick Cavett, and Merv Griffin's TV talk shows to refute Darrach's claims.

Dick Adler wrote, "Denials have since been issued, the most cogent being Hopper's: 'Making a movie is hard work—it would be impossible if I was using hard drugs.'" Hopper was so rankled, he told Guy Flatley, "That story in *Life* about my shooting heroin really bugged me. Man, I never shot anything in my whole life. I never, ever, took a needle," then inadvertently admitted, "Now as far as grass goes, I've smoked that for eighteen years. I get high when I can, but I don't need it. And I've dropped acid. Yet I don't seem to have any brain damage. Well, maybe a little.'"

Evidently, the New Mexico State Legislature's Drug Abuse Study Committee bought Hopper's denials and missed Guy Flatley's column. Hopper appeared before the committee on September 30, 1971, where he said, "Marijuana will have to be legalized because you can't keep making criminals out of the majority of our citizens. Otherwise, the country will fall apart." *The Hollywood Reporter* wrote, "He further stated that legalizing medically controlled use of heroin by confirmed addicts would be a major advance in stopping the wave of crime by addicts, especially with the increase of addiction among returning veterans."

After the dust settled from Hopper's battles with Peter Fonda, scandal-seeking journalists and hippie-haters, he set about editing *The Last Movie*. Surrounded by racks of film reels containing enough footage for four movies, he encountered the same problems he experienced while editing *Easy Rider*. In Peru, Hopper shot an excessive amount of film because he had no way to develop and screen his dailies to evaluate them. He sent the negatives back to Taos where David Hopper developed them and checked to make sure they looked properly exposed. "I brought back forty-eight hours of film," Hopper said. "None of it had I seen, and suddenly, now, I was gonna cut this and make a movie out of it."

Hopper would spend months struggling to carve a comprehensible film out of the superabundant raw material before him. Based on the critical and commercial reaction to *The Last Movie*, it's a problem he never solved. "Editing is like being in prison," he said. "But editing is very painful. It's creative, but there's also something uncreative about it. Sort of like framing a picture. Also, it's painful to throw away footage." Ron Rosenbaum, who spent a week in Taos to write about Hopper, thought that the editing process "seemed to suffer from too many instances of people gathering around the Moviola[7] and gazing with awe and wonder at the nonlinear juxtaposition of images. And from too much reverence for Hopper's."

In 2003, László Kovács said, "I was convinced that we had a good movie in the can, so we all come back, Dennis goes to Taos, New Mexico, and I think he bought D. H. Lawrence estate, which is a beautiful compound and all. He decided he's gonna edit the film there. Of course, he invited all his buddies and everybody, and it was an endless twenty-four hour parties and all that stuff and spending money and all. Everybody was talking into,

---

[7] A Moviola is an electrically powered device that allows an editor to view film while cutting it.

giving advice, 'you should do this, that,' and basically, what happened, Dennis screwed it up in editing. He didn't let anybody, a professional editor come in, and that's what he should have done." (Hopper had experienced editors working with him, led by David Berlatsky. Berlatsky and the other editors lived at the Mud Palace while they assisted Hopper with cutting his film.)

Hopper's concentration on the editing process was constantly broken by a seemingly endless stream of diversions and distractions that resulted from his newfound celebrity and the ongoing renovation of the Luhan house. "To try to get him into the cutting room was really difficult," recalled Berlatsky, "because there were so many people pulling on him. Also, at that time, he was trying to refurbish the Mabel Dodge Luhan house, which is where we lived, and he had tons of Indians around there, fixing the house and stuccoing, and he was always having to sign checks and have these meetings with his brother about needing more money, needing more money, needing more money."

"Essentially, the house was open, and people came," David Hopper said. "You know, Alan Watts, George McGovern, Nick Ray, Leonard Cohen, Bob Dylan, the Everly Brothers, Ricky Nelson, you name it." "It was impossible to keep people out," Dennis Hopper said. "And everybody who came to Taos from Los Angeles wanted to stay with Dennis Hopper or visit Dennis Hopper. I would come in to get a beer out of the refrigerator or to have some breakfast in the morning, and there'd be thirty people sitting in the kitchen—28 of them I didn't know."

"One Thanksgiving," Marin Hopper recalled, "he gave a huge Thanksgiving dinner at this huge table in the dining room, and there were just thousands of people packed in there. It was like an audience. It was incredible. There were people sitting around the main table, but then there were people standing up all around us. He asked me to say a prayer for Thanksgiving."

Bill Dakota, who had been a friend of Nick Adams, used to call Hopper from Ohio and talk about their mutual obsession with James Dean. "His home was filled with Andy Warhol art, paintings and sculptures," Dakota wrote, recalling his visit to Taos to see Hopper. "On the other side of the ranch was a vast desert, and there wasn't one inch of space that wasn't covered with broken beer-bottle glass, and beer caps and cans. It was amazing, like there had been a continual party there for a hundred years, and maybe there had been. When the sun was shining on it, it was beautiful with the colored bottle glass glistening in the sun. Dennis' home was a commune, and several girls were there, cooking and cleaning his house. We had a spaghetti dinner. Nick Ray was wearing an eye patch and was walking around with a bottle of wine in his hand, smoking a joint and popping pills."

A drug-besotted Hopper got no closer to assembling a definitive version of his film after months of effort. One of the many pop-culture luminaries who visited the Mud Palace was Alejandro Jodorowsky, director of the cult favorite *El Topo*, who Hopper summoned to rescue him from his editing quandary. "In Taos," Jodorowsky recalled, "he had four or six editing machines and twelve editors working. At that time, he didn't know what to with *The Last Movie*. And I saw the material, I thought it was a fantastic story. And I said, 'I can help.' I was there for two days, and in two days, I edited the picture. I think I made it very good. I liked it. But when he went to show it to Hollywood, they didn't want it because by then, he was in conflict with them. Later, I think that Dennis Hopper decided that he couldn't use my edit because he needed to do it himself. And so he destroyed what I did, and I don't know what he did with it later.

"I never told that to anybody through the years, but I am sure that if, one day, they found my edit, it was fantastic. Because the material was fantastic. I took out everything that was too much like a love story or too much Marxist politics. For me, it was one of the greatest pictures I have ever seen. It was so beautiful, so different. I don't know what it is like now, how it has been edited, the final thing, I don't know if he conserved anything of mine. But it was a fantastic film. One thing I do remember from back then, though, was how strong the smell of Dennis Hopper's underarm perspiration was. It was so strong, and one day—he had I think ten women there—and I put everyone in a line in order for them to smell the perfume of Dennis Hopper. Because he never changed his shirt for days upon days. He smelled very strong. That I remember."

Hopper couldn't resist when Orson Welles called him away from his Moviola to participate in his film, *The Other Side of the Wind* (1972). In Hopper's mind, it was one genius meeting another. "I was in Taos," he said, "editing *The Last Movie*, and I got a call from Bert Schneider and Henry Jaglom that Orson Welles wanted to shoot some film with me. He was making a 16mm movie. I said, 'Wow, O.K.' So I flew in from New Mexico, got in around 5 o'clock in the afternoon, and Orson picked me up from the airport and drove me to his house in Beverly Hills."

Welles was making the film, about the last day in the life of legendary director Jake Hannaford (played by John Huston) in a piecemeal fashion. Whenever he could raise some money by doing a character part in a film or by filming a wine commercial, he would summon his actors and shoot part of his film. Welles had to work around the availability of his cast, whose personal and professional commitments prevented them from dropping everything the minute he called.

Welles came up with a clever way to get around this for the scene that Hopper participated in, which takes place at a party at Hannaford's house after a hurricane has knocked out the power. Standing in for Huston, Welles lit Hopper with a lantern against a black backdrop and read Hannaford's dialogue off-camera. Welles later repeated this with other young directors, including Henry Jaglom and Paul Mazursky.[8] He planned to cut the scenes together to give the illusion that the guests Hannaford was talking to were all sitting together at the same table.

"We shot from dark 'til dawn," Hopper said, "and he kept asking me questions about what I thought about directing, what I thought about this, what I thought about that. He got all these young Hollywood directors to come and do this. Y'know, I said to him, 'So you're going to play this part?' and he said, 'No, no I hate acting.' I said, 'You *hate* acting?' 'Yeah, I never liked acting. I never wanted to act. I'll get somebody else to play this part.' Yeah, he was incredible. He cooked me a spaghetti dinner. He cooked it, *and* he was running the camera, asking me all kinds of personal things, work things . . . just really an interesting evening. I'd met him before that, but this was a really intense—*more* than intense—night. After that, I went back to New Mexico to work on *The Last Movie* some more."

Hopper's affair with Michelle Phillips, who appears very briefly in *The Last Movie*, was another diversion from his effort to carve a visionary epic out of hundreds of feet of film. You couldn't blame Hopper for his infatuation with Phillips. Her ex-husband, John Phillips, described Michelle as "the quintessential California girl. She could look innocent, pouty, girlish, aloof, fiery." She was the prototypical hippie chick. For her part, Phillips said she was drawn to Hopper by "this Florence Nightingale instinct."

"I was so overloaded emotionally by this point in my life, I didn't know what I was doing," Phillips recalled. "Well, Dennis of course, feels that

---

[8] Excerpts from some of Welles' scenes with Hopper, Jaglom, and Mazursky can be viewed at YouTube at http://www.youtube.com/watch?v=rOVOXhvdKD4

everything he touches is quite magnificent. I got caught up with Dennis' energy, which is fantastic. Dennis is a very, very unusual man. You don't want to necessarily marry him. But you have to give him credit for being a really interesting and maniacal kind of guy."

After about eight weeks together, Hopper and Phillips, who was then going by her birth name, Holly Michelle Gilliam, decided to marry. Their marriage took place in Taos on Halloween, October 31, 1970. With two hundred guests in attendance, Hopper filled the room with candles diffused through paper bags and read to Michelle from his favorite text, *The Gospel of Thomas*. Stewart Stern, one of his wedding guests, said, "It was a whole mixed mystical thing. He read the whole marriage ceremony, and it was just craziness."

Hopper's marriage ended abruptly eight days later. Michelle Phillips fled back to John Phillips, to whom she tearfully related the details of her marital ordeal. She claimed that Hopper accused her of being a witch, handcuffed her twice to prevent her from escaping, and fired guns inside his house. On the morning of the eighth day of their marriage, Phillips grabbed her two-year-old daughter, Chynna, and slipped out of the house while Hopper slept. He pursued her to the airport, driving onto the runway in a fruitless attempt to stop her plane.

Phillips finally called Hopper from Nashville, where she was singing backup vocals for Leonard Cohen, a job that Hopper said he got her so she would have something to do during their marriage. She told him, "I'm not coming back. Music is my life." Hopper whined, "Well, what am I going to do? I love you. I need you. I've been fixing up the new house for you." She replied, "Have you ever thought about suicide?" Hopper paused for a moment and said, "No. Not really." And that was it. Ron Rosenbaum, who visited Hopper in Taos after his marital debacle, wrote, "an aura of romantic tragedy hung over Hopper's place when I was there."

In 2007, Phillips said that her marriage to Hopper was "excruciating." She recalled, "My father dragged me into his attorney's office and said, 'Men like that never change. File for divorce now. It'll be embarrassing for a few weeks, then it will be over.' It was embarrassing for more than a few weeks. Everybody had the same question: 'A divorce after eight days? What kind of tart are you?' " Phillips soon rebounded into the arms of Jack Nicholson and then Warren Beatty.

"Well," Hopper said of his marriage, "the first seven days were pretty good." "Hopper is . . . unconstrained on the subject of wife bashing,"

Ginny Dougary wrote in her 2004 interview with him. Responding to Dougary's mention of Michelle Phillip's allegation about Hopper's "unnatural sexual demands," a reference to handcuffs, he said, "Yeah, first of all, what handcuffs? This is Michelle . . . where did the handcuffs come from? I didn't handcuff her. I just punched her out! Harharharharharhar. I didn't beat any women up. I mean, I've done nothing beyond anything that they did to me. The point is that no one was ever truly hurt by me. And if there's any physical abuse by me, believe me it was after *days* of abuse by them (rueful laugh) so it doesn't really . . . I have no . . . kind of feeling of any kind of guilt about that. I wasn't handcuffing them and beating them to death or anything."

Stern, who arrived in Taos just in time to attend Hopper's wedding, was there to try and help him salvage his film. Stern's ego had been bruised when he read Brad Darrach's article and realized that Hopper had put aside Stern's screenplay in favor of his improvisatory ideas while shooting *The Last Movie*. "I began reading articles," he said, "interviews with Dennis in which he said there was no script, and the film was all his idea . . . that he didn't need a script. Suddenly, improvisation is better than literature." Stern wrote Hopper to tell him that was not an accurate representation.

Hopper later called Stern from Taos and said he was having trouble editing his film. Would he come and help? Stern and Hopper's agent spent about two days in Hopper's editing room viewing all the footage. "It took me two days just to look at the footage," Stern recalled. "Some of it was brilliant, and some was awful. But the end of the film was not there." Stern, who called Hopper "a really wonderful guy," sorrowfully concluded, "Dennis was marvelous during the scriptwriting phase. It was only when he started directing in Peru that he went crazy altogether."

"Mainly," Stern said, "what I felt was very disappointed, not only that he didn't use the scenes as they were written in the screenplay and that he chose to improvise with people who were not up to that kind of improvisation, but also that he hadn't shot scenes that were essential. Including the ending of the picture. Well, I strongly supported the idea of going back and shooting the scenes as written. He wouldn't do it."

At Hopper's invitation, Lawrence Schiller and L. M. Kit Carson followed him around for eighteen days in Taos and recorded his activities on film. The resulting documentary, *The American Dreamer*, is a collection of vignettes of Hopper being, well, Hopper. Originally intended to be exhibited on the college circuit as a companion piece to *The Last Movie*, *The American Dreamer* received few screenings and has acquired the reputation of an underground classic due to Hopper's supposedly outrageous behavior that Schiller caught on camera. (At the beginning of *The American Dreamer*, Hopper says that he welcomes the opportunity to lay his life bare in the film, whether people love him or hate him as a result. After early screenings of the film, he changed his mind. Lois Rudnick wrote that he blocked the film's distribution, though a soundtrack album was issued.)

The American Dreamer begins with Hopper, clad only in a bath towel, greeting Carson and Schiller at the front door of his L.A. home. They follow him as he gets back in the tub to resume washing his hair. Then Hopper arrives in Taos. At this point, the documentary becomes a series of cinematic non sequiturs. Hopper fires semiautomatic weapons in the desert. (He put a picture of FBI director J. Edgar Hoover on one of his targets, though it's not visible in the film.) Hopper makes a "far out" symbolic protest by stripping naked in a suburb of Los Alamos, where the scientists employed in developing nuclear weapons reside. Shaggy and heavily-bearded, he squats in the bushes, explaining that society makes him a criminal for smoking pot while it ignores the white-collar crimes perpetrated by the rest of a hypocritical nation. Hopper muses about his lonely childhood. He says, "I'd rather give head to a woman than fuck them . . . Basically, I think like a lesbian."

Hopper frolics with two girls in the tub. While the film shows a well-endowed nude woman sitting in a rocking chair, an off-camera Hopper philosophizes, "I don't believe in reading. By using your eyes and ears, you'll find everything there is," and blames Michelle Phillips for the failure of their marriage, alleging that she brought the handcuffs.

The film's pièce de résistance is Hopper's sensitivity encounter with an impromptu harem of twenty girls who Schiller and Carson imported from L.A. at his request. After taking their orders—one girl wants a joint, another an orange—Hopper drops trou to allow the girls to grope his ass. Then he teaches them the meaning of mutual trust by getting them to lift up one of the girls and hold her above their heads without dropping her. This surprisingly tame scene typifies this disappointing film, whose notoriety has been generated by its unavailability.

The American Dreamer devotes the least amount of its time to Hopper's work on *The Last Movie* or his experiences in Hollywood, which he barely mentions. Hopper is briefly shown at his editing console, where he quotes Jean-Luc Godard's adage, "A story should have a beginning, a middle, and an end . . . but not necessarily in that order," and says that editing a film is like "having a child and cutting its arms off—putting its eyes out." Hopper also compares himself to Orson Welles when he voices his concern that *The Last Movie* could derail his career in much the same way that the failure of *The Magnificent Ambersons* (1942) jinxed Welles'.

Hopper was conducting the sensitivity encounter captured in *The American Dreamer* when Ned Tanen paid him a visit to see how work on the film was going. "I walked in," he recalled, "and this enormous orgy was going on—I mean, full blown. Buttocks and boobs going in all directions. I went to Dennis and said, 'Can I talk to you?' Dennis was out of his bird, totally gone." Tanen politely asked Schiller to stop filming. When Schiller ignored Tanen's third request, Tanen grabbed his camera and tossed it out the window. Then he grabbed the much-bigger Schiller and said, "You fuck, I'll kill you fucker!" Hopper said, "Man, get me a camera! I want to shoot this!"

Schiller observed some of Hopper's meetings with the functionaries Universal dispatched to monitor his progress. "The encounters were very heated," he said. "He showed them just enough of the movie in just enough of the right way to keep them at bay and never, until the very end, the entire movie. But he didn't know the film was really going to work."

"I went to visit Dennis at his big house in Taos, New Mexico, where he was holed up doing the editing on his film," John Buck Wilkin recalled. "Problem was it was Crazy-ville. Mucho dopa, booze, a constant flow of freaks and hippies. Dennis shot a quarter of a million feet of film, a record at the time, and he was gonna edit it himself. There were telephone wars with Universal Pictures, dinners with LSD around a big table that resembled the Last Supper.

"Slow-motion train wreck, but it didn't matter. It was all cool. He bought the tiny local cinema on the main street in town and screened his 'director's cut' every night. Once, I saw a version that was six hours long. It was a smoke dream, a beautiful travelogue with a plot hidden somewhere, maybe on the cutting-room floor."

"We screened *The Last Movie* at the El Cortez Theatre in Ranchos off and on in 1970 and 1971," Bill Whaley recalled. "When I saw rough cuts anywhere from four to six hours long, I thought Dennis was going to be the next American Fellini. One Sunday, we watched *El Topo*'s American debut followed by four hours of *The Last Movie*, followed that evening by Fellini's *Satyricon* [1969]. In those days, film was king of the arts in America. My eyeballs, stimulated by too many images, continued spinning long after I went to sleep that evening."

In March 1971, *Los Angeles Times* writer Wayne Warga visited Hopper in Taos. "A smaller, more elegant house closer by is Hopper's permanent abode but just now, as though obliged to deny his own basic comforts, he is sleeping on a small bed in his cutting room," he reported. "The cutting room adjoins the main house and contains three Moviolas, hundreds of cans of film, a wash basin, work benches, and several horseshoes tacked on the wall. The beamed Vega ceiling has an Indian arrow stuck into it, a popular New Mexican tradition for safety and security.

"A five-minute drive away is Rancho Taos Theater, the town's only movie house. Hopper bought it, stuffed $11,000 worth of new equipment into it, and uses it during the day to look at his film. At night, the theater is open for business. Hopper initially offered the townspeople—predominantly Spanish—the films of Spain's Luis Buñuel. Business was rotten, and Hopper was disappointed. He then rented a Disney film and filled the theater nightly. He tells about the experience with a head-shaking irony, sorry that customers walked away from great art. He seldom looks at the film in the theater these days because he hasn't time. Instead he watches it on the Moviola in his cutting room. Though he is still in his early thirties, he looks a good deal older. His eyes are ringed red, and the strain clearly shows."

Hopper's appearance was the antithesis of a conventional Hollywood star's. He sported shoulder-length hair and a hermit's beard, and routinely wore a stuntman's macho work outfit of jeans, a denim jacket, and pointed boots. On one wrist, he wore a copper bracelet engraved with the name of Capt. John Hardy Jr., an American pilot held captive by the North Vietnamese.

Warga described Hopper's work regimen. Always accompanied by David Hopper, intern Todd Colombo, and former stuntman-turned-comedic sidekick Eddie Donno, Dennis spent from noon to 2 A.M. in the cutting room. Hopper broke for supper at 8:30, when he and about ten friends would sit around the long dining-room table, relax, and bring out the joints. After finishing editing for the night, Hopper would retire to his guesthouse to watch an old Errol Flynn movie on TV.

By the time Warga arrived, Hopper had spent nine months editing, had fallen five months behind schedule, and had reduced forty-eight hours of footage down to a five-and-a-half-hour version of his film, aiming for an eventual 120-minute cut. He told Warga that he owed Universal a cut of the film the previous October and said the studio was scared he didn't have a film there. "They didn't give me freedom," he said. "I took it. And they can take it back if they want."

Hopper complained about how slowly the editing progressed. He called the editing room a prison, telling Warga, "The mechanics of editing are slow. You see so little progress. You can work all day and not get a scene right. Editing is painful and slow. It's just not fun. It is, of course possible to get into it and not think of other things, but it isn't easy. You're easily distracted and can't have any people around. What I have to do is crawl into the Moviola and think only of the film. At times, it gets really difficult." Hopper promised Warga that he'd finish editing *The Last Movie* in two more months.

"Dennis was at a peak," David Hopper recalled. "He was at a creative peak in his life. But he was also, you know, he'd been divorced, he'd had trouble with women, he was doing a lot of booze, a lot of drugs. He had this seven-day marriage with Michelle Phillips, which kind of turned everything upside down." When Dennis Hopper finally got into the cutting room, he and his brother engaged in drug-fueled marathon editing sessions. "We drank Irish coffee, snorted cocaine, and smoked really good marijuana," David recalled. "We would work three days and three nights at a time."

"Dennis and I had got the film down to around two hours and ten minutes," David Berlatsky said. "When he got the call that they [Universal's executives] were coming out, he said, 'I want you to put back all those other scenes.' I said, 'Why do you want to do that, Dennis?' He said, 'Because I want them to see everything.' I said, 'Yeah, but it's gonna be three hours long.'

"After the screening, we were all gonna go back to the house, and the guys with the suits got in their car and said, 'Well, we'll meet you back at the house.' And we said, 'OK,' and they had a big dinner planned, and David went with them, and Dennis and I wound up staying at the bar, getting loaded, drinking beer and tequila. We got there very late, needless to say. There was no party. There was no dinner. The suits were, I guess pissed off or upset or something, because they left the next morning. I never did see them again. There was a lot of sadness, and there was a lot of depressed feelings about what to do with the picture."

The 108-minute cut of *The Last Movie* that Hopper finally settled on is, in the parlance of its day, a bummer. It's not hard to understand why audiences, critics, and Universal's brass hated it. *The Last Movie* is an enervating allegory of the West's corruption of the innocent Indians and a naïve indictment of the seductive, destructive influence of the violence in Hollywood films and American culture. Stylistically, *The Last Movie* is like the cemetery sequence in *Easy Rider* writ large. Taking Godard to heart, Hopper imposed a nonlinear structure on *The Last Movie,* which has a beginning, a middle, and an ending, but not in that order. The events in the film don't occur in chronological order, as we expect them to.

The Last Movie begins with a miserable, bloodied, and disoriented Kansas standing in church with the Indians at the start of their passion play. The film then switches to a scene of him riding his horse in the countryside while Kris Kristofferson sings "Me and Bobby McGee." Kansas rides into the Indian village, briefly disrupting the filming of the shootout that concludes the Western being directed by a cigar-chomping Sam Fuller. Hopper imported a number of his Hollywood chums to play the actors in the Western, including a bearded Peter Fonda, Dean Stockwell, Russ Tamblyn, Billy Gray, Jim Mitchum, John Phillip Law, and Severn Darden. Then Hopper wasted their talent, using them in the Western's climactic scenes, where he filmed them in long shots that left the actors unrecognizable.

Hopper mostly abandons the nonlinear structure after *The Last Movie's* first fifteen minutes, but still throws the audience into confusion by cutting in titles saying "Scene Missing" and fumbling simple plot elements. When Kansas rhapsodizes about moneymaking schemes to his sunbathing girlfriend, we see what looks like a swimming pool on the terrace below. Is it Kansas' fantasy or his girlfriend's? If it's real, where did he get the money to build it?

Playing Kansas, Hopper is almost a complete washout, playing a wan, uninteresting character, and only briefly showing a flash of his former boyish charm in the otherwise sordid scenes in the nightclub/whorehouse. Even Roy Engel and Rod Cameron, who plays Sheriff Pat Garrett in the Western and converses briefly with Kansas at the wrap party for the film's cast and crew, are warmer and more engaging than Hopper.

What finally sinks *The Last Movie* is Hopper's "far-out" ending. When the Indians shoot Kansas at the conclusion of their ceremony, he runs from them and falls to the ground like a baseball player sliding into base. Hopper steps out of character a moment later. He gets up, claps the dirt off his hands, and sticks his tongue out at the camera. Hopper repeats this scene several times, rubbing the viewer's nose in the revelation that Kansas' story is a fake Hollywood movie starring Dennis Hopper, just like the Western that Kansas worked on. (Mercifully, Hopper abandoned his idea of inserting footage from the films of Mae West and W. C. Fields into the end of *The Last Movie*.)

"Narrative evaporates with Kansas's death, and *The Last Movie* turns into a comic documentary of Hopper and his crew," the film critic J. Hoberman wrote. (Hoberman calls the film "The Lost Masterpiece.") "The death scene is played over and over, actors go out of character, the on-set photographer wanders on camera. This collapse of the fictional story line is superseded by the disintegration of cinematic representation. The movie loses sync, the sound of the camera intrudes, the editing dissolves into black leader, the emulsion is scratched. The shadows refuse to be anything more than shadows, leaving the bemused audience to its own devices. Kansas dies for America's sins, but when *The Last Movie* destroys itself, it is to liberate us all—or at least, make Hopper's point that, so far as the movies go, everyone is an Indian."

Hopper finally emerged from Taos after spending well over a year editing *The Last Movie*, ready to take his brainchild public with a schedule full of promotional activities and future film projects. ("It took us eighteen months," David Hopper claimed, "to edit the film.") On August 17, 1971, *Los Angeles Times'* columnist Joyce Haber reported, " 'Easy Rider's Dennis Hopper has shaved off his beard and is sporting a droopy mustache these days. His and Universal's 'Last Movie,' which Dennis directed on the grasslands of South America, will be screened at the Venice Film Festival on Aug. 29. After attending that one, Hopper hops onto the promotional bandwagon with interviews and personal appearances.

"Next, he reports to Mexico for his starring role in Fox's 'Dime Box.' Fox, in these hard times, is paying Hopper a whopping $400,000 salary, almost unheard of, plus a percentage of the profits. Next, Dennis hopes, will be 'The Holy Net' from a property he owns. Hopper wants to produce, direct, and star in the screenplay by Chilean director Alexandro [sic] Jodorowsky whose 'El Topo' ('The Mole') has been called a masterpiece.

He would costar with Dennis and Dennis' pal, Peter Fonda, who's another easy rider . . ."

In Venice, Hopper was approached with an offer to act in a film adaptation of William Burroughs' *Naked Lunch*. Back home, he was honored with an exhibition of three hundred of his photographs at the prestigious Corcoran Gallery of Art in Washington, D. C., and an exhibit of his personal art collection at the University of New Mexico in Albuquerque.

Universal's executives were horrified by *The Last Movie*. Ned Tanen screened the movie with Hopper and MCA founder Jules Stein, whose daughter was friends with Hopper. The cathedral hush when the lights went up was suddenly broken by the projectionist's review. "They sure named this movie right because this is gonna be the last movie this guy ever makes." When Lew Wasserman went to see the film, he thought that the projectionist had put on the wrong reel. "Well," he said, "it doesn't really matter which reel they put on because this is a piece of shit."

Universal opposed Hopper's plan to take his film to the Venice Film Festival and prevented him from entering it in the New York Film Festival. They grudgingly paid for his flight to Venice, but not for the rest of his cast, and had to be begged by Hopper to provide a paltry supply of publicity handouts for the press. "When it won a prize at Venice, they couldn't believe it," he told James Stevenson. "An executive said to me, 'We must have *bought* the prize for you.' But that prize was the only award given at Venice, and I won it, in competition with Kurosawa, Bergman, and a lot of others.[9]

"I don't respect anyone at Universal except Jules Stein, and he's not really in it anymore. Well, the movie's in their hands now, and their hands are full of blood. Corporate blood. I'm afraid it's like what one of the Universal executives said to me—'Art is only worth something if you're dead. We'll only make money on this picture if you die.' He was asking me to buy the film back. I said, 'Don't talk to me like that. You're talking to a paranoiac.' "

Universal wanted Hopper to make a linear film out of *The Last Movie* and have Kansas die at the end. Hopper refused to comply. Wasserman finally said, "O.K., if you're not going to reedit it, then we're going to distribute it for two weeks in New York, two weeks in L.A., and two days

---

[9] Hopper was wrong. *The Last Movie* was entered out of competition. The festival assigned no awards to films from 1969-1979.

in San Francisco, and then we'll shelve it." "I had final cut," Hopper said, "and cut my own throat."

"I would like to make other kinds of movies," he told writer Mark Goodman in 1978. "But until the world straightens up, I'm going to keep on making movies that torment the world, the same way the world torments me." "It was self-defeating," Hopper later admitted. "The thought was to deliberately alienate the audience, tell them they're idiots sitting there watching a movie. Every time I got them involved in the movie as a story, I'd come back and say, 'Ha. Ha. Ha. You're only watching a movie.' Which is not a very pleasant thing for an audience. I made fun of the audience, and I didn't end the picture with a dramatic ending."

Universal arranged a series of college screenings of *The Last Movie,* hoping that students would understand Hopper's film. Tanen and Hopper decided to have a firsthand look at their reaction to the film at a test screening held at the University of Iowa. Tanen said that Hopper was busy flushing drugs down the toilet before their flight landed. When Hopper stood up after the screening to take questions, students who were angry that he betrayed their expectations for another *Easy Rider* pelted him with improvised projectiles.

Hopper paused on his and Tanen's flight from the auditorium when a beautiful girl manning an old-fashioned popcorn machine called Hopper over and asked if he made the film. He said, "Why yes, my dear," whereupon she hauled off and punched him in the nose, drawing blood, and screamed "You sexist fucking pig" as he and Tanen beat a hasty retreat.

Hopper claimed that *The Last Movie* opened to packed houses in New York and Los Angeles, but the scathing reviews and bad word of mouth for the film quickly killed its initial success. Before *The Last Movie* was released, he told Dick Adler, "I expect everybody to feel that I'm going to fall on my butt with this picture. That's what I thought they would feel; they'd say 'Oh, *Easy Rider* was a fluke.' And a lot of publicity like that did come out while we were in Peru, especially around the time of the Academy Awards." Unfortunately, *The Last Movie's* failure confirmed the predictions of Hopper's enemies, who had their knives out for him.

The Last Movie opened on September 29, 1971, at New York's RKO 59th St. Twin Theater, where it broke the opening day's box-office record. Then the critics slaughtered it. *Time* magazine's Stefan Kanfer, who had been generous in his praise for *Easy Rider,* wrote, "That sound you hear is of checkbooks closing all over Hollywood. The books belong to the smart money; the reason for their action is *The Last Movie* by Dennis Hopper— the same Dennis Hopper who recently opened the checkbook, with *Easy Rider*. His directorial debut may have been adolescent; his second movie is puerile. Formless, artless, it is narcissistic but not introspective, psycho but not analytic—a shotgun wedding of R. D. Laing and the Late Show."

"One would have to be playing Judas to the public to advise anyone to go see *The Last Movie*," *The New Yorker*'s Pauline Kael wrote. "This knockabout tragedy is not a vision of the chaos in the world —not a *Weekend* [1967], not a *Shame* [1968], but a reflection of his own confusion. It's hysterical to blame the violence in the world on American movies. Hopper seems to have worked up a big head of steam about nothing; with all the horrors there are, he has cooked up fake ones. Hopper may have the makings of a movie (perhaps more than one), but he blew it in the editing room. If he was deliberate in not involving the audience, the audience that is not involved doesn't care whether he was deliberate or not. That there's method in the madness doesn't help. The editing supplies so little in the way of pace or rhythm that this movie performs the astounding feat of dying on the screen in the first few minutes, before the credits come on. The movie grinds to a painful halt right at the start; it is visually beautiful, but the editing is so self-destructive that it's as if Hopper slashed his own canvases."

In his exercise in special pleading for the film's merits, even film professor Foster Hirsch had to admit, "The curious problem with *The Last Movie* is that it is unlikely to speak directly or congenially to any particular audience. Its network of religious and literary symbols and its hectically nonlinear structure push the film altogether out of bounds for the mass popular audience, while its almost gleeful preoccupation with Pirandellian puzzles of appearance and reality and its studied concept of life imitating art are likely to seem undigested and sophomoric to informed audiences."

In an attempt to rescue *The Last Movie* from oblivion, Hopper threw himself into a series of college screenings and interviews with journalists willing to hear him defend his film. He appeared on Dick Cavett's show, where he denounced Universal Studios. Attempting to explain *The Last Movie* to reporter Winfred Blevins, Hopper maintained that its failure was not a reflection of its inherent invalidity. Instead, it demonstrated that American audiences lacked the sophistication to understand a work of art that was a comment on the artifice of movies and a critique of the American Dream. ("I don't like the American Dream," he said.)

Hopper admitted that *The Last Movie* angered and alienated the audience by cheating their conventional moviegoing expectations. "*The Last Movie* is a movie in a sense that the paintings of Pollack were paint," he told Blevins. "It's not about anything." "As I talked with Hopper," Blevins wrote, "I noticed that he wound up deflecting the knottier questions and reverting to campaign rhetoric in which he is the misunderstood artist and the audiences are the philistines. He didn't answer the questions. He didn't even absorb just what the questions were. He admits freely, even gladly, that his picture is not for large audiences. 'In Europe, they're far ahead of us in esthetics. They understand 'The Last Movie,' and they like it. Art has always been for an elite. Real art has never been popular, never will be.' Hopper seems to enjoy this notion, and to enjoy having to defend an unpopular film." Blevins noted that he "seems to take a sort of Harvard undergraduate pleasure in thumbing his nose" at conventional movie audiences.

The Hollywood Citizen News' Marilyn Beck wrote, "Universal's motive in exposing Dennis to a saturation publicity campaign? I suppose—and the studio won't deny it—that they are trying to capitalize on all the disastrous 'Last Movie' reviews, hoping audiences will want to see the film to see if it's really as awful as the press has said." "He was terribly tired during our meeting," Beck observed, "weary of having to defend his 'The Last Movie' to everyone, exhausted from the mental effort of explaining over and over and over exactly what it all meant, what he was trying to say in that epic."

"I had the temptation to just back away from it all, but I couldn't," Hopper told Beck. "I still haven't written the movie off—in spite of the American reviews. I believe in it—and hope it will grab a college audience. It's been no fun at all. I loved making personal appearances for *Easy Rider*. Peter Fonda and I must have hit ninety cities and everywhere everyone complimented us. It's a drag having to defend something you believe in, having to remind people it won an award at the Venice Film Festival."

Hopper finally had a glimmer of hope among all the depressing news about *The Last Movie*—he obtained funding for *The Second Chance* from Japan before *The Last Movie* was released and was writing its screenplay. He finally got a good excuse to quit flogging *The Last Movie*. A week after speaking to Marilyn Beck, Hopper headed to Durango, Mexico, to film *Dime Box*, a Western comedy that was released as *Kid Blue* (1973). "It's apple pie and ho ho ho," he told Beck. "And the public will probably eat it up." (They didn't.)

Hopper's reign as Hollywood's latest wunderkind lasted a little more than two years. "It was a moment," he later said, "but it was a brief moment." "Making things is agony," he told Brad Darrach. "I hate to make movies. But I've got to do it. It justifies my existence. If I couldn't, I'd destroy myself." Now box-office poison, Hopper was deprived of his raison d'être. He wouldn't get to direct a major studio film again until 1987, but his self-destruction was just beginning.

· 7 ·

LOST IN TAOS

Finished in Hollywood, Dennis Hopper retreats to Taos and into himself, filling his empty days with booze and drugs. He manages to work occasionally in independent and European films.

"People come into Taos, have a flat tire, and stay the rest of their lives—or they can't wait to get out. It drives some people crazy."

Dennis Hopper, 1971

"Deprived of meaningful work, men and women lose their reason for existence; they go stark, raving mad."

Fyodor Dostoevsky

*B*EFORE DEPARTING TO Mexico for the production of *Kid Blue*, Dennis Hopper returned to Taos to perform some much needed housecleaning. By November 1971, he realized that his dream of a filmmaking commune had failed. "I just threw a lot of people out of the house in the last couple of days," he told James Stevenson. "There were a lot of freeloaders. When I was there for a year editing the movie, we had it all together, but when I left and came back again, it had become a playground. People were very undisciplined. Originally, I hoped everybody would get involved in community business, but there's no work there, no jobs, nothing for them to do. The communes are full, and most of them have to work very hard just to get the food."

In *Kid Blue*, Hopper plays Bickford Waner, a notorious train robber better known as Kid Blue. Following a bungled robbery, Waner tries settling down to a straight life in the border town of Dime Box, Texas, where he works at a variety of menial jobs, including one at the Great American Ceramic Novelty Company where he plants little American flags in kitschy ashtrays (the film's satire of capitalist enterprise). Harassed by the local sheriff (Ben Johnson) and caught two-timing his girlfriend with the seductive wife of a friend, Blue decides to heist the ceramics factory's payroll and escape in the wooden flying machine of a local preacher (Peter Boyle) who touts the benefits of peyote, hemp, and alcohol.

Shock Cinema's Steven Puchalski calls *Kid Blue* a "wrongheaded mix of comedy, crime, and dipsy dramatics . . . When it comes to the sub-genre of Pothead Westerns, this is at the top of a very short list." *Kid Blue's* screenwriter, Edwin "Bud" Shrake, was a novelist who decided he could write a screenplay after seeing *Butch Cassidy and the Sundance Kid* (1969). "In New York publishing, if you write a novel that takes place before 1900, in Texas, and there's a horse, then they call it a Western," he said.

It's too bad that the behind-the-scenes shenanigans during *Kid Blue's* production weren't filmed, instead of what Puchalski calls a "four-star mess" that wastes the talents of a good cast that includes Warren Oates, Ralph Waite, Lee Purcell, and Janice Rule. The fun began shortly after Hopper arrived in Chupaderos, the little town near Durango where *Kid Blue* was filmed. Bud Shrake and a cadre of friends had created Mad Dog Productions, printing up cards that were given to members of their private club of wild men. Hopper was soon inducted into their ranks.

In 1985, Bud Shrake told the *Austin Chronicle's* Louis Black, "Anyway, when we drove down through Mexico and arrived in Durango, first thing that happened was we walked into Dennis Hopper's rented mansion, and there were a whole bunch of people who had taken acid and were carrying guns. And so we thought, well, this is where we belong. This is going to be an adventure. And it definitely was. A life-changing adventure." In an interesting echo of Hopper's *The Last Movie*, Shrake found it surreal, especially while he was on acid, to see the Western town he imagined erected in Chupaderos, complete with a ceramics factory outfitted with working kilns. When the film company left, the locals, having no need for ashtrays, demolished the buildings for firewood.

"About our first week down there, at a Saturday night party at Marvin's house, Dennis came in with this really horrified look on his face," Shrake recalled. "He was really shaken to his boots. He came in and called

Frawley, Marvin, and me and said he had to talk to us immediately in the bedroom.[10] It was really important. We went in the bedroom, we sat down, and Dennis said, 'Look, you guys, I know the movie's already rolling, all this money has been invested, and all you guys are counting heavily on me, but I just can't help it. I've got to get out of here. Got to leave. If you guys have any sense, you'll pack up and leave, too. You'll be out of Mexico by tomorrow morning.'

"We said: '*What*?! What on earth is going on?' Dennis said: 'The revolution has broken out. There's gunfire in the streets. The streets out there are mayhem. I almost didn't get here alive. It's total panic and chaos and hysteria out there right now. People are getting killed right and left. The fucking noise, it's like World War II out there.'

"We weren't sure what to make of all this. But finally, we got to the bottom of it. What had happened is that Dennis had taken acid and on his way over to Marvin's house and had stopped at a carnival. He came away from that carnival, with all the shooting galleries and things—Mexican carnivals are weird anyway—convinced that he had wandered into the Mexican revolution. The next morning after we got all that straightened out, we went ahead with the shooting."

Whatever chances *Kid Blue* had were undermined halfway through shooting when a new regime took control of 20th Century-Fox. "There was such a vast animosity built up against Dennis Hopper in Hollywood that people were just waiting to tear his ass off because he had made saps out of all the old guard with *Easy Rider*," Shrake recalled. "Not only had he made saps out of them, he had gloated over it. If *The Last Movie* had come and been good, then they would have all had to keep their mouths shut. But when it wasn't good, then they all started running around saying who was the asshole and the fool who paid Dennis Hopper $300,000 or whatever it was to star in this movie. They all started blaming each other."

Kid Blue finally premiered at the New York Film Festival in late September 1973 and was given a desultory release by 20th Century-Fox, who were happy to cast off the orphaned film. " 'Kid Blue' is the sort of movie that is likely to sound a lot better than it really is," *The New York Times'* Vincent Canby wrote. "Yet 'Kid Blue' is never very funny or provocative. It tries too hard. It's too insistent. Like the performance of Mr. Hopper (who is getting a bit long in the tooth to play naifs with much conviction), 'Kid

---

[10] Producer Marvin Schwartz and director James Frawley.

Dennis Hopper as Lorenzo, with Roxanne Haug, in San Diego's Old Globe Theatre's 1954 production of *The Merchant of Venice*. (Old Globe)

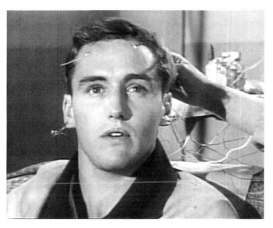

Hopper's performance as a teenage epileptic in "Boy in the Storm," an episode of the TV series *Medic*, won him a contract with Warner Bros. in January 1955.

Hopper and Evelynne Eaton in *Medic*.

Hopper in his uncredited first film role in *I Died a Thousand Times*.

Hopper, second from left, played a gang member named Goon in *Rebel Without a Cause*.

(Left to Right) Corey Allen, Hopper, and James Dean in costume tests for *Rebel* (Hopper's friend, Nick Adams, is at the upper left in the background.)

Hopper, Natalie Wood, and James Dean in *Rebel Without a Cause*.

During a break in filming *Rebel Without a Cause* at the Griffith Observatory, Hopper reads from Stanislavski's *An Actor Prepares*, the bible of Method acting.

(Left to right) Dennis Hopper, Susan Strasberg, and Steffi Sidney at the Chateau Marmont Hotel.

Hopper as Jordan Benedict III, the son of Leslie Benedict (Elizabeth Taylor) and Bick Benedict (Rock Hudson) in *Giant*.

Hopper, Taylor, and Hudson in *Giant*.

A Warner Bros. publicity portrait of Dennis Hopper.

Dennis Hopper and Natalie Wood attend the Los Angeles premiere of *Giant* on Oct. 17, 1956.

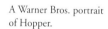
A Warner Bros. portrait of Hopper.

After *Giant*, Warner Bros. didn't seem to know what to do with Hopper. They cast him as Napoleon in *The Story of Mankind* (Marie Windsor at left).

(L-R) Olive Sturgess, Cloris Leachman, and Dennis Hopper in a production of Thornton Wilder's play, *The Skin of Our Teeth*, which opened at the La Jolla Playhouse on June 23, 1958.

Linda Lawson and Hopper in writer-director Curtis Harrington's *Night Tide*.

Peter Fonda and Dennis Hopper in Roger Corman's *The Trip*. The second unit scenes Hopper directed convinced Fonda to hire him to direct *Easy Rider*.

Billy (Dennis Hopper), George Hanson (Jack Nicholson), and Wyatt (Peter Fonda) react to bigoted patrons in a Louisiana diner in *Easy Rider*.

Peter Fonda has a good laugh with Dennis Hopper while filming *Easy Rider*.

Hopper directs *Easy Rider*. Cinematographer László Kovács is behind the camera.

Wyatt, aka Captain America (Peter Fonda) and Billy (Dennis Hopper) in *Easy Rider*, which Hopper intended to be a time capsule of late '60s America.

As Kansas, the stuntman who stays behind in a Peruvian village after a Hollywood film crew leaves, in *The Last Movie*, Hopper's disastrous follow-up to *Easy Rider*.

Dennis Hopper directing *The Last Movie*.

Kansas (Hopper) and the village priest (Thomas Milian) in *The Last Movie*.

Michelle Philips poses for a photo memorializing her infamous eight-day marriage to Dennis Hopper. The writing behind her reads: "TO MY DARLING DENNIS IN MEMORY OF EIGHT GLORIOUS DAYS OF MARITAL BLISS LOVE, MICHELLE."

Dennis Hopper (left) meets Nicholas Ray at the Broome County airport in Binghamton, New York in the fall of 1971. Ray invited Hopper to be a guest lecturer to his film students at Harpur College. (Photo by Mark Goldstein)

Warren Oates and Hopper in *Kid Blue*.

"Stand and deliver, sir!"
As legendary Australian
bushranger Daniel Morgan
in *Mad Dog Morgan*.

Hopper and his friend, Dean Stockwell in director Henry Jaglom's anti-Vietnam film
Tracks, which was released only briefly in 1979. "The only thing Hollywood wanted
less than a Vietnam War movie was one with Dennis Hopper in it," Jaglom said.

Hopper's mugshots when he
was arrested in Taos, N.M. in
July 1975. "He would be in
jail every couple of months or
so for something, and usually
something violent and out of
control," his brother, David
Hopper said.

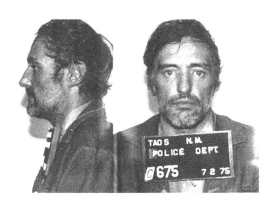

As the frazzled
photographer in
Apocalypse Now.

Bruno Ganz (left) and
Dennis Hopper in
The American Friend.

As gas-huffing psycho Frank
Booth, with Isabella Rossellini in
Blue Velvet, Hopper's spectacular
comeback role.

Gene Hackman (left) and Hopper in *Hoosiers*. Hopper received an Academy Award nomination for playing Wilbur "Shooter" Flatch, the alcoholic father of a high school basketball player.

Kiefer Sutherland (left) and Hopper in *Flashback*. Hopper played Huey Walker, a hippie fugitive from the '60s who surrenders to a conservative FBI agent played by Sutherland.

Hopper as King Koopa in *Super Mario Bros.*, one of his least favorite films.

Hopper played mad bomber Howard Payne in *Speed*, the most commercially successful film of his career.

Hopper played the Deacon, the over-the-top villain in *Waterworld*.

The amazingly youthful-looking Hopper was 59 when he appeared on the March 28, 1996 edition of Charlie Rose's TV talk show to promote his film *Carried Away*, where he played a repressed rural farmer who has a liberating fling with a 17-year-old girl.

Dennis Hopper and his new bride, Victoria Duffy, after their wedding at Boston's Old South Church on April 16, 1996. (Photograph by Mark Garfinkel)

Hopper discusses his role in *Rebel Without a Cause* on a 2001 BBC documentary about the film.

Hopper (right) played poet George O'Hearn, the best friend and confidant of professor David Kepesh (Ben Kingsley) in 2008's *Elegy*. Hopper said it was the first good role he'd gotten in ten years.

Hopper played Death, who is pursuing a photographer (German rock musician Campino, right) in Wim Wender's *Palermo Shooting*.

Blue' is a heavily mannered work, with little or no sense of the spontaneous gaiety that one got from time to time in Eliot Silverstein's 'Cat Ballou.'
'Kid Blue' is a well-meaning, liberal, anti-fascist Western, dressed up with
some good performances by Peter Boyle, Lee Purcell and Janice Rule. But
it's not a very good movie."

Demonstrating the variability of critics, *Time*'s Jay Cocks wrote, "*Kid
Blue* is a quirkish, laid-back, jolly film . . . Bickford, as dexterously played
by Hopper, shows signs occasionally of becoming a kind of surrogate
James Dean, a prairie rebel without a cause. But Hopper is an actor of
quick cunning, and he manages to get the movie back on course whenever
it tends to become a little sentimental about the lot of the misunderstood
loner. He has the uncanny ability to transform himself instantly from a
ravaged outcast into a kid in a cowboy outfit on his way to First Commu-
nion. Mellow and good-humored and not entirely serious about itself, *Kid
Blue* shows it is still possible to bring a newer, fresher, more contemporary
tone to the western while still honoring what is best and strongest in the
traditional form."

Cocks was one of *Kid Blue*'s few supporters. The moviegoing public
ignored the film, which disappeared into limbo until reappearing on cable
TV a few years before Hopper's death. *Kid Blue* would be Hopper's last
role in a major studio film until *Apocalypse Now* (1979), which Hopper
filmed in 1976. Hopper returned from shooting *Kid Blue* to Taos and the
Mud Palace, now quietly bereft of the frantic activity that filled it when he
edited *The Last Movie*.

After *The Last Movie*, Hollywood and Hopper were united only by their
mutual contempt. As far as the Hollywood community was concerned,
Hopper had fallen off the face of the Earth, and he did nothing to remind
them otherwise. Hopper later recognized that exiling himself from Hollywood was a mistake. He said, "I should have said 'O.K., I'm going back
to Los Angeles, like a normal person and say I'm going to make movies,
it's not the end of my career. I should have come back to Los Angeles and
made myself visible.' "

In Hopper's absence, stories about his outlandish behavior circulated to
his detriment, even though plenty of people in Hollywood were consum-
ing as much alcohol and drugs as he was. "I didn't come back and fight,"
he said. "I went to Europe and became an Ernest Hemingway expatriate,
and then I went to New Mexico, and I never came back and faced up to
the fact that I *could* live here."

"I said, 'Well, they should be bringing me movies, I mean I'm, you know, a genius,' " he later told a reporter. "I mean, I'd bought a theater where I had synch sound, I had all my editing equipment, a big complex where everybody could live. I had no product, I had nothing to make. I didn't go back to Hollywood. And I'd get crazier and crazier because I wasn't working, and I wasn't doing the things I wanted."

"I would work, I'd go off and act, I'd do films in Europe and all over the place, but I, you know, I never went back. Saying, 'They've got it against me.' And it was all bull. Because it was me. It wasn't Hollywood. O.K.? It was me. It wasn't the industry. The industry was going along doing fine. It was me."

During his visit with Hopper in 1971, Wayne Warga observed, "On a wall in a corner of the room someone has tacked up a Peanuts poster of Lucy Van Pelt, fists clenched, angrily yelling, 'I don't want any downs. I just want my ups and ups and ups!' " Now it mocked his recent dreams of an unending series of projects, vessels for his boundless creative talent. The failure of *The Last Movie* killed any chance Hopper had of making *Me and Bobby McGee*, *Second Chance*, or *The Holy Mountain*. For Hopper, there would now be plenty of downs.

One of Hopper's few ups was a new relationship with Daria Halprin, then enjoying a brief celebrity after appearing in Michelangelo Antonioni's *Zabriskie Point* (1970), where she could be seen rolling around naked in Death Valley with costar Mark Frechette. Antonioni had seen *Revolution*, a 1968 documentary about the hippie movement in Haight-Ashbury, which showed a nude Halprin reciting poetry. Attracted to what he called her "bratty, free, earth-child quality," he offered the Berkeley anthropology major the female lead in his film. Halprin immediately dropped out of school to star in Antonioni's film.

After making *Zabriskie Point*, Frechette and Halprin joined the astrological commune of harmonica player-turned-LSD guru Mel Lyman in Boston, to whom they donated their earnings from *Zabriskie Point*. Halprin eventually fled the commune, returning to her home in San Francisco in 1971 before meeting Hopper. Like Michelle Phillips, Halprin was another hippie free spirit who was drawn to Hopper's image as a counterculture visionary.

Halprin's appeal to Hopper, or anyone with eyes, was expressed by Frechette's reaction on first seeing her. "The first time I met her," he recalled, "she walks into the MGM office, gorgeous, tan, real long hair, shoulder pads—she must have had shoulder pads . . . I'd never seen shoulders on a chick like that, she sits down on a chair and rolls her eyes at me . . . looks over at me and says, 'I feel like I should rush into your arms and kiss you, but I'm really knocked out from the flight down.' "

Halprin made her second and last commercial film, *The Jerusalem File* (1972), before deciding to marry Hopper. They wed in San Francisco on May 13, 1972, in a ceremony that integrated hippie style into the traditional Jewish ritual. "A trumpet blast," *Time* reported, "and the 55 guests climbed to their seats on a hillside overlooking San Francisco Bay near the home of Bride Daria Halprim [sic], who starred in *Zabriskie Point*. The music began as a composition for synthesizer, ram's horn, flute, and a Yemenite trumpet recorded especially for the wedding. Then, to the melody of a flute song, Daria, in a purple velvet Navajo dress, walked to the bridal canopy designed by her father, Landscape Architect Lawrence Halprin. After the ceremonial crushing of the wineglass under Hopper's foot, everybody danced a hora to the traditional Hava Nagila—arranged for guitar and Congo drum."

Hopper was again desperate for work, as he'd been after losing his battle of wills with Henry Hathaway. Only now, things were even worse. There were no offers for work forthcoming from Hollywood or any other domestic quarter, not even the occasional TV guest appearance or a role in some exploitation film. Hopper hoped that producers would come to Taos to utilize the editing equipment he installed in his home and the movie theater he acquired for postproduction, but there was no reason for them to leave the comfort of Hollywood and the facilities already available there.

In its October 1972 issue, *Oui* magazine ran a small story about Hopper, titled "Dennis Hopper: American Failure." "I got nothing coming up," he said. "He was smiling," *Oui* reported, "but there was more than a touch of bitterness to the joke." Hopper, who was promoting the rerelease of *Easy Rider*, said, "I got nothing, man: I'm a failure. I'm out on the street again."

Hopper's old passions no longer seemed to satisfy his creative drive, and there was nothing else for him to do to kill time. He stopped painting and writing poetry after the Bel Air fire, especially after he turned to photography. But he put away his Nikon when he began directing *Easy Rider*. In 2006, he said, "I didn't take any photographs because I was acting and directing a movie, and I didn't know what to do with the camera. I'd really been taking photographs hoping I was going to direct all these years. Making movies was photography. Movies encompassed all the art that I knew."

Hopper had staked everything on the success of *The Last Movie*, which he hoped would be the beginning of a series of films he would direct and later edit at the Mud Palace, where he would be the paterfamilias of a filmmakers' collective. "Anyway, I didn't succeed at that," he said. "It was a great period of loss."

Though he had become unemployable, Hopper's ambition was as grand as ever. He often spent evenings hanging out in Taos' bars with his friends, fellow Hollywood refugees Dean Stockwell and Russ Tamblyn, whose careers were in about as bad a shape as his. "I remember one night in Taos with Dean and Dennis drinking, and as usual, I usually would just pass out," Russ Tamblyn said. "I just couldn't take it anymore, and Dean and Dennis stayed up. Dennis was . . . God, he was just ranting and raving that night about how much he wanted to direct, and he was weeping at one point that he wanted to direct, and he was just screaming it out, and I just remember in a half of a daze, trying to go to sleep, saying, 'God, give him a film to direct, please!' "

"He was trying all the time," David Hopper remembered. "He was on the phone all the time, trying to get a job. He got more and more depressed, because the same guys that he had made millions of dollars wouldn't give him a job." "I think it was really desperate, desperate times," Hopper later said. "I wasn't really creating. I wasn't really doing anything creative most of the time I was there . . . with the big exception of *The Last Movie*, but after that . . . it was just a lot of bravado, and there wasn't anything behind it, because I didn't have any work, so I find that rather pathetic."

Instead, Hopper turned inward, using drugs to compensate for his forced idleness and creative frustration. "The stories of my drinking, my escapades with guns, my drug dealing and on and on and on go on until the point where Dennis Hopper feels sorrier and sorrier and sorrier for himself," he said. "And he gets farther and farther into addiction and alcoholism."

Hopper rationalized his addiction with the conviction that great art can only result through the derangement of the artist's senses with drugs. Blake's "Those who restrain desire, do so because theirs is weak enough to be restrained" and "The road of excess leads to the palace of wisdom" expressed Hopper's credo. "You see," he later said, "I didn't relate any of the terrible things that happened to me to my using. I thought drinking and drugging were all part of being a tragic artist. No one, certainly none of my friends, even tried to point it out to me. I think they were afraid to. I didn't think I was destroying myself. I had blackouts, of course, and bad trips. But I had great plans. I was going to write a book titled *How to Use Drugs to Improve Your Life*."

Daria Halprin gave birth to a daughter, Ruthanna, in 1974, but divorced Hopper in 1976. "It was during our marriage that Dennis had some of his most difficult years with alcoholism and drug abuse," she said. "Our marriage suffered tremendously." The changes that alcohol and drugs produced in Hopper's already fractious personality, including violent outbursts and his habit of firing guns indoors, finally drove away Halprin, who feared for herself and their daughter in much the same way that Brooke Hayward had.

"He was all Billy [*Easy Rider*] and Frank [*Blue Velvet*] with a dash of Jordan Benedict III [*Giant*]," recalled Bill Whaley, who saw a lot of Hopper during his years in Taos. "But neither you nor his ex-wives and girlfriends or those of us who lived in Taos knew who was going to show up for the party."

Hopper later described a typical day in his life in the mid-to-late '70s. "A lot of sex. A lot of coke. But mainly alcohol. I took a lot of drugs, mainly cocaine, but the problem was drink. I would take cocaine, lines as long as your arm, every five minutes, just so I could carry on drinking. There wasn't a day when I was sober. It was relentless. Part of it was that I was so driven. That driven to genius thing. But a lot of what was going on in my life was just . . . dark."

"My experience in Taos was not a pleasant one," Hopper told his friend Lisa Law in 1989. "I wasn't allowed to create anymore because of *The Last Movie* . . . I became an over-abuser. I am an over-achiever, and I was not allowed to create, so that was the end of my world as far as I was concerned. I felt used and put-upon, and everybody who came to Taos wanted to stay at Dennis Hopper's, and I finally had to move out of my own house, I felt so used. I didn't enjoy the '70s. I went off the Europe for two years, to Mexico City for two years. I didn't have a pleasant time. And coming back to Taos was not pleasant for me."

Hopper's erratic behavior led to several arrests for what his brother

David called "violent infractions." "He would be in jail every couple of months or so for something, and usually something violent and out of control," David Hopper said. Most of these incidents were only reported in Taos' press, but on August 14, 1975, the Hollywood trade paper *Variety* reported on two such episodes. On August 4, Hopper was arrested in Taos' town plaza for carrying a .357 Magnum revolver. On August 11, Hopper pleaded guilty to one count of disorderly conduct, two counts of verbal assault, one count of possession of a deadly weapon, and a further count of resisting arrest. He was fined $300 by Judge Joseph Montoya, who reminded Hopper that he had fined him $300 only a month before for leaving the scene of a car accident without reporting it. *Variety* reported that Dean Stockwell (who they called "Dennis Stockwell") was also fined $50 for failing to report the accident.

"I was surprised that he went that far, that his art didn't kick into gear and save him, as it had with *Easy Rider*," Peter Fonda said. "Every time he'd get really despaired and more and more crazed, the art of making the movie and the art of the movie itself would carry him over into his next inspirational mode." Hopper's momentary salvation from the madness born of isolation, inactivity, and drugs came through the acting work he was offered by filmmakers who were too far outside the Hollywood system to be put off by the failure of *The Last Movie* or Hopper's bad reputation.

In 1974, Hopper flew to Australia to star in director Philippe Mora's *Mad Dog Morgan*, a dramatization of a series of episodes in the life of Daniel Morgan, an Irishman who went to Australia in their gold rush of the 1850s, only to become a legendary bushranger (highwayman). "Well," Mora recalled, "Dennis arrived in Australia, and he was arrested almost immediately over some sort of incident in a bar (laughs). The reality was that Dennis was incredibly famous as Mr. Counterculture and Mr. Easy Rider. He made *Easy Rider*, and it was still playing in cinemas at this point. So every drug dealer and hippie in Australia gravitated to Dennis. They're almost parachuting in to meet Dennis Hopper (laughs).

"And Dennis, this is one reason why I'd rather emphasize his art rather than his personal habits. For me as a director, as soon as I said 'action,' he was totally locked in, and even if I knew he'd had a few things or whatever, he was incredible on things like continuity. I said to him, 'How do you do that? How do you remember all that?' And he said, 'Well, I signed a contract with Warner Bros. when I was eighteen, and they put us through the equivalent of Marine training on technique.' So he was like clock-work, no matter what. I let him improvise a lot, which I enjoyed, because he'd always come up with great things. For me, it was a joy to work with someone who was that good. He told me a lot about James Dean, because he obviously loved James Dean, and could actually do this uncanny thing where he'd actually turn into James Dean, his face would change, and it was just really weird. That's how well he knew him. "

Hopper told Mora that he and Dean smoked pot on the set of *Rebel Without a Cause,* wearing brown paper grocery bags on their heads to mask the smell of the smoke. Then they washed out their mouths with Pine Sol to disguise the odor. "Dennis told me this story a couple of times, once drifting uncannily into the face and emotions of James Dean, in tears for some reason," Mora recalled. "He recalled other random specific details: They used to heat food in cans together, no saucepans."

Hopper was a cornucopia of craziness while shooting *Mad Dog Morgan.* He immediately developed an acute fear of actor Frank Thring, whose character in the film wants to make a tobacco pouch out of Morgan's scro-tum. "Inflamed by Stanislavski, rum, beer, and psychedelics, Hopper hid in fear whenever Thring arrived," Mora recalled. Mora was woken early one morning by the sound of yodeling coming from Hopper's room. "I'd entered Hopper's room and found him drinking Old Spice aftershave with the ultra-Gonzo end of the crew," Mora wrote. " 'We ran out of beer,' said effects man Monty Fieguth, guiltily. 'Want some?' "

The makeup department complained to Mora that Hopper smelled so bad they couldn't approach him. When Mora told him, Hopper shouted, "I'm Mad Dog, man, I don't wash." Mora pointed out that the Mur-ray River, where Morgan had washed, stood behind Hopper. "Far out, man," Hopper shouted as he jumped in, fully clothed. Sometimes Hopper refused to do a second take for Mora until Mora reassured him that he was a true artist and friend.

When he asked Hopper for a second take of a scene where he had been very emotional, Hopper yelled, "I am not a fucking puppet, man, where you just say do it again!" "Remembrances of some work demons emerged," Mora wrote. "I guess some of his bad Hollywood memories were flashing back. We walked into the bush while the perplexed crew waited. Dennis asked me if I loved him. I said, 'I love you, man.' He said, 'I love you, man, let's shoot this fucker.'

"His *joie de vivre* was infectious. I have a fond memory of dawn breaking over the bush as I walked with Dennis to the set. 'Hey man, we are making a MOVIE! Now that is GREAT!' he exclaimed as he danced an Irish jig. Not having seen anyone consume this amount of alcohol and assorted drugs, I convinced myself that Hopper would die before completion and shipwreck my career. Weeks later, I was exhausted, Hopper was healthy, and I was saying goodbye with monumental sincerity."

Hopper celebrated the completion of his final scene in the film, where he rides his horse across the Murray River from New South Wales to Victoria, by going to Daniel Morgan's grave, which is in the Chinese section of a cemetery next to a urinal. In front of Philippe Mora's mother, Mirka Mora, Hopper chug-a-lugged a fifth of 151-proof O.P. rum and poured another onto Morgan's grave before he started tearing up the cemetery. Then Hopper jumped in a car with a bunch of people and roared off with the police on his tail.

After they arrested Hopper, they hooked him up to an instrument that read his blood alcohol level. By all rights, Hopper should have died from alcohol poisoning. "They pronounced me dead," he recalled. "Then they took me in front of a judge, who pronounced that you'll never be able to drive a car in Victoria or be a passenger in a car in Victoria, and you're going to leave now. So I was put on the airplane and shipped out."

"To spell it out," Mora wrote, "Dennis Hopper is a great artist. He is a true free spirit."

Producer Jeremy Thomas sold the film to an American distributor at the Cannes Film Festival, but was disheartened by the film's U.S. release. "I remember going to the opening in New York, and there were three people in the cinema in Times Square," he recalled. "I hated the poster, in fact I have got the poster on my wall It is such a bad poster that I kept it as an example of a shocking piece of artwork. It was very sad. It was a cold, freezing night. I went down there with a couple of people, and there was nobody in the cinema. It was a sad beginning, but you know, it is a school of hard knocks, and it is the best way to start."

Mad Dog Morgan was just one of many instances where Hopper invested himself fully in a performance, hoping it would bring him renewed attention and more work, only for it to go largely unrecognized. In his review of *Mad Dog Morgan*, Jay Cocks devoted only one sentence to Hopper's performance. "Dennis Hopper, in full woolly cry, does rather well as Morgan."

Mad Dog Morgan never really succeeds in its attempt to portray Morgan as a noble savage who is corrupted by the abuse from his sadistic jailers and fellow prisoners and the hounding of vengeful law-enforcement officials who regard him as subhuman. Morgan's haphazard, wandering campaign of revenge against them, where he victimizes the innocent as well as the guilty, loses him our sympathy. While Hopper certainly enjoys himself playing Daniel Morgan, pulling his twin pistols and announcing, "Stand and deliver, sir!" in his inconsistent Irish brogue, he is saddled with trying to animate an undeveloped character. Like other Australian exploitation films of this period, *Mad Dog Morgan* offers some violence and the barest hint of sex, but the repetitive nature of Morgan's exploits don't leave the viewer much by the end of the film.

Reviewers of the recent Troma DVD of *Mad Dog Morgan* hold the film in higher regard than this author. "Dennis Hopper gives one of his strongest performances here," Tom Becker wrote. "While the character is all over the place, Hopper is decidedly focused, almost laser-like. His Irish accent is a bit disconcerting at times, but he offers a complete, and very physical, characterization." "Hopper plays Mad Dog Morgan as a misfit weirdo, a man more at home under the stars than under a roof," Keith Phipps wrote. "While Hopper probably couldn't have played him any other way at that stage of his career, the interpretation fits perfectly into the world Mora creates, one in which a cruel conspiracy of bad luck and inequity easily explains the character's retreat into madness."

Bill Gibron's review suggests how closely Hopper's performance emerged from his own personality. "Hopper plays Morgan as a man possessed by inner demons, a kind of insular anger that arrives in spurts, not drones. When he's subdued, Morgan is a man of quiet dignity and gentle compassion. But instead of going buck wild, Hopper channels his rage into discernible, distinct points. He hardly ever loses control, but when he does, the passionate side of his personality is soon to follow." ("He had a kind of unusual aura, a special energy, a charge around him," Philippe Mora wrote. "There was a creative anger, pounded into a special charm.")

In 1975, Hopper leapt at the opportunity to play the lead role in *Tracks* (1979), writer-director Henry Jaglom's film about a Vietnam veteran, Sgt. Jack Falen (Hopper), who descends into madness over the course of a train journey he takes to escort the coffin of his fallen comrade to his funeral.

(Jaglom had originally written *Tracks* for Jack Nicholson to star in and Bob Rafelson to direct.)

During the trip, the socially uncomfortable, tightly-wound Falen encounters some offbeat passengers and retreats to his compartment, where he listens to oddly anachronistic cassette recordings of rah-rah World War II-era songs like Frank Loesser's "Praise the Lord and Pass the Ammunition." Falen connects with a hip passenger (Dean Stockwell) who may be a deserter, who disappears at the hands of authorities during a stop. While on a picnic, Falen drives away the young woman (Taryn Power, the daughter of Tyrone Power and Linda Christian) passenger he yearns for with his physical advances. Falen grows delusional as the trip wears on. He strides naked through the cars one night and has a hallucination where he witnesses the other men on the train rape the girl he longs for.

At his buddy's gravesite, Falen, the funeral's only attendee, asks officials from the funeral home to leave for an hour. After they depart, he becomes enraged, yelling, "You want to see 'Nam? You want to see 'Nam, you motherfuckers? I'll show you 'Nam!" He opens the casket to reveal a cache of weapons. Falen dons a helmet, grabs two M-16s, and emerges from the grave as sound effects of battle are heard on the soundtrack. The film ends on a freeze frame of Falen moving forward to attack.

Jaglom shot the film on trains running between Los Angeles and San Diego, often without official permission. Jaglom's actors improvised their dialogue and behavior from ideas for scenes that he had written on index cards, a situation that suited Hopper's acting temperament. Hopper was his usual self during production, especially when it came time to shoot his final scene. Hopper took one look at the several pages of a graveside speech that Jaglom wrote for Falen and said, "Fuck It," tore up the pages, and spontaneously emoted Falen's rant. Jaglom agreed with Hopper's instincts, saying that Falen would not be an articulate man given to speeches.

Hopper was also his usual self in less desirable ways. According to Peter Biskind, "He once wrestled filmmaker Henry Jaglom to the ground, threatening to stab him in the neck with a broken ketchup bottle after Jaglom laughingly turned down his offer of a threesome with himself and a female companion." After finishing his last scene, Hopper said, "Now you won't give a shit about me because you don't need me anymore." Jaglom said, "The poor guy had many demons."

Tracks is a film that polarizes audience reaction. You either love it or hate it. *Tracks* earned some strongly positive reviews, including fulsome praise from Anais Nin, who wrote, "Henry Jaglom takes us, with *Tracks,* deep into the heart of the American Nightmare. A terrifying masterpiece." But *Tracks* played only at film festivals and art houses until 1979, when it received a brief theatrical release. "The only thing Hollywood wanted less than a Vietnam War movie was one with Dennis Hopper in it," Jaglom said.

Sheila O'Malley, one of *Track's* rare defenders, wrote, "Nothing happens in the movie for 95 percent of it, and for me, the ending—where something suddenly happens, with a bang—doesn't quite work, but it's forgivable. I understand the impulse, and I understand the point Jaglom is trying to make. It just doesn't work for me because I was so riveted by the rest of the film, its aimlessness, its weird observations of human behavior, and its beauty."

Reviewing the DVD of *Tracks,* David Nusair wrote, "Although *Tracks* starts out well enough—Hopper is initially quite effective as the shell-shocked veteran, while filmmaker Henry Jaglom's idiosyncratic sense of style mirrors the off-kilter subject matter—the film becomes increasingly aimless and flat-out weird as it progresses and essentially mutates into a completely unwatchable piece of work. The baffling conclusion certainly doesn't help matters nor does the inclusion of some seriously dated elements (i.e. what is the deal with that score?)"

"There's no plot, no coherent theme, no character development, no heart or soul," Michael Rankins wrote. "Jaglom clearly wants us to empathize with his hapless protagonist, but how can we, since there's no opportunity or context for us to see Jack Falen as a real human being, and therefore gain compassion for him? Jack, like all of the film's elements—human, locomotive, and otherwise—is merely a device Jaglom uses to hammer the viewer with his muddled message; something about how awful it was when American fighting men came home from Indochina in the 1960s and '70s—but it's buried under one trowel scoop after another of semiotic cement."

After making *Tracks,* Hopper moved to Paris. "I'd been trying to get films together to direct, but it'd been all dead ends in Paris," he said. "I used to resent the fact that all of these guys like Ernest Hemingway went to Europe. I always put them down. But there I was, suddenly in France. I was trying to get some sort of a deal, but nothing worked out, and as that went on for a couple of years, I got deeper into drinking."

Hopper was in Brussels in August 1976, acting in the Belgian-French production *Couleur Chaire* (*Flesh Color*). (*Couleur Chaire,* which also features Bianca Jagger, was shown at the Cannes Film Festival in 1978, but was never released, and remains one of Hopper's most elusive films.) Hopper's agent, Edith Cottrell (Cottrell's husband, Pierre, produced *Couleur Chaire*), who also represented director Wim Wenders, said, "There's somebody who'd like to meet you. He's a young German director. Do you mind having dinner with him?" "I mean, anything to get me out of the state I was in was a good thing," Hopper said. "We had some nice dinners and some wonderful talk."

Wenders was looking for an actor to play the sociopathic character Tom Ripley in *The American Friend,* his film adaptation of Patricia Highsmith's novel *Ripley's Game.* "As much as I was fascinated by the character of Ripley as Patricia Highsmith had invented him, I had no idea of how to portray him," he said. "He's really a very amoral person, a very strange character. I just needed somebody to fill that hole in my imagination how to portray an evil person."

When Wenders spoke to John Cassavetes about playing Ripley, Cassavetes recommended Dennis Hopper for the role. When Wenders asked Pierre Cottrell if he knew someone who could put him in touch with Hopper, Cottrell mentioned that his wife represented him. Wenders knew he'd found the right actor to embody the enigmatic Ripley the moment that Hopper entered Closerie des Lilas (Pleasure Garden of the Lilacs), the beautiful and historic restaurant in Paris where they met. Wenders said, "I'm not gifted in showing bad guys, and when I met Dennis, I knew I had found the one guy who could truly incorporate everything in Ripley's character in his persona."

In *The American Friend,* Hopper plays Tom Ripley, an American expatriate living in Hamburg, whose latest criminal scheme involves selling the "recently discovered" paintings of Derwatt (Nicholas Ray), an American painter who has faked his death with Ripley's help to increase the value of the new paintings he creates in seclusion. When a picture framer named Zimmerman (Bruno Ganz) questions the provenance of a Derwatt at an auction and refuses to shake Ripley's hand, Ripley manipulates him into killing the rival gangsters of his French associate, Minot (Gérard Blain). After Minot sends Zimmerman to a French doctor for a fake diagnosis, he becomes convinced that his chronic leukemia has become fatal. Ripley persuades Zimmerman to kill the gangsters for the payoff that he will leave his wife and child. Ripley and Zimmerman develop a strange kind of bond during their criminal misadventures until Zimmerman finally abandons a muttering Ripley on a wintry beach, only to die on his way back home.

While Wenders was still preparing *The American Friend* for production, Hopper encountered Fred Roos, the coproducer of *Apocalypse Now*, in France. Impressed by Hopper's performance in *Tracks*, Roos offered him a role in *Apocalypse Now* and the chance to work with Marlon Brando, the last surviving member of the Method's Holy Trinity of Brando, Clift, and Dean. "I was not in the greatest shape as far as my career was concerned," Hopper recalled. "It was delightful to hear that I was going to do anything, anywhere."

Though Hopper needed the work badly, he insisted on one condition: that he would have at least one line with Brando. His request was relayed to *Apocalypse Now*'s writer-director, Francis Ford Coppola. Hopper was finishing work on *Couleur Chaire* on August 23 when Robert Raison announced that Coppola had cast him in what *Variety* called a "costar" role in *Apocalypse Now*, which he had already started shooting in the Philippines.

Hopper arrived in Manila on September 2, 1976, accompanied by his latest girlfriend, photographer and writer Caterine Milinaire, who was assigned by the Sygma photo agency to cover him while *Apocalypse Now* was filmed. The daughter of the duchess of Bedford and a former fashion editor at *Vogue*, Milinaire had more than a tempestuous relationship with Hopper.

Robert Mapplethorpe became privy to an unpleasant incident involving the couple when he took a commercial assignment to photograph Hopper. Mapplethorpe, Hopper, and Milinaire went out to a discotheque one evening where they drank and danced until 3 A.M. "Caterine and Dennis were really affectionate toward each other, and it was nice being around them," Mapplethorpe told his biographer, Patricia Morrisroe.

Mapplethorpe arrived at their apartment at 10 A.M., only to find the door ajar. After buzzing several times, he let himself in, shocked by what he saw. In a drunken rage, Hopper had beat Milinaire up and laid waste to the apartment, smashing lamps, mirrors and furniture, and ripping pictures off the wall. Hopper sat in a chair, holding his head in his hands, unresponsive to Mapplethorpe's inquiries about Milinaire.

Mapplethorpe found her whimpering in the bathroom. She begged him, "Get me out of here!" He took Milinaire to her uncle's apartment where she reluctantly allowed Mapplethorpe to photograph her bloodied face as a record of her battering. "In the mid-seventies, people were going to such extremes in their behavior," Milinaire said. "There were so many drugs and so much sex that everybody was pushed to the limit. It seemed fitting that Robert would be there when Dennis and I collided. I can't think of any other photographer who would have captured that moment any better."

Hopper and Milinaire's troubled relationship continued in the Philippines. One evening, crew members saw Hopper hurl a flaming mattress out of his hotel room window into the river below. Hoping to create a romantic mood, he and Milinaire had decorated their room with candles. One of the candles set the curtains on fire. At least one crew member recalls hearing a gunshot during this episode and seeing Milinaire show up the next day sporting a black eye.

Tony Dingman, who was assigned by the film company to look after Hopper, said, "Dennis, Tom Shaw, and I would drink a lot of rum, and two or three times a day, we'd go down to the 'Samurai' massage parlor in the hotel precinct. When they'd finished giving you a massage, they always offered a 'sensation,' and we never refused that!" Another crew member recalled that you could get a hand job for $5 at the massage parlor.

One time, Dingman saved Hopper from the wrath of some soldiers who he had thrown a bottle at. As they cocked their weapons in Hopper's direction, Dingman pretended to fight with him, dragging him away from the area. "When Dennis arrived," Dingman said, "he brought so much laughter and excitement." The Ifugao tribesmen who played the Montagnards in *Apocalypse Now* honored Brando and Coppola as subchiefs, but constructed a special vest made of pine needles for Hopper.

Hopper arrived at the idyllic tourist locale of Pagsanjan, about sixty miles south of Manila, in the midst of *Apocalypse Now*'s production, which had been plagued with difficulties. The Philippines were vulnerable to extreme weather conditions, like Typhoon Olga, which hit the islands on May 21, 1976, washing out a small fortune sunk into sets and equipment. Filming often had to stop when the Philippine army, which lent their helicopters to the filmmakers, took them back to fight communist rebels. Coppola dismissed actor Harvey Keitel after a week of shooting, and his replacement, Martin Sheen, suffered a near-fatal heart attack on March 5, 1977. Shooting without a finished screenplay, and vacillating on creative decisions, Francis Ford Coppola staked his salvation on Marlon Brando's performance as Colonel Kurtz, the renegade Green Beret who Captain Willard (Martin Sheen) has been tasked to "terminate with extreme prejudice."

Before Brando's arrival, Coppola had cast Hopper as a character that was the antithesis of the pixilated photographer he ended up playing in the finished film. "I was there for four or five months," Hopper told Alex Simon. "When I arrived I was signed to play a CIA agent. There was no script. So I started out in a clean uniform being told by Francis [Coppola] that I was going to be second-in-charge to Marlon Brando's army he had in the jungle. I was with these guys about three weeks, and we were training with these Green Beret guys who'd just gotten out of Vietnam, playing war games. We had mortars that we'd play with that were full of powder, and if you got any of the powder on you, that meant you were dead. We had all these war toys we'd play with at night. We'd be assigned to hold a bridge. Would they be coming by the sea? Would they be coming through the jungle? We'd play these incredible war games and just had a ball. We had 250 native Filipinos who they'd brought down from the rice paddies to be my soldiers. They'd never been defeated by the Japanese—they'd never been defeated by anybody. They came down and built the village I moved into where the temple was. So, anyway, I ended up looking more native."

Hopper was no longer playing Daniel Morgan, but he still refused to shower, skipping the scheduled trips the cast and crew took to the hotel to clean up. Doug Claybourne, one of the few Vietnam veterans working on the film, said, "Dennis was known at that time for never taking a shower. You didn't want to stand too close to him."

Hopper's main motivation now was to feed his drug habit. Coppola approached Hopper during a scene and asked, "What can I do to help you play this role?" Dennis said, "About an ounce of cocaine." Coproducer Gray Frederickson said that Hopper was gently crazed, just like his on-screen character. "That's the way he was, on and off camera. But he was fun, and everybody loved him. There wasn't an edge to his craziness at all. Actually, he's a lot more serious and less friendly now that he's not so crazy."

An illustrative example of Hopper's mental state took place when Coppola asked Hopper why he hadn't learned any of his script after five days.

Talking to Coppola, Hopper removed his sunglasses and examined them, saying, "These glasses, I can't see anything through them. But, you know, every crack represents a life I've saved (laughs)."

"Doing *Apocalypse Now* was sheer insanity," he later said. "But it was mostly good insanity. I had a lot of people around me who were just as crazy as I was. But it wasn't all fun. The character you see up there on the screen, that was my state of mind at the time. It was Francis Ford Coppola's state of mind, too, because he was losing everything, his whole life was disappearing down the pipe. Doing that film was like fighting a war for him, and we all got swept up in the madness of battle. I think a lot of us left an awful lot of brain cells back in the Philippines."

Hopper even picked up a disciple during production. Laurence Fishburne (billed in the film's credits as "Larry Fishburne") was only fourteen when he lied about his age to get the role of a crew member on the Navy patrol boat that transports Willard to Kurtz's compound. "All of his performance was improvisational," he said of Hopper. "It was stunning, the stream of consciousness coming out of him. I was just a kid, fifteen years old, but I was blown away by his ability. He didn't pay much attention to me, but I shadowed him for a while because I thought, 'Here's a guy who's free, here's a guy who's really free.' "

Brando's arrival to the set only threw Coppola's plans into further disarray. Coppola had envisioned Kurtz as "a character of a monumental nature who is struggling with the extremities of his soul and is struggling with them on such a level that you are in awe of it." Coppola had not been able to create that monumental character in his unfinished screenplay and relied on Brando to bring Kurtz forth from the wellspring of his creative imagination.

Brando, who coped with boredom by eating, had gained a great deal of weight since Coppola directed him in *The Godfather* (1972). There was now no way that he could play the lean, active Green Beret called for in Coppola's screenplay. Embarrassed to be seen in his bloated condition, Brando spent five days in his trailer until Coppola finally coaxed him to emerge. To disguise Brando's bulk, he resorted to filming him clad in a black poncho in indirect lighting or only in closeups.

It was impossible for Brando, whose interest in acting was now purely financial, to create the depths of Kurtz's character that Coppola needed to animate his film. Brando candidly admitted this after he finished his scenes in the picture. When Coppola realized he'd forgotten to get a closeup of Brando as Kurtz speaking the lines "The horror, the horror," he sent a functionary after Brando, who was in his hotel room, preparing to leave. Asked to film the added scene, Brando demanded an extra $75,000, saying, "I'm in the Marlon Brando business. I sell Marlon Brando." Then again, no other actor could have done what Coppola required. Only inspired writing could have saved *Apocalypse Now*, and Coppola had failed to come up with any.

Dennis Hopper's inauspicious introduction to Brando came when he sat down to the dinner table just as an upset Coppola told Brando, "What do you mean, you haven't read the book?" a reference to Conrad's novella *Heart of Darkness*, the basis for Coppola's screenplay. Coppola had been on Brando's case all day on the subject of his unpreparedness. Hopper told TV interviewer Bob Costas, "I say to Brando, sitting across from him at dinner, 'I bet you haven't read the book,' and he thinks I'm talking about *Heart of Darkness*, but I don't know this at the time. And I'm about to take out the book [a red, pocket-sized Green Beret manual Hopper stashed in his boot], when he gets up, and he's says, 'I don't have to listen to this. I don't have to take this,' and he's screaming and yelling, 'Why do I have to hear it from him? I have to hear it from this punk?' And he's screaming and yelling at Francis, and he storms out of the house.

"So, I take this very personally and start getting in my cups and doing a few other things that we have plenty of down there, and we go into a boxing match, some bantamweights, Philippine bantamweights, who're really good, and they're going to put on a fight that night in Brando's honor, so I go there and I sit behind Brando and I start doin' numbers on him at the boxing match. And then we go to see the *Seven Samurai* [1954] in a movie theater, and I'm sitting then again behind him, and I get up at one point, and I say, 'There's an actor in here that said of a dead friend of mine 'that he wore his last year of Levis, drove his last year of motorcycle, and did his last year of bongo drums,' and I sure would like a piece of his ass.[11] In film, on film, [Hopper gestured with his raised fists, as if pummeling Brando] bah bah bah bah bah bah bah.'

"And I storm out and stagger into some motorcycle and fall over into some bushes or something." Philippe Mora later asked Brando about his experiences with Hopper. Brando said, "What an asshole. He had just shot

---

[11] Asked to comment on James Dean after Dean's first film, *East of Eden* (1955), was released, Marlon Brando said, "Mr. Dean appears to be wearing my last year's wardrobe and using my last year's talent."

a movie in Australia and landed in the Philippines acting like a crazy dog. I was talking privately to Francis, and he interrupted. I told Francis I did not want to see Hopper again or I was outta there."

Coppola shut down production the next day while he and Brando went off on a river excursion on Brando's houseboat, leaving a cast and crew of nine hundred people sitting around on their hands while the meter ticked on Brando's million dollar-a-week salary. *Apocalypse Now* could have been retitled *Waiting for Brando*. Hopper liked to believe Coppola spent the time reading *Heart of Darkness* aloud to Brando. A week later, Coppola and Brando returned from their retreat with a script they had cobbled together. Coppola also gave Brando a tape deck to record his improvisations, which he then culled for Brando's dialogue.

Coppola told Hopper, "We've read the book. We've decided that you're going to be the character of this photojournalist who is sort of mad. He has all of these bags of cameras, but he doesn't really know how to use them." So Hopper said, "You're talking about [P. D.] Ouspensky's tarot-card fool. Ouspensky wrote these tarot cards, but he never visualized them. The fool is the one who knows all of the secret wonders of the world, but can't remember where they are or how to use them." That was the image that Hopper used to guide his performance. Then Brando laid down the law. He said, "I'll work with him [Hopper], but you do your scenes first, and I'll come and listen to you, and we'll never be on the set together."

Coppola made Hopper's character the film's comedy relief, a "foil and a fool to Brando's king," as he wrote in a memo. He festooned Hopper with cameras and film cans slung around his neck, but withheld film from him, worried that his photos of the production might be leaked to the press. In 1978, anticipating *Apocalypse Now*'s release, Hopper boasted, "It's going to be mind-shattering because Brando and I go toe-to-toe for fifteen rounds, and you know what? I think I took the gorilla in Manila! I never had the chance to go the distance with a great actor on an equal footing. But this time, I did, and I think I got him."

That was a figment of Hopper's imagination. Hopper and Brando never performed a single scene together, though Coppola made it appear that they did. After Brando's edict to keep Hopper out of his sight, Coppola cut all but one of their scenes together from the script and reduced their remaining scene to a series of two-shots, which he filmed on alternate evenings.

First, Coppola worked with Brando, recording his performance. Then he played the tape of Brando's previous night's session and guided Hopper's response. One night, a former baseball player threw bananas at Hopper. When Hopper asked why, Coppola said, "Marlon called you a whimpering dog last night and threw bananas at you." In the film, Hopper is explaining Kurtz's philosophy to Willard when Kurtz says "Dog!" and throws a melon in Hopper's direction.

Hopper's quirky whims tested Coppola's patience, which had nearly reached the breaking point before he arrived. "Yes, he offended Marlon, who would not shoot any scenes with him," Coppola said. "I used doubles. Also every time I asked him to say 'Hiroshima mon amour' in dialogue he would say 'Nagasaki mon amour.'" The following exchange took place after an exasperated Coppola spent an entire day shooting thirty-seven takes of the scene where Hopper meets Willard's boat:

Coppola: "For God sakes, we've done thirty-seven takes, and you've done them all your way! Would you just do one for me, Hopper, could you do one for me!"

Hopper: "For Christ sake, Francis. I shot *Easy Rider* for $340,000 . . . look at you sittin' in that chair! I could've made *Easy Rider* five times with the fucking film you've lost here. All right, I'll do one for you!"

Hopper proved he was worth the trouble with his performance of a rambling speech to a caged Willard, incorporating fragments of Kipling's poem "If," a particular favorite of Hopper's.

Photojournalist: "Hey, man, you don't talk to the Colonel. You listen to him. The man's enlarged my mind. He's a poet warrior in the classic sense. I mean sometimes he'll . . . uh . . . well, you'll say 'hello' to him, right? And he'll just walk right by you. He won't even notice you. And suddenly he'll grab you, and he'll throw you in a corner, and he'll say, 'Do you know that 'if' is the middle word in life? If you can keep your head when all about you are losing theirs and blaming it on you, if you can trust yourself when all men doubt you' . . . I mean I'm . . . no, I can't . . . I'm a little man, I'm a little man. He's . . . he's a great man! I should have been a pair of ragged claws scuttling across floors of silent seas . . ."

Dennis Hopper's performance is one of the best things in *Apocalypse Now*, briefly energizing the lugubrious, anticlimactic section featuring Marlon

Brando. Hopper's performances before *Apocalypse Now* were always distinguished by his interesting upper-body language. When Hopper becomes emphatic, he'll typically stretch out one arm and point his finger, a behavior that might have been a carryover from his boxing days, when he would throw a jab at an opponent or use his outstretched arm to fend him off. Whenever Hopper becomes pensive, he touches his fingertips lightly to his face or mouth, appearing tentative.

By the time he made *Apocalypse Now*, Hopper was gesticulating wildly. In an interview that was filmed on location, Hopper kept snapping his fingers just to bring his wandering mind back to the reality of the moment. "Sometimes he was just so wired and so out there, his mind couldn't track what few little tasks we were asking him," Coppola recalled. "When he drank and did these things, he was just a nonstop, manic monologue all the time." It served Hopper's performance as the rambling photographer perfectly.

Hopper finished his work in *Apocalypse Now* on Saturday, November 6, 1976, and became afflicted with the same separation anxiety he experienced on the last day of filming *Night Tide*. He refused to accept that *Apocalypse Now* was over for him. Hopper said, "It's like some films, no matter how big they are or successful they are, or how small they are and unsuccessful they are, some of them are life experiences that cannot be duplicated in any way, and *Apocalypse Now* was one of the great life experiences."

Hopper and Coppola celebrated by getting drunk at the director's house. Hopper attached himself to Coppola, endlessly prolonging his farewell. "Dennis was pretty drunk and in no mood to leave," Eleanor Coppola wrote in her diary. Hopper was already days overdue for his arrival in Hamburg, where he was scheduled to begin making Wim Wenders' *The American Friend*.

Francis Ford Coppola finally found a way to get rid of Hopper. Coppola said, "Dennis, pick anyplace in the world, you'll be the star of the next movie I make. The deal is, I promise I won't think about what the movie is going to be before we start. We'll just make it, we'll make it real fast, in three weeks, and it will be terrific. Pick a place." Hopper finally chose San Francisco, where Daria Halprin and his daughter lived. Coppola said, "O.K., that's the story, that's where the story is. We'll do it." After another half-hour of hugs and farewells, Hopper was hustled into a car with Caterine Milinaire and dispatched to the airport.

As he anxiously awaited Hopper's arrival in Hamburg, Wenders began to fear the worst, worrying if the rumors about Hopper he'd heard were true. "When we first met in Paris, Dennis was sort of relaxed, and I just imagined him exactly like this to be Ripley," Wenders said in 2002 when he and Hopper shared their recollections of filming *The American Friend* for the DVD commentary. "And then I didn't see you for almost for half a year, or nine months. And I just knew he was out there in the Philippines." Wenders was appalled by Hopper's appearance when he stumbled off the plane, stoned out of his mind. Hopper arrived just as he looked and smelled while playing the photographer in *Apocalypse Now*.

"I remember coming back from *Apocalypse*, I was a mess," he said. "I was full of jungle sores, as I remember, and everything else. I flew from the Philippines directly to Hamburg, and I got off the plane and remember you gave me a haircut." "And then he came off the plane from the Philippines, and he was in combat outfit," Wenders said. Hopper came in his wardrobe from *Apocalypse Now*, the cameras dangling around his neck, exactly the outfit that he wore in the movie.

"But I was pretty out of it," he said. "I'd gotten into my part." Wenders told Hopper, "You were in character, and it wasn't Ripley. And I remember you did have these terrible sores, open wounds on your legs, because you'd slept in the jungle all the time. We took you to the specialist for these jungle diseases in the university at Hamburg." "I'd been staying in the village with the Ifugao headhunters, at this village that they built there," Hopper said. "I'd been living next to the pharmacy actually in the village, but I guess I didn't give 'em enough time to take care of me."

Wim Wenders found Hopper totally impossible to work with at the beginning of filming. "Dennis was reckless at the time," Wenders recalled. "He was lethal, suicidal. He took every drug in the book." "My life was a mess at that time," Hopper admitted. Wenders said, "You were waking up passed out on the floor a lot of the time in that rooming house we were in." "I remember waking up one morning," Hopper said. "I was wearing a lampshade over my head, and then you stepped over and said, 'Time to go to work.'" Wenders finally confronted Hopper, asking him, "Are you gonna die tomorrow, or are you gonna become an actor?" "I told him that either we'd get someone else or he'd have to prove to me that he was the great actor that I knew he was," Wenders said. Hopper pulled himself together and chose the latter.

Although Bruno Ganz and Dennis Hopper were in awe of each other's performances, they clashed over their contrary approaches to acting. "We were both working from different areas, but we were both getting the same results in a way," Hopper said. "He was using everything sort of externally, very intellectually, and I was trying to use everything emotionally." "Bruno came always the evening before, and he wanted to discuss the scene, and he wanted to discuss every word of the dialogue," Wenders said. "For Dennis, it was enough to just get to know the scene five minutes before we were to shoot it."

Ganz and Hopper got into a fistfight several days into filming. "I think we got drunk and had a fistfight, and then it was all over," Hopper said. "I just had to stop that day's shooting because all of a sudden, these two were crawling on the floor hitting each other, and that was the end of it that day," Wenders recalled. "And I just remembered that somehow, they escaped together, and the next morning, they came back, and from then on, it was just paradise to work with both of them." "After our initial punch out and then drunk out and passed out together arm in arm, I think we were O.K. the next day to go through it," Hopper said.

"After Dennis and Bruno had their night out together, from the next day on, Bruno never wanted to discuss the movie," Wenders recalled. "He said, 'We do it when were shooting.' And Dennis started to come in the evening, wanted to have his pages and discuss the scene. And Bruno was all relaxed about it, 'No, no, I do it on the fly.' So they really assimilated a lot of each other's approaches. And it was just a pleasure to work with the two of them. And I think the way the film evolved and the way the Ripley character really became so real was also because the two of you really got so close on it."

After a rocky beginning, Wenders and Hopper got along swimmingly, ending up close friends by the time filming ended. "He had an incredible presence," Wenders said of Hopper. Wenders coaxed a skilled performance from Hopper, who shed his frenetic mannerisms from *Apocalypse Now* to return to the attractive naturalism of his earliest performances. In *Out of the Past: Adventures in Film Noir*, Barry Gifford appreciated Hopper's performance. "Hopper doing a bizarre impression of William S. Burroughs when he helps Ganz out by murdering a guy on a train. One of his best scenes takes place in a state of drugged-out, self-absorption one night, snapping photos of himself like masturbating, passing out in a delirious semi-nightmare." That scene, where Ripley lies on his pool table, crying as the photos ejected from his Polaroid SX-70 cascade on him, was just one of the moments that resulted from the structured improvisation Wenders gave Hopper the freedom to indulge in.

Wenders cleverly incorporated Hopper's mannerisms and interests into his characterization of Tom Ripley, creating a resonance with Hopper's own personality. Ripley is an art hustler who decorates his empty villa with an illuminated Canada Dry sign, a jukebox, and a pool table. He eats cornflakes, dresses in denim, wears cowboy boots and a cowboy hat, even indoors (just like Hopper), and drives a vintage white Ford Thunderbird convertible. Wenders even has an amused Derwatt tweak Ripley, asking him, "You'll wear that hat in Hamburg?"

Hopper's Ripley is a displaced, lonely, secretive man who uses a hand-held cassette recorder to tape himself saying, "It's December 6, 1976. There's nothing to fear but fear itself. I know less and less about who I am or who anybody else is," which he later plays back to himself while sitting in his car. (Wenders asked Hopper, "What is the hardest thing for an actor to play?" Hopper said, "Being alone." Wenders then eliminated the part of Ripley's housekeeper.) Hopper even had a bit of fun spoofing *Easy Rider* in *The American Friend.* In one scene, Ripley, clad in mechanic's overalls, gets out of bed and looks out his balcony window. He says, "Even this river, this river reminds me of another river." He walks out on his balcony and plays a recording of himself singing "The Ballad of Easy Rider" in a gently mocking tone.

More an homage to the moody visual atmosphere and moral ambiguity of the characters inhabiting America noirs of the '40s and '50s than a straight-up thriller, *The American Friend* disappointed many viewer's expectations. "This movie seems to confuse people," Barry Gifford wrote. "They find it flawed, verbose, prolix, boring. The real dramatic life of this movie is in the undertow . . ." Though audiences didn't flock to the *The American Friend,* Wenders managed one considerable achievement. He finally elicited some kind words for Dennis Hopper from Vincent Canby, who wrote that Ripley was "the first decent role that Mr. Hopper has had in years. *The American Friend . . .* is enigmatic if one insists on simple logic, which is not something that is terribly rare in movies, even bad ones." "It is fascinating, if you take it on its own terms," Canby wrote, though he felt that Nicholas Ray and Samuel Fuller's cameo performances were distractions.

Dennis Hopper continued traveling the globe, going wherever his next job took him. He left West Germany for Spain, where he appeared in director Silvio Narizzano's *Bloodbath* (1979) (a.k.a. *Las Flores Del Vicio,* a.k.a. *The Sky is Falling*) about a group of burned-out expatriates living in a coastal village who fall victim to a band of Mansonesque hippies. (*Bloodbath* was filmed in the Spanish coastal town of Mojácar, an artists' colony favored by American and British expats where Narizanno resided.)

You have to rely on resources like Michael Weldon's *Psychotronic Video Guide* for information on this bizarre footnote to Hopper's career. Weldon wrote, "Dennis Hopper is Chicken, a grisly-looking junkie poet who hallucinates a lot and has nightmares, religious visions, and frequent disturbing childhood flashbacks." A ten-minute excerpt from *Bloodbath* posted on YouTube should certainly disabuse anyone's fantasies that *Bloodbath* is a lost gem worth reviving. When Chicken's black girlfriend comes home to discover that he has just mainlined heroin, he mutters, "Nothing is real. Everything is permitted." (That could have been Hopper's tag line in the '70s.)

He pushes a broken eggshell in her face, calls her "nigger" and "pickaninny," and makes her sing "Shortnin' Bread." Then Chicken runs outside where he has a vision of his mother singing a religious hymn about being washed in the blood of a lamb. Narizanno not only exploited Hopper's off-screen reputation for its similarity to Chicken's behavior, he also cast faded starlet Carroll Baker as Treasure, an alcoholic ex-star who keeps waiting for the call from Hollywood that will never come.

A resident of Mojácar who blogs as "Rambeau," wrote the following after Hopper's death: "He was working in a film in Mojácar once, called *The Sky is Falling*, which was directed by a local resident called Silvio Narizanno (*Georgie* [sic] *Girl*), who lived with Win Wells (who cowrote the film and acted in it) in the Moño Alto in the pueblo. It wasn't much of a film (to be kind) even though I made my cinematic debut in it. My dad took a strong dislike to Mr. Hopper, fresh from his hit with *Easy Rider*, and when he saw him in a local bar, kicked him forcefully up the arse. This unprovoked attack may have been, on sober consideration, a bit unfair."

In March 1977, Dennis Hopper joined Terry Southern and William S. Burroughs in New York where they spent several months involved in an ultimately abortive attempt to film Burroughs' loosely autobiographical novel *Junky*. The producer was Jacques Stern, a friend of Burroughs from their days together at the Beat Hotel. Connected to the Rothschilds, Stern was wheelchair-bound due to a childhood bout of polio and claimed to be a world-class physicist.

Hopper, who was signed to star in and direct the film, received an initial payment of $20,000, as did Southern and Burroughs. Southern recalled Stern as "a complete decadent drug user . . . he had this hypodermic-type device taped to his wrist. All he had to do was tap this device, and he would get a jolt of speedballs made from heroin and cocaine. He was ultra-lucid. He had these two girls, one black and one white, both wearing short miniskirts, who were his assistants. One was a philosophy student. They were just sort of gofers and when called upon would perform certain unnatural acts for Stern."

"Yeah, well I made a deal with Jock Stern to do a movie of *Junkie* [sic], William Burroughs' first novel, which he put out under a pseudonym and then rereleased under his own name years later," Hopper told interviewer Joan Quinn. "Anyway, Stern wanted to make a movie out of it, so I got him to give Burroughs $45,000, Terry Southern $45,000, and me $45,000 to write a screenplay that I would direct. And so I wrote about three screenplays, Terry about six, Burroughs about five. There was a year that we were together in New York, in the late '70s. I got to spend a lot of time with Bill. He's an incredible man."

Throughout March and April, Hopper, Southern, and Burroughs held script conferences, much like the ones that Hopper and Peter Fonda conducted at Southern's apartment when they developed *Easy Rider*'s screenplay. Once again, Southern sat with his pad and pen while the trio brainstormed. Though Hopper told Joan Quinn that he wrote three drafts of a script, his actual contribution to the picture was insignificant. Victor Bockris, then a writer for the magazines *Interview* and *High Times*, recalled, "I think that Burroughs had a lot of trouble with Hopper in that situation because in the script conference Hopper would be so coked up that he would just talk for hours and hours and not listen to anything Burroughs would say. Bill would say, 'Now listen to me and shut up!' There was a certain amount of annoyance with Hopper." Southern said that Hopper "was just hanging out and hoping to direct it, but at the time, he was just higher than a kite. That was his pre-clean stage." "I did a lot of experimentation with heroin at that time," Hopper told Quinn.

On May 15, Hopper and Southern attended the funeral of novelist James Jones. Southern took Hopper to a reception for Jones' mourners, where Hopper argued with guests and used profanity in front of the children there. Southern, who was proud of his courtly manners, was highly embarrassed when he was asked to take Hopper and leave shortly after their arrival.

Though Southern delivered a first draft of his screenplay for *Junky* on May 25, the whole project fell apart soon thereafter thanks to Stern's erratic behavior. Southern later said that Hopper wasn't really that interested in making the film, and Stern had only enough money to option Burrough's novel and commission a screenplay, but not enough to produce the movie. Southern believed that Stern used the project to work out his love-hate relationship with Burroughs, who Stern claimed had ruined his chance of winning a Nobel Prize by revealing that he was a junky. Victor Bockris observed, "The whole thing from the beginning was a combination of really nutty people who needed someone really together—a practical overseer for the project. Jacques Stern couldn't be that person, so the whole thing broke down. It was a drag because it was a very good idea."

Dennis Hopper and Wim Wenders visited Mexico in August 1977 to scout locations for a film they considering making there. The guest of the Mexican Cosmographical Society, Hopper spoke about environmental preservation and planted several trees at a special ceremony. He also presided over the Mexican premiere of *Easy Rider*, which had previously been banned by government censors. "Now I feel like I'll be presiding over the film's world premiere," he said.

Hopper ruined the visit when he was arrested for firing a gun in a Mexican town's plaza. Thanks to his friendship with the wife of the Mexican president, who was involved in promoting Mexico's film industry, Hopper avoided the cruel indignity of a Mexican jail, and was quickly hustled onto a plane and out of the country.

Hopper returned to Mexico in December 1978, where he planned to coproduce an original screenplay called *A Veces* (*Now and Then*) with the Mexican government. He screened *The Last Movie* to what the *Hollywood Reporter* called "an excellent reception from the viewing audience." At the screening, Hopper made the confusing statement, "The public seems to go for art films with new structures, and I believe they want films like those of the '40s that have a romantic and fantasy theme."

After his expulsion from Mexico on gun charges, Hopper returned to Taos, settling back into his usual routine: hanging with friends, getting high, and nurturing fantasies about film projects he took a stab at getting started. Eager to talk up his role in *Apocalypse Now*, he invited Mark Goodman to Taos in the fall of 1978 to write a profile of him for *New Times*, a free weekly paper. Hopper managed to give the appearance of a busy man with lots of irons in the fire.

Goodman reported what he overheard when Hopper took a phone call from his father. "Dad, how are you? Listen Dad, I need that typewriter to get going on this screenplay. Dad, do you know anything about capital gains? I'm thinking of taking the money from the sale of the house and putting it into the theater here . . . Yeah, hi, Mom, I love you . . . yeah, yeah, I know Mom . . . I'm a weird guy, but what the fuck . . ."

Hopper sat with Goodman at the Sagebrush Inn, drinking Coors beers while regaling him with his old story of his battles with the Taoseños who victimized him and his fellow hippies. Though he was contractually bound not to publicize *Apocalypse Now* before its release, Hopper told Goodman how Francis Ford Coppola told him he was a shoe-in for an Oscar nomination for his performance in the film, which Hopper promised would rival *Gone with the Wind* (1939) in its significance. He said, "It will be the best movie ever made."

Hopper casually told Goodman that he sold the Mud Palace in January for his asking price of $250,000, though he continued living in the rather splendid guesthouse he occupied while editing *The Last Movie*, which he filled with the valuable Spanish furniture he removed from the main house. The guesthouse stood on part of the Taos Indian reservation, giving it an unusual advantage that Hopper explained to Goodman. "It's cool living on Indian land because if you get juiced up in town and get into trouble, the local cops can't touch you," he said. "Dig this, man, the feds have to come out." Pointing to a rickety bridge that connected his guesthouse to the main house, Hopper said, "They have to stand on this side of that little bridge, and they're kind of embarrassed. 'Er, ah, Mr. Hopper, could you possibly come over here for just a moment?' "

Neil Young, Dean Stockwell, and Russ Tamblyn happened to be visiting Hopper in Taos to scout locations with him for their film *Human Highway* (1982) while Goodman was there, providing the writer the opportunity to witness their customary antics at the Sagebrush Inn. Goodman wrote, "Soon there is tequila and beer enough for every living creature in the Rio Grande. (Do not ever, I repeat ever, try to keep up with Dennis Hopper.) While some local dirt-dobber growls out a song about how he's two hundred pounds of swingin' dog, Hopper calls for oranges and starts to juggle.

He's quickly joined by Tamblyn. The Easy Rider is no match for the West Side Story Jet. Hopper then offers a challenge to Neil Young. If Young will sing five songs, Hopper will first recite Hamlet's soliloquy. Agreed, says Young.

"Hopper staggers through the smoky darkness to the dim red-lighted stage, faces down his desert-breather audience and begins: *To be or not to be/that is the question . . .* A madman's gleam in his eyes and a spectral carbine in his hands, he does the whole thing. and he is goddamn terrific—Olivier of the mountain. His audience loves it. Most don't know Stratford-on-Avon from Margaritaville, but they clap like old Billy at the end . . . *That motherfucker Dennis, he can flat get it on . . .*"

While showing Goodman around Taos, Hopper told him about his efforts to rescue *The Last Movie*. Hopper traded Universal the right to use outtakes from his film for their stock footage library in exchange for the film's distribution rights, which he planned to release in Europe and South America. Hopper also took to the road again for college screenings of the film, but found the student audiences he faced just as unappreciative of his film as they'd been seven years earlier. "I've been doing the college lecture tour," he said. "I hit a few schools, show *The Last Movie*, then open the house to questions. Besides trying to get a feel about the film, I'm also interested in seeing what people feel in the universities these days. After all, we're not trying to stop a war anymore. I thought it would mean they could work harder and not be bothered. But I found they're all a little bored—they want a cause to come along. They ask me, 'What are we supposed to do? You're supposed to be our spokesman.'

"So I tell them, 'Look, don't you think I'm a little old to be your spokesman? I'm forty-two, for chrissakes. Why don't you just study and have a good time?' See, I have no bones to pick anymore, no chip on my shoulder. And it's not just because I'm older. Look, I think Jane Fonda and I won the war, but I'm not going to run for the fuckin' Senate. For me, it's over. And hell, I can't say that my politics hurt me in Hollywood. It was probably my own dogmatic personality.' "

Near the end of his visit, Goodman asked Hopper if he was mellowing in his midlife. "I don't think I ever want to do another interview," Hopper suddenly said. "Fuck it. A lot of the great legends didn't—Dean, he never did. I don't think I ever will again, either." Hopper's assistant, Gigi Gray, interjected, "But you got good vibrations from this interview, didn't you

Dennis?" "No," Hopper answered brusquely. "I didn't get good vibrations at all."

Dennis Hopper, Neil Young, Dean Stockwell, and Russ Tamblyn channeled their Sagebrush Inn merrymaking into the film *Human Highway* (1982), a confluence of Young and Stockwell's filmmaking ambitions. Stockwell, who developed a deep friendship with Hopper beginning around 1956, is a fellow artist and a spiritual kin to him in many ways. (Stockwell told an interviewer how he avoided being drafted after dropping out of UC Berkeley. "I took drugs, pretended I was a fag.")

At Hopper's urging, Stockwell wrote a screenplay with Herb Berman titled *After the Gold Rush*, about the day when an earthquake and tidal wave wash away an artists' community in Topanga Canyon, where Stockwell lived. When Neil Young got a hold of a copy of the screenplay, it broke his writer's block, and he composed the album *After the Gold Rush,* which was to be the soundtrack for Stockwell's film. Hopper tried to launch Stockwell's project at Universal when he was still a hot commodity there, but they refused to green light it.

"I think had it been made, it would stand as a contemporary to *Easy Rider*, and it would have had a similar effect," Stockwell said. "The script itself was full of imagery, 'change' . . . It was very unique actually. I really wish that movie had been made because it could have really defined an important moment in the culture." Stockwell later reconsidered, saying, "Now, I look back over at a lot of years, and I don't know if I was really ready to do a movie that, uh, people could follow (laughs). I think I would've stepped out a little too far."

After Dean Stockwell introduced him to the musical group Devo, Neil Young's loose conception of a film about the hippies and sycophants who surrounded him evolved into *Human Highway,* a feature-length in-joke featuring Devo, Young, Hopper, Tamblyn, and Stockwell. Devo's yellow outfits and red plastic hats inspired Young to cast them in *Human Highway* as a radioactive-waste disposal team in a nuclear power plant whose effluents run through the nearby diner where most of the film's action takes place.

Stockwell brought in the rest of the film's cast, who improvised scenes depicting the goings-on at the diner on the day the world blows up in a nuclear holocaust. According to Russ Tamblyn, the film was inspired by an egg fight involving Tamblyn, Young, Stockwell, and producer Larry

Johnson. "The movie was made up on the spot by punks, potheads, and former alcoholics," Neil Young said. "The plan was, there was no plan, no script," Stockwell said.

Devo member Gerald V. Casale recalled, "Hopper I remember as being totally frightening, like the guy in *Apocalypse Now*—a little Frank Booth, too. He wouldn't let you alone. He'd chase you around the set givin' you his rap, whether you wanted to hear it or not—'Devo, you think your shit doesn't stink, don't ya.' And Dean Stockwell would be behind him, laughing at everything he said—'heh, heh, heh'—this evil laughter, like Ed McMahon. You never knew what was going on. A lotta mind-fuck games." When Neil Young's biographer, Jimmy McDonough, brought up the subject of Devo, Hopper sighed, saying, "They'd say, 'Oh, remember him—he's that old actor.' "

Shot over a period of four years on elaborately designed sets on a Hollywood soundstage and also in Taos, *Human Highway* cost Neil Young $3 million to produce. Dean Stockwell, who codirected *Human Highway* with Young (under Young's pseudonym Bernard Shakey) is Otto, the diner's owner, who plans to burn down the place for the insurance money. Sally Kirkland plays a waitress, Young and Tamblyn play a pair of dimwitted gas-pump attendants, and Hopper inhabits the dual roles of Cracker, a fast-talking cook with a pet raccoon, and a cowboy who drives a leopard skin-upholstered convertible.

Throw in some musical numbers performed by Young and Devo, and you have what Steven Puchalski calls "a bafflingly wondrous piece of freaked-out trash . . . starring an overdose of then-unemployable acidheads—a stellar cast of misfits/friends with virtually nothing to do." "Never before have so many people who aren't funny done a comedy," said Elliot Roberts, Young's manager. *Human Highway* premiered in Los Angeles on August 16, 1982. It received bad reviews and closed two days later. "I wanted to go, but I was in the insane asylum at the time," Hopper said. The film was not seen again until its home video release in 1995.

Stockwell said that making *Human Highway* was fabulous fun for those involved. For Dennis Hopper, *Human Highway* became a legal headache that reminded Hollywood not to hire him. On March 4, 1981, actress Sally Kirkland filed a civil suit for assault and battery against Hopper, Neil Young, and the companies involved in producing *Human Highway* for an injury that took place during production, asking $2 million in damages.

Kirkland claimed that Hopper severed a tendon in her arm with his knife-play in the film on February 28, 1980, which could have been avoided if the defendants had heeded the warning about Hopper's drug abuse that she issued at 5 A.M. that day.

Filmmaker Jeannie Field recalled, "Dennis was jabbering chattering and driving everyone crazy because he was doing this little knife trick—he didn't have a prop knife, he had a real knife." Hopper later said that Kirkland "couldn't concentrate on her crying scenes, so she wanted me to be quiet—but in point of fact, she wasn't in the fuckin' scene. It was on me, and I was doing my thing. She grabbed the blade of the knife. I yelled 'Cut! Cut! Cut!' and Neil yelled from outside, 'Only the director yells cut.' I said, 'No man, she's *cut*.'"

Kirkland suffered a severed tendon that required hospitalization, but returned to the set later that day. Her suit alleged that Hopper and others were "smoking and in other ways ingesting dangerous and illegal drugs and drugs known to cause violence and dangerous behavior" and that the filmmakers condoned their drug use, hoping it would enhance the actors' and others' enthusiasm and the film's profitability.

"It seemed like an unhappy time," Devo's Mark Mothersbaugh said. "They were all drinkin' heavily, doin' lots of drugs. Neil was the most grounded of all . . . they had attached their egos onto him." Hopper later joked about his drug use, saying, "She [Kirkland] said I consumed an ounce of amyl nitrate, a pound of marijuana, and drank three quarts of tequila. That was not true. I only did half that amount." Kirkland lost her suit when it went to trial in 1985.

After years of gestation, *Apocalypse Now* finally premiered at New York's Ziegfeld Theater on August 15, 1979. Sent to collect Hopper for his curtain call after the film's screening, Doug Claybourne finally located him in his hotel room, out cold on his bed, naked except for his cowboy boots. Hopper's hopes for renewed attention and an Oscar nomination were deflated by the critical reaction to his performance, which reviewers dismissed as merely an extension of his drugged-out state off screen.

Entertainment Weekly's critic Owen Gleiberman was a college journalist in 1979 when he witnessed Hopper's behavior at the Saturday morning post-screening press conference held at New York's posh Plaza Hotel. He recalled how Hopper "instantly took on the role of flaked-out druggie court jester of the press conference. The more stonerish and cosmic, and the less coherent, he was, the more that he ended up dominating the questions and answers, cracking up everyone in the room, though whether we were laughing with him or at him was, by the end, an open question.

"To this day, I have no idea if he was actually high, but it almost didn't matter. His rambling declarations on everything from filmmaking to the state of America made it sound as if he had never quite stopped playing the jittery, blitzed-out-of-his-noggin, war-fragged photojournalist in *Apocalypse Now*. Or, just maybe, that his performance in the movie wasn't really a performance at all. There's no denying that Dennis Hopper made himself a bit of a joke that day. Listening to him was like looking at the last joint ash of the '60s, hanging in the air and ready to fall. At the same time, you couldn't take your eyes off him. He was a court jester and a train wreck, and he was also every inch a star. In his very dissolution, he played his own legend like a bad-trip virtuoso."

"By the time I first met him in 1979, at the New York press junket for *Apocalypse Now*, Hopper had devolved into a chemically enhanced public spectacle," recalled entertainment reporter Joe Leydon. "Seated alongside director Francis Coppola and costar Robert Duvall, among others, at a standing-room-only press conference, he repeatedly interrupted the proceedings by occasionally and incongruously blurting out, at the top of his lungs, some variation of: 'I just wanna say, this is the greatest fuckin' movie ever made!'

"When he asked the assembled reporters to join him in giving Coppola a standing ovation—all you could hear was the sound of one man clapping. Later, Duvall and Hopper made themselves available for small group interviews at tables scattered throughout a hotel ballroom. When Hopper staggered over to my table after Duvall took his leave—my colleagues quickly scattered, and I found myself having an uncomfortably long one-on-one with an actor under the influence."

A small story about the press conference that appeared in *The New York Times* paints a sad picture of Hopper at the time. "Elsewhere in the Plaza was Dennis Hopper," the *Times* reported, "who observed several times during a brief conversation that he thinks *Apocalypse Now* is 'the greatest movie America has produced since *Gone with the Wind*.' Mr. Hopper, whose shell-shocked manner is not unlike that of the photojournalist character he plays in the movie, said that he now works 'when I'm asked' and had lately been living in Mexico City. He mentioned that he had directed *The Last Movie*, which won a prize at the Venice Film festival in 1971, and repeatedly referred to his direction of *Easy Rider*. "

Most of *Apocalypse Now*'s reviewers didn't bother to mention Hopper's performance. Vincent Canby wrote, "Dennis Hopper, looking as wild and disconnected as ever, turns up briefly at the end as a freelance photographer who has fallen under Kurtz's spell, apparently because Kurtz reads T. S. Eliot aloud (though none too well)." Reviewing *Apocalypse Now Redux* (2001), *Slate*'s David Edelstein called Hopper's performance "linguistic diarrhea."

However much Hopper's acting was a product of his drug intake, he still deserved credit for a notable performance, something you would never get by propping up some randomly chosen junkie before a camera and letting him babble on. Philippe Mora learned that when he cast a clinically insane man who had just been released from an English asylum to play a character who was supposed to be crazy in his first film, *Trouble in Molopolis* (1969). "I thought that since the character was crazy, why not cast a crazy person," Mora wrote. "How could you miss? Well, it was a nightmare, but he got good reviews as a talented 'newcomer.' I told this story to Dennis, and he advised me 'never tell that story to another actor!' "

Deprived of recognition for his performance in *Apocalypse Now*, let alone an Oscar, Hopper again retreated to Taos and the depression that afflicted him between films. Hopper was partially sustained by the companionship of his secretary and girlfriend, Elen Archuleta, who later said, "If I didn't love Dennis, I would have left him long ago." Hopper was fond of quoting a passage from Rilke's *Letters to a Young Poet*, where Rilke asks "If it were denied you to create, would you truly die, must you create no matter what dark despair you're in?"[12] Hopper's despair was undeniable. His alcohol and drug consumption had reached epic proportions. "I was doing half a gallon of rum with a fifth of rum on the side, twenty-eight beers and three grams of cocaine a day—and that wasn't getting high, that was just to keep going, man," he said.

Perpetually high, Hopper would fall into a hypnagogic state, mistake fragments of dreams for reality, and shoot real bullets through the ghosts of D. H. Lawrence and James Dean that stalked him into the walls surrounding him. Hopper was once so startled by what appeared to be the face of a stranger staring back at him that he shot at it with his revolver. When he

---

[12] Replying to a young poet who sought his advice, Rilke wrote, ". . . confess to yourself whether you would have to die if you were forbidden to write. This most of all: ask yourself in the most silent hour of your night: *must* I write?"

turned on the lights, he realized that he had perforated his Andy Warhol silkscreen print of Chairman Mao, where Warhol had tinted a photo of Mao's moon face a deep blue.

When Hopper's art collection was up for auction after his death, his family's spokesman told the Associated Press, "One night in the shadows, Dennis, out of the corner of his eyes, saw the Mao, and he was so spooked by it that he got up and shot at it, twice, putting two bullet holes in it. Andy saw it, loved it, and annotated those holes, labeling them 'warning shot' and 'bullet hole.' "

"People can always say you're your own victim, but there are times that people have great talent," Hopper said in 2003. "And that talent has to be nourished in some way, and if this industry can't nourish it, then they become victims, and then their self-indulgence sometimes takes over, and nobody pulls them up and pulls them out. I mean, if you write screenplay after screenplay after screenplay or deal after deal after deal that you see fall apart and go away, and so on, and you never lose your enthusiasm for wanting to make film, you're a victim, that's all."

Hopper had good reason to despair. The only acting work he got after *Bloodbath* was a cameo in the TV Western miniseries, *Wild Times* (1980), which starred Sam Elliott and veteran character actors Ben Johnson, L. Q. Jones, and Pat Hingle. Hopper was on-screen for only a few minutes in the four-hour series, in a scene where Doc Holliday (Hopper) tries to outgun a sharpshooter (Elliott).

Hopper's rescue from near oblivion came from almost literally out of the blue. Early in 1980, he received a call from his friend, Paul Lewis. Lewis called Hopper from Vancouver, where he was the executive producer of the film, *CeBe* (released in 1982 as *Out of the Blue*), to offer him a part.

Michael Walsh wrote, "The project was developed by Winnipeg film-maker Leonard Yakir, who had written, produced, and directed an inde-pendent feature called *The Mourning Suit* in his hometown in 1975." Written by Yakir and Brenda Nielson, *CeBe* was a drama about a teenage girl who kills the alcoholic father who sexually molests her and is reha-bilitated through the efforts of a benevolent, court-appointed psychiatrist (played by Canadian-born Raymond Burr, the story's narrator).

Lewis wanted Hopper to play the girl's father. "I saw no redeeming qualities in the father whatsoever," Hopper later said, but took the role anyway. "I was there two weeks and never worked." Lewis kept complaining to Hopper that coproducer and first-time director Leonard Yakir's rushes were "awful, terrible, unusable." "After about eight days of shooting," Lewis said, "we just realized that Leonard was very, very inexperienced as a director, and he wasn't getting the footage that really we felt would work on the picture."

"I refused to go the set," Hopper said, "because it was a first-time director and refused to see any of the dailies, and Paul keeps telling me that the dailies weren't working, and it was looking really bad, and I said, 'Nobody said you were a critic of artists, right? The guy's never directed a film, leave him alone.'

"Finally, after two weeks of shooting, he [Lewis] told me he was leaving the picture. He said not to worry, my money was in escrow, but he was closing it down. That was Friday night. By that time, I'd met Linda Manz, and I'd known Sharon Farrell before, and I'd been getting my wardrobe together—I was ready to play the father. So I said, 'Hey, wait a second. Let me see what you got.' On Saturday, I saw the two hours of footage, which was all unusable, and on Sunday, I took over the picture." Despite his misgivings about the script and his character in the film, Hopper said, "I've wanted to direct for so long, I just went for it."

Hopper's costar in *Out of the Blue*, Sharon Farrell, remembers things differently. "I went up to Canada, and the first couple of days, somebody else was directing, and we were going to dailies, and the shots, they were just normal kind of dailies, and Dennis was sitting there saying 'Oh, man, you shoulda done this. Oh, man, oh, man, you shoulda done it this way. What did you do that for? Why did you use that shot?' and it's like in two days, all of a sudden, Dennis was directing this movie. And I kept thinking, why would a director give up his reins? And I thought that guy probably had money in the movie, and you know, Dennis had directed *Easy Rider* with Peter Fonda. And Dennis, really, he started rewriting the script."

Hopper took the opportunity to completely revamp the film to conform to his radically different vision. "I don't do pictures unless I have full autonomy," he said, adding, with irony, "That's why I work so much." "It was made off the cuff. I took over on Friday, redid the script by Monday. I hung out with Linda, learned about her love of drums, used that. I didn't know what punk was—it was just starting—but I had her do that."

Hopper made Manz's character, Cindy Barnes, (nicknamed "CeBe" for her fondness for using Citizens Band radio) a wannabe punk rocker, her mother a heroin addict, added Don Gordon's character, and reduced Raymond Burr's role, junking his narration. Hopper said, "I don't make movies with narration."

Hopper also downplayed the part incest plays in CeBe's story to the point where it is only introduced obscurely at the end of the film. "Dennis had a horrible problem with the fact that he had molested his daughter," Farrell recalled. "I think it kind of changed. It was a story about a girl who was molested by her father. When you see the movie, I don't know whether you really see that. You just see a lot of problems that almost any girl could possibly have. Dennis had a hard time with that, he really did. He was saying things to me like, 'You know, it's really the mother's fault, it's not the father's fault, it's the mother's fault because the mothers always know that this is going on, and they look the other way.' So, we're always trying to figure out how to put that in somehow. It scared Dennis, it scared all of us."

Hopper would have preferred to dispense with Raymond Burr's character altogether, which had no place in his revised dramatic scheme. As originally written, *CeBe* was told from the psychiatrist's point of view. Hopper rewrote the film so that it was told from CeBe's point of view. But the film's investors needed Burr to meet the Canadian government's Canadian Content standards that require the inclusion of a certain number of Canadians in a film to qualify for the government's tax shelter.

Sharon Farrell recalled another reason that Hopper minimized Burr's role. "Dennis said he didn't like the Canadian actors at all," Farrell said, "and he kept firing them, and he brought in Don Gordon. There were just actors he did not like, he just didn't like Canadian actors." "We had problems with the Canadian government," Paul Lewis said. "It was so many actors we brought up from the United States. We just brought people in because we felt they would work better for the picture."

Michael Walsh wrote, "That's when all hell broke loose in the Eastern offices of Canada's cultural bureaucrats, the folks who had devised the point system to determine a movie's national identity (with serious implications for a film's financing). Despite a clearly recognizable Vancouver, the presence of Raymond Burr, The Pointed Sticks, and innumerable stubby beer bottles, the resulting feature was deemed to be not Canadian enough, turning the picture's bleak, dead-end outlook into a fine meta-phor for the cultural alienation faced by both a generation and a region living outside an officially designated 'centre of excellence.' "

"By the time Burr got there to do his part, I'd changed the whole con-cept," Hopper said. "And he didn't know this. He got there, ready to do his thing. He didn't like the script, not knowing that I'd thrown it away, and he was only going to be in two scenes." Paul Lewis said, "I think one of the problems that we did have was we had always worked with people we knew and really good actors, and we got into this thing, and we had Raymond Burr, who had really wanted to use cue cards, pretty much, and wanted to write his own scenes, I think.

"So Dennis and I were sitting in a bar one night with Raymond, and he came down, and he's saying 'I'm not gonna do this picture unless I can rewrite this,' and it's like a horrendous situation. So I turned to Dennis and said, 'What are you gonna do?' and he said, 'Hey, it's your problem.' So I said to Raymond, 'Raymond, come on, we're all street filmmakers, we all came out of the street.' Burr gruffly said, 'No, no, *we* came out of the streets, *he* came out of the low-budget films.' "

Hopper said, "Well, rewrite it—rewrite it any way you want." "And so in three days, for the $50,000 he got, I did a whole television show," he recalled. "I shot everything he rewrote, knowing I was only going to use two scenes. He never knew that he wasn't the star of this film." After fin-ishing his last scene, Burr came over to Hopper and said, "I want you to direct my next picture."

Hopper shot *Out of the Blue* in five weeks in a drug-fueled rush of effi-ciency instead of the six-and-a-half weeks that were originally scheduled. "Everybody was on drugs during at that time, and Dennis was a big drug user," Sharon Farrell recalled. "We [Farrell and Don Gordon] were both scared. We didn't know what Dennis was going to pull, we really didn't. We didn't know what he was going to ask us to do. I mean, it's very hard to enter a room and walk across the floor when an amyl nitrate is stuck up your nose. Number one, you take an amyl nitrate, you get such a rush, your heart flutters and goes so fast you don't even know what's happen-ing. And if you have to walk across the room, you have to get over that to just walk into the room like a normal person. And he was always pulling stuff like that, he was a little scary, you know. I mean, he got drugs for everybody on the set. He's the one that procured the cocaine for everyone.

'Cause we were working really late, late hours and stuff, and he drank, he drank, and he smoked and . . . He started drinking beer at the crack of dawn.

"That movie had a life of its own, it really did. And the script that we went into that movie with was not the script that was done . . . We wrote the picture. Every morning, we'd sit, and we'd write. It was mostly improv. If you weren't in that dressing room where he was rewriting that script, you'd be written out. If somebody didn't show up, they weren't in the scene that day. It was Dennis. Dennis was just brilliant, he just really is. There's part of me that loves Dennis Hopper and part of me that hates Dennis Hopper. I have mixed feelings about that man. But, you know, his talent will out. The fact that he's talented and brilliant, who cares that he's a jerk sometimes."

Dennis Hopper edited the film in six weeks using only one Moviola. He scored *Out of the Blue* with found music, just as he had done with *Easy Rider*. While driving to the set one day, he heard Neil Young's song, "My My, Hey Hey," on his car radio. Hopper contacted Young, who let him use his music for the film. The song's lyric phrases—"Out of the blue and into the black" and "It's better to burn out, than to fade away"—gave Hopper the title for his film and foreshadow its nihilistic ending.

In *Out of the Blue*'s prologue, alcoholic ex-biker Don Barnes (Hopper) is drinking and asking his daughter Cindy to open a bottle of pills when he slams his big rig into a school bus, demolishing it and killing several of the children on board. An unchanged Barnes returns home from prison five years later. He tries to cope with the atomized remnants of his family: his rebellious, thumb-sucking fifteen-year-old-daughter, CeBe (Linda Manz), who's obsessed with Elvis, punk rock, and CB radio, and his heroin-addicted wife (Sharon Farrell), who is having it off with the owner of the diner (nicely played by *Out of the Blue*'s production designer, Leon Erickson) where she waitresses.

The family's precarious situation implodes when the father of one of Don's crash victims gets him fired from his job driving a bulldozer in the city dump. Don and his best friend, Charlie (Don Gordon), waylay the child's father and steal his money. They get drunk and return home. Worried that CeBe might be a lesbian, Don tries to get Charlie to have sex with her, which triggers her memories of sexual abuse at her father's hands. After her pathetically weak mother fails to stand up for her, CeBe lures her father to her bedroom where she stabs him to death. She dons her once-beloved father's leather jacket, applies punk makeup (including a straight pin through her cheek), and blows her mother and herself up in the cab of her father's wrecked truck with a stick of dynamite. "All my movies end in fire," Hopper said.

Hopper wasn't kidding when he told Mark Goodman he wanted to continue tormenting audiences. Granted, there are plenty of dysfunctional families like the one portrayed in *Out of the Blue*, but watching them, accompanied by Neil Young's repetitive whining of the film's leitmotif, "My My, Hey Hey," is an unrelieved exercise in unpleasantness. *Out of the Blue*'s unattractive characters are all irredeemable, trapped in the poisoned amber of their defective personalities. That was Hopper's intention when he rewrote the film's original screenplay.

"Basically," he said, "it was the story of the psychiatrist saving her [CeBe] after she killed her awful father. So, I just made them all despicable and had her kill everybody." Even Linda Manz's CeBe is unlikable. Manz's angular features and hardness, and her character's obnoxious, self-destructive behavior combine to rob CeBe of our sympathy. (Though CeBe was supposed to be in her mid-teens, Linda Manz was actually eighteen when she made *Out of the Blue*.)

"In many ways, it's maybe my best film. People who hate it have a real problem," Hopper told interviewer Kenneth Turan, who noted *Out of the Blue*'s polarizing effect on audiences. "It's better than Bertolucci's *Luna*, and it's dealing with the same subject matter: drugs, incest, and, rather than opera, rock-and-roll. It's about the society of North America. The family unit is falling apart. People who say all this doesn't exist in this country, where have they been?

"I'm a social-protest painter. I can't help it. I don't know much about the past, I'm not really interested in the future, or in space. I like to make things about what I see. I see a corrupt place, which I kind of enjoy." Leaning forward, Hopper whispered conspiratorially, "I'm kind of corrupt myself." Hopper left Turan with the impression that he saw himself as a serious, committed artist who would be redeemed by history for work like *The Last Movie*, whose supposed Venice Film Festival award he made sure to mention to Turan several times.

"I'm not sure what the movie says," Hopper told Gregg Kilday of the *Los Angeles Times*. "I wanted to show a girl wanting to be a boy, emulating her father, but still wanting to put on lipstick and be a little ballerina. But I can't make any moral judgments about the positive and negative aspects of the story. I feel like it's a time-capsule film—it's like a little article on the fourth page of a newspaper that says that a kid's killed her mother and father, and you wonder what that's about and then move along."

Canada's national film board didn't want *Out of the Blue* identified as a Canadian feature when it was entered into competition at the Cannes Film Festival in 1980. "Denied Canadian certification, it played without any official nationality," wrote Michael Walsh. Instead, *Out of the Blue* was introduced as a "Dennis Hopper film." "It was the first entry from Mars at the Cannes Film Festival," Hopper quipped.

Hopper was lucky he wasn't busted by the British authorities when he arrived in England where *Out of the Blue* was being shown at a film festival just outside of London. The moment he got off the plane, Hopper ran over to his daughter, Marin, and confessed, "Oh my God, I've just been through customs, and I've gotta let you know something. I have drugs all over my body. I have drugs all over my body, and I got through customs."

Though *Out of the Blue* was well received in Europe, it wasn't released in the U.S. until November 1982, when the small Discovery Film Corp. distributed it. Dennis Hopper got Jack Nicholson to do him a big favor by recording a radio commercial promoting *Out of the Blue*. Nicholson said, "This is Jack Nicholson. I'm gonna recommend a movie I'm not in that I have nothing to do with. I'd like to tell the people about a movie called *Out of the Blue*, directed by Dennis Hopper. It speaks honestly from the heart of a fifteen-year-old girl. Its milieu is the punk scene. For a young person who sees this film, I absolutely know it may knock 'em back, but they're going to know it's about a real reality that hasn't really been exposed on film before. If Dennis hadn't made another movie, this would do in the '80s exactly what *Easy Rider* did to kind of make the transition from the '60s and '70s. It has everything you can get behind in a movie. Well, I've never endorsed anything, even of my own, but if a masterpiece comes along, people should see it. Ya know, I think that people that love movies would really like to see this one."

"Mr. Hopper's films, particularly this one, are more like *time capsules* than movies anyhow," *The New York Time*'s Janet Maslin wrote, echoing Hopper's own sentiments about the film. "They seem to be collections of free-floating cultural artifacts, assembled roughly but with honesty and passion. The film throws together CeBe's punk aspirations, her adulation of Elvis Presley, her mother's slatternly habits, her father's wild, drunken ravings, and dozens of posters, slogans, and songs. The theme music, from Neil Young's 'Rust Never Sleeps' album, is a haunting accompaniment to Mr. Hopper's sometimes stunning imagery. The best moments of *Out of the Blue* have both the beauty and the banality of *found art*, as when Mr. Hopper is seen working atop a garbage heap, surrounded by hundreds of seagulls, to the tune of Mr. Young's 'Thrasher.' "

"*Out of the Blue* is one of the unsung treasures of independent films . . . a bitter, unforgettable poem about alienation," critic Roger Ebert wrote. Jonathan Rosenbaum's accolades must have been music to Hopper ears, when he wrote that Hopper was the heir to Nicholas Ray's "angst-ridden lyricism" and the mantle of James Dean. Rosenbaum wrote that Hopper had created "a kind of punk remake of *Rebel* [*Rebel Without a Cause*] set in a contemporary working-class environment" that revealed the "bankruptcy of the parents' 1950 generation."

Despite excellent reviews, *Out of the Blue* was poorly distributed and wasn't embraced by moviegoers. "We tried to distribute it," Hopper later said, "but we couldn't get it out for a wide distribution—it's about incest, so no one wants to touch it."

Gregg Kilday wrote, "Nicholson's testimonial notwithstanding, the arrival of a new Dennis Hopper film isn't likely to be regarded as a singular cultural event by the callow teenagers who now comprise the legions of the moviegoing public. For by Hopper's own reckoning, nobody under thirty much remembers him these days."

"It didn't make it back to Vancouver until December 1983," Michael Walsh wrote. "The pre-Christmas playdate indicated that its distributor considered it filler, and its new name, *No Looking Back*, guaranteed that it wouldn't overstay its welcome."

While promoting *Out of the Blue*, Hopper told Kilday that he'd actually moved back to Los Angeles two years before, saying, "I came back here to remind people that I'm still around." Hopper had finally heeded Robert Raison's advice to return, but he told an interviewer that he wouldn't attend Hollywood parties or eat at restaurants frequented by celebrities. After Hopper reluctantly returned to L.A., director Alex Cox offered him the role that eventually went to Harry Dean Stanton in the cult favorite, *Repo Man* (1984).

Hopper turned it down for a higher-paying role in the movie, *King of the Mountain* (1981), about the rivalry between two young hotshots (Harry Hamlin and Joseph Bottoms) who race each other around L.A.'s Mulholland Drive, a winding mountain road like the one where he flipped his convertible with Natalie Wood twenty-five years before. Though Hopper was cast in *King of the Mountain* in March 1980, production on the film only began in September. Looking the worse for wear, Hopper played Cal, a drunken, washed-up mountain racer. Saddled with dialogue like "He's drunk with the speed of his youth," it's no great loss that Hopper's character was a sidebar in a film dominated by racing scenes.

On December 12, 1980, *Variety* reported that *The Second Coming*, costarring Hopper and Michael Moriarty, began shooting in Houston. Directed by Spanish director Bigas Luna, *The Second Coming* (released in 1981 as *Reborn*) tells the story of a phony televangelist's (Hopper) attempt to exploit a young Spanish woman afflicted with stigmata. At the IMDb, Mario Gauci writes, "It's a bizarre and wildly uneven religious satire (with some mild horror/thriller elements added towards the end), but a handful of powerful moments make it worth watching nevertheless. The rushed ending, featuring sympathetic aide-turned-villain [Francisco] Rabal chasing Moriarty and the woman as Hopper flips out at his headquarters, is clumsy and incoherent, but the disjointed whole is held together somewhat by the constant and effectively unnerving synthesizer-based music score."

Francis Ford Coppola proved he was one of Hollywood's few men of his word when he hired Hopper to play the alcoholic father of sons played by Matt Dillon and Mickey Rourke in *Rumble Fish* (1983). Before production began on *Rumble Fish* in Tulsa, Oklahoma, Hopper learned that his father had been diagnosed with cancer. Dennis quit drinking before what he hoped would be a reconciliation with Jay Hopper.

"He wasn't a bad man," Dennis said, "I just didn't understand him, that's all. My father was dying, and I wanted him to see me sober for the last year of his life." Hopper took his father to Paris, hoping they might finally reach an understanding. "I thought, 'This is our chance,' " he quietly told an interviewer in 1990. "He's going to tell me something." Then he roared with laughter. "He didn't tell me a fucking thing. Whatever secrets he had, he died with. The most interesting thing about him was that he wasn't interesting at all."

Hopper's newfound sobriety impressed Coppola, but it threatened to come undone when the director prepared to film the scene where Hopper's drunken character confronts his obtuse son (Matt Dillon). "There are some scenes where you should be drunk, not act drunk," Hopper said. "I told Francis, 'If we don't get it after the third take, I'm going to start taking shots of cognac.' Francis said no, no, he didn't want me to go back to drinking, but I told him it would be O.K.. We shot for eighteen hours, I consumed a bottle of cognac, and I stopped drinking the next day."

Playing the father of actors nearly twenty years his junior prompted Hopper to reflect on the latest stage in his career. "I realized I'm at a transitional age," he said. "I need to work through it as an actor, from being the son to being the father, from being the patient to being the doctor. There are periods in an actor's life: in your twenties you have to play teenagers. If you get through that, in your thirties, you get to play adults. Then in your forties, there's this transition I have to go through now. Especially if you were never a star. A star has maybe three years of being a star, then you never hear about them. There are thousands of guys like that—three years, that's about your basic star period. I didn't really go in for that."

Hopper had just finished his role in *Rumble Fish* and was about to appear in Sam Peckinpah's *The Osterman Weekend* (1983) when he started promoting the U.S. release of *Out of the Blue*, but shrugged off the impression that he was having a career resurgence. "As far as my acting career is concerned, I've really just done the roles that have been offered me. People seem to be lumping them together as if it were all some great plan that I had, but it's all been just waiting for the next job."

In *The Osterman Weekend,* Hopper plays plastic surgeon Richard Tremayne, a college pal of TV journalist John Tanner (Rutger Hauer), who hosts a weekend get-together for his closest friends and their wives at his home each year. Only this time, Tanner's property has been wired for surveillance by a CIA operative (John Hurt), who is convinced that Tanner's friends are Soviet agents. Hopper gives an entertaining performance as Tremayne, who quarrels with his wife (Helen Shaver) over her cocaine habit. Unfortunately, his character gets killed off too early in the film.

The Osterman Weekend was not the great creative collaboration Hopper and Peckinpah dreamed of when they smoked joints in Peckinpah's office while shooting the pilot for the *Rifleman*. Sadly diminished by years of alcohol and drug abuse, both men were now just struggling to survive.

After the debacle of *Convoy* (1978), Peckinpah, an alcoholic, cocaine addict, and heart-attack survivor, was trying to prove to Hollywood that he could be a reliable worker again.

"My problem wasn't working," Hopper explained. "My problem was getting out of the dressing room to the set. Not getting out of the dressing room to the set on time, but the emotional problems I had just to make the walk. My problem was personal. It never seemed to hurt what went on the screen, but it was the process to getting it on the screen that terrified people. You know, you're doing drugs in the dressing room, and spooking everybody on the set and so on, and that's the reputation that should really be talked about, not the work, because I got to the set on time. So at a certain point, my using and my drinking became who's coming out of the dressing room—what, Jekyll or Hyde? You know, what emotional roller coaster is he going to take us on now? I did the work on time. I did good work. So, you know, that's what unfortunately drugs and alcohol did for me, in my life, and my personal life was a shambles."

Though he hid it well, Hopper was drinking and snorting cocaine in his dressing room while filming *The Osterman Weekend*. After his death, Anne Thompson wrote, "I met Dennis Hopper in 1983 on the Robert Taylor Ranch set in Mandeville Canyon of Sam Peckinpah's last film, *The Osterman Weekend*, based on Robert Ludlum's 1972 novel. Both Peckinpah and Hopper were fighting their various addictions; Peckinpah wasn't drinking, but he was doing cocaine. If Hopper was using, it didn't show on set, where he clearly enjoyed being part of the first-rate ensemble that the maverick director had assembled. Like Rutger Hauer, John Hurt, and Burt Lancaster, Hopper had agreed to work for less than his usual fee, playing the part of a plastic surgeon meeting up with his old friends."

While promoting *Out of the Blue*, Hopper told Gregg Kilday that he and Peter Fonda were slated to make a sequel to *Easy Rider*. While Hopper worked in *Rumble Fish* and *The Osterman Weekend*, Peter Fonda carried the ball trying to launch *Biker Heaven*, the sequel to *Easy Rider*. If there was ever a misbegotten project, this was it. *Biker Heaven* was set in a post-apocalypse America, where Fonda's Wyatt and Hopper's Billy descend from heaven, resurrect George Hanson, and save the country. The film was set to be produced by Bert Schneider and directed by *Saturday Night Live*'s Michael O'Donoghue, from a screenplay to be written by Terry Southern and his collaborator, Nelson Lyon.

According to Gail Gerber, "Terry was offended and exclaimed, 'How can they make a sequel when we killed off both the characters?' " The project fell through, only for Fonda to try again in the early '90s. He called Southern in the summer of 1994, a year before the writer's death, leaving a message on Southern's answering machine. Southern played it for Gerber, who recalled, "With a note of desperation in his voice, he said, 'Terry, why don't you want to work with us? I'm offering you $30,000 to take your name off the script so we can make a sequel.'

"A furious Terry said, 'How can they remove my name when I got an Academy Award nomination for the film? He is trying to pull an end run.' I hadn't seen Terry that angry since the last time they tried to make a sequel in the Eighties." Steve Blauner remembers Schneider spending something like $100,000 on *Biker Heaven*, renewing his option on the property several times. Blauner looked at successive drafts of the script, each worse than the last, saying, "It was the worst piece of shit I ever read." The project finally died when Jack Nicholson refused to participate, disputing his proposed salary.

Hopper's return to Los Angeles barely outlasted his brief sobriety as he fled Hollywood once again for the seclusion of Taos. By this time, he was delusional even during waking hours. Convinced that there was a mob contract on his life, Hopper bought a massive Cadillac Seville because he thought it was a tank. Then he decided to stage an insanely risky stunt to promote an exhibition of his photography that was traveling from the Chicago Art Institute to Rice University in Houston, where he was going to screen *Out of the Blue* and give a lecture afterward at the Rice Media Center.

Hopper called his old friend Walter Hopps, who was then directing the Menil Collection in Houston. Hopper said, "Hey, I'm painting again, and I want to show my paintings." "That's crazy after all these years that you'd be painting now," Hopps said. "But Dennis, you can't just turn around after all you've said and announce that you're painting again." "I know," Hopper said, "but I've got a way around it. I've got a way to introduce it, and what I'm going to do is blow myself up and announce that I'm really serious about painting."

"I knew this Mormon guy there named Ollie Anderson who had a wild car-show act called the 'Russian Suicide Chair,' rather like the rodeo stunts I saw as a kid in Kansas," Hopper recalled. "The stunt involves detonating sticks of dynamite arranged in a circle that results in a protective vacuum at the core, but it's a very dangerous act. If even one stick fails to go off, it's curtains. I thought it was worth risking because there was a contract out on me anyway. If they were going to kill me, they would have to do it out in the open. If I lived through it, then I was destined to live for a while."

After the screening of *Out of the Blue* finished, video monitors in the Rice Media Center flickered to life, displaying a glassy-eyed Hopper delivering his lecture. "He was too drunk and stoned to stand in front of us," Christopher Dow said, "so he stayed in the projection booth and rambled on for twenty or thirty bizarre minutes. I couldn't tell you what he talked about. I'm not sure he really talked about anything. The one thing that did register, however, was that he wanted to blow himself up in the stadium parking lot."

Documentary filmmaker Brian Huberman, who videotaped Hopper's dynamite stunt, observed him during his preparations for the event. "The dynamite coffin stunt could not be performed at Rice for safety/insurance reasons," Huberman recalled, "so Hopper hired a fleet of school buses to transport the audience to a racetrack north of town off Hopper Road. My memories of Hopper during his visit include a sad telephone conversation with Jack Nicholson's secretary where Hopper was trying unsuccessfully to speak with Jack the 'star' who was in Houston making *Terms of Endearment*. Rather than a cutting-edge figure, Hopper constantly reflected back to the Hollywood of the '50s telling great yarns about the 'titans' of the film industry including Henry Hathaway, John Wayne, and of course, his great mentor, James Dean. What Hopper liked about this mixed bag of characters was that they did what they wanted and to hell with everyone else. He seems to have modeled his life on this simple value."

The school buses pulled up at the Big H Speedway just as the last race was finishing. "Stick around after the race, folks," the announcer's voice blared over the public-address system. "Watch a famous Hollywood film personality perform the Russian Dynamite Death Chair Act. That's right, folks, he'll sit in a chair with six sticks of dynamite and light the fuse. Will the flagman please come out and flag him as he comes down?" Before entering the arena, Hopper hugged his stunt coordinator while Terry Southern crossed himself. Wim Wenders, holding his 35mm SLR, joked that he'd blow Huberman's video camera up if there was a stick of dynamite left over from Hopper's show.

The moment of truth finally arrived. Hopper crouched in the chair, which was little more than a cardboard box covered with tinfoil and six sticks of dynamite. He struck several matches, which were extinguished by the moist breeze. He finally lit the whole book of matches and ignited the fuse. It sssshed, and then the audience was walloped by the thunderclap of exploding dynamite.

"Dennis Hopper, at one with the shock wave, was thrown headlong in a halo of fire," Dow wrote. "For a single, timeless instant, he looked like Wile E. Coyote, frazzled and splayed by his own petard." As the crowd rushed forward, a miraculously unscathed Hopper emerged from the smoke, exhilarated and amazed by his own survival. As he removed the cotton from his ears, he yelled "Whew!" several times, said he had to piss, and proudly announced, "I didn't crap my pants." (The explosion affected Hopper's inner ear, which caused him balance problems for several weeks after the stunt.)

Though Hopper admitted that one performance of the death chair act was enough, the dynamite's concussive jolt was not enough to exorcise his demons or shock him to an awareness of the dangerous way he was living. Though he narrowly skirted death at the Big H that night, he continued to tempt fate. Soon, fate would answer his pleas, plunging Hopper into his personal hell.

· 8 ·

THE FALL AND RISE OF DENNIS HOPPER

Dennis Hopper goes insane in Mexico and gets committed to a hospital's psychiatric ward. On the brink of suicide, Hopper embraces sobriety. Hopper's role in Blue Velvet *triggers his comeback. Hopper becomes Hollywood's solid citizen, working tirelessly while shamelessly regaling talk show audiences with stories of his past scandals.*

•

*I*F THE DYNAMITE didn't finish him, the mob would. That was Dennis Hopper's crazed state of mind in early 1983. Hopper now pulled what he called a "geographic." "I was moving from one town to another so fast," Hopper said. "And I knew the Mafia was after me." Hopper got his brother to arrange an armed escort to transport him to the Albuquerque airport. Hopper flew from there to Los Angeles where he holed up in a hotel room, invited some friends, and staged something like a condemned man's last orgy. "I shut myself up in a hotel for like three days, went through vast quantities of women," Hopper recalled. Hopper, who once claimed that he went through eight women a day, said, "My biggest drive wasn't alcohol or drugs—it was sex. I used women all my life, just as I used alcohol and drugs. The idea was to break through inhibitions in order to become a better artist. I consider my sexuality to be a tremendous creative source, but at a certain point in my life, I dealt with sex like I was drinking beer."

Hopper was now injecting cocaine intravenously, which gave him an orgasmic, full-body rush that shot straight to the core of his brain. The drug's refractory period was so short that he needed a fresh hit only minutes after the previous shot. "To shoot cocaine is a totally suicidal trip," Hopper said. "You have to shoot it every ten minutes to keep high. I was shooting, like, cocaine and heroin together, just like John Belushi." (John Belushi was found dead on the morning of March 5, 1982, at the Chateau Marmont hotel, after injecting himself with mixtures of cocaine and heroin colloquially called "speedballs.")

Hopper finally stopped in Houston, where he confronted the man he later claimed was a major figure in Texas' organized-crime hierarchy. The meeting took place in a deserted parking lot, a scene right out of a movie. Maybe it was, a movie that played only in Hopper's brain. Hopper asked the mafioso about the contract on his life. "I assumed he wasn't answering correctly, I pulled a knife on him," Hopper later said. Hopper's adversary took a look at that knife and the man wielding it, and decided that Hopper was clearly insane. He shook his head in pity, leaving Hopper and his fantasies behind in the parking lot.

Hopper somehow found his way back to Taos, where a lucrative offer of work awaited him. A West German producer wanted Hopper to play the head of the DEA in *Jungle Warriors* (1984), a film about a group of models on their way to a photo shoot in South America who get captured by a drug lord after their plane is shot down. The film's quality can be gauged by its grab-bag cast, which included Alex Cord, Nina Van Pallandt, Sybil Danning, Marjoe Gortner, and Woody Strode.

Hopper only had a seventeen-line role, but the money was more than he'd ever been offered. So he grabbed it and headed down to Cuernavaca, Mexico, where *Jungle Warriors* was going to be filmed. The job became Hopper's ticket to madness. It began with three complimentary shots of tequila left for him in his hotel room. Naturally, Hopper downed them. He later said that they were spiked with LSD. The LSD-doped tequila was just enough to send the already impaired Hopper over the edge.

"I became convinced that there were people in the bowels of this place who were being tortured and cremated," Hopper recalled. "The people had come to save me, and they were being killed and tortured, and it was my fault." Hopper had to escape the confines of the hotel. He ventured outside into the warm Mexican night, but the hallucinations kept coming. "I masturbated in front of a tree and thought I'd become a galaxy—that was a good mood!" he said. (Hopper roared with laughter when he told the story in 2001, sufficiently distanced from the pain of the events to do so.)

Hopper felt bugs and snakes beneath his skin breaking through it. He tore off his clothes and walked into the countryside. His friends' voices whispered from the telephone wires strung between poles. He saw mysterious lights and thought they were alien spaceships. Hopper recalled, "The Third World War was actually happening, and I was being guided by a spaceship that was controlling my mind, and so I wasn't sure whether I was to walk to the United States naked or all the way down to the tip of South America."

As dawn broke, Hopper wandered back to town, hurling rocks at oncoming cars. The police grabbed him and tried to put a robe on him. Thinking they were his pursuers, he threw it off. "When the police tried to get me dressed, I refused," he said. "I said, 'No, kill me like this! I want to die naked.'" The police jailed Hopper while they figured out what to do with him.

"I heard friends of mine being lined up outside and machine-gunned," he said. Transferred to a hospital, Hopper reacted with terror when doctors approached him with a syringe, convinced they were trying to kill him. Then he thought his lungs had been replaced with "these things." Some of the film crew managed to get him on a chartered flight back to Los Angeles. "On the plane, I was hallucinating, and I crawled out on the wing in midair," he recalled. "I decided that Francis Ford Coppola was on the plane filming me. I had seen him, I had seen the cameras, so I knew that they were there. The crew started the wing on fire, so I crawled out on it knowing that they were filming me. I was out there, and a bunch of stuntmen grabbed me and pulled me in."

After Hopper returned to L.A., some of his friends checked him into Studio 12, a drug-and-alcohol rehabilitation facility for people in show business. Withdrawing from alcohol gave Hopper delirium tremens. He became psychotic. While clipping hedges around the facility, he began hearing voices. Hopper went on a rampage, convinced that he could only keep the voices at bay with his incessant clipping. He was subdued and put in a straitjacket. Doctors gave him the antipsychotic drug, Prolixin, which causes the symptoms of Parkinson's disease in rare cases. Hopper became one of those cases. The doctors gave him Cogentin to counteract the Prolixin, but the inadequate dose was insufficient to reverse his Parkinsonian syndrome. Hopper's body became frozen. He couldn't make gestures, form sentences, or turn his head. It took him minutes to agonizingly get food or a cigarette into his mouth. "It lasted for three months without them know-ing what had happened," he recalled. "I was in lockup cleaning toilets and shaking so badly I screamed, 'I can't do it.' And the guard said, 'You're going to do it!' but I couldn't hold the rag."

The doctors made Hopper into a living public-service announcement. They marched him in front of three sobriety meetings a day, saying, "See, this is what happens when you drink and use drugs." Ben Irwin wrote, "The night before I met Dennis Hopper for the first time, he had burst stark naked into a meeting at a recovery center where I was working as an alcoholism-and-drug counselor. He was a resident at the center, and he was escorted none too gently back to his quarters. That did not keep him from repeating the performance, once again unclothed, a week later. No character he had ever portrayed on-screen, including the doper in *Easy Rider*, came close to projecting the dazed, lunatic quality that characterized Dennis Hopper. If he was not totally deranged at this time, he was giving an Academy Award performance."

Hopper checked himself out of Studio 12 and flew to Las Vegas, where Elen Archuleta was waiting to drive him to Taos. "We were driving back to Taos, and on the way there, I told her that I'm going to kill myself because I obviously wouldn't be able to act again," he recalled. Archuleta flew him back to L.A. to see his doctor. After examining Hopper, his doctor exclaimed, "My God, they didn't give you enough Cogentin!" He injected Hopper with several doses of the drug and said, "There, that ought to do it." Hopper got up and put his hand in his back pocket in one fluid move. Suddenly released from his nightmare, he cried tears of joy, saying, "My God, I'm back."

Hustler publisher Larry Flynt, who was launching a bizarre campaign for the presidency of the United States to hype *Hustler*'s sales, contacted Hopper while he was in Studio 12. "I got an offer from Larry Flynt to do the first celebrity shoot for *Hustler*," Hopper later said. "I was so out of it, I thought it was some sort of code. It sounded really interesting to me. So Flynt moved me into his house, and I became like his top advisor. And here I was, just out of a fucking mental institution. I'd agree with anything he said. 'Oh yeah, run for President, sure, why not? Wish I'd thought of it, Larry.' "

Hopper spent about three weeks in Flynt's twenty-room mansion on St. Cloud Road in Bel Air, which formerly belonged to Sonny and Cher.

Hopper was just part of Flynt's motley crew of eccentrics, which included professional atheist and full-time resident Madalyn Murray O'Hair, Native American activist Russell Means (Flynt's vice-residential candidate), former Black Panther leaders Stokely Carmichael and H. Rap Brown, JFK-conspiracy author Mark Lane, and Frank Zappa. LSD burnout Timothy Leary and Watergate ex-con G. Gordon Liddy rehearsed the two-man debate act they were touring the country in at Flynt's and hung around to play cards with Flynt and his circle. Flynt's mansion was outfitted with all sorts of security devices and swarmed with his private army of Uzi-wielding bodyguards recruited from Gold's Gym.

Flynt, who was partially paralyzed after falling victim to an attempted assassination, wore a diaper made from an American flag and zipped around the mansion in his gold-plated, $85,000 electric wheelchair, doped to the gills to quell the pain from his damaged spinal nerves. To keep her from annoying him, Flynt encouraged his drug-addicted wife, Althea, a former teenage stripper from one of his clubs who had been *Hustler*'s July 1975 centerfold, to develop her pet project, a biopic of Jim Morrison. Althea enlisted Hopper to consult on the project and direct the film. Hopper picked up the phone and called Terry Southern in Connecticut. He told Southern, "I've sent you a first-class, round-trip ticket, and I want you to come out. I have a proposition for you. Take my word, it's a good thing. I'll meet the plane."

After Southern settled in at Flynt's mansion, where he and Hopper occupied adjoining suites, Hopper told him, "We'll write the script together. I already asked them for $25,000 apiece up-front." In 1970, Southern, who was in dire financial straits after the IRS descended on him, wrote Hopper a letter begging him for even one point of the profits from *Easy Rider*. Hopper never answered his letter. Prodded by a guilty conscience, Hopper now handed Southern an envelope stuffed with $100 bills, telling him, "Here, here's yours. I'll show you mine—see, they're the same." Southern asked, "Where should we keep it?" Hopper said, "I don't know, I'm keeping mine behind this book. The other day, I got so stoned I couldn't remember which book it was. I tore the place apart."

"Dennis and I were there about three weeks," Southern recalled. "He did his shoot for the *Hustler* series called 'Celebrity Porn' where a movie actor is invited to set up an erotic storyboard. Den, being a poet of the lens, shot it himself. He created a gallerylike situation with some paintings he had done, and then he had these girls posing on a couple of settees. Two girls doing lez-type lovemaking with some of his paintings in the background. So it served his sort of aesthetic purpose. And a big photograph of him. I was there for part of the shoot. Hot stuff at first, then it got too predictable."

Hopper insisted that the girls actually engage in sex with each other, but they refused. "Finally Flynt had them bring in the guy who'd been sending the girls over, and the security guard starts hitting him with a stick and pounding him," Hopper said. "Then he takes out a .45 and says he's going to shoot him if he tries to run. And Flynt is yelling and screaming. Terry wouldn't look, he didn't want to see it. I was watching. 'Nothing's happening,' I said, 'he's just yelling at him.' But it was really weird, it was awful."

Hopper said, "Then you start thinking, 'How do I get out of here?' I'm living in this house like a monk. Sex must be going on everywhere, but none for me. And Terry and I were sitting there like angels. I swear to God, it's true. I guess we were just the weirdos upstairs." The Morrison project went nowhere. Hopper shot video screen tests with some actors, but the whole thing fell apart when Southern informed Althea Flynt that they'd need to acquire the rights to use Morrison's music and get permission from the members of The Doors to portray them in the film.

Hopper awoke one morning to the sound of helicopters buzzing the mansion and turned on the television. Local news shows were broadcasting live coverage showing Flynt's home surrounded by federal agents who were seeking video tapes Flynt had of car manufacturer John DeLorean's FBI cocaine sting and the tapes Flynt claimed to have of President Reagan's advisor, Alfred Bloomingdale, engaged in sex orgies with his mistress, Vicki Morgan, and other prominent Reagan advisors. (The tapes never surfaced.) "I got this part to play this CIA guy in Sweden [in *Slagskämpen* (1984), a Cold War thriller costarring Hardy Krüger], so I left," Hopper said. "Larry went to prison. Althea came in and destroyed the metal detector at the federal prison in Missouri. So she was put in prison. And then I never saw any of them again."

Hopper spent the remainder of the year in Taos, staring at the TV to stave off boredom and stay away from the bottle. He worked in Robert Altman's *O.C. and Stiggs* (1987), a barely released comedy about two rebellious teenagers out to get revenge on an insurance executive for canceling one of their grandfather's policies. Hopper played a shell-shocked Vietnam vet, an intentional parody of his character in *Apocalypse Now*. "I'd known Robert Altman for a long time, too," he later said. "Again from the grass association." Hopper recalled how Altman, an incurable gambler, was constantly visiting a greyhound track to place bets. "He would have great parties to watch rushes, with food and drink and hours and hours of dailies," he said. "It was a very joyous time. I wish the film had been good." *Variety*'s staff reviewer called the film tedious nonsense, but wrote, "Performances are uniformly good, with Dennis Hopper once again excelling as a madman."

In October 1983, two weeks after he started Altman's film, Hopper convincingly played the part of a reformed man for *People* magazine's Michael Heaton, who visited him in Taos. Hopper made light of his freak-out in Cuernavaca and offered readers some friendly advice, saying, "Never drink tequila that is set in your room, man." Accompanied by twenty-seven-year-old Elen Archuleta, Hopper maintained that he was sober, didn't take drugs, or smoke anything stronger than tobacco since he joined Alcoholics Anonymous in May. He said, "I'm enjoying reality now." Archuleta said, "Dennis is a person entirely in control of everything around him now." Hopper said he'd even given up guns. Showing Heaton the bullet holes marking the walls of his bedroom, he said, "What can I say? I was a fun guy."

Hopper's apparent recovery made a good story for public consumption, but it was just a pretense. "I went into an alcohol-drug rehabilitation place, and when I came out of it, I decided, 'Well, right. Alcohol drove me insane," he said. "It's obvious: It was alcohol, and it wasn't drugs.' So I wasn't drinking—because my whole life had been to have the martini before the meal, have the beer, have a beer with the meal, have an Irish coffee, cognac afterwards, and then drink the rest of the night. My whole orientation had been: 'Where's the drink, where's the drink, where's the beer!' I was in total denial. I thought other people had problems—not me. I would look at other people falling down and slurring words, and I would say, 'I don' know what's wrong with these people. Why can't they handle their drinks?' Other people were getting drunk and falling on the floor. I was just drinking all day, and if I felt drunk, I would do some more cocaine. It would sober me up. If I wanted to get drunk, I would have neat tequila. Then I'd black out."

"So to get through that I decided I would just continue doing drugs, so that rather than having a beer in the morning, I would have cocaine.

And I'd always thought, 'Well, I can stop cocaine anytime I want. It's not an addictive thing. The point is not that cocaine is addictive or that beer is addictive; I'm an addictive personality. So I just stared using cocaine like I was drinking beer all day. Suddenly, I became a secret person about it because now I was going to be straight.

"So I wouldn't let people know I was doing cocaine. I had a half an ounce every two days, two-and-a-half days, three days at the most. I was getting dealer's price—fifteen dollars a gram—when everybody was paying a hundred and fifty. There are a lot of dealers and people that were never my friends but that I dealt with because I had to."

"I did a year like that, without drinking. I carried on taking coke, and I was even nuttier than before. I'd turn up at AA meetings with half an ounce of cocaine in my pocket. Then I'd go to Narcotics Anonymous, not really sure where I was, stand up and say, 'My name is Dennis, and I'm an alcoholic.' I was clinically insane. When the radio starts talking to you, then you know you're in deep shit. Even then, I didn't act on it. The point when I first suspected that something had to give was when I sat in my house, completely alone, in the middle of the night, surrounded by guns, my German shepherd chained to the bed, the doors and windows boarded up, and I'm ready to shoot the first person who tries to get through that door."

And then Hopper went totally crazy. "Again I started hearing voices," he recalled. "People came to see me. After they left, I'd hear them being tortured and murdered. It's really amazing when the telephone wires start talking to you. I was going to celebrate my first birthday in A.A. and decided I was a drug addict, also." In April 1984, Hopper checked himself into Century City Hospital's drug-and-alcohol treatment program. Doctors there told his daughter, Marin, that her father might never regain his sanity. They placed him on antipsychotic drugs and transferred him to the psychiatric ward at Cedars-Sinai Medical Center, once the home away from home for celebrity nutjobs like famed actor, pianist, and wit Oscar Levant. Pumped full of the heavy tranquilizer Thorazine, Hopper shambled around the ward like a lobotomy victim.

Hopper discovered that checking out of the psych ward was harder than checking in. California law prohibits the release of patients who pose a danger to themselves. Hopper's doctors decided he was not responsible for his own safety. Hopper had no family to rely on to get him released.

His father was dead. His mother had remarried and had her own life. If it hadn't been for Bert Schneider, Hopper would have remained committed for at least two years, which was the determination of his doctors.

Hopper recalled, "He [Schneider] came down and saw me and said, 'What the hell are you doing in here?' I said, 'Oh hell, I can't get out of here.' He said, 'Bullshit.' He signed me out and got me up to his house. He said, 'You have to see a shrink for a while.' And I said I didn't know whether I could drive a car. He said, 'You can drive a car. Just take the car and go.' So he got me started."

"I said, 'Thank God I'm back. Thank God it's over,' " Hopper recalled. "So it was a sort of erase and rewind. The experience had really humbled me, and I had gotten the message." Hopper threw out his antipsychotic drugs and returned to Alcoholics Anonymous. "Certainly the 12-Step programs are the most important things that I've found anywhere," he said.

To understand how he had fallen into the abyss of polydrug addiction, Hopper had to retrace the road that led him there. "As far as my family and the life that I had, that wasn't why I was drinking. No one was hiring me," he recalled. "I was wondering why people were calling me difficult, but that's not why I was drinking. I was drinking because I was an alcoholic. I started as a kid, you know, hanging out with the guys. In Kansas, we used to go out in the pickup truck and get a bunch of beer. We would all make a circle with the trucks in the middle of a vacant lot or the field and drink beer. When I was a kid, I worked on the harvest, and the farmers used to give us beer because the sun was so hot. They fed us salt and the beer to cut the wheat. When I was eighteen years old, my agent gave me a martini. He said, 'This is a martini, extra dry.' I went, 'God, this is awful,' and he said, 'It's an acquired taste.' Boy I acquired that taste real quickly.' "

Hopper soon acquired the taste for more exotic drugs like the marijuana and peyote he did with James Dean. "I'd taken peyote when I was a kid," Hopper recalled. "There was a period of time in the '50s when I had an apartment, and there was peyote cooking on the stove all day and night like a pot of coffee, and people would come by, and we'd partake. I finally did that for five years until I had a very bad trip and stopped." Hopper resumed taking peyote after his marriage to Brooke Hayward and began taking LSD in 1967 after playing an LSD dealer in *The Trip*. He finally added cocaine to his drug regimen around the time that he and Peter Fonda began collaborating on *Easy Rider*.

In order to achieve sobriety, Hopper finally had to question the rationale for his alcohol and drug use that kept him in denial for thirty years. "I had built in such a strong endorsement for drinking and using drugs because, after all, I was an artist, and it was O.K. for artists to do that," he said. "All my heroes as painters, poets, or actors were all alcoholics or drug addicts. You see, I didn't relate any of the terrible things that happened to me to my using. I thought drinking and drugging were all part of being a tragic artist. It became my task. I had to do it, or I would never achieve the things I wanted, so I thought. I never thought that was possible without drugs and alcohol because, again, I was an artist, and that's what artists do.

"If you argued with me, I'd point to Fitzgerald and Hemingway and Thomas Wolfe and Tennessee Williams and Modigliani and Jack London. I used to quote Van Gogh, who said, 'I had to drink that whole summer to find the yellow.' Now I say it's probably because he couldn't find the fucking paintbrush! I think that when you start dealing with the arts and people in the arts, it's beyond denial. Many people think it's their right. They have to go and seek the bottle. They have to seek the drugs and disorienting themselves. That's a tragedy in itself. With that kind of rationale, it is almost impossible for anybody to talk to you about it and say you have a problem. In my mind, I was an artist and writer. The reality was that I was just a drunk and a drug addict. It wasn't helping me create. In fact, it hindered me. It stopped me from getting jobs. I dealt with the rejection by taking more drink and drugs. All alcohol and drugs got me was a lot of misery."

Alcohol and drugs robbed Hopper of the very senses that are the Method actor's instrument. "You can only do that sober," he explained. "If you're an alcoholic and drug addict, there's only a moment when drinking and taking drugs work. After that, you're working for the drink and drugs, they're not working for you. I'm talking as a creator. Then pretty soon, if you're really involved in drugs and alcohol, you don't have your senses at all. You don't have any sensibility of your own. You become a schizophrenic, you become more and more paranoid—which you probably were anyway—until you lose sight of yourself. So the mere fact of just stopping—not drinking and not doing drugs today, and being able to maintain that—causes the rest of the miracles to open up because you start becoming normal again. Your senses quiet down, and your vulnerability, your patience, and your understanding start coming back." Afraid that he wouldn't be able to create again without alcohol and drugs, Hopper discovered, "I can do it so much better. My work is so much cleaner. I can utilize all of my senses. Everything is clear now."

"I have not had a drink or hard narcotic in twenty-five years," Hopper told *The Sunday Times'* Garth Pearce in August 2008. A chink in Hopper's carefully managed facade appeared in October 1999 when he was arrested in the airport at Calgary, Alberta, for possession of twelve grams of marijuana. Hopper was there to appear in the film *Knockaround Guys* (2001). Hopper's Canadian attorney, Edward Greenspan, entered a plea of guilty on the actor's behalf in his absence. Judge Doug McDonald granted an absolute discharge, imposing no penalty on Hopper, in consideration of his age, the small amount of marijuana, and the actor's cooperation with the police. "It's fair to say, in terms of Canadian justice, he got the easiest ride possible," Greenspan said. Although the Associated Press picked up the story, and *The San Jose Mercury News* published a small item on the incident, it wasn't widely circulated, especially in Hollywood.

Hopper parsed his words with Garth Pearce very carefully. Evidently, he didn't consider marijuana to fall within his definition of what a hard narcotic was. He never told Pearce that he still snuck a joint in now and then among the cigars and coffee he told journalists he restricted himself to. In their report on the 2005 Cannes Film Festival, the British magazine *Uncut* ran the following tidbit: "Our favourite Hopper story went something like this: when asked whether he still took drugs by a friend of *Uncut*, the *Easy Rider* star admitted he still smokes weed 'because it keeps the bowels regular.' Haven't you heard of dried apricots, Dennis?"

Hopper justifiably called his lifesaving recovery from drugs and alcohol a miracle. "I should really be dead," he said, referring to his lost years in Taos. "I got so insane and crazy out there. I should have just died. Or been killed by a number of people. I don't know how I made it." By the mid-'80s, Hopper had survived enough personal and professional catastrophes to become a one-man *Hollywood Babylon*. That he didn't die a dozen times over from some alcohol or drug-related misadventure is remarkable. Hopper would soon be blessed again when his agent got him some much needed work that jump-started the comeback that introduced the most prolific period in his career.

Hopper moved back to Los Angeles, this time for good. He quit renting Tony Luhan's guesthouse in Taos, though Dennis and his brother converted the El Cortez Theatre into an apartment and studio where Hopper occasionally returned to paint. "When I was still in rehab, the doctor suggested I leave Taos and come back to reality," he said with a laugh. "Reality? In L.A.?"

Dennis had fond memories of the funky atmosphere of Venice, California, recalling the Beat culture, coffeehouses, and jazz clubs that he experienced when he filmed *Night Tide* there. "Anyway, Venice was the only place in L.A. I could remember enjoying because all my painter and poet friends lived here," he said. Hopper purchased one of three 1,200-square-foot, two-story homes designed by celebrity architect Frank Gehry, which he snagged for the bargain price of $90,000. The buildings had been on the market for several years when Hopper came along because Venice's gang problem deterred buyers. Hopper had architect Brian Murphy renovate his home's interior, giving it the imprimatur of trendy modernity that he required.

Around this time, fellow Venice resident Richard Stayton, a writer for the *Los Angeles Herald Examiner*, began seeing a vaguely familiar figure hanging around the periphery of the gallery openings in West L.A. that Stayton attended. Could the "ghostly, anxious loser" that Stayton saw be Dennis Hopper? Indeed he was. Stayton approached Hopper and interviewed him for an article about his comeback for Stayton's paper. "He rarely laughed and cautiously measured every move," Stayton observed. "He worried that one false step might plunge him back into the hell of his 1970s decade."

"I thought I'd never come back to Los Angeles," Hopper told Stayton, explaining his move to Venice. "I really enjoy being in Venice and seeing my friends and also not being in a place where I'm the only person in town. People who were going through Taos kept saying, 'Oh, let's look up Hopper, we can stay at his place.' It became a really expensive proposition. It's nice to be back where things are more leveled out and to be around the industry."

Stayton reported that Hopper had just finished acting in the TV movie *Stark* (1985) and secured a European distribution deal for *The Last Movie* at the recent Cannes Film Festival. Hopper said he had been cast in *The Two Jakes,* the sequel to *Chinatown* (1974), had played the lead in the film *The American Way* (1986, a.k.a. *Riders of the Storm*) in England, directed an MTV music video for Bob Dylan, and played an American video director in an fifty-minute MTV movie starring Mick Jagger. (*The Two Jakes* was finally filmed in 1989 with Tracey Walter taking the role originally intended for Hopper.) Phil Spector was considering Hopper to head his music-video division, Hopper was painting again, and *Vanity Fair's* California editor, Caroline Graham, persuaded him to get his camera out of mothballs for a photo shoot. Hopper was also trying again to get *Biker Heaven* rolling, this time with himself as director. Stayton said that Hopper's phone rang constantly during his visit with the actor.

Hopper also candidly discussed his past alcoholism and drug abuse with Stayton, telling him that he had gone without alcohol for two years, and had just celebrated his first drug-free year. "Well, it's partly that I'm still alive," he told Stayton, explaining the resurgence of his career. "I survived all the experimentation that we went through in the 1960s and 1950s, and most didn't. Then *Apocalypse Now* was on television the other night. *Easy Rider* just played cable. *The American Friend* has a following, and there are a number of people now directing who really loved *Easy Rider*, *Rebel Without a Cause*, *Giant*. And it's partly because I'm around again."

Hopper's comeback began with a role in the teen comedy *My Science Project* (1985), where he played an ex-hippie science teacher who activates a time machine, which turns him into a parody of his character from *Easy Rider*. "It's something I never thought would happen," he said, "but the role offered me an opportunity to return to filmmaking in Los Angeles. Before *My Science Project*, I hadn't worked on a Hollywood soundstage in over twenty years. I wanted the part. I'm anxious to work. It's a real gag. I'm right out of the '60s, spouting the same rhetoric like 'Hell no, I won't go,' 'flower power,' and I even get carted off to jail. It was, well, sort of déjà vu." Hopper followed *My Science Project* with a supporting role as a police lieutenant in *Stark* and reprised the role in *Stark: Mirror Image* (1986). Hopper might have continued playing these bottom-drawer roles for eating money for the rest of his life, but for the next turn of fate that favored him.

Director David Lynch, a master of the grotesque with a genuine gift for infusing banal situations with the dread of imminent horror, was casting his latest production, *Blue Velvet* (1986), whose villain, Frank Booth, would join the pantheon of great movie monsters in a human guise. *Blue Velvet* told the story of Jeffrey Beaumont (Kyle MacLachlan), a college student who returns to his seemingly idyllic hometown after his father suffers a heart attack. After discovering a severed human ear in a field, Jeffrey becomes involved with local chanteuse Dorothy Vallens (Isabella Rossellini), the sex slave and punching bag of psychotic, gas-huffing drug dealer Frank Booth (Dennis Hopper), who kidnapped Vallens' husband and child. Jeffrey enlists the help of his wholesome girlfriend's (Laura Dern) father, a police detective, to defeat Booth and his scuzzy gang.

After Lynch's first two choices, Robert Loggia and Willem Dafoe, rejected the role of Frank Booth, Lynch turned to Hopper, whose enthusiastic acceptance has become a classic Hollywood story. "I had a manager at the time who said this was a career-stopper, that Booth had no redeeming character," Hopper said. "Yeah, I guess! I knew Booth perfectly. Lynch is such a talent, I didn't care if it was commercial or not." Hopper solicited Richard Stayton's advice. Stayton read the script and urged him to take the role, which Stayton thought was a dream role for any actor.

"I had just come out of drug addiction and alcohol," Hopper recalled. "I wasn't even sober like a month and a half. I had just gotten out of rehab. I called David when I read the script for *Blue Velvet*, and he cast me without ever having met me. When I got the part, I wanted to reassure David that I could handle the role, that I understood the character. I called him while he was having lunch with Kyle MacLachlan and Laura Dern and Isabella Rossellini, and I said, 'David, don't even worry about casting me in this. You did the right thing because I *am* Frank Booth.' And he went back to the table and said, 'I just talked to Dennis Hopper, and he said he *is* Frank Booth. I guess that's really good for the movie, but I don't know how we'll ever have lunch with him.'"

"While his name had come up early on, the casting people told me, 'You can't work with Dennis. It'll be a disaster,'" Lynch recalled. "But nobody knew then that he had gone sober, and after I spoke to his agent, he called me personally. We first met face to face on the set of Dorothy Vallens' apartment. A day later, we were filming."

During his drug-fueled years in the wilderness, directors never knew which Dennis Hopper would emerge from the dressing room. "I had incredible mood swings, so no one knew who exactly they were going to be dealing with on any given day," Hopper said. Those days were now behind him. Hopper's professionalism during the making of *Blue Velvet* allayed any fears about him that Lynch and his other actors may have harbored. Kyle MacLachlan's apprehensions about Hopper were put to rest when he saw him arrive on the set in Wilmington, North Carolina carrying a briefcase, looking like a prosperous businessman.

Hopper later explained his declaration that he was Frank. "I'd come out of a heavy drug life and had known a lot of people like Frank," he said. "I didn't mean that I was literally Frank Booth, but I'd known a lot of guys like Frank and understood him very well. I understood his sexual obsession. I was known to abuse people when drunk or high, but not exactly this way. But Dennis Hopper in reality is more a masochist than a sadist.

"You can call Frank Booth a deviant, a pervert, a madman, whatever. But I saw him as a man who would go to any lengths to keep his lady. He might slice off ears and kidnap children. But it's essentially a love story. Maybe some people find that strange. But they didn't play Frank Booth. To play Frank, you need to understand him, and to understand him, you need to have Frank's point of view."

"I don't think actors have to die to do a death scene, but in *Blue Velvet*, Dennis touched something personal with Frank Booth's dark side," David Lynch wrote. "No one could have topped his Frank Booth. After seeing Dennis walk that dark edge, I don't think anyone could have even come close." "*Blue Velvet* was wonderful," Hopper said. "David Lynch was terrific to work with. There was no improvisation—David had written the screenplay and stuck to it. David kept me up really high, pushing all the time. He insisted I keep playing it at a high level. But I had a terrific time." "I love what I do in the film, and what David did with me," he said, calling *Blue Velvet* the first American surrealist film.

Hopper even served as a technical advisor of sorts to Lynch, who was a naif when it came to drugs. In the film, Frank Booth huffs some substance from a handheld inhaler. "I'm thankful to Dennis," Lynch said, "because up until the last minute it was gonna be helium—to make the difference between 'Daddy' and the baby that much more." "A big discrepancy came the first day we were shooting the big scene where Kyle is hiding in the closet and I come in demanding my bourbon and tell Isabella to spread her legs," Hopper remembered, "and then this sort of horrendous rape scene occurs against her. None of us had met at this point, and that was our first scene (laughs). David had helium on the set because in the script, the tank that Frank was constantly taking hits from was written as helium, which makes your voice really high, like Donald Duck. But it doesn't disorient you in any way, it just makes you talk funny.

"So I said to David, 'You know I always thought of this as being nitrous oxide or amyl nitrate or something.' He said, 'What is that?' I said, 'Something that disorients your mind for a few minutes. I'm also having trouble acting with my voice sounding like this. So could I just show you what it would look like with the other stuff?' " "But I didn't want it to be funny," Lynch recalled. "So helium went out the window, and it became just a gas. Then, in the first rehearsal, Dennis said, 'David, I know what's in these different canisters.' And I said, 'Thank God, Dennis, that you know that!' And he named all the gases." "If you want to put the [helium] voice in later, in post, we can, " Hopper recalled telling Lynch, "and of course, we didn't. So that was the only real contribution I made to that film, I guess."

Hopper was amused by Lynch's propriety. "David was like a Boy Scout," he said. "He doesn't take drugs. He meditates. He'd give direction like, 'Dennis, if you say that, when you say *that* word . . .' And I'd say, 'David, that word is fuck.' He'd be like, 'Yes, I know, and when you say that word . . .' He wouldn't even say it. But he'd written this film . . . You know, you'd do this very, very dark scene, and he'd be like, 'Howdy-doody! Solid gold! Let's do one more!' It makes you think that whatever he has inside, he really keeps buried."

If the spectrum of Hopper's film career can be spanned by two roles, then his performances as Jordan Benedict III in *Giant* and Frank Booth in *Blue Velvet* represent its polar opposites. Hopper made *Giant* barely a year after leaving high school. Jordan Benedict III was the closest he got to playing a conventional leading man, and his screen presence in *Giant* conveys what Oscar Wilde called "all the hope and joy and glamour of life before him."

Hopper's Frank Booth is the monster from the id that rampages through Lynch's allegory of the duality of good and evil, light and darkness. By the time that he played Booth, Hopper's face mapped the changes wrought by the last thirty years of his roller-coaster life. Gone was any trace of his boyish softness and tentative gestures. Hopper's Booth is all hardness and seething anger. Hopper's head, with its broad expanse of forehead exposed by his receding hairline, looks disproportionately large on his short body, almost like a bobblehead doll, magnifying his malevolent presence. His most expressive feature now was his brows, which knit together above the bridge of his nose with each explosive outburst he made.

"He was physically small, lean, with a large head," Philippe Mora wrote, recalling his impressions of Hopper. "His electric charisma made him big. It reminded me of when I had dinner with Richard Burton, who had a similar physicality. He had a great face, and as Samuel Fuller said: 'The human face is the greatest landscape of all.' Starting out as a pretty boy was a burden for him, and so he relished acting nasty. His face then became a weapon."

Time's Richard Corliss called Frank Booth "maybe the vilest sadistic creep in movie history." "I think it's my best movie performance," Hopper said in 2005. "I got voted Best Movie Villain in the 1994 MTV Awards for that role, and I was flattered out of my pants. I was there above Jimmy Cagney in *White Heat* [1949] and Edward G. Robinson in *Little Caesar* [1931]. How's that for a farm boy from Kansas? That doesn't make any sense to me. It's so great."

Hopper's inimitable performance of Frank Booth became his signature role, eclipsing everything he had done before. The impact his performance had on audiences caused him to recall the advice Vincent Price gave him thirty years earlier when they worked together in *The Story of Mankind*. Price told Hopper, "You should play bad guys. You're going to make a great bad guy." "I thought, 'Boy is he crazy," Hopper said. "Just because he plays bad guys, he thinks I'm going to be playing bad guys.' But he was right. I make a pretty good living playing the bad guy." Hopper's iconic turn in *Blue Velvet* vindicated Price's prophecy. *Blue Velvet* would prove to be both a blessing and a curse for Hopper. Though he worked constantly after *Blue Velvet*, Hopper became trapped playing endless variations of Frank Booth for the rest of his life.

Hopper appreciated the irony of his new situation. Straight out of rehab, he played a drug-inhaling psycho in *Blue Velvet*, the town drunk in *Hoosiers* (1986), and a one-legged, pot-dealing ex-biker in *River's Edge* (1986). Filmed in Indianapolis, Indiana, *Hoosiers* tells the feel-good story of former college basketball coach Norman Dale (Gene Hackman), who was suspended from college ball after hitting a player. Twelve years later, in the fall of 1951, he gets hired to replace the recently deceased coach of a rural town's high-school team. Dale overcomes the initial resistance of the town's citizens and the teacher (Barbara Hershey) who becomes his love interest, and leads the underdog team to win the state championship.

Hopper played Wilbur "Shooter" Flatch, who blew the winning shot in his high-school championship game, becoming an alcoholic and a humiliation to his son, who now plays on the school's team. When the assistant coach suffers a heart attack, Coach Dale enlists Shooter to become his new assistant in the face of the town's opposition on the condition that he stays sober. Shooter relapses, creates a drunken scene during his son's game, and is hospitalized. The home team goes on to victory while Shooter listens to coverage of the championship game on the radio.

Hopper initially refused *Hoosiers*, reluctant to play an alcoholic so soon into his own recovery. "I didn't want to do this movie," he said. "I didn't think it was right for me. I was gonna do *Blue Velvet*, and Anspaugh [*Hoosiers'* director] kept bugging me to do this. I told them to get Harry Dean Stanton." Stanton asked Hopper, "Aren't you from Kansas?" Hopper said, "Yeah." Stanton asked, "Didn't you have a hoop on your barn?" Hopper said, "Yeah." Stanton said, "I think you may be the guy that David Anspaugh's looking for."

"Finally, fuck it, I did it," Hopper said. "I did *Blue Velvet*, then flew right to Indianapolis to do this, and I knew this guy so well it's ridiculous. And I knew that James Dean had played against this team as a boy in Indiana. Nice touch. Also, myself being a recovering alcoholic helped." Hopper objected to a scene in *Hoosiers'* screenplay where Shooter breaks out of the hospital to cheer his son on at his championship game. "Being an alcoholic, I felt that it was really destructive to have Shooter leave," he said. "Maybe he'll never get sober, but he ain't going to get sober if he goes to the game. I said, 'Just do a shot of me in the hospital jumping up and down while listening to the game on the radio.' I sacrificed a lot of movie time up there on the screen."

Hopper told reporters why he found his role in *Hoosiers* appealing. "I liked it on a number of levels. I thought it was a nice little part, that it had charm to it. It had a certain beginning, middle, and end to it, that the character was realized in its own way. I also like the fact that it was an alcoholic who ended up in treatment because that is what happened to me three years ago. I bottomed out, and my character bottoms out in this and is put into treatment."

At the same time, he said, "I know about how to be a drunk real well. I don't think it probably helps anyone that Shooter ends up in treatment because unfortunately most drunks are charming, devious people. So I don't know that it helps anyone to see what happens to him, except that he's a terrible embarrassment to his son and he's hurting people around him—and he's hurting himself." Most reviewers found *Hoosiers* corny, but affecting, and praised Hackman and Hopper's performances.

"To me, the performance in *Hoosiers* was the best thing that I've seen from Dennis," Stewart Stern said in 1988. "I long for Dennis to start dealing with the things that really, really have touched him. Kansas, the farm in Kansas, his grandparents. I always told him that I didn't know how deeply his connection to other people really ran. And that until he could feel what they really felt, he couldn't be an artist. I saw some of that in *Hoosiers*, a vulnerability. And I wish that he would let himself be moved again by his own childhood. There's a side of him which is authentic and certainly much simpler than Robert Frost. That is absolutely American. Not just America at its hippest, but America at its most traditional."

River's Edge, the third film in Hopper's comeback trifecta, tells the story of a teenager who kills his girlfriend and the apathetic reactions of the killer's circle of disaffected classmates. In *River's Edge,* Hopper played Feck, a pistol-wielding, pot-dealing hermit who lost a leg in a motorcycle accident years before. Feck (a great character name that sounds like an expression of disgust) once killed his own girlfriend and now lives in a locked shack with an inflatable sex doll he calls Ellie. Feck could very well be *Easy Rider's* Billy gone rotten, if he had survived that film, or even Hopper himself in an alternate universe. Hopper once speculated that he could have easily become a criminal if things had gone differently for him. Hopper was even given a line of dialogue that harkened back to his admission in *The American Dreamer* that he preferred going down on women to fucking them when Feck says, "I ate so much pussy in those days, my beard looked like a glazed doughnut."

"I love that movie," Hopper said, ten years after making *River's Edge.* "It was beautiful, but tough, and [Crispin] Glover gives a great performance. It's a real story out of Sacramento. You know, when I was young, I wanted movies that shocked me. Now, they go to *Speed,* and that is wonderful, but it's just a big ride in an amusement park." "It is another of Hopper's possessed performances, done with sweat and the whites of his eyes," Roger Ebert wrote in his review of *River's Edge.* In her review, Janet Maslin wrote, "And Mr. Hopper, whose scenes with the party doll ought to be thoroughly ridiculous, once again makes himself a very powerful presence. For better or worse, Mr. Hopper is back with a vengeance."

Time magazine made it official in their November 17, 1986, issue: Dennis Hopper was back. *Time's* article, "Dennis Hopper: Easy Rider Rides Again," reported that he had completed nine movies in the two years preceding the article, but acknowledged that the singular nature of *Blue Velvet* and his performance in it vaulted him back into the limelight. "But one film—David Lynch's *Blue Velvet*—cannot be dismissed," *Time*'s Gerald Clarke wrote. "An illustrated guide to Krafft-Ebing, *Blue Velvet* is perhaps the first film since 1972's *Last Tango in Paris* to scandalize its audience. At the end, people are as likely to erupt in boos as to burst into applause."

Time's article also set the template for all the future articles that would be written about Hopper. *Time*'s piece had the potted biography, noting the key events in his life: his Kansas boyhood, James Dean's mesmeric influence, Henry Hathaway's blacklisting, Hopper's first comeback in *Easy Rider*, his flame-out in *The Last Movie*, his lost years in Taos on drugs, his miraculous recovery, and his desire to play a character that isn't deviant or psychotic. *Time* even got the notoriously interview-averse Jack Nicholson to endorse Hopper's cultural significance. "As an actor, Dennis stands out because of his edge, his sincerity, the honesty he conveys," Nicholson said. "But Dennis also paints. He takes pictures. He's got an extremely fine eye for life. He's a great appreciator with a great vision. And he does things his way."

Time suggested that some of Hopper's recent films, like *My Science Project* and *The Texas Chainsaw Massacre, Part 2* (1986), were best left off his resume. Hopper was the only big name in *The Texas Chainsaw Massacre, Part 2*, a black comedy gorefest that was the sequel to *The Texas Chainsaw Massacre* (1974). Hopper played former Texas Ranger Lt. "Lefty" Enright, who's been investigating the connection between the disappearance of his niece and nephew thirteen years earlier and a recent series of chainsaw murders. Enright even goes chainsaw to chainsaw with Leatherface (Bill Johnson), the killer from the original film.

Roger Ebert, who respected the original film, had none for its sequel, writing, "This movie goes flat-out from one end to the other, never spending any time on pacing, on timing, on the anticipation of horror. It doesn't even pause to establish the characters; Dennis Hopper has the most thankless task, playing a man who spends the first half of the movie looking distracted and vague, and the second half screaming during chainsaw duels." "I was lousy—it's a lousy film, but I had fun doing it," Hopper said.

It didn't help any that writer L. M. Kit Carson, who couldn't make it all the way through a screening of *The Texas Chainsaw Massacre* in 1974, was churning out pages of his script to the sequel while Tobe Hooper was directing it. Hopper's consolation prize for making the film came when the cast and crew surprised him with a birthday cake decorated with one candle for each of his fifty years and a chainsaw with which to cut it. Another incidental benefit of filming in Texas was the opportunity it gave Hopper to play in his friend Willie Nelson's golf invitational at his Pedernales Country Club, in which Hopper won the second-place trophy.

Bud Shrake introduced Hopper to golf after he looked Shrake up in Austin when he was shooting *The Texas Chainsaw Massacre, Part 2*. When the recently sober Hopper heard that Shrake had quit drinking, he asked him, "How do you spend your days? How do you fill up all this time that we used to spend in bars and running around and doing shit?" Shrake said, "Playing golf." Hopper said, "Well, I better start." Shrake took Hopper to buy a set of clubs and drove him to Willie Nelson's golf course for his first round. "He became a golf nut," Shrake said. "It's happened that you see a lot of the time with show business and musicians, that people replace those hours they spend drugged out and they become addicts of another kind. And a lot of them become addicted to golf. Not long ago, I saw a big full-page, color photograph in *Golf Digest* magazine with Dennis Hopper standing out at the first tee wearing knickers, plaid socks, a little cap, leaning on his driver, and it said 'Mr. Golf.' Hopper."

Hopper followed *The Texas Chainsaw Massacre, Part 2* with a role in James Toback's *The Pick-Up Artist* (1987), a vehicle for teen star Molly Ringwald that Warren Beatty produced. Hopper played Ringwald's father in the film. Roger Ebert complained that *The Pick-Up Artist* was so derivative, it even had actors playing inferior imitations of characters they'd played before in better films. Ebert wrote, "Dennis Hopper, for example, is the drunken father, a shambles of ruined self-loathing, drinking himself into oblivion while his child tries to help him. This is a guest shot from 'Hoosiers.'"

With each new film he completed, Hopper became more prosperous. Richard Stayton, who accepted Hopper's invitation to write the actor's biography, observed how the quality of his life improved, even if his roles didn't. "There is often someone else present, usually a woman and always a new one," Stayton wrote. "They grow in beauty as his career accelerates. Most appear to be putting their clothes on when I arrive."

Sometimes, one woman wasn't enough to satisfy Hopper's sexual desire. In the scurrilous tell-all, *You'll Never Make Love in This Town Again*, a prostitute accustomed to servicing Arab sheiks and high-profile celebrities recounts the time she and a friend answered Hopper's call for two women.

After some chit chat, he asked the women to strip down to their lingerie and engage in some lez-type lovemaking, which they performed with the assistance of various sex toys. Hopper was content to merely watch them, until one woman brought the other to a loud, simulated orgasm which he was satisfied was authentic, ending the session. As Hopper was paying them and seeing them to his door, he invited them to be his guests for lunch at a nearby restaurant where he was meeting a producer. He asked only that they not tell the producer they were whores, a condition they happily complied with.

Hopper outgrew the home he bought when he first relocated to Venice. He purchased the two remaining Gehry buildings, which he had connected by elevated walkways covered with wire mesh. He acquired the adjacent vacant lot, where he commissioned Brian Murphy to build his main house, which one writer called Hopper's "art barn." He added a lap pool and Jacuzzi outside. In 2001, he finally acquired the Craftsman home near the main house after the elderly woman who owned it died. Hopper turned it into a guest cottage. Hopper was finally able to give his wife at the time, Victoria, a backyard to plant her roses, and somewhere his son, Henry, could play with his new German shepherd.

Hopper's main house was fittingly idiosyncratic. The street-facing facade is a surface of corrugated aluminum with a diagonal roofline, broken only by a single recessed, heavy door that looks like something out of a '30s Warner Bros. prison picture. The house can only be entered by punching in a code on an electronic keypad by the front door. That door leads to a cavernous interior big enough to include an indoor garage separated from the living area by a retractable steel shutter.

Illuminated by a skylight, the interior space served as a gallery for Hopper's art collection, his own art and photographs, and framed awards. Metal staircases led to rooms upstairs connected by catwalks. An elaborate security system allowed him to follow events outside through a number of video cameras that observed the neighborhood.

"It's been described as a floodlit fortress," Brian Murphy said. "It's an interior landscape bereft of windows with sliding walls that can showcase his enormous art collection on both sides. The entire structure keeps morphing to suit his changing lifestyle. Dennis is a very sophisticated person in terms of aesthetics, and he's been very involved in aspects of the design."

The fortress-like appearance of Hopper's home was appropriate, since it was located in a graffiti-scarred, gang-ridden part of Venice. Ben Irwin, who interviewed Hopper in his Venice home, wrote, "Hopper's studio in Venice is located on a sad-looking street in a rundown neighborhood that looked as if it might not be the safest place in the world in which to wander at night." "There are gangs," Joe Rhodes wrote. "But there are also artists nearby, warehouse lofts where painters and sculptors have been living for years, places where artists like Ed Ruscha and Kenneth Price got their start. It's a neighborhood where art and danger, two things that always have attracted Dennis Hopper, live side by side."

Richard Stayton arrived at Hopper's house one afternoon just as he was concluding a phone conversation with Warren Beatty, who Hopper held in awe. "Imagine, Warren Beatty on a car phone in the Cahuenga Pass talking to Dennis Hopper in Venice. Wow," he told Stayton. It was great news for Hopper, who was hoping to do some sort of movie deal with Beatty, but bad news for Stayton when Hopper told him he was backing out of the book project on Beatty's advice. He told Stayton, "You know, Warren says I shouldn't do it." A flabbergasted Stayton said, "Warren Beatty? You're asking him for advice on your life story?" Hopper said, "Who else? He's the only actor in Hollywood who's had as many women as me. He says people in this town never forget. Warren's smart about these things. In my spare time, I gotta concentrate on directing a film. There's a chance if I play things right that I'll finally direct a studio picture. That's gotta be my focus."

Nineteen eighty-seven was Hopper's year. He would be nominated for an Academy Award, grace the cover of *Vanity Fair*, and direct Sean Penn and Robert Duvall in a film for a major American studio. The Los Angeles Film Critics Association had just given him their award for Best Supporting Actor for his performances in *Blue Velvet* and *Hoosiers* in mid-January when Ron Rosenbaum followed Hopper around to profile him for *Vanity Fair*.

Hopper had recently returned from New York, where gallery owner Tony Shafrazi gave him an exhibition of his photos, throwing Hopper a party attended by such hip glitterati as David Byrne and Jim Jarmusch. "And Dennis' show, the photographs were nothing special," Andy Warhol wrote in his diary entry for Saturday, December 13, 1986. "I guess Tony just wanted publicity with a movie star. Everybody kept telling Dennis how great he was in *Blue Velvet*." Two days later, Warhol noted how Julian Schnabel "sat himself right down next to Dennis Hopper at Tony Shafrazi's dinner for Dennis over the weekend and then made the speech about Dennis although he didn't know him." Schnabel, who became a star of the art scene by gluing broken crockery onto his canvases, became Hopper's friend and painted a witty, affecting portrait of Hopper, whose long, melancholy face in the painting is fractured by the cracks in the underlying plates.

The sunny morning following the L.A. Film Critics ceremony found Hopper sitting on his sofa, drinking coffee, and smoking Marlboros, surrounded by the perks of his renewed success. A coffee table held copies of *Variety* and *The Hollywood Reporter*, strategically opened to full-page ads from Orion Pictures recommending Academy members nominate Hopper for an Academy Award for Best Supporting Actor for his performance in *Hoosiers*. A souvenir program from a black-tie event honoring Lew Wasserman's fiftieth year in show business, where Hopper escorted Jennifer Jones and Jean Stein, MCA founder Jules Stein's daughter, lay on the sofa beside him. A carton containing copies of *Out of the Sixties*, a slick coffee-table book collecting Hopper's photos from the period, sat on his other side. Hopper's desk was stacked with screenplays he was offered, including one for *Colors* (1988), a drama that Penn wanted him to direct, about a veteran cop and his young partner dealing with warring inner-city gangs.

Penn was one of the latest generation of "bad boy" stars, known for his dustups with intrusive paparazzi and his marriage to Madonna. He was also a huge fan of Hopper's work and rebel spirit. Penn first approached Hopper to direct a project starring himself and Madonna shortly after they married in August 1985. David Geffen called Hopper and told him the couple were impressed by *Out of the Blue* and wanted to meet him. During their first meeting, Hopper noticed that Penn was carrying a book by Charles Bukowski. Hopper told Penn that he'd be the perfect actor for *Barfly* (1987), a screenplay Bukowski had written for director Barbet Schroeder. Penn asked Hopper, "Will you direct it?" Hopper said, "There's no way to get this from Barbet Schroeder—I ended up enemies with him when I told him he couldn't direct traffic." "So we had a meeting in which Bukowski said no to me," Hopper recalled. "He wanted Sean to do it really badly—with Barbet—but Sean said, 'Unless Dennis directs, I'm not going to do it.' This was really incredible to me, Sean being that kind of stand-up guy."

Penn developed *Colors* with producer Robert H. Solo, from a screenplay by Richard DiLello about cops fighting a fictitious gang in Chicago which has invented a dangerous new drug. "I read the script, and we had a meeting at Orion, and I told them it was awful, terrible—that it wouldn't even make a bad television show," Hopper recalled. "It was about a white cop that had to bust a black gang that was selling cough syrup, and if this wasn't stopped, there was going to be a cough-syrup epidemic across the country. So, to me, it was bad news, and I told them we couldn't make it. Bob Solo told me I'd just rode in like a gunslinger from out of town and shot down a sure deal."

Orion's executives asked Hopper, "Well, what would make it good?" Hopper, who lived in gang territory, said, "Have you read the fucking newspaper? You set it in Los Angeles, and you make it about an older cop and a younger cop. And make it about *real* gangs and *real* drugs." The executives at Orion Pictures didn't want Hopper to direct, but they wanted Penn, and Penn insisted on Hopper. "It was really a privilege directing Sean in *Colors*, a wonderful creative experience for me," he said later. "And it was also a really wonderful thing that he did in hiring me to direct that movie, basically. It was an Orion picture, but it was Sean who put me in there. That's something that a guy like me never forgets." Though colleagues routinely express similar thoughts about each other while publicizing a film, Hopper really meant it. A photo taken of Penn and Hopper walking together shows him following Penn, beaming with pride at his young disciple. The old rebel was passing the torch to his young successor.

"Dennis made it happen," Penn said. "And when Dennis talked about L.A. gangs, he talked about a particular culture, and it was a visual culture, too." Penn brought in screenwriter Michael Schiffer to revise DiLello's script when Hopper was signed to direct. Hopper and Penn worked with the Los Angeles County Sheriff's Operation Safe Streets team and rode with members of the LAPD's anti-gang CRASH unit for research. Hopper said, "We had cooperation from both the Crips and the Bloods [L.A.'s opposing gangs], just on the level that they were aware it was happening and that we were using real gang members as extras. I mean, my feeling from the start was that if you had real cops and real gang-bangers, then you were probably going to get a pretty real picture."

Though Hopper, Penn, and Duvall worked with actual gang members and shot the movie on gang territory in South Central Los Angeles, it was Penn's temper, not gang violence, that threatened to derail the production. Penn had already pled no contest in February to charges of misdemeanor assault and battery for an altercation in April 1986 with a musician he suspected of having an affair with Madonna. On April 2, 1987, Penn assaulted an extra who photographed him on the set of *Colors*. Penn managed to stay out of jail during the remainder of the shoot, but later served thirty-three days behind bars for violating probation and for reckless driving (running a red light).

Hopper attended the 59th Academy Awards on March 30, 1987, with guarded anticipation. "I'm just going to have a good time, just like when I went in 1970," he told an interviewer before the ceremony. "Then I knew the Academy wouldn't give somebody like me an Oscar, not for *Easy Rider*. So I enjoyed myself. Now? Well, to win would be nice, but so much has gone down in my life that just to be nominated by my peers in the acting community is great. I would accept every year being in this kind of conversation and never winning, honestly." When Michael Caine won the award for *Hannah and Her Sisters* (1986), Hopper was magnanimous in defeat. "I felt Michael Caine would win, and he did," he said. "I mean, he had been nominated seven times and never had one. I just feel that adds up and ought to be recognized."

Hopper also acquired a new girlfriend, who would go on to become his fourth wife. In March 1987, he attended the opening-night performance of the Karole Armitage ballet company, where he was taken by the appearance of twenty-one-year-old dancer and actor Katherine LaNasa. Hopper went backstage where he told her, "This is really embarrassing, but you have a really great ass!" "This led to other things, and the next night, I was back at the ballet," he said. "He wasn't like Mr. Suave who pulled some big number," LaNasa later said. "When he took me back to the hotel, he took my face in his hands and kissed me all over like a puppy." "I loved her the first time I saw her," Hopper said. "She was snappy, strong, not sentimental. She wasn't impressed by things. Katherine is very well versed in art, which is the only thing I am very well versed in." Hopper and LaNasa dated for nine months. By Christmas of 1987, LaNasa was living with Hopper and had become his fiancée.

The release of *Colors* in April 1988 revived the old controversy about the role violence in movies plays in stimulating violent behavior in viewers. The LAPD and experts on street gangs feared that *Colors* would ignite gang violence at screenings, like the three killings that followed screenings of Walter Hill's gang-war film, *The Warriors,* in 1979. After picketing Sean

Penn's Malibu home, the self-promoting Curtis Sliwa and his red beret-wearing Guardian Angels protested outside Hopper's home. Carrying seven mock coffins and a toilet seat with Hopper's picture taped to it, they hectored Hopper to donate the film's profits to neighborhood antigang groups. They drew the chalk outlines of two imaginary victims of gang violence on the sidewalk in front of his house and affixed yellow police tape to his white picket fence. Hopper did not emerge from his home to answer their charges, but a man who identified himself as Hopper spoke over an intercom, saying, "The movie is great. This [the protest] is bogus. They're just out for publicity. It's too bad, unfortunate."

Addressing the issue of whether movies made viewers violent, Hopper said, "Blame the killing on the movies? Blame it on kids with guns. Blame it on police who don't have enough guns. Blame it on rock cocaine. Blame it on poverty. But don't blame it on the movies. Films don't kill; people do." Where was the Dennis Hopper who made *The Last Movie*, which blamed Hollywood for the impact of media violence on innocent viewers?

"There's nothing romantic about gangs," he said. "None of that *West Side Story* stuff works anymore. There's no glorification of that life in *Colors* at all. *Colors* is about more than gangs. The story is really about an older cop and a younger cop. Boy, if I'd made a story about the gangs, I'd have never gotten the movie released. Yet people who haven't seen the film say it shouldn't be seen. 'Bodies are going to be strewn from one end of this town to the other,' they say. Well, bodies are being strewn from one end of this town to the other now, and while we were making the film, it was happening."

Jay Boyar, the *Orlando Sentinel's* movie critic, concurred with Hopper, writing, "People who blame the approaches taken by these movies for the violence at the theaters are taking too simple a view. Make a movie about dentists, dentists will go to see it. Make a movie about kindergarten teachers, kindergarten teachers will show up. And if your movie is about street gangs, members of gangs will want to see it. Even if a film's approach is not in the least inflammatory, the presence of gangs at the movies may very well be. Only a disturbed mind could see the gang violence in the movie as glamorous. Anyone sick enough to join a gang based on the horrors portrayed in *Colors* is most likely beyond help anyway." Fortunately, serious violence related to *Colors* was limited to a single incident where a nineteen-year-old was shot in a dispute with a moviegoer outside a theater showing the movie in Stockton, California.

Though *Colors* was a substantial commercial success, critical reaction to it was mixed. Roger Ebert praised the film's strong performances and the authenticity of its portrayal of gang life, but criticized the triteness of the relationship between the sage older cop (Robert Duvall) and his hotheaded partner (Sean Penn), and found Hopper's direction routine. Jonathan Rosenbaum was so disappointed by Hopper's return to directing that he checked his enthusiastic review of *Out of the Blue*, almost refusing to accept that both movies were made by the same man. "The script is terrible," Rosenbaum wrote, citing a scene where Duvall and Penn's police cruiser flips over while pursuing gang members, whose cars collide in a playground. "As they're hanging upside down in their car," Rosenbaum wrote, "Hodges (Duvall) says to McGavin (Penn), 'My wife says she wants to meet you. She says you can bring a date'—and the scene abruptly shifts to McGavin with a date visiting Hodges and his family. Who got killed in the last scene, and who got caught? The movie doesn't care, and, thanks to such indifference, neither do we. The project was developed by Sean Penn, who brought in Hopper as a director; without Hopper's name in the credits, I doubt anyone would recognize his participation."

Pauline Kael complained that Hopper didn't take the viewer inside the material: the cops are the only characters we get to know. "Despite the film's kinetic style, it feels slow and long and tame," Kael wrote. "He's a visual aesthete—less a director than an artistic arranger of people in the frame. He takes us on an art tour of the graffiti-covered walls in the ghettos and barrios." In 2008, Hopper said *Colors* was merely "alright."

Though Hopper would only direct three more films, he worked nonstop as an actor after *Blue Velvet* until October 2009, when terminal cancer forced him to retire. Hopper acted in fifteen feature films and TV movies from 1985 to 1990 alone, not counting his voice acting for a series of children's videos and his narration for a TV movie. Most of these were potboilers, where producers used Hopper as a cinematic Mrs. Dash®. Hopper might get a supporting role in a decent, if undistinguished studio production, a higher profile part in an independent film, or be the main attraction in a film whose backers hired him knowing he was their only bankable asset.

Hopper played an eccentric toymaker who falls victim to serial husband-killer Theresa Russell in the mediocre *Black Widow* (1987), directed by his friend Bob Rafelson. Though *Black Widow* was a major studio production starring Debra Winger, Hopper's role was a cameo that gave him no chance to develop or sustain a character. Sometimes Hopper took a bite-sized part as a lark, like his role as I. G. Farben in Alex Cox's spaghetti Western spoof *Straight to Hell* (1987). Hopper worked one day on the film's Spanish location. Five actors were required to act in the scene. Twenty-five showed up just to watch Hopper.

Hopper's participation in *Straight to Hell* gave Roger Ebert a flashback from *The Last Movie*. Ebert wrote, "*Straight to Hell* was 'filmed in three weeks on a shoestring budget of $1 million,' but looks more as if it were filmed in one week on Cox's MasterCard. The cast is littered with familiar faces who dropped in for the fun: [Joe] Strummer, Elvis Costello, Grace Jones, Jim Jarmusch, and Dennis Hopper—whose mere presence should have sent up some sort of a warning light. It was Hopper who went to Peru in 1970 and made *The Last Movie*, another shapeless gonzo Western starring lots of rock stars and personal friends, and the backlash from that movie put his career on hold for years. Cox seems to have staged the same sort of come-as-you-are party."

What can you say about *Blood Red* (1989), where Hopper hauled his Irish accent out of storage to play William Bradford Berrigan, a railroad magnate out to get the land of winemaking Sicilian émigrés in 1890s California? The film represents the only on-screen pairing of siblings Eric and Julia Roberts, but didn't merit a single review from a major periodical. "Let's just say I'm a man who takes care of business," Hopper said of his role. While promoting the second season of their TV series, *Crash*, in August 2009, Hopper teased Eric Roberts about *Blood Red* and *Luck of the Draw* (2000), where they were also paired. Hopper reminded Roberts, "We did a movie together, too." "We don't want to talk about that, Dennis," Roberts said. "Terrible movies. I made a couple." Hopper said, "I made more than a couple."

Hopper played a wily inmate in a hellish state mental institution in *Chattahoochee* (1990), but was second banana to Gary Oldman, a champion scenery chewer who, like Hopper, has made a specialty of quirky characters. "I was there for three weeks, for something that should have been eight weeks," Hopper said, recalling director Mick Jackson's no-nonsense approach. "I had no idea what I was doing. I would suggest that we rehearse something, and Mick said, 'No, I have three cameras on you right now. You must stay right where I put you.' "

"About the closest thing to actual movie entertainment comes when the camera wanders within range of Dennis Hopper, who manages to inject his own personal weirdness into even the most innocuous encounter," the *Washington Post*'s Hal Hinson wrote. "The rest of the picture is torturously routine. When, at last, the movie declares its true subject, our worst fears are confirmed. Yes, *Chattahoochee* is the story of a crusader whose battle against the state's inhumane treatment of its mental patients provokes widespread reforms."

Since Hopper could play roles like that of the inmate in *Chattahoochee* in his sleep, it's surprising how much game he brought to them. Producers recognized this. They also recognized how valuable he was in publicizing their films. Hopper no longer resented giving interviews. He often seemed to enjoy himself hugely while doing them. His shameless willingness to discuss his past foibles made him a publicist's dream. After *Blue Velvet* gained Hopper a new audience, he made practically a second career out of his appearances on TV talk shows, where he reveled in telling colorful stories of his drinking and drug use and his friendships with James Dean, Natalie Wood, and Elvis, all punctuated by his inimitable dirty chortle. With the kind of films Hopper was making, the interview *was* the performance.

While appearing on *Late Night with David Letterman* during the 1988 presidential campaign, Hopper revealed that he was supporting George H. W. Bush in his bid for the presidency. This surprised viewers who assumed Hopper's counterculture past had cemented his allegiance to the Democratic Party. Hopper later explained his decision. "My whole family were Democrats, and I was a Democrat until Reagan. I've always been political, but I haven't always been a Republican. I was with Martin Luther King and at the Free Speech Movement in Berkeley. I was a hippie. I was probably as left as you could get without being a Communist. I never cared for Reagan, very honestly. I thought he was a bad actor. I never thought he was a great communicator, didn't think he was a great speaker, and I didn't know what kind of a president he'd be.

"But I was reading a lot of Thomas Jefferson at the time, and Jefferson said that every twenty years, if one party has stayed in power, it's your obligation as an American to vote the other party in. But the idea of changing the Congress, changing the Senate, getting the Democrats out, getting the Republicans in, also the idea of having less government—which didn't seem to work out. At that time, I wanted to see Congress change, and we did change Congress. The idea of less government, more individual freedom, is something that I liked. I started believing it. So I started voting. I voted that time for Reagan, and I've voted on the straight Republican ticket ever since. I don't go to meetings, I don't go to things. I just go to the polls and do it. Then I just stayed with the Republicans. I voted for both the Bushes."

Hopper's role in *Flashback* (1990), where he played an unreconstructed hippie, seemed a perfect fit for the actor, but wasn't initially offered to him. Marin Hopper discovered the script and told her father the role was tailor made for him. When Hopper's agent told him that Chevy Chase and Dan Aykroyd were being considered, Hopper thought he was out of the running until director Franco Amurri eventually chose him.

Yippie Huey Walker (Hopper) decoupled Spiro Agnew's railroad car during his whistle-stop tour in the 1968 presidential campaign, stranding Agnew in a deserted part of Idaho. Walker then became a fugitive after his arrest for malicious mischief. Twenty years later, Huey decides to turn himself over to the FBI to publicize his upcoming memoir. The FBI assign conservative, buttoned-down agent John Buckner (Kiefer Sutherland) to return Walker to custody.

Once on the train, Huey plays mind games on Buckner so he can escape again. He convinces Buckner he's slipped him acid, then tells him that the only antidote is plenty of beer and tequila. (Hopper could have written this film.) Walker, who starts the film looking like Hopper in his '70s Taos period, cleans himself up, switches clothes and identities with Buckner, and turns him over to the authorities in his place.

Once Buckner's real identity is discovered, he threatens to have the corrupt sheriff holding him prosecuted. The sheriff, who is running for Congress, decides to solve his problem by killing Buckner and Walker, who escape to the commune where Buckner was raised. It all ends happily ever after. His inner hippie awakened by revelations about his parents that he discovers at the commune, Buckner takes off to California on a motorcycle to find himself. The last shot in *Flashback* is of Huey walking out of San Francisco's City Lights Bookstore, where his book is on display in the front window.

If Hopper's political conversion gave his fans grounds to wonder what happened to one of the counterculture's standard-bearers, then *Flashback* was seen by those who remained loyal to the political and social ideals of the '60s as his betrayal of everything they held dear. Really nothing more than a composite of *Trading Places* (1983) and *Midnight Run* (1988), *Flashback* used Huey's counterculture values as just a plot gimmick to propel yet another comedy-chase buddy film.

Critic Karl Williams cut to the heart of the problem, writing, "The highly contrived plot is certainly annoying, while Dennis Hopper appearing as an aging radical in handcuffs is somehow just sad for those who remember the actor's rebellious politics and spirit of creative invention in *Easy Rider* (1969). Despite Hopper's energetic performance and a nostalgic, well-constructed soundtrack of genuine '60s rock music hits, *Flashback* is a phony and artificial piece of work built on a precarious foundation of clichés regarding the generation gap between yuppie and hippie."

Hal Hinson called *Flashback* a "beastly stew" of "treacherous embarrassments." Hinson termed Hopper's performance a "tawdry spectacle," writing, "When it's revealed that Huey's capture was a publicity stunt designed to promote the book he's written about his life, we feel that some circle of awfulness has been completed. Hopper plays Huey as a kind of cartoon version of himself—he's playing his own legend, which in addition to being grotesquely square, seems a tad premature. The main features of the performance are lifted from the outer-limits photographer he played in *Apocalypse Now*—that and the antiheroic biker in *Easy Rider*. All in all, what he indulges in here qualifies less as acting than as self-cannibalism."

"The best thing in the movie is the Hopper performance," Roger Ebert wrote, "which is quick and smart and oddly engaging. It's hard to play a character with charisma, since the charisma has to seem to come from the character and not from the actor, but Hopper does it here. He's convincing, and his dialogue actually sounds like the sorts of things an unrepentant hippie might say—not like the clichés someone might write for him. Credit is obviously due to the filmmakers, but Hopper puts the right spin on a difficult character and makes the movie special."

Vincent Canby, usually stingy with praise for Hopper, wrote, "The film's biggest surprise is the secure, richly comic performance of Dennis Hopper as Huey Walker, who appears to be a leftover from the Yippie movement. Mr. Hopper, a terrifically intense actor, has never before been so light of touch and so disciplined. Though the name of Huey Walker suggests the serious militancy of the '60s, Huey's spirit recalls the unrepentant verve of Abbie Hoffman."

Perhaps if someone other than Hopper had played Huey Walker, critics like Hinson and Williams may not have reacted to *Flashback* with such deep-seated antipathy. Did Hopper sell out? Hopper's old frenemy, John Gilmore, certainly thought so, writing, "Voices obsessed him. God was talking to him, telling him that he had failed—he was a failure. The perfection of art had eluded him. It would forever remain out of reach. He heard the voices talking about torture and death. Alcoholism and drug abuse had taken their toll: Dennis the Menace was going crazy. After some time in and out of psychiatric wards, his juice gone, but his brain cooling down, Dennis was pandering to Hollywood with hat in hand, promising to be good.

"Afraid of going down like Barbara Payton,[13] he'd give them the soul along with the body. He promised to behave—he'd wear suits, dress proper. He'd adopt conservative thoughts. He'd be able to talk to people like Clint Eastwood and Charlton Heston. He'd be sort of interested in politics. He'd give interviews and eat salads and play golf, dovetailing his lobotomized Mr. Nice Guy behavior into a run of mediocre acting roles nobody would remember.

"Dennis the Menace had died, shrieking somewhere down the corridor of some loony ward, shrugged off like a snake's skin to blow away in the wind. He wouldn't cause any more trouble, and the new Dennis wouldn't feel any more pain—it was simple logic."

Hoppers transformation from a cultural rebel to a bourgeois conformist was hardly uncommon for the boomers who came of age in the '60s. In fact, it became the norm. "I think I just made the natural curve," he said, explaining the shift in his political affiliation. "You've got to start one place and go all the way around."

Hopper's attraction to the counterculture may have meant little more than a shared interest in hedonistic excess, especially when it came to the use of drugs. When Lisa Law asked him to sum up the '60s, he said, "Free love and drugs and rock 'n' roll . . . free love . . . "I think it was part of the

---

[13] Barbara Payton (1927–1967) was a blond bombshell who enjoyed a brief career as an actress, giving her best performance in the James Cagney vehicle *Kiss Tomorrow Goodbye* (1950), an unfortunately apt description of the trajectory of her adult life. Her career declined rapidly when she was embroiled in numerous scandals, including an infamous love triangle with actors Franchot Tone and Tom Neal, who nearly beat Tone to death. After making her final film in 1955, the alcoholic Payton eventually turned to prostitution to support herself until her death.

rebellion against the other culture that wasn't using drugs," he said. "We felt free to use them, and that was part of our life." "We all thought we were hip, slick, and cool, but we were really, really terribly naïve," Hopper told Philippe Mora in 2008. "I mean really naïve. I think we were politically naïve . . . And the idea that cocaine—Freud had used cocaine, and it must be great—and everbody's getting addicted to cocaine, and it's just one big party, you know. It's wonderful, until the down side of it, and everybody realizes they are addicted, and this is not going anywhere. In the beginning, all the drugs were free, the acid was free, the grass was free, and the cocaine and so on . . . and then suddenly, the dealers came in, and it was the dealers that I saw who, really, like, destroyed the '60s.

"When it started costing money, and suddenly you realized you were addicted, or didn't realize you were addicted, just kept on drinking and doing more cocaine. That was really the downfall, I think, the drugs, and the fact we were like cannon fodder. Back in those days, we were all like guinea pigs. We were always waiting for the next new drug. It was like, 'Hey, gimme some of that!' The drugs that were free suddenly weren't free anymore. Everybody was addicted. The party was over. We were all going to hold hands, take LSD, find God—and what happened? We ended up at the drug dealer's door, carrying guns and in total madness. But then the people around me straightened up, and I never saw them straightening up. I just got lost in it."

Though he remained busy acting, Dennis Hopper was always trying to get back in the director's chair. He succeeded when Vestron Pictures, an offshoot of the home-video distributor, Vestron Video, hired him to direct *Catchfire* (1990) (a.k.a. *Backtrack*), a suspense story about Anne Benton (Jodie Foster), an artist who witnesses a mob hit one night when her car breaks down. Benton flees to Mexico, pursued by the police, who need her testimony, and by Milo (Hopper), a hit man who digs jazz and modern art. Infatuated with Benton because of their mutual affinity for art, Milo turns from her pursuer to her rescuer.

Hopper added his personal touches to *Catchfire*, giving his friends Julie Adams (from *The Last Movie*), Bob Dylan, Dean Stockwell, and Vincent Price roles in the film, which was shot in the summer of 1988 in Los Angeles, Seattle, and Taos. "Jodie hides out in Taos, in an old movie theater where I do my painting," he said. "I changed the first hit-man script a lot, made her an artist instead of a secretary." Alex Cox, who rewrote the script with his wife for Hopper, wrote, "*Backtrack* is, in a way, his homage to the Venice artists' community of which he felt a part: Jodie Foster plays a Cindy Sherman-type artist-entrepreneur—her character lives in Dennis's hangar—and Dennis cast Bob Dylan as a chainsaw-wielding Venice artist modeled after Laddie Dill. When Jodie goes on the run in *Backtrack*, her destination is Taos—Dennis's other home."

All did not go well during filming when Foster tried to arrogate Hopper's directorial prerogative. On the first day of shooting, he set up a long tracking shot of Foster in the shower. After he yelled "Action," the camera began slowly dollying in on Foster. Foster, who had her own directorial ambition, became dissatisfied with something about the scene, and abruptly said "Cut." Hopper approached her, and after discussing the setup, said, "Don't ever do that again." And Foster didn't.

Alex Cox said, "Dennis the actor specialized in chaotic, drug-crazed, out-of-control roles, but as a director, he was always disciplined, always in control." In 1996, Hopper told Charlie Rose, "I have a problem with Jodie, and it was not a problem when I was working with her and directing her in the movie. She did something that wasn't very pleasant to me. I had a picture I wanted to use Meryl Streep in, and I wanted to direct her in a movie, and Jodie went out of her way to call her and tell her she shouldn't work with me, and I can't really come to grips with that one. I called her a number of times. She's refused to call me back. It blew what I thought at the time was a go project a few years ago. 'Cause Meryl suddenly said no. She [Foster] thought that I had this AA mentality where I was really just doing this sober drunk or something, and I just couldn't possibly understand women. But she didn't say that, confront me with that on the set, so I didn't know where that was coming from, 'cause I thought I treated her rather well."

True to form, Hopper reportedly turned in a three-hour cut of *Catchfire*, which Vestron reedited to their liking, but not to his. Hopper removed his name from the film's credits and replaced it with the name Alan Smithee, the pseudonym mandated by the Directors Guild in situations where a director refuses credit on a film. "I did a beautiful fucking movie," Hopper said. "Strange, intense, slow—not Antonioni, but with a lot of wonderful, unspoken behavior between Jodie and me. But Vestron, being a schlock outfit, totally reedited and rescored the movie to go for the meat, the action." Vestron released their ninety-eight-minute version of the film in Europe, but Hopper won a pyrrhic victory when their version of *Catchfire* went unreleased here after the company went bankrupt.

Reviewing Vestron's version of *Catchfire*, *Variety*'s staff reviewer wrote, "Somewhere in here is a dark, sassy picture, but final product is more like a jigsaw with half the pieces. Apart from Foster, who's strong, shrewd and sexy, thesping is vaudeville all the way. [Joe] Pesci rants and raves, Stockwell shows a nice line in low-key comedy, [Fred] Ward looks like he hasn't been shown the whole script, and Hopper has a go at Humphrey Bogart in shades."

A 116-minute version of the film crediting Hopper as the director was released on VHS video under the title *Backtrack*. Fernando F. Croce called *Backtrack* "a wacky rumination on creating, selling out, and Jodie Foster cheesecake." "Naturally," Croce wrote, "she [Foster] falls for him, and the two take off for the open wide spaces of New Mexico—if Hopper and Fonda were the new cowboys in *Easy Rider*, Hopper and Foster here make a postmodern frontier couple idyllically holed up in a log cabin, chopping wood, rescuing baby lambs, and making love on beds covered with pink Hostess Snowballs, until it's time for the helicopter chase. 'Fuckin' artists,' an exasperated Hopper mumbles at the wood murals chain-sawed by Bob Dylan (just one of many hipster-bud cameos: John Turturro, Dean Stockwell, Vincent Price, Julie Adams, Charlie Sheen, Helena Kallianiotes), though the movie itself is nothing if not a piece of pop art or maybe a conscious essay on types of art, barely preoccupied with story."

Greg Wroblewski wrote, "It's a mediocre film, with often illogical, even incomprehensible plot twists and poor character development. Jodie is not especially good in it and is even responsible for some of the problems. She isn't awful, but she shows none of the spark and imagination that you'd expect if you hired the best young actress in the world, which many people considered her at the time. Bad movie, but Jodie is often naked or in skimpy clothing, so it's worth a look for that reason."

After living together for two years, Dennis Hopper finally decided to make a legitimate woman out of Katherine LaNasa. "Living together was wonderful, but I really didn't like the way she was being treated publicly," he said. "We would go to a premiere, and she would be pushed away. The press would say, 'Who is this girl? Is she your daughter?' That wasn't the kind of relationship we had. I thought it would be much better for us to be married."

Why did Hopper, who had already left three broken marriages behind him, enter into yet another one? "Each time, I was marrying for life," he told an interviewer. "I also know that I am the first one to ever get divorced in my family. I've more than made up for it, haven't I?" LaNasa's forty-six-year-old father, Dr. James LaNasa Jr., a plastic surgeon in Baton Rouge, was violently opposed to the union at first, bothered by the age difference between his daughter and Hopper and by Hopper's career.

"It was a big mess for a while," LaNasa's seventeen-year-old brother, Steven said. "The parts that Dennis has played bothered him." (Dr. LaNasa hadn't even seen *Blue Velvet* yet.) LaNasa's forty-three-year-old mother, Anne, an artist, was crazy about Hopper and admitted that her favorite of his films was . . . *Blue Velvet*. LaNasa's father eventually gave in, telling his daughter, "You accept." "I can't tell her who to love," he said. "I have a friend who's sixty-four and married to a woman thirty-four, and they're doing fine. So you never know." "He seems like a real fine man," Dr. LaNasa said of Hopper.

Dennis Hopper and Katherine LaNasa married on June 17, 1989, at the Wayfarers Chapel in Rancho Palos Verdes, thirty miles from his Venice home. The one hundred guests included Hopper's *Flashback* colleagues Kiefer Sutherland and Carol Kane, while Roddy McDowell served as the ring bearer. Hopper's oldest daughter, Marin, served as one of three bridesmaids. "I am going to work on this one," Hopper vowed. "It was love at first sight."

Five days after wedding LaNasa, Hopper was in Texas directing Don Johnson, Virginia Madsen, and Jennifer Connelly in *The Hot Spot* (1990), a neo-noir thriller based on Charles Williams' intricately plotted, compulsively readable 1952 pulp novel, *Hell Hath No Fury.* In *The Hot Spot,* a drifter (Don Johnson) gets a job as a used-car salesmen in a small Southern town, schemes to rob the town's bank, and gets entangled with two women, blackmail, and extortion.

The project came to Hopper after writer-director Mike Figgis dropped out. Hopper installed his longtime factotum, Paul Lewis, as the film's producer. Alex Cox called Lewis Hopper's "No. 1 henchman," writing, "Paul was loyal to Dennis, and Dennis was loyal to Paul, and from their relationship, I learned the importance of having someone experienced and trustworthy among the ragtag pack of 'producers' who attach themselves to an independent film. On Dennis' films, Lewis was always the real producer: making sure hotels were booked, actors got fed, trucks had gas, and the production didn't run out of money." Hopper also hired his wife as the film's set designer.

When Hopper showed Figgis' script to Lewis, he recognized it as the same film he planned to make twenty years earlier with Robert Mitchum. Lewis managed to unearth the screenplay that Charles Williams adapted from his own novel in 1962. "We did some rewrites, but I preferred the Williams screenplay to the one by Figgis," Hopper said. "This is *The Last Tango in Texas*. It's a very seedy, sultry, hot piece. And it's not just the sex—it's the characters."

Hopper recast the film after his first choices in actors—Sam Shepard, Anne Archer, and Uma Thurman—dropped out. Choosing Shepard's replacement took some deliberation. "One thing we're light on these days is male and female sex symbols," Hopper said. Dennis Quaid, Patrick Swayze, and Richard Gere turned down the film. Then someone suggested Don Johnson. "I'd heard a lot of stories about how Johnson carries so much baggage that it's almost impossible to talk to him," Hopper said. "But he was right for this part. He is an amoral used-car salesman who's led around by his cock. He knows women are his downfall, and he'd like to stop, but he can't. Ingmar Bergman said, 'Actors are objects and should be treated that way. If you have the right object for a part, you have the right actor.' I did." Hopper may have felt an affinity for *The Hot Spot*'s horndog protagonist, telling an interviewer, "I'm a sensualist, not a well-balanced person on any level. My moral ideas are totally confused. And I'm a womanizer, which is not popular right now. But that doesn't make me unhappy."

Starting in the late August of 1989, Hopper, his cast, and his crew sweated out the production of *The Hot Spot* for ten weeks in the blazing Texas heat in Taylor and Muldoon, two small towns near Austin, where Hopper and his wife were scouting locations for a second home. "I'm from Kansas, which is flat without trees," he said. "Texas is flat with trees. I enjoy the life here with friends like Waylon Jennings and Willie Nelson." "And this place holds a lot of movie memories for me," Hopper said, referring to the time he spent in Texas making *Giant* with James Dean.

Though Hopper eventually got a performance from Don Johnson that satisfied him, there were reports of friction on the set between them over their contrasting approaches to acting. "Johnson has a lot of mannerisms and things that make me uncomfortable," he said. "He acts smoking cigarettes. He acts drinking drinks. But I got him working real. He doesn't over-amp. I'm not saying he's going to be great in other films or whether he'll ever be good in a film again. But I took a lot of painstaking trouble making sure that he was good in this film. It was a lot of work that I wouldn't do for a lot of people. Because I care that much. He should have a healthy career for a while because of this movie. Everybody on this movie has something to prove. I just want a hit movie."

Hopper called *The Hot Spot* "The best I've ever made—hot, way overboard, and one step from soap opera." *The Hot Spot* opened in September 1990 at the Toronto Film Festival, but performed poorly at the box office, grossing only $1.3 million domestically. Hopper blamed the film's failure on its stars' unenthusiastic promotional efforts. He said that Virginia Madsen was "very embarrassed" by her on-screen nudity. Hopper later blamed the film's commercial failure on Orion Pictures, saying, "Orion was going broke this time around. And they put all their money into *Dances with Wolves* [1990] and *Silence of the Lambs* [1991], so we got cut off the list. So many of my films were not backed."

Hopper gave reporter Joe Leydon an earful about Johnson at the Toronto Film Festival. "But the man is so insecure, he has to arrive with ten people, an entourage of ten people, that go on salary," he said. "It cost us between $600,000 and $800,000 just for his baggage that he brought with him. Like, a helicopter pilot. Two bodyguards. Two drivers. A cook. A trainer. His own wardrobe person. His own hair person. His own makeup person. I never saw anybody come on a set like that. Never. The only guy I ever saw like that was Elvis. And the guys around him, they were his cousins! You know what I mean? At least they were his family. They weren't bodyguards.

"He [Johnson] walked onto the set every day with five people. This is all insecurity to me. I mean, who's trying to kill him? The man was paid $2.5 million to act in this film. That's a lot of money—way over anything I've ever seen or thought about seeing. And yet he looks at it, admits that it's the best thing he's ever done, but he will not come out and do any publicity on the picture until he sees the reviews. This is bullshit to me." Johnson later said that he was prevented from attending the festival because he was committed to filming *Harley Davidson and the Marlboro Man* (1991) at the time.

Roger Ebert enjoyed the film, which he regarded as a welcome throwback to B-movie noirs. "The movie is all style and tone, and a lot of the tone is set by the performance of Virginia Madsen as Dolly Harshaw, the boss' wife," he wrote. "Hopper regards both women with the visual imagination of a cheesecake photographer, which is kind of refreshing. And maybe his sensibility is attuned to this kind of material, to the notion that an ordinary guy can stumble into some pretty strange stuff. The movie has been compared in some quarters with the work of David Lynch, but it's less self-hating and more stylistically exuberant."

Hal Hinson thought the film was "stylishly silly," writing, "Early on, as Hopper lays out the relationships, the movie is teasingly entertaining. Hopper slides us into the narrative, and at first, his pacing is brisk and efficient. His images have a honeyed brightness, and as long as he's working on the level of innuendo and suggestion, Hopper generates some genuine heat. But as soon as the action becomes more explicit and the actual sexual gymnastics begin, the movie's fire goes out. Hopper wants to be tough but doesn't have the guts for it. In *The Hot Spot*, he sends up his material as he stages it, signaling us that the universe he's created is an anachronism, a collection of quotes from an antique form, and in the process turns his story into lurid kitsch. Where he needs to shove in the knife, he turns cute, giving us overblown production design and gaudy effects—complete with existential thunderclaps on the soundtrack—instead of bare knuckle. In this circle of the Inferno, the down-and-outers wear $500 slacks."

Hopper continued to be a whirlwind of activity following the completion of *The Hot Spot*. He spent Christmas in Baton Rouge with Katherine and her parents, along with his mother. "I still don't like her," he said. "I'm just giving her one last chance." When he sat for an interview with *Movieline* magazine's Stephen Rebello at the beginning of 1990, Hopper had just come off the plane from Tokyo, where he was attending a retrospective of his films. He had devoted the previous months to directing *Backtrack* and *The Hot Spot,* and acting in *Flashback, Chattahoochee,* and *Backtrack.* Hopper also squeezed in a trip to New York, where he lectured on the '60s' impact on contemporary art. "It's alarming that nothing of importance has really changed in music or the visual arts since the '60s," he said. "I find it hard to believe that we did everything in the '60s."

"At this point, I'm going to do things that I know I can do," Hopper told Rebello and explained his compulsion for work. "Work is all I want to do, and I'm just going to keep doing that. I don't feel I've left a body of work." Pausing, he added, "I must leave a body of work." Though Hopper staked his legacy on the films he directed, he was aware that he had been strictly a director for hire since his comeback, directing films he had no role in developing. Hopper longed to direct films that expressed his personal vision, like his latest project, *Kilo*.

According to Rebello, *Kilo* "tracks the last days and nights of a young, world-class surfer who, as a sideline, ounces out coke to everyone from downtown Los Angeles gangbangers to movie and record hotshots in Beverly Hills, but dreams of getting out." "An *Easy Rider* can't be made by a committee company that keeps watering things down," Hopper said. "Here's a movie that shows what this time is about, and, when I bring it up to executives, they change the subject." Hopper was unable to get *Kilo* produced. The story probably hit too close to home for many of the studio gatekeepers, themselves customers of coke dealers like *Kilo*'s protagonist.

Hopper would spend the next twenty years stuck on the treadmill of Hollywood mediocrity, dreaming of one last shot at greatness. He would act out the most surprising drama of his life, not on a Hollywood soundstage, but within the confines of his Venice home only months before his death.

· 9 ·

MAKING THEM SAY "WOW!"

Dennis Hopper divorces his fourth wife, only to marry his fifth. Hopper pursues his legacy in movies, television, art galleries, and museums. As Hopper lies dying of cancer, he divorces his wife while the press has a field day reporting new stories of guns, drugs, and a family feud to divide his estate.

"It's always been about wanting to prove something. The desire, the determination to be great. If I was determined to be a genius at nineteen, then I'm still as determined now."

Dennis Hopper, 2005

*H*OPPER HAD SOMETHING besides *The Hot Spot* to celebrate in September 1990. On September 11, his new wife, Katherine, gave birth to a boy, christened Henry Lee Hopper, at Cedars-Sinai Medical Center in Los Angeles. Though Hopper attended Lamaze childbirth classes with her, he wasn't present when Katherine delivered her child a week earlier than expected, while he was filming the made-for-cable movie, *Paris Trout* (1991) on location in Atlanta, Georgia. Hopper started crying when his wife informed him of the news during a call he made from a phone booth on the film's soundstage.

Two months later, *People* magazine published a sweetness-and-light feature on the new parents. "I give him the baby to hold; he does do that," Katherine said, shrugging her shoulders. Though not a doting father, Hopper was making a two-room addition to his home for the baby and his nanny. "Whether Hopper or Katherine will be spending much time there is the next question," *People* reported. "She hopes to start up her own ballet troupe, Umbrella Forest Dancers, early next year, and he has already finished performing in another new film titled *Indian Runners* [sic], written and directed by his pal, Sean Penn. 'Hopefully I'll be directing a movie a year until I'm seventy,' Hopper says, as Henry snoozes in the crib nearby. 'If I could act in a movie a year besides, I could be very happy.' "

Based on Pete Dexter's National Book Award-winning novel of the same title, *Paris Trout* is set in the South of 1949. The film tells the story of Paris Trout (Dennis Hopper), a sadistic, bigoted storekeeper who kills the twelve-year-old sister of a young black man after he refuses to pay Trout for a used car that Trout knew was defective. Trout believes he has impunity from prosecution because he's white, but is put on trial for the crimes. His lawyer (Ed Harris) becomes romantically involved with Trout's abused wife (Barbara Hershey). Even as he learns of Trout's depravity from his wife, the lawyer must still defend him. Realizing that he went too far by murdering the girl, Trout goes insane.

While plugging the HBO movie, *Doublecrossed* (1991), in July 1991, Hopper told Joe Rhodes, "When I was in France promoting *Paris Trout* [which was released as a theatrical film in Europe], some guy said to me, 'You've finally come full circle with this part, haven't you?' And I didn't understand what he said. He said, 'You finally played the guy that shot you in *Easy Rider*.' I thought that was pretty funny." "Harris has a look of suffering that is affecting," Marshall Fine wrote, "while Hershey simmers with both passion and resentment—and Hopper embodies the pure evil of unredeemable bigotry." *Variety* wrote, "Hopper, beefy and aged for the role and sporting a clipped redneck haircut, gives an extraordinary portrayal of the tortured madman."

Hopper followed *Paris Trout* with a small role as a bartender in Sean Penn's *The Indian Runner* (1991). In August 1992, Hopper was back to Wilmington, N.C., where *Blue Velvet* was filmed, to play King Koopa in *Super Mario Bros.* (1993), the first film adaptation of a video game. After hitting it big by creating the character of Max Headroom for a British TV series, animators Rocky Morton and Annabel Jankel were lured to America by the Walt Disney Company to direct *D.O.A.* (1988), a remake of the 1950 film noir, and *Super Mario Bros.*

Bob Hoskins minced no words when he said, "The worst thing I ever did? *Super Mario Bros.* It was a fuckin' nightmare. The whole experience was a nightmare. It had a husband-and-wife team directing, whose arrogance had been mistaken for talent. After so many weeks, their own agent told them to get off the set! Fuckin' nightmare. Fuckin' idiots."

John Leguizamo and Bob Hoskins drank their way through the making of *Super Mario Bros.*, a coping mechanism Hopper couldn't resort to. Hopper hated the experience of making *Super Mario Bros.,* and his performance in it. "It was a nightmare, very honestly, that movie," he said. "It was a husband-and-wife directing team who were both control freaks and wouldn't talk before they made decisions. Anyway, I was supposed to go down there for five weeks, and I was there for seventeen. It was so over budget. My son, who's now eighteen years old, was six or seven when I did that movie, and he came up to me after he saw it, and he said, 'Daddy, I think you're probably a really good actor, but why did you play King Koopa?' And I said, 'Why?' And he said, 'Well, he's such a bad guy, why did you want to play him?' And I said, 'Well, so you can have shoes.' And he said, 'I don't need shoes.' So that was my seven-year-old's impression."

Alienated by his directors, and required to play a video game blip in a nonsensical script that suffered daily rewrites, Hopper gave the worst performance of his career. *Super Mario Bros.* is to Hopper's career what *Cruising* (1980) is to Al Pacino's. If you only saw those films, you'd dismiss their stars as unattractive no-talents. Critics and audiences reviled *Super Mario Bros.* "Dennis Hopper is disappointing," James Berardinelli wrote. "His role as King Koopa cries out for an over-the-top performance, but, for some inexplicable reason, Hopper plays him straight, creating a dull and uncharismatic villain. This guy is so boring that we find it difficult to root against him—that is, when we can unravel enough of the murky plot to figure out why we're not supposed to like him." "*Super Mario Bros.* devotes half its run time to lumbering exposition, yet still makes no fucking sense," Nathan Rabin wrote. The lone critical voice praising *Super Mario Bros.? The Washington Post*'s Hal Hinson!

Hopper, who had plenty of free time while filming *Super Mario Bros.,* went looking for a rental space in Wilmington that he could use as a painter's studio. A real-estate agent showed him what one reporter called a "monumental eyesore," a recently condemned five-story, 61,000-square foot sandstone building constructed in 1887 that once housed a Masonic temple. For Hopper, it was love at first sight. He looked at the huge, high-ceilinged rooms that suggested theaters and thought, "This is incredible. It would be a great place to teach acting."

He spent $144,000 to acquire the old wreck and invested an additional $1 million "just getting the pigeons out and getting the roof fixed," as he later told Charlie Rose. Ever since he studied with Lee Strasberg, Hopper dreamed of opening an acting academy where he could pass on the lessons he learned from Strasberg to a new generation of students. "I've always thought it would be nice to end up that way, teaching acting," he said. Hopper planned on opening the school in 1996 and personally supervising it when he turned seventy.

Wilmington seemed an odd second home to Hopper, who said, "I agree it's a little weird, but I like it here." A town of 62,000 residents on the Cape Fear River, Wilmington was then the second most active center of film production in the United States. "A lot of technicians are moving into the area here," Hopper explained, "so you can come in and bring a movie company and find almost everybody you need to do your film, except for actors. It's not guaranteed you'll be in the movies if you come to school here. But I think there are actors who will be trained here who could actually go into productions."

Two years after buying the building, Hopper had finished his loft, complete with a dazzling kitchen, the requisite Frank Gehry corrugated cardboard chair, and a sound system playing the music of Miles Davis that he had marinated in during his New York nights, but much of the rest of the building remained in disrepair.

Hopper's continued professional success was not matched by equal success in his private life. Hopper and Katherine LaNasa divorced in April 1992. He complained constantly to Richard Stayton about his ex-wife during the shooting of *Super Mario Bros*. "I've never been so badly treated by a woman in my life," he told Stayton. Denying LaNasa's allegations of physical abuse at his hands, he fought her for custody of their young son, who he got to see for five days every two weeks. "No, I didn't use violence on Katherine LaNasa," Hopper said, "even though she used it as an excuse in court. I was sober, and I used no violence on her. I missed my daughters' upbringing, and I tried to be so involved in this one, but karma has dealt me the same kind of hand again—it's been hard on me."

A week after LaNasa left him, Hopper turned around and found his next lover, who went on to become his fifth and last wife. While dining at Rebecca's, one of his favorite restaurants in Venice, he was approached by the hostess, petite, red-haired, twenty-four-year-old Victoria Cane Duffy.

"I had been separated from my last wife for just a week, and I was eating alone," he later said. "She seated me and then came over and said, 'I don't want to bother you now, but when you're finished, would you mind if I asked you about your art. I just saw your show at the James Corcoran Gallery and I'd like to discuss it with you.' " Duffy soon replaced LaNasa in Hopper's bed and moved into his Venice compound.

A small batch of Hopper's paintings inspired by gang graffiti was exhibited at the Corcoran Gallery in Santa Monica in January 1992. He began painting again between breaks from professional commitments, but not in his Venice home. "I don't paint here, it's too schizophrenic, the acting and the photographing," he said of L.A. When he wanted to paint, Hopper escaped to Taos, to his studio in the El Cortez Theatre.

Pauline Kael was indeed astute when she observed that Hopper's interest in the gang culture he depicted in *Colors* was primarily aesthetic. *Los Angeles Times*' art critic William Wilson wrote, "Filming *Colors*, he became fascinated with the vandalized walls he saw around L.A. The painter within was attracted to the extra visual interest added by the city's dogged attempts to efface the defacement. Bad boys do their thing with spray cans followed by stolid citizens wielding censorious paint rollers that blot out the graffiti but leave behind unruly rectangular Rothkoesque shapes. Gang members then seem to take mordant pleasure in spraying more offensive matter on top of them. Hopper's exhibition consists of some forty enlarged Polaroids of defaced walls and ten large paintings based on them. The photos aestheticize these signs of urban civil war into a kind of poetry of the absurd." (Hopper was fond of quoting Jean Cocteau's adage that 90 percent of art is accident.)

The single painting shown in Wilson's article is a square canvas with a muted, dark-red background. Centered on the background is an irregular white square with a thin line of paint dripping from one corner. Imposed on the white square are six irregularly arranged purple rectangles. It's an innocuous, if uninspired exercise in abstract expressionism.

Wilson praised all but two of Hopper's paintings, writing, "Hopper is a deft colorist and placer of shapes in muted, matte-finished compositions. A virtuoso Rorschach-like orchestration of tans, olives, and blued slate grays evokes the urbane spirit of Robert Motherwell. There is a real tension between Hopper's sweet sophistication as a painter and the jolt of the underbelly allusions. Put together they are like a melding of jazz and rap." In 1997, *Los Angeles Times* critic Susan Kandel called them "a rather ghastly six-canvas pastiche that includes graffiti on simulated stucco and photographic imagery derived from Hopper's *Colors*."

Though director Tony Scott's *True Romance* (1993), from a screenplay by Quentin Tarantino, was studded with stars like Val Kilmer and Brad Pitt in cameos, Dennis Hopper quietly stole the film, playing the father of the film's unlikely hero, Clarence Worley (Christian Slater). When comic-book fanboy Clarence and his new bride (Patricia Arquette) abscond with $5 million of the mob's cocaine, Mafia *consigliere* Vincenzo Coccotti (Christopher Walken) and his henchmen (one of whom is played by a pre-*Sopranos* James Gandolfini) visit Clifford Worley (Hopper), determined to force him to reveal the whereabouts of his son. When Coccotti declares his intention to torture Worley to force him to reveal Clarence's location, Worley provokes Coccotti into killing him by telling him a racially offensive story about the origin of Sicilians' mixed-race heritage.

Hopper's performance of Tarantino's infamous "eggplant" monologue has justifiably become a cult classic, thanks not just to Tarantino's dialogue, but also to Hopper's perfectly controlled gem of a performance. While the famous flower duet for sopranos from Léo Delibes' opera *Lakmé* plays faintly in the background, Hopper, adopting an understated, effective Boston accent, plays Worley as a man quietly enjoying the opportunity to show his contempt for the murderous Coccotti as he denies him the information he urgently demands.

Val Kilmer recalled the exact technique Hopper employed in the scene. "That twinkle in his eye was as movie-star as it gets. That grin and the way he looked away, then slashed you back with a laserlike look, then a quick nod. He practiced that a lot, you could tell. Actors practice the stuff that works on people. And he worked on people."

For Hopper, Tarantino's monologue was like suddenly getting a slice of rare roast beef after subsisting for years on stale crackers. "First of all, you don't see speeches like this as an actor in film anymore," he said. "It was just pages and pages of this great dialogue. It was just wonderful. The only improvisation in the whole thing, because Tarantino's script was so good, was the bit about the eggplant and the cantaloupe. Walken and I went out later, selling the piece as a team. And someone said to us 'Oh, you guys are great actors!' And Walken says 'I don't know if we're great actors or not, but I started out as a dancer, and Hopper and I partner real well together.' And I thought that was a great line."

Hopper's next role was in writer-director John Dahl's *Red Rock West* (1994), an overly mechanical series of plot twists and reversals about a hapless schmo (Nicolas Cage) who gets caught in the labyrinthine scheme of a double-crossing sheriff (J. T. Walsh) and his wife (Lara Flynn Boyle) after being mistaken for a hit man. Dressed in black and driving a black, retro Oldsmobile Toronado, Hopper is "Lyle from Texas," the real hit man. Unfortunately, Hopper's attire and car are the most interesting thing about his character, who exhibits the same implacable sense of purpose and lack of personality as Arnold Schwarzenegger's robot killer from *The Terminator* (1984).

Red Rock West sat on the shelf for about two years until it gained a cult following after airing on cable TV and being released on home video. *Red Rock West* received an enthusiastic critical reception when it was finally theatrically released in 1994. "*Red Rock West* is a diabolical movie that exists sneakily between a western and a thriller, between a film noir and a black comedy," Roger Ebert wrote. "Hopper plays a version of the character he has become famous for: The smiling, charming, cold-blooded killer with a screw loose." "Dennis Hopper, whose latest few efforts in front of and behind the camera have been rather unimpressive, enjoys himself immensely as the real Lyle, and his scenes with Cage crackle with suppressed energy," James Berardinelli wrote. "Hopper seems to be at his best playing this sort of character, as was made abundantly clear in David Lynch's *Blue Velvet*."

The only thing Hopper mentioned about making *Red Rock West* was the discomforting location where it was filmed, a small Arizona town whose name he couldn't recall only a couple of years later. "It was all done in Arizona," he said. "It was a place called Winslow or something. It wasn't Winslow. It was in a terrible part of Arizona, like it's too high to be warm and too low to be cold, like 3,800 feet, and the wind never stops blowing. It's, like, eighty miles from Tucson, which is just far enough not to be able to go to a movie. And you go, and you say, 'What do people do in this town?' And they go, 'They work at the prison.' Then you find out there are, like, twenty-five prisons in the radius of fourteen miles. It's Prescott or something, I don't know what it is." (The film was shot in Willcox, Arizona.)

Hopper's priorities were always to direct, then act. Directing gave him the greatest involvement in making a film and the greatest control. "I have tried every year to direct," he said, "but could not get financing." Alex Cox recalled, "The pictures he wanted to make were *Ambrose Bierce Meets Pancho Villa*, a megawestern set in the Mexican revolution, and *The Monkey Wrench Gang*, based on Ed Abbey's immortal novel. Dennis the Republican directing a spirited tale of ecoterrorism starring Woody Harrelson and several other stellar names! *The Monkey Wrench Gang* would have been quite a picture, but not entirely surprisingly, it was not to be. Dennis regretted not having made more features. Directing films was, to him, his principal work."

"You know, I've been scraping the bottom of the creative bowl here in Hollywood for so long that I don't really get any of the roles that one gets nominated for," Hopper told Lynn Barber of the British *Observer*. "I'm not on their A list at the studios, nor on their B list nor their C list nor their D list. So I have to go out and do independent films that most of the time never see a theatre, go directly to video or Home Box Office. Some of them turn out very well, but you don't win Academy Awards for things that go straight to television. I was in a producer's office the other day with a script he wanted to do of mine and he said, 'Now if you can get these actors'—and he gave me a list—'I can get you $90 million. If you can get these actors, I can get you seventy; these forty, and these fifteen to twenty.' And my name wasn't even on the list! I'm not bankable on any level. And it's been that way for my entire career, except for one moment after *Easy Rider*."

"This business is so uneven you can be up one second and the next year wonder why you can't get a job," he told another interviewer. The old adage, "You're only as good as your last film" applied to Hopper's prospects as a director. *Colors* had been a solid success, *Backtrack* went unreleased, and *The Hot Spot* flopped. "These last directorial efforts were works-for-hire," Alex Cox noted, "scripts that had been kicked around for a while. Dennis made them because he needed money for houses, alimony, wives, trips, kids."

There's another old Hollywood adage—"You can't polish a turd." (Stanley Kubrick once said, "You could if you froze it first.") Even Hopper couldn't polish *Chasers* (1994), the last film he would get to direct. In this unacknowledged ripoff of *The Last Detail* (1973), Tom Berenger and William McNamara played Navy Shore Patrol officers assigned to transport an ensign (*Playboy* Playmate and *Baywatch* babe Erika Eleniak) from a Marine base in the Carolinas to a military prison in California. Eleniak repeatedly tries to escape as the trio encounter a series of eccentric characters, all played by Hopper's cronies: Gary Busey, Seymour Cassel, Frederic Forrest, Crispin Glover, and Dean Stockwell.

"As a director, Dennis Hopper can be counted on to fill the sidelines of a film with amusing wild-card diversions, even if he has more trouble holding together a central plot," Janet Maslin wrote. "In the amiable, loose-knit *Chaser*, which opened yesterday at local theaters, all the fun is in the digressions. Mr. Hopper thoughtfully gives himself this story's King Pervert role, as an underwear salesman who barks like a dog and picks up Ms. Eleniak in his Cadillac convertible. No one familiar with Mr. Hopper's oeuvre will be surprised to see an inflatable party doll come out of the Cadillac's trunk."

Critic Derek Armstrong wrote, "A strange choice for Dennis Hopper—and an unfortunate choice for whatever director had gotten stuck with it—*Chasers* is a failed little military comedy that everyone involved with would likely prefer to forget." With deference to Maslin and Armstrong, I can't resist quoting from an anonymous customer's one-star review at Amazon.com. With Zen-like wisdom, they wrote, "It is always easy to judge a comedy. A good one makes you laugh, a bad one does not. This is a bad comedy. Dennis Hopper could not stage a comedic scene to save his life. He has no idea how to direct physical comedy. The tampons in the gas-tank scene is awkward and obvious. The truck stop escape scene has Toni (Eleniak) in a bad wig associating with Eddie and Rock, who have no earthly idea who she is! She looks the exact same, she is not Lon Chaney! Hopper populates this nightmare with tons of character actors in bit and cameo parts. Hopper's own cameo, with a fake nose that makes him look like Karl Malden, is as funny as a prostate exam. Do not pursue *Chasers*." Amazon customer Eric James Cooper cut to the chase, writing, "Well, if you are a fan of nude Erika Eleniak then you watch this movie. Really that's the good part of this flick."

Hopper shrugged off the failure of *Chasers,* which he blamed on poor distribution, and went straight into *Die Hard* (1988) cinematographer Jan de Bont's directorial debut, *Speed* (1994). Seeking revenge on the LAPD bomb squad officer (Keanu Reeves) who foiled his earlier extortion scheme, diabolical bomber Howard Payne (Dennis Hopper) plants a bomb on a city bus that is set to explode if its speed falls below 50 mph. Hal Hinson described *Speed* as "brainless, substanceless, and noisy," but thought that its worst sin was that it was "leaden and strangely poky. It never seems to shift into overdrive and let fly." "But even Hopper," he wrote, "who's spent his career driving on the wrong side of the road, seems to keep it between the lines. Every now and then, we hear his mad cackle, but in this case, he's literally just phoning it in, and in his overalls, he looks about as threatening as the Maytag repair man."

"The often imitated, never duplicated, sarcastic, psychotic disgruntled ex-cop Howard Payne is Dennis Hopper at his Hopper-ist; practically parodying himself," the critics at the website, *The Playlist,* wrote. "Delivering his cliché action movie one-liners as if tearing into a juicy steak, Hopper is the perfect foil for Keanu Reeves' languid SWAT cop. He lets himself be as hammy as the role calls for, but imbues it with his trademark live-wire energy."

Following the release of *Speed,* Hopper reached his widest audience yet playing a crazy NFL referee in a series of TV commercials for Nike athletic shoes. Hopper's Nike commercials earned him one of the best reviews of his career. In the 1994 edition of his *Biographical Dictionary of Film,* David Thomson ended his entry on Hopper by writing, "Late in 1993, Hopper did a series of commercials for Nike, playing a football freak, so precise, so funny, and so daring (and perverse—sniffing Bruce Smith's shoe), they may be his finest work." *The New York Times* reported, "The ads . . . created a squall last winter when advocates for the mentally disabled objected to the character. But according to Nike, the reaction from the public was overwhelmingly positive, and a new series of ads is slated for this fall. Mr. Hopper's wickedness, once brazenly antisocial, is now the stuff of popular consumption. 'I just judge from going to airports,' he said about his current public profile. 'I'm getting a squarer group of people coming up to me than I used to get in the old days.' "

Hopper followed *Speed* with *Waterworld* (1995), a science-fiction story that takes place in an unspecified future where global warming has completely melted the polar icecaps, inundating all land except for the top of Mount Everest. *Waterworld* was a thinly disguised imitation of *The Road Warrior* (1981), where oil became the most precious commodity after a resource war went nuclear. In *Waterworld,* dry land is the holy grail. Hopper played the bald, one-eyed Deacon, the messianic leader of the Smokers, cigarette-smoking pirates who live on the infamous *Exxon Valdez* oil tanker and worship a photo of its former shipmaster, Joseph Hazelwood. The Deacon and the Smokers pursue and capture an orphan child with a map tattooed on her back. They believe the map will lead them to the mythical Dryland, where the Deacon hopes to drill for oil and play golf. The Deacon and his followers are eventually vanquished by the Mariner, played by *Waterworld*'s star, Kevin Costner.

Waterworld began life as a low-budget Roger Corman film until the script came into the hands of its star, Kevin Costner. With Costner's involvement, the film's budget rapidly escalated when it was filmed on location in Hawaii and parts of California. *Waterworld*'s production became the subject of the kind of transient controversy that fills the pages of celebrity magazines, which reported how hurricanes, script rewrites, and conflicts between Costner and his friend, director Kevin Reynolds, caused overruns that made *Waterworld* the most expensive American film then made. (Such records are made to be broken. *Titanic* passed *Waterworld* in 1997 to become the costliest domestic film.)

"Costner wanted to play both parts, the good guy and the bad guy," Hopper said. "But when it turned out he couldn't, he said he might as well be eaten alive by Hopper as by anybody else." Hopper grabbed the role of the Deacon after Gene Hackman, James Caan, Laurence Fishburne, and Gary Oldman all turned it down. He prepared for the film in early September 1994 by shaving his head the day before *The New York Times*' Bruce Weber interviewed him in Wilmington, N.C. Hopper, who Weber described as "professionally weird," said, "I understand why people wear yarmulkes now," while feeling his scalp with both hands. "Feeling your head is really bizarre, and I find by covering it, it mellows me down. If you put your hands on your head, you can feel different temperatures. You can feel how uneven the shape of your head is. I don't like it."

Hopper spent four glorious months in Hawaii performing in *Waterworld*, apparently oblivious to the problems plaguing the production. "I've never been on a picture that ran smoother," he told *Parade* magazine's James Brady in July 1995. "Making movies is sort of like being in a family. And because of the size of this film, I saw people I knew from *Apocalypse Now*, even people from *Giant*. There were a few weather problems and delays, but they were minor. We were on the big island in Hawaii, and a storm they called something like 'the big salami' came, with killer waves, and we were working out on the water, with two hundred to five hundred stuntmen working every day. I knew Kevin from before, and I know he was going through a lot of personal problems, but he never showed them on the set, never was anything but professional. My stuff is great, the technical stuff I've seen looks great. The word of mouth at the studio is great. I hope we kick butt!"

Most critics reacted to *Waterworld* with a shrug of their shoulders and a "Meh," but agreed that Hopper earned his pay. "It's one of those marginal pictures you're not unhappy to have seen, but can't quite recommend," Roger Ebert wrote. "The leader of the Smokers is Deacon (a chain-smoker, of course), played by Dennis Hopper as another of his violent cackling loonies. Hopper is the standard-issue villain of the 1990s, and his appearances would grow tiresome if he weren't so good at them, adding weird verbal twists that make his characters seem smarter and more twisted." The *San Francisco Chronicle*'s Mick LaSalle added, "He is over-the- top and theatrical, mugging and raving, but never more than a touch away from sarcasm: 'Don't just stand there, kill something!' At times, he seems to be in a different movie from Costner, and it's a tossup which of theirs is the better one."

Speed's success didn't prevent Hopper from expressing his frustrations on the December 21, 1994, edition of Charlie Rose's TV talk show. Agreeing with Rose that this was the best of times for him, he said, "I tell you very honestly, Charlie, I don't feel I've done it yet. I don't feel that I've ever really done the great part, I don't feel like I've ever really directed the great movie, and I just feel that I'm just getting myself into the position where I may have the opportunity. I don't feel I've ever really had the great role, and I don't feel I've ever really been in the great movie. I look at Anthony Hopkins now, and I look at *Remains of the Day* [1993], and I go, where is the part and where is the movie like this that I could do? Why am I never ever even seeing these kind of scripts or they ever even come close to me? Anthony Hopkins is doing part after part after part. I'm very envious. And uh . . . Harvey Keitel. Harvey Keitel is doing wonderful work.

"I'm not saying I'm not doing wonderful work. I think *Speed* is terrific, and I love it, and Jan de Bont did a sensational job directing this movie, and it set a new kind of genre for action films. But there's no backstory to my character. There's no backstory to any of the characters in that movie. It's not like *In the Line of Fire* [1993], where you know more about Malkovich's character than my character. My character is just there to push the action on. And it's wonderful, and I love the movie, and I love to see it. I love to watch this movie over and over and over, it's so exciting.

"But, the great role I don't feel I've ever really had and the kind of films

I want to direct, studios say, 'Oh they're too dark, or they're too this, or they're not commercial or . . . ' I feel that I'm still at a place where . . . I look at Woody Allen. And the real filmmaker for me is the filmmaker who writes his own things, he's the author of his own . . . He's the auteur film-maker, he writes his stuff and does it. And I did that with *Easy Rider* and *The Last Movie*, but after that, I was not allowed to do any of the projects that I wrote. I could never get financing for them.

"So I feel a little uneasy about that. I feel I haven't really finished the work." Rose said, "But you feel ready to do it. Do you think you'll get it?" Hopper said, "Yeah, absolutely." "Yeah, I gotta think that," he said, smil-ing. "I'm at a place now where the success of something means something to me. Listen, if my life went on the way it is now, I couldn't complain, and it's a good thing to feel you still gotta do it, you still gotta prove it."

Nineteen ninety-four was probably as good as it would get for Dennis Hopper. *Speed*'s popularity renewed his hopes for a shot at the great role he coveted or a chance to direct one of his pet projects. He had a new woman in his life, was constantly in demand as an actor, and appeared on the TV series, *Inside the Actor's Studio*, a homecoming of sorts for Hopper, who was still an enthusiastic disciple of Lee Strasberg and an advocate of the Method. He even had the dubious honor of attracting his own celebrity stalker.

"A fanatic has been writing Hopper bizarre letters claiming to be the reincarnation of James Dean," Richard Stayton wrote. "Somehow this stalker had climbed onto Hopper's roof and was trying to sneak in through a skylight." He discussed the stalker with Stayton when he ran into him at a bookstore. " 'How did he get up there?' Hopper asks me, stunned that his fortress had been breached," Stayton recalled. " 'There's no way. The police had to do it with helicopters, man, it was like—weird. Not totally wrapped. Know what I mean?' I knew all about the stalker. I had heard the helicopters and sirens after midnight, had walked into my street and looked downhill toward his home."

Hopper put a blot on what should have been an otherwise fine year when he appeared on *The Tonight Show* on May 31, 1994, to promote *Speed*. Mentioning the twenty-fifth anniversary of the release of *Easy Rider,* host Jay Leno innocently asked him how Jack Nicholson came to replace Rip Torn in the film. "Well, at dinner he [Torn] pulled a knife on me," he told Leno. "He thought I was cutting him out of the picture, as he put it." Leno asked, "Is that the best way to settle an argument?" Hopper said, "Yeah, well, it was, uh, it was, uh, it was one way for me to say, 'We're not working together. That was pretty easy' "

The Tonight Show's audience laughed appreciatively. Rip Torn was not amused at being portrayed as a dangerous hothead since it could imperil the recent career resurgence he was enjoying with his role in HBO's *The Larry Sanders Show* (1992–1998). On August 23, 1994, Torn filed a lawsuit against Hopper for slander, offering to withdraw the claim if Hopper published a retraction in five publications of Torn's choosing. "Rip Torn can't sleep at night because of this?" Hopper asked *People* magazine. "Give me a break." Unwilling to retract his story, he said, "I said to my lawyer, 'I am not taking out three fucking pages anywhere saying I'm a liar about something I remember very vividly.' "

"My lawyer keeps saying, 'I just can't understand why Hopper's had it in for you,' " Torn said. "The whole thing did cripple my career, there's no doubt about it. I've spent twenty-five years outliving this rumor that I always quit. It still comes up. It seems like I'll never get rid of it. It may have been because I was a witness to the fact that Terry Southern actually wrote the script. Maybe that's why it was necessary for me to be out of the picture."

Southern, who was ill and would die the following year, spent five hours giving his deposition in the offices of Torn's lawyer, Robert S. Chapman. "Well, that's supremely ironic, isn't it, that he should tell it exactly backwards?" Southern told Gail Gerber, after hearing Hopper's version of the knife story. That wasn't the only thing Hopper had backwards. Torn's lawsuit unmasked Hopper's shameless attempts to aggrandize credit for writing *Easy Rider*. The authorship of *Easy Rider*'s screenplay became an important component of Torn's case when Hopper mentioned it in his deposition, and Torn's attorney decided to use it to impugn his credibility.

"Dennis was still insisting that he and he alone wrote *Easy Rider*," Gerber wrote. "He boasted that he wrote it in three weeks after becoming frustrated with Terry and Peter's supposedly slow progress, but didn't have the script any longer, or maybe he put it on tape, but he didn't have that, either." At trial, Hopper even accused the late Southern of perjury for taking credit for writing *Easy Rider*. When he learned that Southern's deposition supported Torn's account of the knife incident, he said, "It broke my fucking heart. Because I considered Terry Southern one of my best friends."

During pretrial depositions, Chapman asked Hopper, "When it came to the physical writing, you did it all by yourself?" He replied, "I did it myself." Chapman asked Hopper if he had a copy of the screenplay. He said, "No. I don't know that one exists, actually." On the witness stand, Gerber produced Southern's personal copy of his script, complete with his marginalia. In his decision for Torn, the judge wrote, "not a single witness nor piece of evidence supported Hopper's story that Torn pulled a knife on him," adding, "Hopper was not a credible witness."

"If Den Hopper improvises a dozen lines, and six of them survive the cutting-room floor, he'll put in for a screenplay credit," Southern told interviewer Mike Golden. "That's the name of the game of a certain Den Hopper. It would be almost impossible to exaggerate his contribution to [*Easy Rider*]—but, by George, he manages to do it every time. In *Interview*, he pretty much claimed credit for the whole script. I called him, and I called the woman who interviewed him. He said he didn't remember saying it. Then I heard he said it somewhere else."

One has to consider the context of Southern's harsh comments about Peter Fonda and, especially, Dennis Hopper in judging the extent of their contributions to *Easy Rider*'s screenplay. Southern voiced his damning opinions years after his involvement in the film, after Hopper ignored the financially strapped Southern's plea for 1 percentage point of the film's profits, and after Fonda attempted to bribe an ill, needy Southern to erase his credit on the film to make way for its sequel. Southern told Gail Gerber that they were motivated by "vicious greed." In 1994, Robert Chapman asked Southern, "Do you still consider Mr. Hopper a good friend?" He said, "No, not at all." Asked, "When did you reach the conclusion that he was not a good friend?" Southern replied, "Well, it was a cumulative thing of being refused time after time of beseeching his help. And I guess it was the proverbial last straw, you know."

"After the movie became an enormous success, lots of people got compensated," Bill Hayward told *The New Yorker*'s Mark Singer in 1998. "Bert Schneider gave little pieces of it to Jack Nicholson, to his secretary, the editor, the assistant editor. All these people got tastes, and the only person who didn't get a taste was Terry Southern. He deserved it before all these other people. I always thought this thing never would have got written without him."

Recalling the days when Fonda, Hopper, and Southern swapped ideas in his apartment, Gerber wrote, "Terry loved collaborating with other people. He always felt that two heads were better than one when creating a story or screenplay. Terry was really in his element sharing concepts with Peter and Dennis. He just loved to work in this free-for-all fashion with people yelling out story ideas while nestled on the sofa. He jotted down the better ones in pencil on his yellow legal pad. Peter once remarked that Terry agreed to work on *Easy Rider* on a handshake 'just for the sake of having the freedom to play with an idea that appealed to his individual nature.' This statement is oh so true."

"Through a really monstro and misguided sense of generosity," Southern said in 1972, "it seems I invariably tend to *offer* sharing the screenplay credit with almost anyone who happens to be around. You see, theoretically I believe a film should have a *single credit*—'A Film By . . . ' and then simply list, alphabetically, the creative people involved. Unfortunately, the Dickensian structure of the filmmaking labor organizations doesn't yet provide that possibility, so we are still faced with this primitive and irrelevant attempt to break it down into categories—like who's responsible for what—whereas in any really good film these things are bound to overlap."

In his memoir, Fonda recalled how elated he was when Southern agreed to write the film—"*Terry fucking Southern!*"—and admitted that he was "certainly doing more than just putting an idea into script form." (If Fonda and Hopper thought they could write the screenplay, why did they enlist Southern?) "He gave us the title," Fonda told Nathan Rabin in 2003. "Dennis and I had a slew of titles, some of which were hilarious and would make us both erupt with laughter, and some were serious. Terry came up with *Easy Rider* and explained what it was. That was definitely a major gift, that title. He gave us guidance. He gave us a great wall to bounce off of. He gave us dark humor and a literary panache that Dennis and I did not have. Having him with us as a writer on the script put it above periscope depth. People would say, 'Wow, Terry Southern cowrote that. I wonder what that's about?'" Fonda said that Southern's function during the story meetings was "keeping it on track, keeping the story flowing properly, making shooting notes, narrative directives."

"*Easy Rider* was written by three fucking loaded guys in a room . . . ," Bill Hayward told Mark Singer. "Somebody has the pencil and piece of paper, and that somebody wrote it all down. Dennis's position is he had the piece of paper. I would tend to believe that Terry would more likely have had the piece of paper than Dennis would." Singer had the opportunity to examine Southern's screenplay. "The screenplay is unquestionably Southern's handiwork," he wrote, "distinguished by detailed scene descriptions and by dialogue with a crispness and rhythm familiar to any reader of his fiction."

The legal judgment in Torn's favor only stopped Hopper from saying Torn pulled a knife on him. But Hopper continued to claim that he wrote *Easy Rider*. "*Easy Rider* is the film by which he must stand or fall. He says it is his masterpiece, his pitch for posterity, and it is his, all his," Lynn Barber wrote, after interviewing Hopper at his home in 2001. "He wrote, directed, acted in it. No matter that the writing credits read Peter Fonda, Dennis Hopper, Terry Southern."

"Terry Southern never wrote one fucking word of *Easy Rider*," Hopper insisted. "Only the title *Easy Rider* came from him. He broke his hip. He couldn't write. I used his office, and I dictated the whole fucking thing in ten days." Barber asked, "Surely Peter Fonda made some contribution?" Hopper said, "He did. He had a name. He had a credit card. And he loved motorcycles. [Barber noted that Hopper hated them.] But Jack Nicholson was the one who put the deal together, he went in and told them there was no way they could lose money on a motorbike picture. I was a productive one! And they were a bunch of pussies. I went out and made a movie and put it together, and they posed a lot and afterwards took a lot of credit for doing absolutely nothing. And then when they suddenly realized I'd gone and made the masterpiece, they all started talking about how much they'd done on it."

"Peter and I will never patch anything up. He has made my life so miserable," he told writer Elizabeth Snead. "He tried to take away the one thing I created—*Easy Rider*. The story is partly his, but I wrote the screenplay, and Terry Southern didn't write any of it. He even gave me his percentage of it. Peter and I talked out the script on a tennis court, and he and Terry were supposed to go off and write the screenplay. I went out with Paul Lewis and scouted locations, and when I called and asked, 'How's the script?' they had three pages. I went to New York, kicked them out of the office, hired a woman, dictated the script in ten days. It wasn't a masterpiece, but it was something so we could go make the movie."

Hopper's lone supporter in his claim to sole authorship of *Easy Rider* is his longtime friend and producer, Paul Lewis. "Terry never wrote a word and did not even want his name on the film," he told Snead. "Dennis wrote that script, and I should know because I spent eighteen days in a car with him. Much of it even came from things that happened to us. There may have been editing, and it came from an idea that Dennis and Peter had. The picture made a lot of money, and so people started saying, 'Why aren't I making money?' It was all about greed."

"Terry never broke his hip—where does Dennis come up with this stuff?" Gail Gerber wrote, decrying Hopper's continued "delusional outrageous ranting." "If Fonda and Hopper's claims about writing *Easy Rider* without much input are true, then why haven't they written anything of merit since? Hopper received story credit for his disastrous film, *The Last Movie* and Peter cowrote the screenplay for the forgettable film called *Fatal Mission* [1990]. That is the extent of their screenwriting careers." (Hopper rewrote at least part of the screenplay for *Out of the Blue*, but did not receive screen credit.)

In Southern's opinion, Hopper was suffering from a severe case of what he called "one-shot syndrome." He said, "There are people of so little confidence—most frequently not without good reason—in their own abilities that they're inclined to regard any successful endeavor with which they're connected as a *fluke*, a *one-shot*, something unlikely ever to happen again—consequently, they're pretty anxious to make the most of it and very loathe to share . . . it seems to be a terrible kind of *hunger* which brings out their worst, or at least most desperate, qualities."

For Dennis Hopper, *Easy Rider* was a well that never seemed to go dry. He sued Peter Fonda in 1992 contesting his screenwriting credit on *Easy Rider* and demanding a greater share of the film's profit. Hopper said that he received just 33 percent of *Easy Rider*'s profit from 1969 to 1992 instead of the 41 percent he claimed was due him. Fonda and Hopper's attorneys reached an agreement in 1992 that raised his share of *Easy Rider*'s profit to 41 percent. Hopper sued Fonda's Pando Company again on December 13, 1995, claiming that Fonda breached their 1992 agreement by giving Hopper only 33 percent of the money when Columbia Pictures purchased the rights to *Easy Rider* in 1994. Hopper's attorneys settled the case in 1997 without revealing further details.

Hopper's peevishness toward Fonda was on full display on the evening of March 23, 1998, when he attended *Entertainment Weekly*'s Academy Awards party at New York's celebrity restaurant, Elaine's, with his wife,

Victoria, and his daughter, Ruthanna. His *Easy Rider* costars, Peter Fonda and Jack Nicholson, were both nominated that year for Best Actor.

The New York Observer reported, "Everyone has their favorite picks on Oscar night, even an aging crazy man like Dennis Hopper, whom you'd think would have gotten over this kind of Hollywood industry schmaltz years ago. He gazed in stony silence from behind gray shades as Mr. Fonda's clips from *Ulee's Gold* [1997] were played, but then beamed from ear to ear when Mr. Nicholson's scenes from *As Good as It Gets* [1997] came on-screen.

"When Mr. Nicholson won—for the third time in Academy history— Mr. Hopper let out an enthusiastic 'Yeah! Woo!' and banged his hands on the table. As Mr. Nicholson gave the smarmiest speech of the evening, thanking the Academy and 'all you people for looking so good tonight,' Mr. Hopper doubled over in laughter, covering his mouth with one hand." When the *Observer* asked him if he and Fonda were still friends, he replied, "We weren't friends when we shot the movie. Jack Nicholson and I are friends."

Hopper was still at it as late as 2008. The website contactmusic.com reported, "Dennis Hopper is tired of others taking credit for his *Easy Rider* movie—because he and costar Peter Fonda are the only people who made the cult 1969 film. The veteran movie star wants to clear any confusion about those responsible for the road trip movie before the film's fortieth anniversary celebrations next year (09)."

Hopper was pictured standing outside Beverly Hills restaurant Mr. Chow's, nattily attired in a black tie and tuxedo, happily signing autographs. "I wrote and directed *Easy Rider* with Peter," he said. "Terry Southern, who gets a writer's credit, broke his hip, and he didn't write anything. He gave us the title, *Easy Rider*, but I called it *The Loners*. Peter and I talked out the screenplay, and then I wrote it. We made it for $340,000 all across the United States and filmed it in four and a half weeks. After it became famous, there was a hundred million people who took credit for making it. I don't know how that happened."

It's ironic that Hopper's 1995 legal complaint against Fonda stated, "In the years since the release of the picture, Pando Company's continuing breach of the *Easy Rider* agreement (promising Mr. Hopper the two-fifths share) has harmed the relations among the parties, forcing Hopper to engage in litigation and to threaten continued litigation among the parties." The only person taking credit for making *Easy Rider* was Dennis Hopper, who was solely responsible for keeping the controversy over its authorship alive. Terry Southern never went public with his side of the story or sued Fonda and Hopper for a percentage of the film's profits, as his friends urged him, even when his career declined and his financial problems mounted soon after *Easy Rider* was released.

But Hopper's sporadic legal skirmishes with Fonda were merely a diversion from his acting career. Lamenting his status as the go-to guy for playing villains, he told an interviewer, "I keep saying I'd like to play a professional man, like a doctor or an architect whose problems are not internal but external, and he has to face his external problems." Laughing, he said, "But I'll never get that part, so what am I talking about?"

He got his chance with *Carried Away* (1996), which was filmed in Dallas in early 1995. Hopper played Joseph Svenden, a small-town farmer and teacher trapped in a stultifying routine. Hobbled by a childhood accident, Svenden admits that he isn't a very good farmer or teacher. He tends to his dying mother (Julie Harris), and visits his fellow teacher and lover, Rosealee (Amy Irving) on the same day each week for their ritual lovemaking, which their modesty forbids being conducted with the lights on.

Svenden's life is shaken up when he is seduced by the seventeen-year-old daughter (Amy Locane) of a newly arrived retired Air Force officer (Gary Busey). Svenden's roll in the hay with the girl liberates him enough to convince Rosealee to disrobe with him and look at each other with the lights on, giving Hopper and Irving a chance to do full-frontal nudity. When Svenden breaks off the affair, the girl burns down his barn, killing the horse she stabled there. We expect some kind of violent confrontation between the girl's father and Svenden when he learns of the affair. Instead, the story fizzles out with the surprisingly understanding father telling Svenden his daughter must have been partially responsible for the affair. At the end of the film, Joseph and Rosealee go see the ocean for the first time, where he dares to roll up his pants, bare his damaged leg, and walk into the surf. Woo hoo!

Too desiccated to be camp, *Carried Away* feels like a Southern Gothic drained of its flamboyant juiciness. It's the kind of competently made, but dull film that gets respectable reviews from critics calling it honest for daring to show male nudity, before quietly fading away on home video and cable TV.

Hal Hinson called *Carried Away* "crushingly earnest," writing, "The pace of the picture is funereal, and, visually, Barreto [director Bruno Barreto, Amy Irving's husband] has composed his images in only the most depressing shades of brown and slate. Think Dennis Hopper has played too many crazies? Well, you'll wish he'd stuck to blowing up buses after you see him in *Carried Away*. Though Joseph is only forty-seven, Hopper plays him as if he were seventy. Given a chance to demonstrate his range, Hopper tackles this drab, defeated man with everything in him. And when he's not clomping around with his cane as if he were Long John Silver, he manages to create some lovely effects that, indeed, show what a fine, subtle actor he can be. The whole time, though, you feel as if Hopper were about to explode. His spirit is too big for a small man like Joseph. What you want him to do is come alive and bust the film's creaky premise wide open. It never happens, of course. Instead, the drama is resolved in a flood of weak, greeting-card sentimentality. Oh, if only Hopper hadn't misplaced his detonator."

Hopper returned to Charlie Rose's show on March 28, 1996, where he made *Carried Away* sound better than it was, telling Rose how pleased he was being able to play a reflective character in a film with a European sensibility. He told Rose that Jack Nicholson exhorted him to go out and sell the film hard because it contained his best performance. He praised Bruno Barreto's Andrew Wyeth-like images and said that director James L. Brooks told him that *Carried Away* was the first American art film.

Hopper was nicely attired in a forest-green jacket, a light blue shirt, and a green-and-gold tie. With his carefully styled salt-and-pepper hair, he looked well fed, relaxed, and elegant, like a hip executive who was comfortable with himself, but not smug. When he briefly donned reading glasses, he looked almost professorial. Hopper said he had everything except for that one great role, telling Rose, "I just want the work to get better and better. I'm in a place where I'm doing my best work, I'm doing really accomplished work, so I want to make sure this continues. And also, I've got to direct that next movie, which I'm going to."

Charlie Rose made sure to hold up the May issue of *Elle* magazine, so that Hopper could plug his Mexican fashion shoot of German model Nadja Auermann and praise his daughter Marin, who was the magazine's fashion director. Rose held up a couple of pages of Hopper's photos for the studio's camera, showing Auermann posed against artfully weathered, paint-splotched walls. These were essentially the same abstract-expressionist photos of doors and walls that he was taking more than thirty years ago, now with the addition of an attractive woman.

After making *Carried Away*, Hopper was off to Ireland to film *Space Truckers*, a science-fiction comedy Nathan Rabin called "little more than a bland *Spaceballs*-like mediocrity." Though produced directly for video, *Space Truckers* was so undistinguished, it only made it to the small screen in 2002. Hopper would spend the next fourteen years after shooting *Carried Away* taking anything that came along, appearing in fifty films and TV movies and four TV series. He also made commercials, narrated documentaries, and supplied voices for video games and GPS navigation devices. He said, "I try to be as good as I can in some bad movies. Then, occasionally, I get a part in a good movie, but a lot of movies I have done have been pretty grim."

In the early '90s, Hopper told interviewers his love for work explained his prolific output. "I want to work, man," he said. "Work is fun to me. Involvement is fun. I will always be scared. If you've ever had a period of time where you weren't allowed to work—maybe because you were doing drugs and alcohol, but you didn't know that was their reason—then the fear of not being able to work is always with you. It's disastrous for an actor or a director to sit around thinking about why he isn't working. I'd rather have sleepless nights thinking creatively than sleepless nights wondering if I'm ever gonna do it again."

A decade later, he bluntly admitted, "The '90s, especially, was a difficult time for me work-wise. To survive, I needed to take on every job I was offered. The unfortunate thing was that, well, I got married, and I couldn't turn anything down at one point because of financial needs. I've always had a family and always had to work. All those marriages keep you working. I'm on my fifth wife. There's no escape. And, for every divorce, there's a price to pay to lawyers and everyone, including alimony. I think I did a lot of damage, very honestly, to my career because I never had the opportunity to say, 'No, I don't want to do that. I should wait for something else.'

"What happened is I became hopelessly typecast. By the '90s, all I was getting offered was psychotic nuts. Then, after *Speed* and *Waterworld*, even those roles started drying up because the moment I appeared on the screen, everyone knew I was the lunatic. So even that started working against me. A lot of the time, I was taking shit and trying to turn it into gold."

He told one interviewer, "I'd love to be in a Coen brothers film or something by Curtis Hanson—did you see *8 Mile* [2002]? A terrific little movie—but I've never worked for Lucas or Spielberg. You could name most of the directors in Hollywood I've never worked for. Hollywood has never embraced me despite the fact I went and lived there. Some of my friends now run the studios. But they still have a star system. They still think younger people can do it better. I am not offered any of the roles that Jack Nicholson gets or Warren Beatty gets or any of these people get, and never have been and never will. So when you ask me about playing villains and would I like to play other things, I think, God, I'm just lucky if I get a villain part every once in a while."

After cohabiting for four years, Dennis Hopper and Victoria Duffy married on April 13, 1996, at Boston's Old South Church, in a traditional ceremony, accompanied by his six-year-old son, Henry, but not before she was exposed to a glimpse of Hopper's dark side. Right before the high-profile wedding, Hopper demanded Victoria sign a prenuptial agreement, which her attorney called a "draconian and unconscionable agreement which provided Victoria with no security in the event of a divorce." (Her attorney dumped her when she signed the agreement.)

In March 2011, Victoria's attorneys attempted to have the court declare the prenup invalid. In her legal declarations, she said that Dennis "berated, belittled, threatened and intimidated" her into signing the prenuptial agreement after she suffered "hours of threats, sleep deprivation, and intimidation" from him. She claimed that he even threatened to "publicly destroy her" if she did not sign it. "Dennis Hopper had a history and reputation for spousal abuse, violent and/or erratic behavior, but this was one of the first times such behavior had been directed at Victoria," her brief stated.

Hopper worked religiously to enjoy the comfortable life of a Hollywood D-list celebrity who greeted interviewers wearing fine Italian suits and butter-soft leather loafers. It took money for him to add satellite houses to his Venice compound, all designed by America's most famous—and expensive—architect, Frank Gehry. Hopper and his new wife had expensive hobbies. The world of modern art had become far more expensive since the years when he could snatch a Warhol for $75. It took money for Hopper to buy back the pop art he lost to Brooke Hayward in their divorce. It took money to commission Julian Schnabel to paint his and former wife Katherine LaNasa's portraits. It took money to buy a condemned building for more than most people earn in a year and then spend a $1 million renovating it. Hopper spent $40,000 just for the privilege of membership in a golf club whose course was built over a landfill that occasionally vented malodorous gases from the decaying garbage underneath.

Victoria Hopper became accustomed to the finer things in her husband's life. He gave her two credit cards, each with a $5,000 credit limit, which she maxed out on a monthly basis. (Hopper's annual income in 2008 was about $1.26 million.) Victoria always wanted to be a champion horsewoman. Now she owned three horses and competed in three-day equestrian events. She attended showbiz functions and gallery openings on Dennis' arm attired in pricey haute couture. Victoria became a top Democratic Party fundraiser, rubbing shoulders with presidential candidates Sen. John Kerry and John Edwards, and was invited to President Barack Obama's inauguration. On March 26, 2003, Victoria gave birth to a daughter, Galen. Nurses, nannies, famous-name children's furniture and clothes, and private preschool all took money. It took money not to be concerned with the quotidian costs of just getting by.

Hopper's marriage appeared to have tamed him, at least to the *Daily Mail's* correspondent Glenys Roberts, who observed the newlyweds in Morocco when Hopper performed in director Nicolas Roeg's TV movie *Samson and Delilah* (1996). "The couple were holed up in their desert bungalow," she reported, "enjoying each other's company so much that the other stars, including Elizabeth Hurley, who had been expecting displays of Hopper's legendary roistering, were left sorely disappointed. Here was the infamous Hollywood hell-raiser, variously known as a genius and a maniac, in nesting mode, his only arguments confined to benign exchanges with the local carpet sellers as he haggled for soft furnishings to take back to the marital home in L.A."

Elizabeth Snead described Dennis and Victoria's domestic scene in 2001. "Victoria Duffy, his wife of five years, is a striking, slender brunette. She heads out clad in gray jodhpurs and boots to train her thoroughbreds, Time Point, Samba, and Red Night. Before she leaves, she gives him a kiss, calling him 'Mr. Beautiful,' her pet name for him taken from a character in a video game he played. "Victoria just knows how to deal with me," Hopper said. "If she sees me in a mood, she comes over, touches me and says, 'How are things going?' But if she needs to stay away, she stays away. She has an understanding. We just don't get into confrontations." "Victoria has put me on a good path. I have a very stable life," he told reporter Ruth La Ferla a year later.

"He was definitely the most interesting man I had ever met," Victoria said. "That's basically why I married him. I loved him, but he was just great. I was always called the love of his life, until Galen, and then he said, 'She's the love of my life, I hope you don't mind.' I said, 'No, I love that. That's great.' We were in the pod hurtling through space, the two of us. We were always on the road, always traveling. We regularly traveled five to nine months of the year. He was voracious for life. Actually, me too. We got along that way. Wanted to see everything, do everything, be everywhere—cultural stuff. There was a lot that was great."

The couple traveled not just to locations where Hopper was engaged in fulfilling his professional obligations, but to the many exhibitions of his art and photography held at galleries and museums in the U.S. and abroad after his career resurgence spurred a renewed interest in his art. What triggered it? After all, there was nothing particularly new about Hollywood celebrities who were art collectors, Sunday painters, or shutterbugs photographing their celebrity friends. But they were staid members of the Hollywood establishment, whose unadventurous taste in art ran to safe choices like 19th-century impressionists.

Dennis Hopper was different. Andrew Karp, a friend of this author, once said, "People are fascinated by everything that comes out of an artist." That was certainly true of Hopper, whose art emanated the allure of his reputation as Hollywood's self-destructive rebel outlaw and hip tastemaker who discovered the pop artists of the '60s. Hopper had been involved with and photographed many of the leading figures in art, movies, and politics in the '60s. "My art dealer says I have the mythic eye of the '50s," he told writer Cree McCree in 1988. "He tells me, 'It wouldn't matter *what* you do. People just wanna know what it's like to look out your eyes.' "

Hopper received an artist's homecoming in San Diego when their Museum of Contemporary Art in La Jolla exhibited a selection of his art and photography from November 19, 1996 to February 23, 1997. Standing in the museum's gallery, he told society columnist Burl Stiff, "I think this is probably the most important thing in my life. I've done a lot of stuff, but this is where my heart is. Always has been. This is really important to me." When Stiff asked if he had opening-night jitters, he said, "Not at all. I'm very relaxed here. I'm familiar with these objects. I feel they really look good, and I'm very confident of their importance." The art exhibit was accompanied by a retrospective of thirteen of Hopper's films screened at the museum's theater. Hopper, who selected the films, said, "I think the series gives a good sense of things on which I had some major involvement." He made sure the series included all of his directorial efforts, even *Chasers*.

Hopper brought Victoria and his mother to the preview of the exhibit and the reception afterward, along with his artist friends, Ed Ruscha and Chuck Arnoldi and their wives. Hopper was the guest of honor at the party, where seventy of San Diego's business and social elite were feted with a catered dinner of Asian and Southwestern specialties. Two of the guests even reminded Hopper of his teen years in Lemon Grove. Robert Nugent, president of the museum's board, was an executive with the Jack in the Box fast-food chain where Hopper worked as a teenager at their drive-thru restaurant located at the intersection of Massachusetts and University. "I fried a lot of hamburgers," he said. "Saw some pretty good fights, too." Guest Russell Forester said that he met Hopper in 1952—"When he was a gofer at the La Jolla Playhouse, and I was a young architect doing some work there."

Hopper's show at San Diego's MOCA was the beginning of his campaign to become recognized as a serious artist by the fine-arts community. He had already achieved some recognition overseas, in no small part because of his rejection by Hollywood and the public after *The Last Movie*. "Europe loves a bad story," he said. "The fact that I stopped making films, that I had a huge hit with *Easy Rider* and then made *The Last Movie*, which won the big award at the Venice Film Festival and then flopped in the US—that sort of thing resonates with, particularly, the French. It's like when rock and roll took over the airwaves in the U.S., all these jazz musicians went to Europe and were treated like royalty. That's the way I felt. I guess if you're a big enough failure, they really take you to heart! (laughs)"

The MOCA exhibition was followed by another at Fred Hoffman Fine Art in Santa Monica that opened on June 13, 1997. "Yet, there is something troubling about the particular works selected for display, most of which are of recent vintage," the *Los Angeles Times*' Susan Kandel wrote. "On one hand, these works play up the popular conception of Hopper as a histrionic daredevil, and on the other, Hopper as someone whose visual art is parasitically dependent upon his film work. It probably would have made more sense to schedule a film series."

Kandel offered qualified praise for a 16mm film of Hopper's 1983 Russian Suicide Death Chair act, which he had taken to calling a performance-art event, and *Bomb Drop*, a seven-foot-long box-shaped construction of wood, Plexiglas, and neon that incorporated the components of the bomb-release mechanism from a WW II bomber, which occupied a corner of Hopper's dining room in the Mud Palace when he edited *The Last Movie*. A writer described the thing, which looked like a wacky pinball machine in action: "*Bomb Drop* is written across a large sheet-metal phallus with stainless-steel balls that switch from positions of 'safe' to 'arm' as colored lights flash from inside the base."

Prefiguring critics' reactions to Hopper's many subsequent shows, Kandel wrote, "Indeed, it was as a photographer that Hopper did his best work, chronicling in black-and-white images throughout the 1960s the creative and political world around him. One wishes more of those seminal images had been included here; their wry wit, not to mention their modesty, is sorely missed."

The most recent photographs Hopper showed at Hoffman's gallery were large, highly detailed images of walls in Europe and North Africa. "What interests me more than anything is photographing the paint on the wall," he said. "I love the irony of reproducing paint through a photograph." *The Guardian*'s Los Angeles correspondent, Dan Glaister, described these photos when they were included in a major retrospective of Hopper's art put on by L.A.'s Ace Gallery in 2006. "Half the show is given over to Hopper's colour photographs of fragments of walls: from close-ups of brightly coloured walls in Florence, Venice and Prague to bits of graffiti, torn-up posters, and even some Europa Foods price stickers on a slab of wall in London. The pieces are aesthetically pleasant and sometimes quirky, but lack the bite and caustic humour of his best work. Similarly, his paintings of graffiti draw on the abstract expressionists and Pop, but lack the punch. Portrait photography is his forte."

"This is a thrilling moment in my life," Hopper told writer Peter Clothier while overseeing the installation of his works at Hoffman's gallery. "I have a wonderful opportunity to fall on my ass. It's a beginning. The story is beginning to be good. I like the idea that there's a story here, and I can see the trajectory." The trajectory he was referring to included upcoming exhibitions in France and Denmark. Hopper planned to relax by spending June painting in Julian Schnabel's studio in Venice, Italy. Then it was on to Kassel, Germany, for another show before he returned to L.A. to make a personal appearance at a U2 concert. He told Clothier that he was looking forward to a retrospective of his work at the Andy Warhol Museum in Pittsburgh scheduled for 1998.

"I want my life to be more joyous," he said, adding, "A lot of art comes out of misery, pain, and sadness. One comes to the conclusion that one's a compulsive creator, and I'm feeling more comfortable with that. But there's a problem being an actor: Actors aren't taken seriously when they make art. For a while I was thinking of changing my name. There has never been an actor showing in the arena in which I'm showing now."

Hopper told Clothier that art gave a continuity to his life that his work in films failed to supply. "But I'm off on location most of the time, in some trailer somewhere," he said. "I live a gypsy life, moving from one film family to the next. So art is something I felt I could focus on and follow, it seemed like a simple history. You know who your grandfather and your father are. For me, that's Duchamp and Pollock. That's where I came into it, trying to find my own way."

As the '90s gave way to the new millennium, Hopper continued to toil away in thankless film and TV roles that did nothing to advance his legacy, only giving the impression that he was now in the business of selling Dennis Hopper. "I've made a lot of movies that are only shown in Eastern European countries and Fiji," he joked. Movies like *Luck of the Draw*, from which Mickey Rourke was fired when the producer overruled the director's decision to allow Rourke to use Bojack, his pet Chihuahua, in a scene.

Hopper's itinerant film work saw him working in what Nathan Rabin called "depressingly perfunctory" direct-to-video action films like *Top of the World* (1998); *Straight Shooter* (1999), a German action film where Hopper was the only English-speaking actor (even the director was German); *Lured Innocence* (2000), where he looks bored playing an adulterous husband planning to murder his ailing wife (Talia Shire); and the unreleased *The Venice Project* (1999), with Lauren Bacall and Dean Stockwell.

In the ridiculous teen comedy, *Meet the Deedles* (1998), Hopper played a demented former Yellowstone Park ranger who lives in a cave and employs a herd of trained prairie dogs to divert the geyser Old Faithful to a new location, which he plans to make into his own profitable tourist attraction. *The New York Times'* Anita Gates, who actually liked the film, wrote, "That man is Frank Slater (Dennis Hopper, in all his usual glory), a disgruntled former park ranger who lives underground and spends his days in a big red comfy chair, surrounded by video screens, with a Smokey

Bear doll in his lap. There isn't nearly enough of Hopper in the film, but what there is, is fun."

The Web's Mr. Cranky wrote, "It boggles the mind to think that somebody wrote this script, somebody else read it, some executive at Disney green-lighted it for production, and then it actually got made. I can understand two losers like Paul Walker and Steve Van Wormer taking these roles, but what is Dennis Hopper doing here? Doesn't he have better things to do? It's just one more example of one of our nation's most tragic news stories: What happens to guys when they stop smoking ganja and move on to harder things? Hey, if it's *Meet the Deedles* or LSD psychosis, I'll take psychosis any day." Unlike so many of Hopper's other films, *Meet the Deedles* had the virtue—if, indeed, it was a virtue with a film like this—of being a Disney production that actually got to run through the projectors of more than a few movie theaters.

Hopper finally landed an important supporting role in a respectable, big-budget film when he was cast as Christof, the imperious director of the television show starring the unwitting Truman (Jim Carrey) in *The Truman Show* (1998). Hopper was fired and replaced by Ed Harris after one day of shooting. "I did months and months of preparation," he told Tony Shafrazi in 1999 while they were preparing a collection of Hopper's photos to be published in book form. "I went down and saw Peter Weir twice in Florida. I spent six months on that picture and then did one day shooting, and Scott Rudin, the producer, who I'd never even met, he never wanted me for the part. He said he would wait for one day's rushes, and if he didn't want me in the picture, he was going to fire me—and he did. Anyway, that's my story. But I enjoyed the picture, and I thought Ed was really good in it. I think he's a terrific actor. But it was the first time . . . It was the only time in my life I've ever been fired."

After being fired from *The Truman Show*, Hopper played the father of Matthew McConaughey's character in *EDtv* (1999), which had a premise similar to that of *The Truman Show*. McConaughey's Ed Pekurny is a video-store clerk who agrees to have his life filmed for a TV show. *EDtv* might not have had the pretensions to seriousness of *The Truman Show*, but at least it wasn't as embarrassing as so many of Hopper's other films. Directed by Ron Howard, with a decent cast, the film was a theatrical release from a major Hollywood studio, Universal Pictures.

Now sporting a mustache and a chin beard, Hopper appeared in a recurring guest role in several episodes of the first season of the TV series *24* (2002). He played Yugoslavian terrorist Victor Drazen, who breaks out of a secret Department of Defense prison to take revenge on government agent Jack Bauer (Kiefer Sutherland), who Drazen believes was responsible for the deaths of his family in Kosovo years before. Drazen wasn't much of a role for Hopper. He was a one-dimensional baddie from Central Casting. His screen time was limited by the show's format, which alternated several subplots during each episode. Hopper gave a rote performance, delivering his hackneyed and predictable lines in a road company Boris Badenov dialect. At least it kept his name before a viewing audience and on casting agents' radar.

The only reason to watch the Australian oddity, *The Night That We Called It a Day* (2003), is the oddball casting of Dennis Hopper as Frank Sinatra. The film is about a half-assed Australian rock-music promoter who manages to pull off the coup of getting Sinatra to give a concert in Australia. Barely off the plane, Sinatra insults an Australian reporter and gets confined to his hotel suite when the Australian unions conspire to deny him essential services. The film was loosely based on Sinatra's actual visit to Australia in 1974, but spends most of its time on the promoter's love life and his attempt to one-up his prosperous mobster father.

Hopper said his initial reaction to the script was, "I didn't see any way that one could play Frank Sinatra and come out of it successfully." He decided to take the role after discovering that Melanie Griffith would play Sinatra's girlfriend, Barbara Marx. "I always wanted to work with Melanie Griffith," he said. "Playing him was really difficult, but I am very good at Sinatra actually." This was of those occasions when Hopper, usually a good judge of his own performances, was wrong. Hopper is very bad as Sinatra, actually. He bears no physical resemblance to Sinatra, and his own screen persona is too recognizable to be ignored. Worse yet, in the scenes where he lip-syncs Sinatra's songs, Hopper's rigid body language, with his arms held close to his torso, is the antithesis of Sinatra's loose-limbed, finger-poppin' style.

If Hopper's endless variations on Frank Booth made him acting's leading one-trick pony, then he met his directorial match when he appeared in *Land of the Dead* (2005), director George Romero's fourth entry in his deathless zombie series. Made for $17 million in Toronto by Universal Pictures, *Land of the Dead* was Hopper's first film for a major studio since

EDtv. He played Kaufman, the ruthless owner of a walled-off high-rise called Fiddler's Green, whose comfortable residents are provided for by slum dwelling mercenaries who scavenge goods from the zombie-infested city surrounding Kaufman's development.

Hopper said that he chose to do *Land of the Dead* because of Romero, saying, "*Easy Rider* came out the same time as his first film. They both came out in '69. [Romero's first film, *Night of the Living Dead,* was released in 1968.] We both made them in '68, and we both wrote them in '67. They're the same sort of pattern. George is a historic figure in film in my mind, the whole genre of zombie movies. Also the political references that are always inherent in his work.

"They were very much metaphors about how we saw our society at that time. We were looking with the same eyes, but we were talking about it in a different way. Today, I think that probably . . . you know, this is George Romero's movie, and I came in and just played the part. The politics of this movie, if one sees them, are not necessarily my politics. I just want to make that clear."

Hopper was asked, "Since George Romero's films have a political overtone, it has been said that Kaufman could be a representation of the Republican Party. What is your take on that?" He said, "I think that's a little unfair because Kaufman does things that are immediately illegal and very vicious. I don't really see that as representing the Republican Party.

"People have called my character Rumsfeldian. The character I play in this is a very evil person. I do not see Donald Rumsfeld as an evil man. I just want to make that clear. I see him as a very hard-working man, with a very hard job, and doing the best job he can. I live in a very open society where it's OK to disagree. My wife's a Democrat, I'm a Republican; we do not have fights in my house about politics. She raised over a million dollars for Kerry, and I sat quietly as a silent majority. I used to go down and have parties for them in my house, and I'm a Republican! I voted for Bush's father, and I voted for Bush. It's OK in my country to be like that. So that's the way it is."

Hopper, who started *Land of the Dead* right after finishing a film in Italy, told an interviewer that producer Brian Grazer called him in Toronto to hire him to narrate the documentary, *Inside Deep Throat* (2005). "I think everything is political in one way or another," he said. "It's an amazing documentary. But it was amazing how political that was. Film is political.

Even if it's a comedy, it seems to end up being political. If you remember the comedy, *All in the Family*, it was a very interesting political show. So I think it's hard to get away from politics, especially right now. There's a very conservative movement going on in the United States, and there's a very liberal movement going on in the United States. Both of these things are obviously going to make films. They're going to make films for their side, and maybe it's a very interesting moment. Maybe we'll get some really interesting things happening. I hope so. I'd rather think of it positively than negatively at the moment."

Hopper also said that he was going to direct a film called *Genuine Article,* though it never got made. "It's a complicated story," he said. "It's a heist, a political movie." Though reviewers greeted Romero's latest film enthusiastically, they spent most of their time summarizing its story and complimenting Romero on his allegory of class warfare. Only the *San Francisco Chronicle*'s Peter Hartlaub mentioned Hopper's performance, writing, "The best lines are saved for the postapocalyptic Donald Trump figure played by Dennis Hopper, who hasn't had this much fun since he was rigging commuter buses with explosives in *Speed*." Hopper's proficiency playing villains was so practiced, it was taken for granted.

Hopper returned to the grind of a TV series in *E-Ring* (2005–2006), playing a hard-ass senior military officer at the Pentagon who helps a younger officer (Benjamin Bratt) navigate Pentagon politics to resolve international crises. You'd think that Hopper would have had enough of TV after *24* and the little-seen *Flatland* (2002), a twenty-two-episode mash-up of *The Matrix* (1999) and *Crouching Tiger, Hidden Dragon* (2000) that was financed by and filmed at Shanghai China's Hweilai Studios.

While touting *E-Ring* at the NBC Upfronts[14] in New York on May 16, 2005, a gaunt-looking Hopper, accompanied by his wife, told a reporter from *Access Hollywood* that he got involved in the series after encountering the pilot episode's director, Taylor Hackford, at an Academy Awards party earlier that year. Hackford said, "Wow, you look really good. Have you ever thought of doing episodic television?" Hopper said, "Absolutely fucking not." He told *Entertainment Weekly* that TV didn't really appeal to him. "My wife watches *Desperate Housewives*, *Sex and the City*, *The Sopranos*, whatever," he said. "I'm a news nut, and I watch sports. I watch The Golf Channel."

---

[14] The Upfronts are an event where a TV network previews its new shows for prospective sponsors.

He told *Access Hollywood* that he was impressed by *E-Ring*'s great pilot, great scripts, and producer Jerry Bruckheimer's involvement. Plus, he'd only need a fifteen-minute commute to get to the show's Santa Monica studio, keeping him close to home and his two-year-old daughter, Galen. Hopper clowned around for *Access Hollywood*'s TV cameras, taking photos of the photographers shooting him, and mentioned his latest art exhibit in Beverly Hills, which he hoped would go to the Guggenheim Museum in spring 2006.

"I am overwhelmed by my dialogue: I have diarrhea of the mouth," he told *Variety*'s columnist Army Archerd about his role in *E-Ring*. "And he loves it," Archerd reported. "He is also planning big-screen work and is writing the script of *The Last Tango in Venice*, which he will also direct. It's based on a real incident he witnessed in Venice, and he's spoken to Javier Bardem to star. Does he tango? 'He can do anything,' Hopper enthused. Hopper is also readying a 50th anni show of his photos and paintings skedded for the Ace Gallery in BevHills around Oscar time (March 5, 2006)."

Entertainment Weekly pointed out the apparent incongruity of the once draft-shy, anti-Vietnam war protester now playing a military officer. "He is now an avowed Republican who voted twice for President Bush." "I made the natural curve that everybody talks about," Hopper said. "I went from the left to the right—and rather gracefully, I think." "The controversy about me," he told another interviewer, Kate O'Hare. "I don't think it's going to stop me. However, a lot of people treat me differently, and they do bring it up. I'll be at a dinner party, and somebody will say, 'Well, you couldn't be thinking that . . .' And then you realize that everybody at the table is looking at you, and they're like, 'You're kidding! You're not really for Bush.' And it goes around the table. It can only stop me from eating, not working."

Hopper told O'Hare that he intended his role as an homage to his late father, saying, "I never was in the military. I was an age group that was between the Korean War and the Vietnam War, and then the draft came. I was under contract to Warner Bros., and there was no war going on, so I did everything to get out, so I got out. But my father was in the OSS. He was in China, Burma, India. Anyway, I just felt, when I read the thing, this seems like a reasonable way to pay my dues."

USA Today's Robert Bianco called *E-Ring* "a hokey, clunky bit of macho claptrap that is the first Jerry Bruckheimer TV series to call to mind the worst of the Jerry Bruckheimer movies. Imagine *Top Gun* without the planes, the action, or any other conceivable draw. The bizarrely paired stars here are Benjamin Bratt and Dennis Hopper, competing to see who can deliver the more grating, scenery-chewing, testosterone-crazed performance. Bratt wins, but it's a close contest. It's hard to imagine what Hopper is doing in a show like this, but whatever it is, he's not doing it well." "Hopper, meanwhile, almost cartoonishly channels a cross between Jack Nicholson in *A Few Good Men* [1992] and George C. Scott in *Dr. Strangelove*," *Variety*'s Brian Lowry wrote. Hopper's presence didn't save *E-Ring* from cancellation after its first season.

Only a handful of the sixteen films Hopper made between 2005 and early 2009, when terminal cancer forced him to retire, are worth mentioning. Hopper paid homage to his biker film past with a small role in actor-writer-director Larry Bishop's *Hell Ride* (2008), an intentionally campy, lurid throwback to the AIP biker films Bishop acted in throughout the '60s and '70s. Most reviewers lacerated *Hell Ride*, which was executive produced by Quentin Tarantino, whose insatiable and indiscriminate appetite for this type of film is legendary.

Keith Phipps wrote, "Any film that gets Dennis Hopper back on a motorcycle can't be all bad, but *Hell Ride* sure tries to be." James Berardinelli was *Hell Ride*'s kindest critic, writing, "*Hell Ride* has been made with a very specific audience in mind, and those who fall outside of the perimeter may call this the worst film of 2008. I see what Bishop is going for, and I recognize that he understands how inane, derivative, and cheesy all of this is. Nothing about it quite gels. Dennis Hopper and David Carradine get the joke and seem to be enjoying it."

"But, it is a fun romp," Hopper said. "I enjoyed it. It's not much of a part that I had in it, but it was fun." Gary Dean Murray noted, "Kudos also go out to Dennis Hopper in what is basically a cameo role. There is this 'awe shucks' grin on his face as he delivers his lines, as if he is just pleased as can be about being in another biker flick." Evidently, Hopper really did enjoy simply working.

Oscar winner Charlize Theron received star billing in 2008's *Sleepwalking*, but wasn't on-screen very long in this bleak drama, which she produced. Neither was Hopper, playing the cruel father of white trash pot-dealer Joleen Reedy (Theron), whose young daughter and brother seek refuge at his farm after she abandons them. Hopper attempted to understand his character's actions by relating them to his own childhood experiences with corporal punishment. "He has a really tough life out there. I didn't see him as an evil man. I saw him as a person that was probably disciplined strongly as a child and given a work ethic, whether right or wrong, and that's the way he treated people. That place, if you look at that farm, boy, working that farm alone is not a joy. . . . I was raised in a similar situation. When I did something I got punished, man. It wasn't a spanking. I'd say more like a whipping. That's just the way it was in those days, especially if you were out on a farm like that. You had to keep discipline, and your kids were born to work. That's just the way people were treated in those days, and I'd say it's only the last forty or fifty years that we've been so concerned about disciplining our children, that it was wrong to spank them or wrong to hit them."

Though Hopper's role was small, he made an indelible impact on reviewers. Dustin Putman described Hopper's character as "a sad, pathetic monster of a man who doesn't exactly have the best parenting skills. Dennis Hopper is so believable, he's scary as Mr. Reedy Sr., unflinchingly disappearing behind the eyes of a man who is without remorse in making other people's lives a living hell." *Salon's* Stephanie Zacharek's led her review by writing, "If you've been longing to see Dennis Hopper as an unhinged rancher barking at a young girl to get on her hands and knees and clean up that horse manure, *now*, then *Sleepwalking* is the movie you've been waiting for. Apparently, at some point even Hopper has to scrape the bottom of the barrel when it comes to perversions: Snorfeling amyl nitrite and stuffing scraps of velvet into his mouth? Been there, done that."

Hopper returned to Europe to work with Wim Wenders in his film, *Palermo Shooting* (2008). "Well, Wim is a great old friend," he said, "and I just love him, and he's a terrific guy. And, in *Palermo Shooting*, I played Death. I shaved off my hair and my eyebrows, I'm all in gray. It's really a terrific role. We showed it in Cannes, and we got an eight-and-a-half-minute standing ovation. But, the movie really is twenty minutes too long, and Wim went back to Germany and recut it. I just got a message from him a couple of days ago, saying that he had reedited it and had taken twenty minutes out, which he really needed to do. And, hopefully, we'll see it soon."

It's no surprise that *Palermo Shooting* remains unreleased, considering the reactions of the very few American critics who reviewed it. *Variety's* Todd McCarthy wrote, "Twenty-eight pop songs go looking for a drama to accompany them in *Palermo Shooting*, which suffers from being both pretentious and inconsequential." Matt Noller wrote, "*Palermo Shooting* is one of the biggest train wrecks I've ever seen projected in a theater. It's slow, pretentious, and mind-blowingly stupid. These ideas are explored by the story of a photographer (Campino) who escapes dying in a car crash only to have Death (Dennis Hopper, sporting a bow-and-arrow and a ridiculous gray cloak) start hunting him down. The battle is fought through hilariously overwrought dream sequences and turgid voice-over, climaxing in a showdown in Death's library that is quite possibly the single most ill-conceived and badly written scene I've ever seen in a film."

The only comments on Hopper's performance come from user reviews at the IMDb, which range from the high of hpark5's "played to perfection by a wise old Dennis Hopper" to fucyeah's "Dennis Hopper was too lame in it. Let's not forget that this was the role that predated his performance in *An American Carol* [2008] so this is not exactly rock bottom."

It would have been interesting for a producer to use Hopper, a man known for his mutable political orientation, in an intelligent political film, always a rarity in Hollywood. Instead, he ended up in *Swing Vote* (2008), a Capraesque comedy about good-natured alcoholic slob Bud Johnson (Kevin Costner). Devoted to his twelve-year-old daughter, Johnson gets courted by the Republican and Democratic presidential candidates (Kelsey Grammer and Dennis Hopper, respectively) when the election hinges on his single vote.

"By the way, I was very disappointed in *Swing Vote* when I saw it, unfortunately, even though I think it's a charming movie, and I think Kevin [Costner] is wonderful in it," Hopper said in an interview with the website, *Ain't It Cool News*. "My part was just totally ripped out of it. I mean, I had this whole subplot where a young Mexican waitress wants me to come to her grandfather's funeral. And, I shake off the secret service, and I go to the funeral, 'cause we marched with Chávez [César Chávez (1927-1993), the cofounder and leader of the United Farm Workers, a labor-rights group representing agricultural workers] together, and I give this speech in the church, and this whole thing where I come to my realization of who I am, because my character is so off, doing all these things, and so I come back with this strength. And that was all taken out of the film. So, when I saw it, I went, 'Oh, no!' " What did critics think of Hopper's performance in *Swing Vote*? They didn't. In their reviews of *Swing Vote*, Roger

Ebert, Nathan Rabin, and Stephanie Zacharek didn't bother to mention his performance. Once again, it was that kind of role for Hopper.

As a favor to fellow Republican Kelsey Grammer, Hopper appeared briefly in *An American Carol*, a right-wing comedy based on Charles Dickens' *A Christmas Carol*. Kevin Farley plays Michael Malone, the movie's stand-in for Michael Moore. Malone is a leftist agitprop film-maker whose latest cause is to abolish the Fourth of July. He's visited by the ghosts of Gen. George S. Patton Jr. (Kelsey Grammer), George Washington (Jon Voight, whose political statements make Hopper sound like a statesman), and JFK (Chriss Anglin), who show him the error of his liberal ways.

The filmmakers' (including director and cowriter David Zucker of *Airplane!* (1980) and *The Naked Gun* series) puerile idea of satire is to make Malone a clueless clown who makes documentaries like *Die, You American Pigs* and *No Country for Anyone*, and an anti-American dupe who lets Afghani jihadists plant a bomb at his anti-Fourth of July rally. Hopper provided his own review of the film, saying, "I did one day on it. Kelsey Grammar got me involved. I came in and did a day, playing a judge shooting ACLU lawyers. I haven't seen it. Doubt I will."

In *Elegy* (2008), Hopper played poet George O'Hearn, the friend and confidant of David Kepesh (Sir Ben Kingsley), an aging literary lion who enjoys a rejuvenating fling with an admiring young graduate student (Penélope Cruz). Giving a nicely modulated performance, Hopper provided one of *Elegy*'s two highlights. (The other was Penélope Cruz's topless scene.) Hopper, who had been diagnosed with prostate cancer in 1997 and died at the end of May 2010, may have even informed his character's death scene with a presentiment of his own impending mortality.

Hopper said that *Elegy* offered him his first decent role in a decade. "When I saw this movie, however, I went, 'Wow, what a wonderful film.' And, not just because I'm in it, but I just thought it was a really wonderfully mature piece of work that we just don't have the pleasure of seeing very often."

It's a shame there wasn't more of Hopper in *Elegy*. His performance earned him his first string of good notices in ages. While *Salon*'s Andrew O'Hehir wrote that *Elegy* "is a muted, pretty, anesthetic concoction that's never fully satisfying," he noted the "Pulitzer-winning poet played delightfully by Dennis Hopper." Roger Ebert wrote, "I also liked Dennis Hopper as George, the old pal he has coffee with, who attempts to bring sanity to David's behavior, but despairs." James Berardinelli wrote, "Strong supporting performances are provided by the always reliable Patricia Clarkson and Dennis Hopper, who is suddenly ubiquitous (see also: *Swing Vote* and *Hell Ride*). The *San Francisco Chronicle's* Ruthe Stein wrote, "For once, Dennis Hopper underplays his role." (I suppose that passes for some sort of compliment.)

Two days after returning from the Cannes Film Festival in late May 2008, where he promoted *Elegy* and *Palermo Shooting*, Hopper's agent called to offer him the lead in the cable channel Starz' TV series *Crash* (2008-2009), based on the Oscar-winning film of 2004. Hopper had only two days to consider the offer. Even suffering from prostate cancer, the seventy-two-year-old Hopper seemed indefatigable. He accepted Starz' offer and took off to Albuquerque, where he put in horrendous seventeen-hour days in the summer heat playing an outrageous music producer named Ben Cendars.

"It's a drag because I have to leave my family, but the work is good. I have to be in Albuquerque three days a week, so that was a big decision, too, but we're working through it. Yeah, I'm having a joyous time, even though it's difficult. But we have our three days off and four days off every two weeks, whatever. I've taken a hotel room. I used to live in Taos, new Mexico, so my brother and my cousins all live up in Taos. So I have a choice of coming back to L.A. where my family is or going up to Taos where my family is. So it's beginning to work out, haven't quite figured it out yet.

"I've had a lot of dialogue in this series, so that's been the most difficult part for me. I have all these speeches to memorize, which really, if you look at them, mean nothing at all! (laughs) They're just these stream-of-consciousness rants. I'm like a little kid sitting in the corner memorizing this stuff all day and all night. I'm working a little harder than I enjoy right at the moment because I'm doing a television series. But, nobody's complaining, because the writing is so good. Boy, the scripts have been incredible."

Hopper denied that Cendars was based on notorious record producer Phil Spector, who he shared office space with in the '60s, telling one interviewer, "No. I'm doing me!" "I'm playing a Phil Spector-type music mogul who has orgies, plays with guns and knives, and abuses drugs and alcohol," he said at a press conference for the show. Hopper laughed at one interviewer's suggestion that Cendars was what Frank Booth would have been if he had survived *Blue Velvet* and become a record producer. "Yeah, right!," Hopper said. "My first conversation with my penis in the limo with the young woman driver, it's pretty hairy. When I hire the new driver, who's black, and say 'Gorillas in the mist, that's what the LAPD call you,' he has no stop switch, my character. He says everything and insults everybody. He just goes for it."

The *San Francisco Chronicle*'s Tim Goodman panned the pilot episode of *Crash*, writing, "It feels like one-thirteenth of a story you won't really care to follow. The first hour of *Crash* is mostly about Dennis Hopper, the marquee name (all the other actors are essentially unknowns). Hopper, as a music producer, obediently gives Starz what it undoubtedly wants: the full Hopper. He's crazy, man, crazy. He's Dennis Hopper, he's supposed to be crazy. Brain-damaged, drug-addled and just plain weird—it's the role the world wants him to play, right?

"If it weren't so utterly devoid of surprise, it might even be funny. But luckily Hopper has yet to cross over into total self-parody a la William Shatner. That's because he's a great actor, has a mind for the business of theater and gives you enough—even in bad roles with undistinguished writing—to keep his dignity. Then again, he opens *Crash* talking to his penis, so it might not be prudent to make bold predictions about quality or dignity."

Two days after completing the first episode of *Crash*, Hopper touched down in Paris to take in a retrospective of his films and art at the Cinémathèque Française, where he would be awarded France's order of Commander of Arts and Letters by their minister of culture. The exhibit employed twenty video screens, playing Hopper's feature films, commercials, and the experimental films he made with Andy Warhol and Bruce Conner.

Hopper said "They worked on it for three and a half years, it's the whole fifth floor of the Frank Gehry building on the Seine River. You walk through and you see the things I was doing —TV, movies—at every part of my career, while you're also seeing part of my art collection. And alongside you see the political things that were happening in the country—the Kennedy assassinations, Malcolm X, Martin Luther King, and the last thing is Obama running for president. They're doing a whole virtual reality of my nightmare life (laughs). And, then Wim Wenders and I are doing a workshop. And Julian Schnabel and I are going to do a workshop. So that'll be fun."

The Cinémathèque show was Hopper's nineteenth since San Diego's MOCA exhibition in November 1996 and came after he was honored by having his art exhibited at St. Petersburg's legendary Hermitage Museum in 2007. "I had five rooms," he proudly told Garth Pearce. "I became the only living American artist to show there. Andy Warhol was shown there, but he's dead." Thomas Krens, the director of the Guggenheim Museum, asked Hopper, "How does it feel to be the most successful artist in Russia—but no one knows you in the United States?"

Why did Hopper court the approval of the art world so zealously? He regarded himself as an artistic genius and wasn't shy about his ambition to have that genius recognized by others. "I do it totally out of an ego problem, that's all," he told Lynn Barber in 2001, saying he wasn't making any money from his art. (By 2006, that had changed. He told Dan Glaister that he had sold about half a million dollars worth of his work from his latest show, mostly to collectors in New York.)

"I'd like to establish a place in time," he said. "I went to a party the other night—Nic Cage and Francis Ford Coppola had a party—and I said, 'This house is really familiar,' and they said, 'Well, it's Dean Martin's house.' They didn't say it was Coppola or Nic Cage's house. It was Dean Martin's house. The only reason you go into art is that you hope you can cheat death a little by leaving something that's going to last a little bit beyond your own time.

"You have to want to express something, to create something that lives beyond you own lifetime. It's a pretty lonely concept, an object you're leaving after you're dead." Hopper believed the creative drive "comes out of a lonely, sad place. It's a way of looking for acceptance, which is almost impossible to find. Acting comes out of that place, too." Hopper was still the lonely, unhappy child who thought he could win the love of others by getting them to say "Wow!" in reaction to his art. In "Look At Me, Mama," a song that John Buck Wilkin wrote and performed in *The American Dreamer*, he sings, "Look at me mama, look at me papa, look at me, it's your boy."

Hopper's bid for artistic recognition even saw him eagerly participate in high-profile events that mingled high art with the blatant promotion of brand-name products like BMW motorcycles and Hugo Boss suits.

In 1996, the German clothing company Hugo Boss began awarding a $50,000 prize every other year to an artist working in any medium. Hopper became their celebrity-artist frontman, hosting a dinner for the lucky recipient the evening before he presided over the presentation ceremony at the Guggenheim museum. Hopper told *People*, "I have been involved with Hugo Boss for a long, long time because of their involvement in the art world. I wear their clothes because I get them free and I love them. But I got involved with them because of the arts." He also got Jaguar automobiles gratis from Hugo Boss.

In July 1998, New York's Solomon R. Guggenheim Museum presented "The Art of the Motorcycle," an exhibition of 114 motorcycles sponsored by BMW. On July 28, Hopper drew a standing-room-only audience at the museum for "An Evening With Dennis Hopper," where he discussed the making of *Easy Rider*. Hopper even overcame his documented aversion to motorcycles to join the Guggenheim Motorcycle Club, a group of celebrities, including the Guggenheim's director, Thomas Krens, Jeremy Irons, and Laurence Fishburne, who participated in cross-country rides to publicize openings of "The Art of the Motorcycle" at the Guggenheim museums in Bilbao, Spain, and Las Vegas. (In 2006, *New York* magazine called Hopper "the Goog's Hollywood star-in-residence," noting his membership in the "Guggenheim Motorcycle Gang.")

In the summer of 2008, the seventy-two-year-old Hopper rode from the Hermitage in St. Petersburg to the Pushkin Museum of Fine Arts in Moscow. "It was an incredible thing," he said. "It took us five days to get from St. Petersburg to Moscow, but it was wonderful. We opened '300 Years of American Art' at the Pushkin Museum in Moscow and the Guggenheim. So it was cool." Such excursions were not without their hazards, as demonstrated by the accident involving actress and model Lauren Hutton, a later addition to the Guggenheim Motorcycle Club. Hutton was participating in a 100-mile ride near Las Vegas with Hopper and Jeremy Irons when she lost control of her bike on a curve, suffering a collapsed lung, multiple fractures of her arms and legs, and broken ribs.

Following Hopper's death, a commenter to the online edition of the *Los Angeles Times* wrote, "When Dennis Hopper took the stage at the Guggenheim SoHo, New York, in 1998 to announce the winner of the Hugo Boss Prize, the audience was filled with joy. The audience, composed of individuals from the visual arts, the performing arts, the world of business, etc., cheered him on, as if we were acknowledging him for simultaneously being one of us and one of the greats in the world-at-large. I've seen polite applause and such at art-world events, but I've never seen such glee as I had on that summer evening twelve years ago."

In May 2002, Hopper opened an exhibit of his paintings at the Hugo Boss flagship store on New York's Fifth Avenue. Artistically, his latest work returned him to the pop heyday of the '60s. Hopper turned some of his photos of Andy Warhol and other artists into huge, billboard-sized paintings. *The New York Times* reported, "He agreed to exhibit his paintings at the Boss store because, he said, it was one way of ensuring that they would get the kind of attention he craves. His paintings have been shown at the Stedelijk Museum in Amsterdam. The Boston Museum of Fine Arts and the Philadelphia Museum have expressed interest in his recent work, Mr. Hopper said. 'But I would like the Whitney to take them,' he added, clearly hoping to be asked. 'I don't know where I fit in, in the art world,' Mr. Hopper said. 'I'm an actor, and actors don't fit in anywhere—people say we are always acting, right? Still, I want to be considered. Maybe on my gravestone that's what it will say: 'Consider me.' "

Hopper seemed unaware of the irony of his situation that evening. Flanked by his wife, who wore an Yves Saint Laurent leopard-print creation, he sat on a sofa in the clothing boutique's upstairs VIP room, safely sequestered from the celebrity gawkers below. Hopper, who had just appeared in a Gap commercial directed by Joel and Ethan Coen, told the *Times*' style reporter, Ruth La Ferla, "Marcel Duchamp and Andy Warhol were all in the tradition of artists who finger-pointed. They exposed the ills of a too-commercial culture."

Hopper's campaign to advance his legacy as an artist bore fruit. He told Lisa Law that he had recognized his destiny as an artist in many ways. "I've been closer to artists and closer to the art world than the film business . . . Leo Castelli and I are tight. I know all these people. I know Larry Gagosian really well. I know all the top dealers and all the top people. I know the art world. I have never been allowed into the movie business in that kind of sense. I've never been taken into the inner sanctums of the studios, but in the art world, I have. In the art world, I've also maintained an aesthetic and maintained a position that has importance. In the film business, you're sort of like yesterday's newspaper whenever they want you to be."

Hopper had something beside his genius to announce at the opening of his Cinémathèque Française show on October 13, 2008. In another surprising political reversal, he told journalists he planned on voting for Sen. Barack Obama in the upcoming presidential election. "I pray God, Barack Obama is elected," he said, criticizing what he called the "lies" of the administration of President George W. Bush. He repeated his announcement when he appeared on the TV talk show *The View* on November 4, 2008.

"I voted for both the Bushes," he told *The Onion A. V. Club*'s Noel Murray on Election Day in 2008. "Things really started falling apart when President Bush said our financial structure was strong. And then McCain later repeated the same thing, my God. So it started crumbling down. Also, my wife's a big supporter of Obama, and I met him. I had marched with Martin Luther King in the South, and I felt a great empathy and obligation to that movement. Still, I stayed with McCain until he picked Palin. I couldn't quite go on any longer with this cartoon. And also, I really resent the negative stuff the Republican Party is putting out on Obama. I just think it's really disgraceful. Then I ditched. I'm happy I did. We'll see what happens today."

Hopper's support for Obama was motivated by something other than the Republicans' choice of Sarah Palin and their campaign tactics. "My wife's been a big fan of Obama, and we met him the day he announced he was running for president. We saw him in Chicago. I was in an elevator with him. He turned to me and said, 'I know that your mother died a couple of months ago. I know your mother was from Kansas, my mother was from Kansas. I know what it's like losing a mother.' My wife had obviously said something to him, but I thought the fact the man had the presence in mind to think of me at that time when he had so much going on—the day he announced he was running for president—it moved me."

Hopper spent some of his time off from filming the second season of *Crash* to return to Taos for the city's Taos Summer of Love 2009, a series of musical, art, and film events celebrating the fortieth anniversary of the original summer of love, when the city canceled its planned festival. Taos, like the rest of the country, chose to forget the hostility with which they once greeted members of the counterculture. The hippies and their communes were gone. (The Lama Foundation, a spiritual community in San Cristobal, twenty miles north of Taos, is the lone exception.) Dennis Hopper no longer stalked the town square wielding a gun. Now Taos' cultural celebrity and honorary mayor, he kicked off the festivities by hosting a fundraising dinner on May 3.

The festival would not have been complete without a screening of *Easy Rider*, which was held outdoors at the Taos County Sheriff's Posse Arena on June 20. Hopper also curated two concurrent exhibitions at Taos' Harwood Museum of Art. The first exhibit, "Dennis Hopper Photographs And Paintings," was self-explanatory. "Hopper at the Harwood: L.A. to Taos 40 Years of Friendship" showcased the work of Larry Bell, Ron Cooper, Ronald Davis, Ken Price, and Robert Dean Stockwell, artists who moved from Los Angeles to Taos, where Hopper befriended them and supported their work.

"Dennis did look a bit enervated, almost pale last year at the Harwood," Bill Whaley recalled. The most notable thing about Hopper's appearance at the opening of the exhibitions was his touching self-effacement when he spent his time with interviewers talking about the work of his fellow artists. Years before the Harwood exhibitions, Ron Cooper said, "The most interesting thing about Dennis Hopper for me is his reverence for art and other artists, total reverence and respect for art itself and for its makers."

In 1994, Hopper contemplated retiring when he turned seventy to teach acting. Instead, the beginning of 2009 saw the nearly seventy-three-year-old actor back on a film set in Queens, New York, starring in *The Last Film Festival*, where he played a desperate, Robert Evans-like producer, who has taken his latest film to the only film festival that would have it, the last on a list of hundreds. The circumstances of the film's production were in keeping with those of Hopper's character in the film. *The Last Film Festival* was such a low-budget affair that Hopper and his fellow cast members, including Jacqueline Bisset and Chris Kattan, were each assigned a classroom in the high school of the city where the film was being shot in lieu of trailers. (Director Linda Yellen was still seeking money to complete the film in November 2010.) Yellen said, "He was in great health and had enormous charisma when we were shooting. He eagerly worked long days." Hopper's next and final film role was in the animated 3D film *Alpha and Omega* (2010), where he supplied the voice of the wolf named Tony.

Hopper was in New York on September 30, 2009, where he was scheduled to make the rounds of TV talk shows to promote the second season of *Crash*, when he suddenly fell ill with stomach sickness and flulike symptoms as he was about to appear on the political chatfest *Morning Joe*. He was rushed by ambulance to a nearby hospital wearing an oxygen mask and was seen to have various tubes inserted into him to sustain him until he reached the hospital's emergency room. Hopper's publicist, Sheila Feren, said that he was being treated for dehydration. (Dehydration has become one of the catchall explanations that press agents use when their celebrity clients suddenly become indisposed, no matter what the actual reason.)

Hopper was released the following day, feeling better, according to his manager, Sam Maydew, who said that he looked forward to returning to work on *Crash*. Hopper had recently finished shooting his second-season episodes for *Crash* and was preparing to fly to Australia to attend "Dennis Hopper and the New Hollywood," an exhibition of his artwork and photography at the Australian Centre for the Moving Image in Melbourne celebrating "the work and life of an extraordinary filmmaker, artist, and key figure in the evolution of Americas cultural scene from the 1950s to today," when he called off his trip. On October 29, 2009, Maydew announced that Hopper was suffering from prostate cancer and had canceled all travel plans in order to focus on the medical treatment he was receiving through a special program at the University of Southern California.

As the editors of print and online publications instructed their writers to bring Hopper's obituary up to date, he surprised everyone one last time. Rather than bowing out with a dignified farewell appearance with Leno or Letterman, he dropped a bombshell tailor made for a tabloid scandal. *The Huffington Post*'s January 15, 2010, headline read "Dennis Hopper Divorce Shocker," reporting that he had filed a motion in court the previous day requesting a divorce from Victoria Hopper, his wife of fourteen years. In a press release issued several days later, he said, "I wish Victoria the best but only want to spend these difficult days surrounded by my children and close friends."

No one outside of the Hoppers' private life saw it coming, but his shocking announcement was the eruption of long simmering tensions between the couple. Hopper's fourteen-year marriage seemed proof that he had finally managed to solve his problems with women, but it wasn't really so. "Dennis was a very difficult man to be married to, and I loved him, but he was really tough," Victoria Hopper said. "He had a lot of issues with women. It was born out consistently in his whole life." Even drug free, "He didn't magically become better. He was the same guy. I was just, I think, a calmer, stronger person than most. My friends used to call me 'The Diplomat.' "

Hopper's attitudes toward women contributed to his unsuccessful relationships with them. He tended to view them as servile sex objects. Charlotte Hopper said that the women who were part of the support staff at his house when he edited *The Last Movie* were expected to be on call at all hours to serve the film's all-male crew and any other men on the premises. When she asked Dennis to thank these women by crediting them in *The Last Movie*, he refused. Hopper viewed anything less than unconditional love and total compliance with his wishes as part of a continuous pattern of betrayal by women that began with his conflict with his mother.

"To be loved is a desperate primary need for Dennis, and he's never really been able to satisfy it," a woman familiar with him told journalist Brad Darrach. "He doesn't know how to ask for love because that would involve accepting a woman as an equal. Too dangerous. I think that to Dennis, a woman is either a whore or a madonna. Or both. Anyway, he wants you to be a fantasy creature, and he leaves you if you try to become real."

"My relationship with Dennis was always very difficult," said Victoria Hopper. "He is not an easy person, but we definitely did love each other." That may have once been true of the couple, but they were already living separate lives under one roof some time before the divorce. Reportedly, Victoria found Dennis cruel and controlling. Dennis thought Victoria was cold and materialistic. Their marriage had become sexless.

Hopper became increasingly angry and irritable after learning that his cancer had metastasized in the summer of 2008. In October 2008, he lashed out at Victoria in their hotel room while they were vacationing in Paris. "You're a human garbage can," he screamed at her. "I can dump anything on you." "I hadn't gotten a lawyer, but in my mind, our marriage was irrevocably broken," she recalled. Two days after he returned home, Hopper learned that his cancer was terminal. "I dropped any idea of leaving and decided to stay and take care of him," Victoria later said. When he became sick while promoting *Crash* in October 2009, she rushed to New York to comfort him. While Victoria was caring for him in their hotel room following his release from the hospital, he became enraged, and accused her of causing his cancer. When she said she was going to get her own room, he said, "I will never let you leave me."

Victoria's decision to stay by her husband's side throughout his ordeal may have been motivated as much by pragmatic financial considerations as a sense of devotion. The couple's prenuptial agreement specified that Victoria would be the beneficiary of 25 percent of her husband's estate and a $250,000 life-insurance policy, but only if they were married *and* living together at the time of his death.

After returning from his aborted publicity tour for *Crash*, Hopper stopped working and spent much of his time at home. When he worked, his frequent absences acted to relieve some of the stresses of his marriage. Now, Dennis and Victoria were constantly together, often at each other's throats. Their ongoing conflict was complicated by the presence of Hopper's children, Marin and Henry, who resided at his Venice home. Henry, who dabbled in expressionist painting, lived in one of his father's two-story Gehry-designed homes. He had spent two years studying at Cal Arts, an exclusive private art academy located thirty miles north of Los Angeles in Valencia, and had a fledgling career as an actor, having appeared in Gus Van Sant's *Restless* (2011).

Marin Hopper and her young daughter had moved into a second Gehry home two-and-a-half years before her father's divorce, after she experienced trouble in her own marriage. Dennis gave her a job booking his paid appearances at film festivals and other events. Marin and Henry got involved in Dennis' marital disputes with Victoria, taking their father's side against Victoria's in the couple's fights. Hopper reportedly enjoyed seeing his two children verbally beat up Victoria, who he took his frustrations out on.

In October 2009, Victoria learned that Hopper had modified his estate plans in violation of their prenuptial agreement. She claimed that when she confronted him about her discovery, he told her that he did not want to divorce her, but was being pressured to do so by his advisors and his adult children. Dennis told her that other people were insisting that he take care of them upon his death. In the spring of 2009, he told Victoria that Marin accused her of stealing Marin's inheritance.

According to Victoria, Hopper's adult children were attending his legal appointments and reading everything. "It's so horrible, Dennis is at home, Victoria and Galen are living there as well, and Marin is pulling her father out of his bed and driving him to the divorce lawyers. The poor guy has no idea what is going on," a friend of the couple told *The Huffington Post*. "Even his lawyers are telling people he is on painkillers and is essentially sleeping all the time."

Hopper received an experimental cancer treatment for several months that concluded without success in early January 2010. He spent much of that time in bed, shrouded in the smoke from the medicinal marijuana he smoked, woozy from the marijuana and heavy doses of prescription painkillers he took to relieve the unremitting pain of the cancer eating away at him. According to Victoria, Hopper required twenty-four-hour nursing care to assist him with his basic needs.

The TV was constantly on, tuned to news and crime shows. Victoria once entered Dennis' room as he was about to show Galen one of his films on TV that contained graphic sexual content. When she complained to Dennis that it was unsuitable for the girl, he said, "She should hear this. She should learn what the world is really like." Victoria said that he also smoked pot in front of Galen. Until his cancer metastasized, Hopper had shown little interest in the daily chores involved with raising Galen, delegating them to Victoria. According to Victoria, he took Galen on only one outing by himself and never spent more than a few hours alone with her in their home. Now Hopper fought Victoria over Galen's upbringing.

As his cancer worsened, Hopper became increasingly volatile, verbally abusive, and threatening to Victoria, who sought safety by sleeping behind locked doors in her daughter's room. Hopper's behavior escalated to direct threats to Victoria's safety and well-being. "Something bad is going to happen to you, and you won't see it coming," he told Victoria during one argument. She started to fear for her life. When Victoria once tried to discuss getting therapy for Galen, Hopper became infuriated and aggressive, jumped from topic to topic, and made extraordinarily exaggerated statements, telling Victoria he would "end her" if she tried to leave him, even though she never threatened to. Though Hopper had discouraged his wife's attempts to pursue an independent career during their marriage, he told her he would never let her divorce him and would leave her and Galen destitute if she left him.

Victoria always knew that Hopper kept guns in the house. In October 2009, she was alarmed to discover a loaded pistol and several rounds of ammunition in their unlocked bedside drawer and a loaded shotgun in their bedroom closet, which were all accessible to a small child. She removed them to a safer location and later gave them to the police. One night in mid-October, as she was putting Galen to sleep, Victoria heard firecrackers outside the house. Dennis rushed into the bedroom, demanding his pistol. When Victoria reminded him it had been removed, he became enraged. He screamed and swore at her in Galen's presence and promised to get more guns.

The tension between the couple culminated in Christmas of 2009. Sources close to Victoria alleged that Hopper's children moved him into a suite at the Beverly Hills Hotel under an assumed name to get him away from her. Victoria took Galen with her on a trip to Boston to visit her mother, seeking relief from her exhausting conflict with her husband. The *New York Post* insinuated that Victoria was there to visit Democratic Party strategist James Boyce, who they suggested was having a romantic relationship with her. The tabloid alleged that they worked together on liberal causes and attended President Obama's inauguration together when Dennis Hopper was too ill to attend. Boyce denied the paper's allegations.

Upon returning to Venice, Victoria moved into a bungalow on the property in January with Galen. On January 12, Galen was sent home from school due to illness. Victoria kept her in the guesthouse to protect Dennis, whose immune system was compromised by his chemotherapy. On January 14, the day she was served with Dennis' petition for divorce, Victoria attempted to return to the main house with Galen, who was well enough to return to school. She was asked to leave by Hopper's adult children and others who were present, distressing Galen, who told her mother she didn't feel safe there. Victoria's last face-to-face encounter with Dennis took place on January 19. "We spoke calmly, and I said my final piece," she recalled. "I told him that I would always have love for him because of our daughter. His response was, 'I don't need forgiveness from you.' Then he held a cross up to my face and said, 'Now get out.' "

On January 25, 2010, Victoria Hopper responded to her husband's divorce petition, filing a motion requesting sole custody of the couple's six-year-old-daughter, spousal and child support, and reimbursement for therapy for Galen, who was stressed out by the ongoing family psychodrama. She also requested that she be made a joint beneficiary with Galen of her husband's $1-million life-insurance policy. This was the beginning of a series of claims and counterclaims by Victoria and Dennis Hopper in their legal declarations that were then circulated by the tabloid press.

The main thrust of Victoria's claims was that Dennis Hopper's adult children were taking advantage of his vulnerable state to compel him to divorce her in order to increase their share of his estate. In her legal response to Dennis Hopper's petition for divorce, Victoria declared that he was "more often than not incapable of handling his legal and financial affairs." A family confidant told *The Huffington Post* "that his eldest daughter Marin is engineering a deathbed divorce and sending lies out to the media to try to bleed extra millions out of his sizable estate."

Victoria Hopper told me, "He was definitely not in control of his personal affairs. He was not in control of his personal affairs in the fall of '09. In the last few months of the court case, he didn't even sign his 'declarations' that they put in. He couldn't read, and he couldn't concentrate. Not making him innocent or blameless for some of the bad things that happened, but it was not him. None of the press stuff was him."

Victoria visited Hopper the same day that he supposedly issued the press release stating, "I wish Victoria the best but only want to spend these difficult days surrounded by my children and close friends." "The day that the statement was issued, my sister, who is a minister, and I, we saw Dennis that day, and talked with him quietly and very gently, and he had no idea that any statement had gone out, he had no idea why anyone would know we were getting divorced. He was begging not to get a divorce. He was under terrible pressure from his kids, and he reported that, which is reported to the court. Which isn't to say that our relationship was great at that point. It was really sad, what happened. And sadly, I think the filing was just about the kids wanting more money when he went. They knew there was a chance they could leave me with nothing because of the prenup, and they went for it, which is really sad. I mean, very sad for me, very sad for Galen, and really sad for Dennis."

Dennis Hopper answered his wife's allegations on February 11, 2010, when his attorney, Joseph Mannis, filed declarations in Los Angeles Superior Court from the actor, his adult children, his doctors, and his assistant in support of his motion for divorce. The declarations claimed that Dennis Hopper was the victim of Victoria Hopper, portraying her as an emotionally out-of-control gold digger. The declarations described her as "volatile," "insane and out of her mind," and "inhuman."

Hopper disputed Victoria's contention that his adult children pushed him to divorce her, stating that he filed for divorce "clearly and deliberately, without any pressure or influence exerted upon me by any other person." His doctors attested to his mental competence. They also said that he weighed 120 pounds and vomited after taking his medication. Hopper claimed that Victoria's mother, who had come from Boston to live with and support Victoria ". . . told me in November of 2009 that I should simply leave the bulk of my property to [Victoria] as I was going to die soon. I found this statement distressing, inappropriate, bizarre, and disturbing." He also claimed that Victoria and her mother woke him up in the middle of the night and badgered him to reveal how much money and property Victoria would get when he died.

Hopper's son said, "Victoria has made my father's life a living hell over at least the last six months." Henry Hopper claimed that Victoria had accused him of stealing a Warhol portrait of Dennis Hopper and a small sculpture of a spray-painted TV on a plaster pedestal by the street artist Banksy, and then changing the locks on the compound's five houses. (Victoria Hopper told me that she and Henry had a terrible argument, where he accused her of stealing the works in question. "Dennis' children presume everything belongs to him because he's the king and I'm the 'waitress,' " Victoria explained to a friend at the time.)

Dennis Hopper said that he spent Christmas 2009 "in utter distress" after Victoria took their daughter to Boston without informing him. "This malevolent act . . . has caused me to miss what may very well be my last Christmas with my daughter Galen," he declared. Hopper's personal physician, Dr. David Agus, stated, "The presence of his estranged wife is hampering Mr. Hopper's present cancer care. It is my belief and recommendation that the less Mr. Hopper has to do with his estranged wife at this time, the more likely he is to have his life extended."

The judge in the case granted a restraining order preventing Victoria Hopper from communicating directly or indirectly with her husband by any means except with regard to matters concerning their daughter. Victoria was also restrained and enjoined from "harassing, attacking striking, threatening, disturbing the peace, keeping under surveillance, or blocking the movements of the Petitioner (Mr. Hopper), Petitioner's son Henry Hopper, Petitioner's daughter, Marin Hopper, and Petitioner's assistant Emily Davis, directly or indirectly." She was ordered to stay at least 120 feet away from them, and was restricted from entering her husband's home or any of the other buildings on his compound except the bungalow where she was residing. The judge awarded Dennis Hopper daily visitation rights with Galen between five and seven P.M. if he agreed to refrain from smoking marijuana at least one hour before every visit.

On March 23, Dennis Hopper filed an affidavit in court that alleged Victoria had taken artwork and other personal property with her when she left that was worth $1.5 million. He claimed that his wife "surreptitiously removed from my home very valuable personal property while I was extremely ill, refused to tell me where the property was when I asked her, and then left town." She said that the Warhol was in a museum in Australia and insisted that Banksy gave her the sculpture as a birthday gift (with a certificate of authenticity) when she and Dennis met him in London. (In e-mails sent to *The Daily Beast*, Banksy's representatives confirmed her story.) "I removed my own property," Victoria told the *New York Post*. "He is making a big deal about me removing things that are legally mine from the house. I have legal letters saying they belong to me."

On March 25, Hopper's attorney filed declarations from his doctors in which they reversed their earlier optimism about his recovery after undergoing last-ditch chemotherapy. They claimed that he was now too ill to undergo further chemotherapy and his debilitated condition prevented him from being deposed by Victoria Hopper's attorney. Dr. David Agus stated that Hopper weighed 100 pounds, was unable to continue long conversations, and that a deposition "could actually threaten his ability to survive his current health crisis."

Victoria said that Dennis was using his illness as an excuse to avoid being deposed in his divorce case. "They were just trying to run out the clock on the case," she said. (She told me that "things got very weird" in the last two months of his life. She claims that Hopper was practically being held incommunicado. People had to sign an agreement before seeing him, and he wasn't accepting calls.) She said that he made his own weekly runs to a medical-marijuana dispensary and wasn't too sick to accept his star on Hollywood Boulevard. She also learned that he had recently chartered a jet and took his children with him to Taos to show them his old stomping grounds there. (Hopper also managed to make a trip to New York, where he was interviewed by Peter M. Brant and Tony Shafrazi for *Interview* magazine at Shafrazi's art gallery in Chelsea.)

While Hopper was busy dying and battling his wife through legal proxies, his friends in Hollywood worked feverishly to get him his star on Hollywood Boulevard's Walk of Fame while he could still attend the ceremony, even though he had rebuffed efforts to award him the honor years before. On March 25, the Hollywood Chamber of Commerce announced that the ceremony would take place the following day. Dr. Agus told the court that he approved of Hopper's appearance at the Walk of Fame because it would likely be a positive experience.

Few expected Hopper to show up at the ceremony. But Dennis Hopper surprised his skeptics, rallying enough to accept his star in person. Flanked by Jack Nicholson, whose American flag-patterned shirt intentionally brought *Easy Rider* to mind, a cadaverous Hopper, wearing a tweed golfing cap and bandages on his hand and head to cover a recent injury, was visibly delighted by the occasion. Hopper, who remained seated much of the time, was introduced by his friends, producer Mark Canton and actor and artist Viggo Mortensen.

Hopper then shakily stepped up to the podium to deliver his acceptance speech. He joked, "I want to thank the paparazzi. Because yesterday, I got up, I've been workin' for this date to look as good as possible, to be as strong as possible. So I got out of the house yesterday, and I'm in the middle of the road and going to the van, and I was walkin', and somebody yelled from down the block, 'Hey Dennis!' I thought I recognized the voice, so I kept walking, and I turned around, but I didn't see the little ridge line in the road, and I took a terrible fall because I have no muscle thing. So I fell directly on my face, and I had my glasses in my hand. I got pretty screwed up. But anyway, I know you [the paparazzi] have a tough job, but sometimes you oughta be a little more sensitive."

Hopper continued by thanking the Starz network, who sponsored the award, the Hollywood Chamber of Commerce, his friend Satya de la Manitou "for having this dream for forty years," and his son-in-law, John Goldstone, for working for a year to get him the star. "Now, I've written a little something here," Hopper said. "Let's see if I'll be able to read it. Everyone here today that I've invited, and obviously some that I haven't invited, have enriched my life tremendously. You've shown me a world I would never have seen being a farm boy from Dodge City, Kansas. Learning things I would never have learned. I went under contract to Warner Bros. when I was eighteen years old, so my college and everything I learned, I learned from Hollywood. And I've never been treated better by anyone. You shared your life with me and my talent and your talent. Everything I learned in my life, I learned from you and the wonderful world that I traveled and saw. Well, I got it all from you. So this has been my home and my schooling. And I love all of you. Well, I just want to thank you, that's all I can do. This means so much to me, and thank you very much, everyone."

Hopper knelt down by his star to take pictures with his sunny daughter Galen, making a touching scene on what happened to be her seventh birthday. Hopper's son became upset and fled when someone asked him about his father's health. After the ceremony, Hopper attended a private luncheon at the Beverly Hills villa of Marin Hopper's friend, Coca-Cola heir Alex Hitz, where he spent nearly three hours with friends before returning home, even standing outside Hitz's home for photos which were later posted on the Internet.

Dennis and Victoria Hopper's attorneys appeared in Los Angeles Superior Court on April 5, 2010, to argue her requests for child and spousal support. Hopper, who was undergoing radical chemotherapy, did not attend the proceedings. In a sworn statement, his doctor maintained that he was too sick to undergo questioning by attorneys. Despite his attorney's claims that Hopper was spending $26,000 monthly on medical expenses and was low on cash, since his illness prevented him from working, Judge Amy Pellman ordered him to pay his wife $8,000 a month in spousal support and $4,000 in child support. She also ordered him to pay his wife's mortgages, utilities, and half the $5,000 she spent every month to stable her horses. Pellman awarded Victoria Hopper $200,000 in attorney's and accountant's fees. While Hopper's attorney again asserted that Victoria's residence in the guesthouse on his compound was detrimental to his client's health, Judge Pellman ruled that she be allowed to continue living on the property as long as she didn't enter the main house.

Judge Pellman was most concerned with the effects of the Hoppers' acrimonious squabble on Galen. Addressing his adult children, who were seated in the back of the courtroom, Pellman said, "If you care about this little girl who is about to experience the death of her father, having an extended war with her mother is not in her best interests. Make every effort to sit down with each other, or with a third party, and try to put your feelings aside. It's never one-sided. There needs to be street cleaning on both sides of this street." Standing on the steps outside the courthouse, Victoria told reporters, "It's heartbreaking, and I hope it can be amicably resolved." Joe Mannis said that he was pleased with the judge's ruling, except for the award for legal and accounting fees, and added that his client would not contest the decision on custody and spousal and child support.

Though Hopper gave innumerable interviews throughout his life, he seemed determined to make sure his final thoughts on a variety of subjects were recorded for posterity when he sat for what *Vanity Fair* later claimed was his final interview shortly before his death. (His last complete interview was given to *Interview* and was published posthumously. Though he didn't provide any new revelations about his life and career, he added some interesting new details to old stories and seemed to be in remarkably good spirits, considering his condition.)

Photographed surrounded by his children, the grey-skinned Hopper looked like a disinterred mummy, whose golf cap seemed like an oversized gag prop on his withered head. "I'm sorry, I'm not feeling well," he told writer Bob Colacello, before giving him the requisite tour of the live-in art gallery inside his home. Perhaps alluding to his tumultuous divorce, he pointed to some of the paintings, which were askew, and said, "We've been rearranging."

Until stomach pain caused Hopper to excuse himself from completing the interview, he gave the same answers to the same questions he'd been asked innumerable times before. When asked if he would make *Easy Rider* again, or make it differently, his answer was typically grandiose. "Would I make it *now?* It was about *then.* And I think a filmmaker's responsibility is to show his time. Brueghel, I think, was the first artist to show his time."

Hopper never directly addressed the subject of his divorce except to say, "Who would have ever thought I'd be getting a divorce in this state? It was a big shock." He only mentioned his wife while discussing politics. "Victoria got very involved with the Obama campaign, and I stepped back out of it. I thought it was good for her to get some glory. It's hard being married to a celebrity."

Hopper explained his vote for George W. Bush, telling Colacello, "I looked at the two of them and said, 'Who would I rather have on my side in a fight?' Bush. That's a true story." Then he said, "I like Clinton, I like Obama. I hate what's happening to the country. I think we're in the worst shape I've ever seen. Just think how conservative this country has become. It's like the '60s never happened." That was a peculiar observation from someone who had voted the Republican Party ticket for the last twenty years.

Liver failure, probably induced by the toxicity of his chemotherapy, brought Dennis Hopper's life to an end on Saturday, May 29, 2010. Surrounded by his children at his Venice home, he peacefully expired at 8:15 A.M., probably one of the few things in his entire life he did quietly. Perhaps he would have appreciated the plentitude and length of the obituaries that followed his passing. A number of Hopper's colleagues paid tribute to him, most notably Peter Fonda, who said, "Dennis introduced me to the world of pop art and 'lost' films. We rode the highways of America and changed the way movies were made in Hollywood. I was blessed by his passion and friendship."

"He was one of the world's all-time cool guys," David Lynch wrote. "Dennis was the strongest rebel we had, and I think his drug use and rebelliousness played a big part in his on-screen charisma. He was a painter, photographer, filmmaker, and art collector. He knew absolutely every artist around. He swam with the hippest and celebrated them all in such an honest way."

Sadly, the bitterness between Dennis and Victoria Hopper didn't end with his death. A letter from his attorney disinviting her from his funeral reportedly reached her just hours before the ceremony commenced. Written by Joe Mannis, the letter states, "As your client knows, the funeral for Mr. Hopper will be where he wanted to be buried in Taos, New Mexico. As your client also knows . . . she is not invited to the funeral. It was Mr. Hopper's specific wish that Ms. Hopper not attend his funeral. Ms. Hopper has indicated that she is not going to allow Galen to attend the funeral unless she attends. Mr. Hopper's family (particularly after what was said about them in the press by Ms. Hopper) does not wish that Ms. Hopper attend the funeral. On the family's behalf, I request that [her nanny] be allowed to bring Galen to the funeral and return her thereafter. Please let me know whether your client will consent to do what I can only call the 'decent thing.'"

Victoria Hopper did not send Galen to her father's funeral. Hopper's funeral ceremony commenced at noon on June 2, 2010, at the historic San Francisco de Asis adobe chapel in Ranchos des Taos. Hopper's *Easy Rider* costars Jack Nicholson and Peter Fonda, and Val Kilmer and Dean Stockwell joined Hopper's family members and mourners as his simple wood casket was carried into the church.

Henry Hopper brought many of those in attendance to tears with his dramatic readings from Walt Whitman's collection of poems, *Leaves of Grass,* and Rilke's *Letters to a Young Poet* during the two-hour memorial and mass. Dennis Hopper was also eulogized by his daughters, Marin and Ruthanna, and his brother, David. He elicited knowing laughter and scattered applause when he read the lyrics of Kris Kristofferson's song, "The Pilgrim: Chapter 33," whose subject bears an uncanny resemblance to the Dennis Hopper of the '70s, "Runnin' from his devils, lord, and reachin' for the stars/Takin' ev'ry wrong direction on his lonely way back home." (The resemblance was intentional. Kristofferson wrote the song with Hopper, Johnny Cash, and a number of his friends in mind.)

Jack Nicholson remembered his friend by saying he was "an all-around guy." "It was a very singular relationship I had with him," he said, "like nobody else. We were soul mates in a way. I really miss him." Nicholson, who retained his composure during the ceremony, finally lost it when a distant chorus of bikers gunned their engines as Hopper's casket was removed from the chapel for a private burial. "When they set their engines off, that set me off, too," he said.

Two of Hopper's influential friends in the art world combined forces to mount the first retrospective of his art held at a U.S. museum to celebrate his importance as an American artist. In the winter of 2009, New York gallerist Jeffrey Deitch met with Julian Schnabel, who had just visited Hopper. Impressed by Schnabel's report on the severity of his illness, Deitch came up with the idea of organizing the exhibit quickly enough for Hopper to attend its opening. Though Deitch wasn't scheduled to take the reins of Los Angeles' Museum of Contemporary Art (MOCA) as its newly appointed director until July 1, he arrived in L.A. on April 15, announcing that his first exhibition would be "Art Is Life," a survey of Hopper's art. "We're rushing this exhibition because Dennis is ailing," Deitch said. "He saw the space with us last week. Dennis was very happy and gratified to be having an L.A. museum retrospective."

In a statement following Hopper's death, Deitch said, "The reason for doing the exhibition 'Dennis Hopper Double Standard' at MOCA at this time in Dennis' life was so that he could be closely involved. Dennis participated in the selection of works and how the show would be presented, working closely with myself, exhibition curator Julian Schnabel, curatorial consultant Fred Hoffman and with the Tony Shafrazi Gallery. He was involved with the exhibition press release, the choice and approval of every image for every magazine, in the design of the print advertisements—in every aspect of the exhibition."

When the show opened, Schnabel said, "I wanted to do this before he died, and he almost made it to this moment. Dennis was an inspiration for me as a person in every way. I mean, he was like my brother. Somebody's trying to figure out how to mediate the world, somehow, by making objects, by making films, by using things that are around them. I think that you see what his world was like. I think this is a pretty good portrait of him."

"Dennis Hopper Double Standard" opened on Sunday, July 11, 2010 at L.A.'s Geffen Contemporary, an adjunct to the Museum of Contemporary Art. The exhibition's title referred to Hopper's best known photo, "Double Standard," taken in 1961. Shot through the windshield of a car, it shows a Standard Oil gas station with two Standard Oil signs facing the V-shaped intersection where the station stood. The car's rearview mirror shows the hood and windshield of the car behind it.

Art critic Edward Goldman wrote, "In recent years, this image has become almost iconic; in 2006, it was chosen for the banner greeting visitors approaching the Pompidou Centre in Paris, with its groundbreaking exhibition celebrating thirty years of Los Angeles art, from 1955-1985. French curators deserve credit for being coolly objective in assessing Hopper's artistic career as an interesting photographer, while passing on his derivative paintings and sculptures." While Goldman believed that Hopper deserved respect as an artist, he wrote, "he's treated uncritically as a celebrity whose every step is of importance, and in that, the museum reveals, unwittingly, its own double standard."

"Dennis Hopper Double Standard" exhibited 250 of Hopper's works in every medium. His commercial films were deemphasized, with a video monitor playing a Schnabel-edited selection of film clips positioned at the back of the exhibit space. The show's selling point was its abundant selection of Hopper's photographs. Visitors went to see his photos of friends who were already stars when he took their picture or became stars afterward.

Isabel Wilkinson wrote, "The show is a walking tour through the Dennis Hopper ecosystem—the films, friends, places and parties that made up his life. At the focal point of the exhibition are his black-and-white photographs from the early to mid-1960s, hung salon-style from floor to ceiling. On one wall there is Paul Newman, slouched in the sun; on another is Dr. Martin Luther King, Jr.; there's Jane Fonda in a leopard-print bikini with bow and arrow; on another, Ike and Tina Turner at home. Together, they're a portrait of Hopper—an assortment of memories and places organized around his cinematic and painterly eye."

The *LA Weekly*'s Tom Christie dismissed Hopper's paintings and sculptures. For Christie, Hopper's photos *were* the show. "A lot of these photos are nice, some very nice, a few memorable, one or two perhaps even iconic. Hopper had a decent eye. But for the most part, if you take in each photo ... there's nothing particularly interesting about the photograph. Likewise with the Italian walls, which Schnabel hangs with edges cropped and unframed in a row, as if they are special. They're not—they're Italian walls, very nice, textured!

"The exceptions are the titular "Double Standard"—pretty great—and Hopper's shots of the Ferus Gallery crowd (early Warhol, Ruscha, Rauschenberg, even Hockney if I'm not mistaken). But then these are photos of interesting people, which is to say, people, faces we are interested in. It is hard, if you have a good eye, to miss with shots such as these. To Hopper's credit, he didn't miss. But the great irony of this show is the one face missing—Hopper's. The truth is, there's more life in one still of him on the set of *Apocalypse Now* than in any of Hopper's own photographs. This was Hopper's one true talent."

"Failed promise characterizes this mostly listless art, however celebrated the actor-director's movie career," the *Los Angeles Times*' Christopher Knight wrote. "But he just isn't a very interesting artist. And for anyone who saw his large 2006 survey at L.A.'s Ace Gallery or the smaller one at Hoffman's old Santa Monica space in 1997—not to mention Shafrazi's September show—the MOCA presentation will be largely redundant. Artistically, though, movies like *Giant* or *Blue Velvet* are better than anything here. Their brilliance diminishes the show."

Members of Hopper's family and friends held a memorial for him on the Santa Monica Pier the Monday after "Dennis Hopper Double Standard" opened. Dennis' ex-wife Brooke Hayward, his daughter Marin, and his friends Eli Broad, Wendy Stark, Michael Chow, Barbara Davis, Peter Brant, Nikki Haskell, Alex Hitz, and Ed Ruscha listened as Dwight Yoakam and Tony Shafrazi eulogized their late friend.

Though Hopper's death mooted his action for divorce, legal observers expected the battle over his estate to continue in probate court. Instead, attorneys for Victoria Hopper and the estate of Dennis Hopper reached a partial settlement in November 2010. Hopper's trust was free to sell his art collection, 40 percent of which would be placed in trust for his daughter, Galen. The settlement didn't specify how the remaining 60 per cent would be divided. Victoria Hopper would receive $4,000 a month for Galen's support and an additional $6,000 a month in family support. Victoria would also get $10,000 in moving expenses. A ranch house in Brentwood, which Hopper purchased for Victoria to use to train and stable her horses, was put in trust for Galen.

The settlement cleared the way for Hopper's trust to begin liquidating his personal and real property. Hopper's Venice property went up for sale on Friday, July 23, 2010, for the asking price of $6.2 million. Coldwell Banker Previews' listing agent Jane Gavens said that buyers could choose to purchase only Hopper's 4,900-square foot main residence, designed by Bryan Murphy, instead of the entire 15,500-square foot compound, which included the three townhouses designed by Frank Gehry. The asking price was subsequently dropped twice, but Hopper's homes were still on the market as of early April 2011.

Next to go was Hopper's personal art collection. Christie's auctioned forty pieces from what it called "The Dennis Hopper Collection" during its Post-War & Contemporary Evening and Day Sales in New York on Nov. 10 and 11, 2010. The stars of his collection, Basquiat's *Untitled 1987*, worth an estimated $5 to $7 million, and Warhol's *Portrait of Dennis Hopper 1971*, worth an estimated $800,000-$1,200,000, were sold on November 10 along with contemporary art from collections of others. An additional lot was auctioned the next day.

Hopper once said, "My idea of collecting is not going out and buying bankable names, but buying people that I believe are really contributing something to my artistic life." The bankability of his collection was not lost on auction attendees Marin Hopper and Victoria Hopper when it fetched slightly more than $10 million. Victoria Hopper brushed off reports that she was involved in a new romance with charter-jet executive Eric Lang. They were spotted dining together while she was in New York with Galen to peruse her late husband's art at Christie's before the auction. "We are really great old family friends," Victoria told the *New York Post*. "We met in Vermont when I was seventeen years old."

Three hundred pieces of fine art Hopper owned and his personal memorabilia were auctioned at Christie's on January 11 and 12, 2011. The highest priced item was the Warhol print of Chairman Mao that Hopper shot at his home in Taos one night in the '70s. Cathy Elkies, Christie's director of iconic collections, said that Hopper's Venice Beach house was filled "literally from floor to ceiling with art, and realistically they [the children] couldn't take that on. This really was his calling."

One of the more interesting items was a photo Hopper took of Michelle Phillips, holding finger cymbals in one outstretched hand, with the message "TO MY DARLING DENNIS IN MEMORY OF EIGHT GLORIOUS

DAYS OF MARITAL BLISS LOVE MICHELLE" handwritten and stamped on the wall behind her (it sold for $5,625). The auction also offered an unbound, 158-page screenplay of *Easy Rider* that Hopper had annotated on two pages, the framed plaque awarding him his star on Hollywood Boulevard, and posters from his films. Alex Hitz said, "It was Dennis' wish to sell everything," but Elkies said that Hopper's children were keeping certain sentimental pieces, including his own photographs and paintings.

The auction did not proceed without a hint of drama when Victoria Hopper filed a last-minute legal action against Hopper's trust, asserting that she owned thirty-two of the items up for auction. A Los Angeles Superior Court justice issued a temporary restraining order prohibiting the sale of the items in question, forcing Christie's to remove them from the sale. The auction still went smashingly, exceeding Christie's estimates. The Warhol Mao, estimated at $30,000, sold for $302,500 on the first day, contributing to a first day's total of $1.8 million.

The remaining items auctioned the next day brought in a more than respectable $148,682. Most were film memorabilia. Items related to *Easy Rider* inspired furious bidding, including the *Easy Rider* screenplay, which fetched $20,000, ten times its estimated price, and a copy of the film's poster, which sold for $5,250. Like his friend, Andy Warhol, Hopper never threw anything away, especially any kind of award, on which he placed a particularly high value. The Frontier Award that the Texas Hall of Fame bestowed upon Hopper for his performance in *Giant* pulled in $4,750 on a $200-$300 estimate.

While it was easy to put a price on Hopper's tangible possessions, it is tougher to render a definitive judgment on his character and his legacy. "Over a prolific career with many ups and downs, marred at times by drug use, Hopper, at his best, seemed a man in the grip of an ecstatic vision that ultimately had nothing to do with chemicals or substances," Mick LaSalle wrote in his obituary of Hopper. "In his acting, he often reached beyond the pedestrian to find the truth right at the edge of madness. He called life 'this miracle we all exist in,' and his finest performances suggested an affectionate respect for the various and telling ways people receive reality."

The Austin Chronicle's Louis Black concluded his tribute to Dennis Hopper by writing, "Dennis Hopper sped through most of his life with a pedal to the metal intensity that left not just normalcy behind, but just as often acceptable human behavior. Driven by a commitment to personal vision and an unshakable integrity, he really had no other choice as how to live. Always inner-directed, Hopper was never in thrall or even very respectful of the social mores, whims, infatuations, and ever-shifting sensibilities of the outside world. He lived in a world that was of and as defined by Hopper. Neither his vision nor integrity were deeply rooted in any ideology, traditional body of philosophical thought, or religious belief. Instead, as certain, unbendable, and controlling were his beliefs, they were also nonspecific, often shifting characteristics and mores. Despite uncertainties, he was certain. In spite of his changing perceptions, he was unchanging. Everything about Hopper's career is greater than the sum of its parts, but it is hard to imagine he would have wanted it any other way."

Dennis Hopper was often asked by interviewers to take stock of his achievements. His answer often depended on his mood. On more than one occasion, he reflected, "There are moments that I've had some real brilliance, you know. But I think they are moments. And sometimes, in a career, moments are enough. I never felt I played the great part. I never felt that I directed the great movie. And I can't say that it's anybody's fault but my own. The high points have not been that many, but I'm a compulsive creator so I don't think of the children first, I think of the work. Let's see, I guess, *Easy Rider, Blue Velvet,* a couple of photographs here, a couple of paintings . . . those are the things that I would be proud of, and yet they're so minimal in this vast body of crap—most of the 150 films I've been in—this river of shit that I've tried to make gold out of. Very honestly."

And yet, at other times, Hopper seemed more content with himself. "I am just a middle-class farm boy from Dodge City and my grandparents were wheat farmers," he said. "I thought painting, acting, directing, and photography were all part of being an artist. I have made my money that way. And I have had some fun. It's not been a bad life."

Dennis Hopper memorized and recited Rudyard Kipling's poem, "If", while in high school. Though Hopper had little fondness for books, he appreciated poetry. Kipling's poem made a lasting impact on him, providing him with a philosophy of how one should live one's life. Hopper performed "If" on Johnny Cash's TV show in 1970, and used it in his dialogue in *Apocalypse Now*.

If

If you can keep your head when all about you
Are losing theirs and blaming it on you;
If you can trust yourself when all men doubt you,
But make allowance for their doubting too;
If you can wait and not be tired by waiting,

Or, being lied about, don't deal in lies,
Or, being hated, don't give way to hating,
And yet don't look too good, nor talk too wise;

If you can dream—and not make dreams your master;
If you can think—and not make thoughts your aim;
If you can meet with triumph and disaster
And treat those two imposters just the same;

If you can bear to hear the truth you've spoken
Twisted by knaves to make a trap for fools,
Or watch the things you gave your life to broken,
And stoop and build 'em up with wornout tools;

If you can make one heap of all your winnings
And risk it on one turn of pitch-and-toss,
And lose, and start again at your beginnings
And never breath a word about your loss;

If you can force your heart and nerve and sinew
To serve your turn long after they are gone,
And so hold on when there is nothing in you
Except the Will which says to them: "Hold on";

If you can talk with crowds and keep your virtue,
Or walk with kings—nor lose the common touch;
If neither foes nor loving friends can hurt you;
If all men count with you, but none too much;

If you can fill the unforgiving minute
With sixty seconds' worth of distance run,
Yours is the Earth and everything that's in it,
And—which is more—you'll be a Man my son!

FILMOGRAPHY

2011	*The Last Film Festival* (postproduction)
2010	*Alpha and Omega*
2008–2009	*Crash* (TV series)
2009	Deadly Creatures (voice, video game)
2008	*An American Carol*
2008	*Palermo Shooting*
2008	*Swing Vote*
2008	*Elegy*
2008	*Sleepwalking*
2008	*Hell Ride*
2007	*Entourage* (TV series)
2006	*Memory*
2005–2006	*E-Ring* (TV series)
2006	*10th & Wolf*
2006	*Hoboken Hollow*
2005	*The Golden Years of Advertising: The Roaring 90's of Separating People from Their Money* (video)
2005	*Land of the Dead*
2005	*The Crow: Wicked Prayer*
2005	*Americano*

2005	*House of 9*
2004	*The Last Ride* (TV movie)
2004	*Out of Season*
2004	*The Keeper*
2004	*Bad Boy's 10th Anniversary . . . The Hits* (video, uncredited)
2004	*Las Vegas* (TV series)
2004	*Legacy*
2003	*The Night We Called It a Day*
2003	*Suspense* (TV movie)
2002	*The Groovenians* (TV short)
2002	*Grand Theft Auto: Vice City* (voice, video game)
2002	*The Piano Player*
2002	*Leo*
2002	*24* (TV series)
2002	*Unspeakable*
2002	*Space Truckers*
2002	*Firestarter 2: Rekindled* (TV movie)
2002	*Flatland* (TV series)
2001	*L.A.P.D.: To Protect and to Serve*
2001	*Knockaround Guys*
2001	*Choke*
2001	*Ticker*
2000	*Held for Ransom*
2000	*The Prophet's Game*
2000	*Tycus* (video)

2000	*Jason and the Argonauts* (TV movie)
2000	*Luck of the Draw*
2000	*The Spreading Ground*
2000	*Michael Angel*
2000	*Lured Innocence*
1999	*Bad City Blues*
1999	*The Venice Project*
1999	*Jesus' Son*
1999	*Straight Shooter*
1999	*Edtv*
1999	*Justice* (TV movie, uncredited)
1999	*American Masters* (TV series documentary)
1998	*Meet the Deedles*
1998	*Black Dahlia* (video game)
1997	*Road Ends*
1997	*Top of the World*
1997	*The Blackout*
1997	*The Making of 'Super Mario Brothers'* (TV short)
1997	*The Good Life*
1996	*Samson and Delilah* (TV movie)
1996	*The Last Days of Frankie the Fly*
1996	*Basquiat*
1996	*Carried Away*
1995	*Waterworld*
1995	*Search and Destroy*
1995	*Hell: A Cyberpunk Thriller* (voice, video game)

1994	*Witch Hunt* (TV movie)
1994	*Speed*
1994	*Chasers*
1993	*True Romance*
1993	*Red Rock West*
1993	*Super Mario Bros.*
1993	*Boiling Point*
1992	*The Heart of Justice* (TV movie)
1992	*Sunset Heat*
1992	*Nails* (TV movie)
1992	*Rabbit Ears: Jonah and the Whale* (voice, uncredited/video short)
1992	*Rabbit Ears: Annie Oakley* (voice, uncredited/video)
1992	*Rabbit Ears: Rip Van Winkle* (voice, uncredited/video short)
1991	*Eye of the Storm*
1991	*Doublecrossed* (TV movie)
1991	*The Indian Runner*
1991	*Paris Trout*
1991	*Rabbit Ears: King Midas and the Golden Touch* (voice, uncredited/video)
1990	*Catchfire*
1990	*Flashback*
1990	*Rabbit Ears: Paul Bunyan* (voice, uncredited/video)
1989	*Chattahoochee*
1989	*Blood Red*

1989	*Rabbit Ears: How the Leopard Got His Spots* (voice, uncredited/video short)
1989	*Black Leather Jacket* (TV movie)
1989	*Rabbit Ears: The Fisherman and His Wife* (voice, uncredited/video short)
1989	*Rabbit Ears: Thumbelina* (voice, uncredited/short)
1987	*Santabear's High Flying Adventure* (voice, TV short)
1987	*The Pick-up Artist*
1987	*Straight to Hell*
1987	*Rabbit Ears: The Tale of Peter Rabbit* (voice, uncredited/video)
1987	*Black Widow*
1987	*Rabbit Ears: The Tale of Mr. Jeremy Fisher* (voice, video)
1987	*Running Out of Luck*
1986	*Hoosiers*
1986	*Blue Velvet*
1986	*River's Edge*
1986	*The Texas Chainsaw Massacre 2*
1986	*Stark: Mirror Image* (TV movie)
1986	*The American Way*
1985	*My Science Project*
1985	*Stark* (TV movie)
1985	*Rabbit Ears: The Ugly Duckling* (voice, uncredited/video)
1985	*Rabbit Ears: The Steadfast Tin Soldier* (voice, uncredited/video)

1985	O.C. and Stiggs
1985	A Hero of Our Time (short, uncredited)
1984	Slagskämpen
1983	White Star
1983	The Osterman Weekend
1983	Rumble Fish
1982	Human Highway
1981	King of the Mountain
1981	Reborn
1980	Out of the Blue
1980	Wild Times (TV miniseries)
1979	Bloodbath
1979	Apocalypse Now
1978	Last In, First Out
1978	Flesh Color
1977	The Sorceror's Apprentice
1977	The American Friend
1979	Tracks
1976	Mad Dog Morgan
1973	Kid Blue
1972	The Other Side of the Wind
1972	Crush Proof
1971	The Last Movie
1969	True Grit
1969	Easy Rider
1968	Head (uncredited)

1968	*Panic in the City*
1968	*Hang 'Em High*
1968	*The Glory Stompers*
1967	*The Big Valley* (TV series)
1967	*The Guns of Will Sonnett* (TV series)
1967	*Cool Hand Luke*
1967	*The Trip*
1967	*Combat!* (TV series)
1966	*The Time Tunnel* (TV series)
1966	*Queen of Blood*
1966	*The Legend of Jesse James* (TV series)
1965	*Convoy* (TV series)
1965	*The Sons of Katie Elder*
1965	*Gunsmoke* (TV series)
1964	*Bonanza* (TV series)
1964	*The Lieutenant* (TV series)
1964	*Arrest and Trial* (TV series)
1964	*Petticoat Junction* (TV series)
1964	*Tarzan and Jane Regained . . . Sort of*
1964	*The Thirteen Most Beautiful Boys*
1963	*The Greatest Show on Earth* (TV series)
1963	*Espionage* (TV series)
1962–1963	*The Defenders* (TV series)
1963	*Wagon Train* (TV series)
1963	*The Dakotas* (TV series)
1963	*Twilight Zone* (TV series)

1962	*Surfside 6* (TV series)
1962	*G.E. True Theater* (TV series)
1961	*The Investigators* (TV series)
1961	*87th Precinct* (TV series)
1961	*Night Tide*
1961	*Naked City* (TV series)
1960	*The Barbara Stanwyck Show* (TV series)
1960	*Key Witness*
1960	*The Millionaire* (TV series)
1960	*The Betty Hutton Show* (TV series)
1959	*The Lineup* (TV series)
1959	*The Young Land*
1958–1959	*The Rifleman* (TV series)
1958–1959	*Zane Grey Theater* (TV series)
1958	*Pursuit* (TV series)
1958	*Swiss Family Robinson* (TV movie)
1958	*Studio One in Hollywood* (TV series)
1958	*From Hell to Texas*
1957	*Sayonara* (voice, uncredited)
1957	*The Story of Mankind*
1957	*Sugarfoot* (TV series)
1957	*Gunfight at the O.K. Corral*
1957	*Conflict* (TV series)
1956–1957	*Cheyenne* (TV series)
1956	*Giant*
1956	*The Kaiser Aluminum Hour* (TV series)

1956	*Screen Directors Playhouse* (TV series)
1956	*Kings Row* (TV series)
1955	*I Died a Thousand Times* (uncredited)
1955	*Rebel Without a Cause*
1955	*The Loretta Young Show* (TV series)
1955	*The Public Defender* (TV series)
1955	*Medic* (TV series)
1954	*Cavalcade of America* (TV series)

ACKNOWLEDGMENTS

I AM GRATEFUL FOR the generous assistance of the following individuals in contributing to this book: R. G. Armstrong, Stephen Blauner, Jacquelyn Craig, Maria Giraco, Phyllis Gollehon (aka Trinity Mason), Frankie Harris, Brooke Hayward, Victoria Hopper, the late Lamont Johnson, Rurik Kallis, Michael Kay, Michael Macready, Bob Merada, Cecil Munsey, Don Murray, Dean Otto and Jill Vuchetich at the Walker Art Center, Gerald Palmer, Lawrence Schiller, the late Steffi Sidney-Splaver, Ed Sorrels, and Bob Turnbull.

I wish to thank Louis Black for permission to quote from his article, "In Memory of Dennis Hopper," originally published in *The Austin Chronicle* on June 4, 2010.

I also wish to thank Nile Southern for permission to quote from Terry Southern's article, "The Loved House of the Dennis Hoppers," originally published in the August 1965 issue of *Vogue* magazine.

I would like to express my thanks to my literary agent, Robert G. Diforio, and my publisher, Carole Stuart, for sharing my enthusiasm for this project and helping it become a reality.

I would also like to thank Sandra Stuart for her editorial contributions and wish to express my great appreciation for the work of Suzanne Henry in assisting me in the preparation of my manuscript for publication.

BIBLIOGRAPHY

Books

Adams, Leith, author, and Keith Burns, editor, with an introduction by Dennis Hopper. *James Dean: Behind the Scenes.* New York: Carol Publishing Group, 1990.

Alexander, David. *Star Trek Creator: The Authorized Biography of Gene Roddenberry.* New York: ROC/Penguin Books, 1994.

Baker, Carroll. *Baby Doll: An Autobiography* New York: Arbor House, 1983.

Baker, Fred, editor, with Ross Firestone. *Movie People: At Work in the Business of Film.* New York: Douglas Book Corporation, 1972.

Biskind, Peter. *Easy Riders, Raging Bulls: How the Sex-Drugs-and-Rock 'N' Roll Generation Saved Hollywood.* New York: Touchstone, 1999.

Carter, Graydon, editor. *Vanity Fair's Tales of Hollywood: Rebels, Reds, and Graduates and the Wild Stories Behind the Making of 13 Iconic Films.* New York: Penguin Books, 2008.

Coppola, Eleanor. *Notes.* New York: Simon and Schuster, 1979.

Corman, Roger, with Jim Jerome. *How I Made a Hundred Movies in Hollywood and Never Lost a Dime.* New York: Random House, 1990.

Cowie, Peter. *The Apocalypse Now Book.* New York: Da Capo Press, 2001.

Coyote, Peter. *Sleeping Where I Fall: A Chronicle.* Washington, D.C.: Counterpoint, 1998.

Dalton, David. *James Dean: The Mutant King.* San Francisco: Straight Arrow Books, 1974.

Dodd, David and Tai Babilonia. *Playing It Straight: Personal Conversations on Recovery, Transformation and Success.* Deerfield Beach, Florida: Health Communications, 1996.

Engel, Joel. *Gene Roddenberry: The Myth and the Man Behind Star Trek.* New York: Hyperion, 1994.

Finstad, Suzanne. *Natasha: The Biography of Natalie Wood.* New York: Three Rivers Press, 2002.

Fonda, Peter. *Don't Tell Dad: A Memoir*. New York: Hyperion, 1998.

Flynt, Larry, with Kenneth Ross. *An Unseemly Man*. Los Angeles: Dove Books, 1996.

Frascella, Lawrence and Al Weisel. *Live Fast, Die Young: The Wild Ride of Making Rebel Without a Cause*. New York: Touchstone, 2005.

Gerber, Gail and Tom Lisanti. *Trippin' with Terry Southern: What I Think I Remember*. Jefferson, North Carolina: McFarland & Co., 2009.

Gilmore, John. *Laid Bare: A Memoir of Wrecked Lives and the Hollywood Death Trip*. Los Angeles, California: Amok Books, 1997.

Gilmore, John. *The Real James Dean*. New York: Pyramid Books, 1975.

Hardin, Nancy and Marilyn Schlossberg, eds. *Easy Rider: Original Screenplay by Peter Fonda, Dennis Hopper, Terry Southern*. New York: Signet Books, 1969.

Hayward, Brooke. *Haywire*. New York: Alfred A. Knopf, 1977.

Hickenlooper, George. *Reel Conversations*. Secaucus, New Jersey: Citadel Press, 1991.

Hill, Lee. *A Grand Guy: The Art and Life of Terry Southern*. New York: HarperCollins Publishers Inc., 2001.

Hinkle, Robert, with Mike Farris. *Call Me Lucky: A Texan in Hollywood*. Norman, Oklahoma: University of Oklahoma Press, 2009.

Hopper, Dennis. *Out of the Sixties*. Pasadena, California: Twelvetrees Press, 1986.

Hopper, Dennis, edited by Marin Hopper, with an introduction by Brooke Hayward. *1712 North Crescent Heights: Dennis Hopper Photographs 1962-1968*. Los Angeles, California: Greybull Press, 2001.

Howlett, John. *James Dean: A Biography*. New York: Fireside Books, 1975.

Hunter, Tab with Eddie Muller. *Tab Hunter Confidential: The Making of a Movie Star*. Chapel Hill, North Carolina: Algonquin Books of Chapel Hill, 2005.

Kael, Pauline. *5001 Nights at the Movies: A Guide from A to Z*. New York: Holt, Rinehart and Winston, 1982.

Kelly, Richard T. *Sean Penn: His Life and Times*. New York: Cannongate U.S., 2004.

Lambert, Gavin. *Natalie Wood*. New York: Back Stage Books, 2005.

Law, Lisa. *Interviews With Icons: Flashing on the Sixties*. Sante Fe, New Mexico: Lumen Books, 1999.

Robin, Liza, Linda, and Tiffany as told to Jennie Louise Frankel, Terrie Maxine Frankel, Joanne Parrent; preface by Lois Lee; editor's introduction by Joanne Parrent. *You'll Never Make Love in This Town Again.* Beverly Hills, California: Dove Books, 1995.

McDonough, Jimmy. *Shakey: Neil Young's Biography.* New York: Random House, 2002.

McGilligan, Pat, editor. *Backstory 2: Interviews with Screenwriters of the 1940s and 1950s.* Berkeley and Los Angeles, California: University of California Press, 1991.

Morrisroe, Patricia. *Mapplethorpe: A Biography.* New York: Random House, 1995.

Riese, Randall. *The Unabridged James Dean: His Life and Legacy from A to Z.* Chicago: Contemporary Books, 1991.

Rodriquez, Elena. *Dennis Hopper: A Madness to His Method.* New York: St. Martin's Press, 1988.

Rudnick, Lois Palken. *Utopian Vistas: The Mabel Dodge Luhan House and the American Counterculture.* Albuquerque, New Mexico: University of New Mexico Press, 1996.

Russo, William. *The Next James Dean: Clones and Near Misses, 1955-1975.* Bloomington, Indiana: Xlibris.com, 2003.

Scott, Toni Lee, edited by Curt Gentry. *A Kind of Loving.* New York: World Publishing Co., 1970.

Strasberg, Susan. *Bittersweet.* New York: G. P. Putnam's Sons, 1980.

Warhol, Andy, edited by Pat Hackett. *The Andy Warhol Diaries.* New York: Warner Books, 1991.

Weldon, Michael. *The Psychotronic Video Guide.* New York: St. Martin's Griffin, 1996.

Zicree, Marc Scott. *The Twilight Zone Companion.* New York: Bantam Books, 1982.

Magazines and Newspapers

"Actor Hopper Denies Claims of Drug Use." *Los Angeles Times,* July 16, 1970.

Adler, Dick. "The Young Directors." *Los Angeles Times' West,* Nov. 15, 1970.

"Ailing Dennis Hopper had film-set charisma." *New York Post,* April 30, 2010.

Archerd, Army. "E-Ring Nearing." *Variety,* Aug. 17, 2005.

Arthur, Robert Alan. "Hanging Out." *Esquire,* February 1975.

Applebaum, Stephen. "Dennis Hopper: Land of the Dead." *BBC Entertainment*, Sept. 19, 2005. <http://www.bbc.co.uk/films/2005/09/19/dennis_hopper_land_of_the_dead_interview.shtml>

Bacon, James. Untitled story about a screening of *The American Dreamer*. *Los Angeles Herald-Examiner*, Mar. 30, 1971.

Barber, Lynn. "American psycho." *The Observer* [London], Jan. 14, 2001.

Beck, Marilyn. "Confused Hopper Mexico Bound." *Hollywood Citizen News*, Nov. 11, 1971.

Beck, Marilyn and Stacy Jenel Smith. "Jacqueline Bisset Hoping Money Can Be Found to Complete Hopper's Final Film." *Beck/Smith Hollywood*, Nov. 21, 2010. <http://becksmithhollywood.com/?p=3048>

Bernstein, Jacob. "New Twists in Hopper Divorce." *The Daily Beast*, June 7, 2010. <http://www.thedailybeast.com/blogs-and-stories/2010-06-07/dennis-hoppers-divorce-a-bitter-feud/?cid=tag:all4>

Bianco, Robert. "Grating egos, little action in 'E-Ring.' " *USA Today*, Sept. 20, 2005.

Birnbaum. Jane. " 'Easy Rider' Gets Lost." *Entertainment Weekly*, May 15, 1992.

Black, Louis. "Bud Shrake's Adventures in the Film Trade." *The Austin Chronicle*, Oct. 18, 1985.

Black. Louis. "In Memory of Dennis Hopper." *The Austin Chronicle*, June, 4, 2010.

Blevins, Winfred. "Dennis Hopper: In Apologia." *Los Angeles Herald-Examiner*, Nov. 21, 1971.

Blevins, Winfred. "Dennis Hopper In Peru On Location With 'The Last Movie.' " *Entertainment World*, May 1, 1970.

Bockus, Kim. "Double standards: an interview with Dennis Hopper." *ArtUS*, March-April 2007.

Bonner, Michael. "50 Greatest Lost Films: #1: *The Last Movie*." *Uncut*, July 2010.

Boyar, Jay. " 'Colors' Isn't The Problem–Violence Is The Problem." *Orlando Sentinel*, April 29, 1988.

Brady, James. "In Step With Dennis Hopper." *Parade Magazine*, July 16, 1995.

Brandum, Dean. "A Legacy Went Searching for a Film . . . Dennis Hopper and *Easy Rider*." *Senses of Cinema*, April 4, 2010. Issue 54. <http://www.sensesofcinema.com/2010/feature-articles/a-legacy-went-searching-for-a-film%E2%80%A6-dennis-hopper-and-easy-rider/>

Brokaw, Francine. "Crash Season Two: Dennis Hopper and Eric Roberts Talk about the Show." *suite101.com*, Aug. 30, 2009. <http://www.suite101.com/content/crash-season-two-a143914>

Bryan, Susan Montoya. "Dennis Hopper's Funeral Draws Jack Nicholson, Val Kilmer & More." *Associated Press*, June 2, 2010.

Burke, Tom. "Will Easy Do It for Dennis Hopper?" *The New York Times*, July 20, 1969.

Canby, Vincent. "Film Festival: 'American Friend' Tops Day's Fare." *The New York Times*, Sept. 24, 1977.

Canby, Vincent. "Film Festival: Frawley's 'Kid Blue,' a Western: Dennis Hopper Stars as Unlucky Robber Polish 'Illumination Comedy Tries Too Hard, Lacks Spontaneity." *The New York Times*, Oct. 1, 1973.

Canby, Vincent. "Review/Film; Liberal Old vs. Conservative Young in 'Flashback.' " *The New York Times*, Feb. 2, 1990.

Canby, Vincent. "Screen: 'The Last Movie': Hopper Cast as a Mythic Film Cowboy in Work He Directed in Peru." *The New York Times*, Sept. 30, 1971.

Canby, Vincent. "The Screen: 'Apocalypse Now': Faces of War." *The New York Times*, Aug. 15, 1979.

Caruso, Michelle. "Hopper Isn't Fonda 'Easy Rider' Deal." *NYDailyNews.com*, Dec. 15, 1995. <http://articles.nydailynews.com/1995-12-15/news/17990343_1_dennis-hopper-pando-punitive-damages>

" 'Catchfire.' " *Variety*, Dec. 31, 1990.

Christie, Tom. "Dennis Hopper at MOCA: Double Trouble." *LA Weekly*, July 23, 2010.

Cinegram Magazine. Report on Hopper's plans and personal state. Summer 1978.

Clarke, Gerald, and Elaine Dutka. "Dennis Hopper: Easy Rider Rides Again." *Time*, Nov. 17, 1986.

Clark, Jayne. "Taos hosts a 'Summer of Love' celebration." *USA Today*, April 23, 2009.

Clothier, Peter. "HIP HOPPER: Profile of Dennis Hopper." *ARTnews*, September 1997.

Cocks, Jay. "Cinema: Desperado for Hire." *Time*, May 14 1973.

Cocks, Jay. "Cinema: Shaggy-Man Story." *Time*, Oct. 18, 1976.

Cohen, Sandy. "Dennis Hopper Has Prostate Cancer." *Associated Press*, Oct. 29, 2009.

Colacello, Bob. "The City of Warring Angels." *Vanity Fair*, August 2010.

Conley, Mike. " 'Wanda,' a film by the late Barbara Loden of Marion is getting star treatment." *The McDowell News*, Oct. 9, 2010.

Constable, Collin. "Mickey Rourke." *Mean Magazine*, November/December 2000.

Corliss, Richard. "Cinema: It's a Strange World, Isn't It Blue Velvet." *Time*, Sept. 22, 1986.

Cox, Alex. "I was Dennis Hopper's henchman." *The Guardian* [London], June 3, 2010.

"D. Hopper's Wife Sues For Divorce." *Hollywood Citizen News*, March 4, 1967.

Darrach, Brad. "The Easy Rider Runs Wild." *Life*, June 19, 1970.

Davis, Gwen. "Remembering Dennis Hopper." *VF Daily*, June 1, 2010. <http://www.vanityfair.com/online/daily/2010/06/remembering-dennis-hopper.html>

"Dennis Hopper." *Movies Now*. Volume 1, Issue 2. 1971.

"Dennis Hopper: American Failure." *Oui*, October 1972.

"Dennis Hopper art collection up for auction in NYC." *Associated Press*, January 4, 2011.

"Dennis Hopper Buys Theatre In N.M. Village. *Variety*, June 15, 1970.

"Dennis Hopper Cast In 'Apocalypse Now.' " *Variety*, Aug. 24, 1976.

"Dennis Hopper family and wife told to resolve their differences." *San Francisco Chronicle*, April 6, 2010.

"Dennis Hopper Gets Off Pot Charge." *Associated Press*, Sept. 1, 2000.

"Dennis Hopper–Hopper Explodes Easy Rider Myths." *contactmusic.com*, March 15, 2008. <http://www.contactmusic.com/news.nsf/story/hopper-explodes-easy-rider-myths_1062599>

"Dennis Hopper Hospitalized with Flu-Like Symptoms." *People*, Sept. 30, 2009.

"Dennis Hopper Was Moved By Obama." *starpulse.com*, Nov. 4, 2008. <http://www.starpulse.com/news/index.php/2008/11/04/dennis_hopper_was_moved_by_obama_>

"Dennis Hopper's Widow Settles Up With Estate." *TMZ.com*, Nov. 17, 2010. <http://www.tmz.com/2010/11/17/dennis-hoppers-widow-settles-settlement-estate-victoria-hopper-artwork/>

"Dennis Hopper: Wife 'stole' valuable art." *New York Post*, March 24, 2010.

"Dennis the 'Dreamer.' " *The New York Times*, Mar. 11, 1971.

"Divorce Won By Wife Of Actor Hopper." *Los Angeles Herald-Examiner*, Feb. 2, 1969.

"Drag Race Film Takes A Detour." *New West*, Sept. 9, 1980.

Dougary, Ginny. "Born to be wild: but now I vote Bush and I only swing on the golf course." *The Times* [London], March 12, 2004.

Dougherty, Steve and Vicki Sheff. "With a New Wife, Son and Movie Uneasy Rider Dennis Hopper Hopes to Find the Hot Spot Back on Top." *People*, Nov. 12, 1990.

Christopher Dow. "Dennis Hopper Blew Away Houston With 1983 Dynamite Death Chair Act." *Rice News*, Sept. 14, 1995.

Duke, Alan. "Judge asks Hopper family to put aside differences." *CNN Entertainment*, April 5, 2010. <http://articles.cnn.com/2010-04-05/entertainment/dennis.hopper.divorce_1_prostate-cancer-pellman-cancer-doctor?_s=PM:SHOWBIZ>

Ebert, Roger. "Colors." *Chicago Sun-Times*, April 15, 1988.

Ebert, Roger. "Flashback." *Chicago Sun-Times*, Feb. 2, 1990.

Ebert, Roger. "The Hot Spot." *Chicago Sun-Times*, Oct. 26, 1990.

Ebert, Roger. "Out of the Blue." *Chicago Sun-Times*, Jan. 1, 1982.

Ebert, Roger. "The Pick-Up Artist." *Chicago Sun-Times*, Sept. 18, 1987.

Ebert, Roger. "Red Rock West." *Chicago Sun-Times*, May 6, 1994.

Ebert, Roger. "River's Edge." *Chicago Sun-Times*, May 29, 1987.

Ebert, Roger. "Speed." *Chicago Sun-Times*, June 10, 1994.

Ebert, Roger. "Straight to Hell." *Chicago Sun-Times*, July 1, 1987.

Ebert, Roger. "The Texas Chainsaw Massacre, Part 2." *Chicago Sun-Times*, Aug. 25, 1986.

Ebert, Roger. "Waterworld." *Chicago Sun-Times*, July 28, 1995.

Ebiri, Bilge. "Dennis Hopper on Elegy, James Dean, and Being Big in France." *nymag.com*, Dec. 4, 2008. <http://nymag.com/daily/entertainment/2008/12/dennis_hopper.html>

Edelstein, David. "Acid redux." *Slate*, Aug. 10, 2001. <http://www.slate.com/id/113476>

Elliott, David. " 'Blue' and other hues: a short history of Hopper." *The San Diego Union-Tribune*, Nov. 17, 1996.

Finnigan, Joe. "A Rebel? Hopper Says No," *Los Angeles Examiner*, Jan. 23, 1960

Finkel, Jori. "Dennis Hopper was 'closely involved' in upcoming MOCA show, says museum director Jeffrey Deitch." *Los Angeles Times*, May 31, 2010.

Finkel, Jori. "Jeffrey Deitch's first show at MOCA: Dennis Hopper, curated by Julian Schnabel." *Los Angeles Times*, April 15, 2010.

Flatley, Guy. "…. D-e-n-n-i-s H-o-p-p-e-r!" *The New York Times*, Oct. 18, 1970.

Foote, John. "INTERVIEW: Dennis Hopper." *incontention.com*, Nov. 6, 2008. <http://incontention.com/2008/11/06/catching-up-with-dennis-hopper/>

Freeland, Bridget. "Dennis Hopper's Widow Fights His Family Over Actor's Estate." Courthouse News Service, Mar. 7, 2011.

Gates, Anita. " 'Meet the Deedles': Disney Formula Piece Brings Surfers to Wyoming." *The New York Times*, Mar. 27, 1998.

Glaister, Dan. " 'I'm just an art bum …' " *The Guardian*, April 5, 2006.

Gleiberman, Owen. "Dennis Hopper was the most visionary of all Hollywood bad boys." *Entertainment Weekly*, May 29, 2010. <http://moviecritics.ew.com/2010/05/29/dennis-hopper-a-visionary-bad-boy/>

Golden. Mike. "Now Dig This: Interview with Terry Southern." *Reflex*, September 1992.

Goldman, Edward. "MOCA's Double Standard." *The Huffington Post*, July 15, 2010. <http://www.huffingtonpost.com/edward-goldman/mocas-double-standard_b_648075.html>

Goodman, Dean. "Dennis Hopper's divorce battle getting uglier." *Reuters*, Feb. 11, 2010.

Goodman, Mark. "Rebel Without a Pause." *New Times*, Oct. 2, 1978.

Goodman, Tim. " 'Crash' wrecks the small screen." *San Francisco Chronicle*, Oct. 15, 2008.

Goodwin, Michael. "In Peru with Dennis Hopper making the last movie." *Rolling Stone*, April 16, 1970.

Granberry, Michael. "Hopper's Hometown Saw a Bright Future for Him." *Los Angeles Times*, April 26, 1988.

Grigoriadis, Vanessa. "The Furious Life & Final Days of Dennis Hopper." *Rolling Stone*, July 8, 2010.

Haber, Joyce. "Hopper to Hop On Promo Bandwagon." *Los Angeles Times*, Aug. 17, 1971.

Hartlaub, Peter. "Not dead yet! Romero's zombies come back to life–again. *San Francisco Chronicle*, June 24, 2005.

Hattenstone, Simon. " 'The Method? Living it out? Cobblers!' " *The Guardian*, Aug. 3, 2007.

Hayward, Brooke. "Once Upon a Time in L.A." *Vanity Fair*, September 2001.

Heaton, Michael. "It Hasn't Been An Easy Ride, But Hard-Living Dennis Hopper Is Out Of Trouble–For Now." *People*, Oct. 24, 1983.

Hill, Lee. "The Vox Interview with Terry Southern." *Vox* (Canada), September 1990.

Hinson, Hal. " 'Carried Away' Slowly." *The Washington Post*, June 5, 1996.

Hinson, Hal. " 'Chattahoochee.' " *The Washington Post*, May 4, 1990.

Hinson, Hal. " 'Flashback.' " *The Washington Post*, Feb. 3, 1990.

Hinson, Hal. " 'The Hot Spot.' " *The Washington Post*, Oct. 26, 1990.

Hinson, Hal. " 'Speed.' " *The Washington Post*, June 10, 1994.

Hirsch, Foster. "You're Wrong If You Write Off Dennis Hopper." *The New York Times*, Oct. 24, 1971.

Hoberman, J. "Drugstore Cowboy." *The Village Voice*, Aug. 8, 2006.

Hollywood Citizen News. Untitled, anonymous story where Hopper voiced his unhappiness with Warner Bros. March 1, 1957.

The Hollywood Reporter. Untitled, anonymous story about the Mexican premiere of *Easy Rider*. Aug. 9, 1977.

The Hollywood Reporter. Untitled, anonymous story about Hopper's sale of the Mud Palace. Feb. 16, 1978.

The Hollywood Reporter. Untitled, anonymous story about Hopper's Mexican coproduction deal. December 19, 1978.

The Hollywood Reporter. Untitled, anonymous story about Sally Kirkland's lawsuit against Hopper. March 13, 1981.

"Hopper, Bottoms Team On 'King Of Mountain.' " *Variety*, Mar. 22, 1980.

"Hopper Pleads Guilty In Taos, N.M., Incident." *Variety*, Aug. 15, 1975.

"Hopper Says He Uses Nothing More 'n' Vitamins." *Variety*, July 23, 1970.

"Hopper the Popper." *TV Guide*, October 9-15, 1965.

"Hopper wife's liberal friend." *New York Post*, Feb. 12, 2010.

Hopkins, Henry. "Dennis Hopper's America." *Arts in America*, May-June 1971.

Horkins, Tony. "Renaissance Easy Rider." *New York Post*, July 15, 2010.

In Re Marriage of HOPPER Los Angeles Superior Court Case No. BD 518 046.

"The Indian Runner." *Variety*, Dec. 31, 1990.

Irwin, Ben. "Dennis Hopper Traveled the Long Road Back." *Sober Times*, Sept. 1990. Vol. 4 No. 9.

Jones, Oliver. "Dennis Hopper Divorce Drama 'I Felt Scared for My Life.'" *People*, March 29, 2010.

Kael, Pauline. "Movies in Movies." *The New Yorker*, Oct. 9, 1971.

Kandel, Susan. "Troubling Flashbacks From Dennis Hopper." *Los Angeles Times*, June 13, 1997.

Kanfer, Stefan. "Cinema: From Adolescent to Puerile." *Time*, Oct. 18, 1971.

Kanfer, Stefan. "New Movies: Space Odyssey 1969." *Time*, July 25, 1969.

Kashner, Sam. "Here's to You, Mr. Nichols: The Making of *The Graduate*." *Vanity Fair*, March 2008.

Kay, Michael. "Kallises' lives intertwined with Hopper's." *The Union Democrat* [San Diego], June 8, 2010.

Kelley, Kate, George Gurley, and Carl Swanson. "Easy Riders Feud as Dennis Hopper Cheers Peter Fonda's Non-Oscar." *The New York Observer*, Mar. 29, 1998.

Kilday, Gregg. "Dennis Hopper returns from 'Out of the Blue.' " *Los Angeles Herald-Examiner*, Nov. 12, 1982.

King, Susan. " 'True Grit' memories from Kim Darby and Glen Campbell." *Los Angeles Times*, Jan. 4, 2011.

Knight, Christopher. " 'Dennis Hopper Double Standard' @ MOCA's Geffen Contemporary." *Los Angeles Times*, July 11, 2010.

La Ferla, Ruth. "Dennis Hopper; Consider the Outsider." *The New York Times*, May 12, 2002.

LaSalle, Mick. "Dennis Hopper, director of 'Easy Rider,' dies." *San Francisco Chronicle*, May 29, 2010.

LaSalle, Mick. "Kevin Keeps It Afloat." *San Francisco Chronicle*, July 28, 1995.

Lee, Ken. "Dennis Hopper Files For Divorce." *People*, Jan. 15, 2010.

Leydon, Joe. "Dennis Hopper likes it 'Hot.' " *www.movingpictureshow.com*, Oct. 21, 1990. <http://www.movingpictureshow.com/dialogues/mpsDennisHopper.htm>

Leydon, Joe. "My 31 years with Dennis Hopper: A once-cornered critic reflects." culturemap houston, June 30, 2010. <http://houston.culturemap.com/newsdetail/05-30-10-my-31-years-with-dennis-hopper-a-once-cornered-critic-reflects/>

Linderman, Lawrence. "Playboy Interview: Peter Fonda." *Playboy*, Sept. 1970.

Love, Damien. "The Mole Man." *Bright Lights Film Journal*, Aug. 2008. Issue 61. <http://www.brightlightsfilm.com/61/61jodorowskyiv.php>

Lowry, Brian. "E-Ring." *Variety*, Sep. 19, 2005.

Lynch, David. "Dennis Hopper." *Time*, June 14, 2010.

Maddox, Garry. "Dennis Hopper does Ol' Blue Eyes . . . his way." *The Age* [Melbourne, Australia], Nov. 28, 2002.

Mahoney, John C. "Hopper's 'Last Movie' a Film Within a Film." *Los Angeles Times*, Mar. 15, 1970.

Marill, Alvin H. "The Television Scene." *Films In Review*, May 1980.

Martin, Edwin. "How to crash the movies; Dennis Hopper, ex-Globe actor, gets promising film roles." *San Diego Union*, Nov. 17, 1955.

Maslin, Janet. "Digression And Color Are All of It For Hopper." *The New York Times*, April 23, 1994.

Maslin, Janet. "River's Edge." *The New York Times*, May 8, 1987.

McCarthy, Todd. "Palermo Shooting." *Variety*, May 25, 2008.

McCree, Cree. "Uneasy Rider." *The Cable Guide*, May 1988.

McKay, Hollie. "Frail Dennis Hopper Receives Walk of Fame Star." *FOXNews.com*, Mar. 26, 2010. <http://www.foxnews.com/entertainment/2010/03/26/frail-dennis-hopper-receives-walk-fame-star/>

Miller, Edwin. "Dennis Hopper Makes 'The Last Movie' In Peru." *Seventeen*, July 1970.

Moore, Frazier. "Dennis Hopper Out Of The Hospital." *Associated Press*, Oct. 1, 2009.

Mora, Philippe. "Dennis Hopper: A remembrance by Philippe Mora." WeHoNews.com, June 10, 2010. <http://wehonews.com/z/wehonews/archive/page.php?articleID=4928>

Mora, Philippe. "The shooting of Mad Dog Morgan." *The Sydney Morning Herald*, Jan. 31, 2010.

Morgan, Spencer. "Tough Guys Are on Time: Rip Torn on Males, Mailer, McCain And That Barfight in Lakeville." *The New York Observer*, June 3, 2008.

Murray, Noel. "Betty White In Black And White/Dennis Hopper: The Early Works/Trek Stars Go West." *The Onion A. V. Club*, Jan. 12, 2011. <http://www.avclub.com/articles/betty-white-in-black-and-white-dennis-hopper-the-e,49930/>

Murray, Noel. "Random Roles: Dennis Hopper." *The Onion A.V. Club*, Dec. 2, 2008. <http://www.avclub.com/articles/random-roles-dennis-hopper,2549/>

The New York Times. Anonymous story about Hopper's appearance at the *Apocalypse Now* press conference. Aug. 31, 1979.

Noller, Matt. "Cannes Film Festival 2008: Days 9 and 10." *The House Next Door*, May 30, 2008. <http://www.slantmagazine.com/house/2008/05/cannes-2008-days-9-10/>

"O.C and Stiggs." *Variety*, Dec. 31, 1986.

O'Hare, Kate. "(Dennis) Hopper Evolves From Rebel to Republican." ZAP2*it*.com, Oct. 27, 2005. <http://tv.zap2it.com/tveditorial/tve_main/1,1002,271>

O'Hehir, Andrew. " 'Elegy' for a topless bombshell." *Salon*, Aug. 8, 2008. <http://www.salon.com/entertainment/movies/beyond_the_multiplex/feature/2008/08/08/elegy>

O'Malley, Sheila. "5 for the Day: Dean Stockwell." *The House Next Door*, Dec. 3, 2007. <http://www.slantmagazine.com/house/2007/12/5-for-the-day-dean-stockwell/>

O'Neill, Ann W. "No Easy Ride for Hopper Over Rip Torn's Lawsuit." *Los Angeles Times*, April 5, 1998.

Palmer, Robert. "The Pop Life." *The New York Times*, Mar. 18, 1977.

"Paris Trout." *Variety*, Dec. 31, 1990.

Parsons, Spencer. "From Mad Dogs to Mister Golf." *The Austin Chronicle*, April 25, 2008.

Patterson, John. "Fighting Talk." *The Guardian*, Jan. 30, 1999.

Pearce, Garth. "Dennis Hopper's life: a hell of a ride." *The Sunday Times* [London], Aug. 31, 2008.

Peers, Alexandra. "Guggenheim Presents Hugo Boss Prize; Winner Gets Cash, Show, Dinner Next to Dennis Hopper." *nymag.com*, Nov. 15, 2006. <http://nymag.com/daily/intel/2006/11/guggenheim_presents_hugo_boss_1.html>

"People, May 29, 1972." *Time*, May 29, 1972 (A brief account of Dennis Hopper and Daria Halprin's wedding ceremony).

Phipps, Keith. "The Easy Rider Road Trip: Retracing the Path of the Iconic Movie on Its 40th Anniversary." *Slate*, Nov. 16, 2009. <http://www.slate.com/id/2233176/entry/2233171/>

Quinn, Joan Agajanian. "Dennis Hopper." *Interview*, Dec. 1985.

Rabin, Nathan. "Pixelated Case File #139: Super Mario Bros." *The Onion A.V. Club*, June 10, 2009. <http://www.avclub.com/articles/pixelated-case-file-139-super-mario-bros,29032/>

Rabin, Nathan. "Space Truckers." *The Onion A.V. Club*, Mar. 29, 2002. <http://www.avclub.com/articles/space-truckers,19564/>

Rabin, Nathan. "Top Of The World." *The Onion A.V. Club*, Mar. 29, 2002. <http://www.avclub.com/articles/top-of-the-world,19670/>

Rabin, Nathan. "Interview: Peter Fonda." *The Onion A.V. Club*, Oct. 1, 2003. <http://www.avclub.com/articles/peter-fonda,13835/>

Ray, Nicholas. "Story Into Script." *Sight and Sound*, Fall 1956.

"Re Dennis Hopper." *Variety*, Aug. 20, 1975.

Rebello, Stephen. "Dennis Hopper: The Hopper Agenda." *Movieline*, March 1990.

Rhodes, Joe. "The Wild World of Dennis Hopper." *Los Angeles Times TV Times*, July 14-20, 1991.

"A Rip-Roaring Feud." *People*, Sept. 12, 1994. Vol. 42 No. 11.

Rosenbaum, Jonathan. "Out of the Blue." *Video Movies*, Aug. 1984.

Rosenbaum, Jonathan. "Social Criticism." *Chicago Reader*, May 6, 1988.

Rosenbaum, Ron. "Riding High: Dennis Hopper Rides Back." *Vanity Fair*, April 1987.

Rosenthal, Donna. "Hopper's Progress." *Los Angeles Times*, Nov. 5, 1989.

Rottenberg, Josh. "Lord of the E-Ring." *Entertainment Weekly*, Sept. 16, 2005.

"Sally Kirkland Sez Hopper 'Injured' Her." *Variety*, Mar. 4, 1981.

Sanello, Frank. "Hopper picks himself up, starts all over again." *Star-Free Press*, Jan. 28, 1990.

Saroyan, Strawberry. "Dennis Hopper: Disneyland Memories." *Variety*, April 8, 2005.

Shapiro, Walter. "Lew Wasserman: the man who ruined movies." *Slate*, June 6, 2002. <http://www.slate.com/id/2066690/>

Shafrazi, Tony and Peter M. Brant. "Dennis Hopper." *Interview*, Aug. 1, 2010.

Sharp, Rob. "Hopper's estranged wife pulls star's art from sale." *The Independent* [London], Jan. 12, 2011.

Silverman, Jason. "Riders on the Storm." *Santa Fean Magazine*, June-July 2009.

Silverman, Stephen M. "Hopper Gets Bossy." *People*, July 2, 1998.

Simon, Alex. "Dennis Hopper Is Riding Easy." *Venice Magazine*, Nov. 2008.

Singer, Mark. "Whose Movie Is This?" *The New Yorker*, June 22, 1998.

Snead, Elizabeth. "Dennis Hopper: Renaissance Rebel." *Cigar Aficionado*, Feb. 1, 2001.

Stan, Alexandru. "Sleepwalking Dennis Hopper on Sleep Spanking Anna Rob." *www.inoutstar.com*, Dec. 3, 2008. <www.inoutstar.com/news/Sleepwalking-Dennis-Hopper-On-Sleepspanking-Anna-Rob-5442.html>

Stayton, Richard. "Dennis Hopper in Conversation with Richard Stayton." *Los Angeles Herald-Examiner*, May 20, 1985.

Stayton, Richard. "Waiting For Dennis." *The Los Angeles Times*, May 14, 1995.

Stein, Jean. "At Home With Larry Flynt." Grand Street Issue 36.

Stevenson, James. "AFTERNOONS WITH HOPPER." *The New Yorker*, Nov. 13, 1970.

Stiff, Burl. "Museum exhibits actor's other side." *The San Diego Union-Tribune*, Nov. 17, 1996.

Soule, Berenice. "To See or not To See." *Southwestern Jewish Press*, Aug. 6, 1954.

Southern, Terry. "Letter: Exact Genesis." *The New York Times*, June 7, 1970.

Southern, Terry. "The Loved House of the Dennis Hoppers." *Vogue*, Aug. 1965.

Susman, Gary. "Hog Heaven." *Entertainment Weekly*, Sept. 27, 2002.

"Taking a Young, Fourth Wife Actor Dennis Hopper Promises That This Time He's Playing for Keeps." *People*, July 3, 1989. Vol. 32, No. 1.

Thomson, Katherine. "Dennis Hopper Divorce Shocker." *The Huffington Post*, Jan. 15, 2010. <http://www.huffingtonpost.com/2010/01/15/dennis-hopper-divorce-sho_n_424589.html>

Thomson, Katherine. "Dying Dennis Hopper Divorce Details: The Daughter At The Center Of The Split." *The Huffington Post*, Jan. 19, 2010. <http://www.huffingtonpost.com/2010/01/19/dennis-hopper-divorce-det_n_428253.html>

Topel, Fred. "Dennis Hopper. Eric Roberts: Crazy in Crash." *Dish Magazine*, Issue 100. <http://dishmag.com/issue100/celebrity/10732/dennis-hopper-eric-roberts-crazy-in-crash/>

Topel, Fred. "Dennis Hopper on Sleepwalking." *CanMag*, Mar. 13, 2008. <http://www.canmag.com/nw/10692-dennis-hopper-sleepwalking>

Trebbe, Ann. "Hopper, hopping mad at Johnson." *USA Today*, Sept. 11, 1990.

Tully, Judd. "Christie's Sale of Dennis Hopper's Movie Mementos Does Boffo, Despite Legal Challenges." *ARTINFO*, Jan. 13, 2011. <http://www.artinfo.com/news/story/36738/christies-sale-of-dennis-hoppers-movie-mementos-does-boffo-despite-legal-challenges/>

Turan, Kenneth. "Dennis Hopper, a Survivor of the 60's, Tries Again." *The New York Times*, April 3, 1983.

"Uneasy Hopper's 3% Suit Of 'Rider.' " *Variety*, June 24, 1970.

Universal Studios. "DENNIS HOPPER–Biography." Aug. 6, 1971.

Veiga, Alex. "Dennis Hopper's Estate in SoCal to Go on Sale." *Back Stage*, July 20, 2010. <http://www.backstage.com/bso/content_display/news-and-features/e3ic2e2d16144df098a7fabb498fd982775>

"Victoria Duffy dines with an 'old friend' at The Lion." *New York Post*, Nov. 17, 2010.

Warga, Wayne. "Dennis Hopper Wound Up in Cutting Room." *Los Angeles Times*, March 7, 1971.

Weber, Bruce. "Dennis Hopper; A Wild Man Is Mellowing." *The New York Times*, Sept. 8, 1994.

Weber, Christopher. "Dennis Hopper, creator of hit 'Easy Rider,' dies."*Associated Press*, May 29, 2010.

Weller, Sheila. "California Dreamgirl." *Vanity Fair*, December 2007.

Whaley, Bill. "(Honorary) Mayor Hopper To Be Memorialized in Ranchos de Taos." *Taos Friction*, June 1, 2010 <http://www.taosfriction.com/?p=224>

Wilde, Jon. "Man On Fire." *Uncut*, Feb. 2005.

Wilkin, John Buck. "My uneasy ride with Dennis Hopper." *Nashville Scene*, Oct. 14, 2010.

Wilkinson, Isabel. "Dennis Hopper's Cinematic Art." *The Daily Beast*, July 13, 2010. <http://www.thedailybeast.com/blogs-and-stories/2010-07-13/dennis-hopper-show-at-moca-in-los-angeles/>

Wilkinson, Tracy. "Guardian Angels Picket Director's, Actor's Houses Over Gang Movie." *Los Angeles Times*, April 11, 1988.

Willis, Ellen. "See America First." *The New York Review of Books*, Jan. 1, 1970.

Wilson, William. "More Than Meets the Eye." *Los Angeles Times*, Jan. 14, 1992.

Zacharek, Stephanie. "Sleepwalking." *Salon*, March 14, 2008. <http://www.salon.com/entertainment/movies/review/2008/03/14/sleepwalking/>

INDEX